Y0-AFX-755

KEEPING PACE PLUS
AN ACTIVE READING STUDY GUIDE
FOR

LEFTON

PSYCHOLOGY

SIXTH EDITION

Prepared by
Andrew H. Ryan, Jr.
University of South Carolina

Allyn and Bacon
Boston · London · Toronto · Sydney · Tokyo · Singapore

Copyright © 1997 by Allyn and Bacon
A Viacom Company
160 Gould Street
Needham Heights, Massachusetts 02194

Internet: www.abacon.com
America Online: keyword: College Online

All rights reserved. No part of the material protected by this copyright may be reproduced or
utilized in any form or by any means, electronic or mechanical, including photocopying, recording,
or by any information storage and retrieval system, without the written permission from the
copyright owner.

ISBN 0-205-26328-3

Printed in the United States of America

10 9 8 7 6 5 4 3 2 1   00 99 98 97 96

To Meghan, Caitlin and Mary.

Contents

Preface

Keeping Pace Plus has been written with one goal in mind: to help students learn more from *Psychology, Sixth Edition*. Proven learning strategies are incorporated throughout the study guide in a easy-to-use format that will encourage students to become active participants in the learning process. The focus will be on learning, not on memorizing. Each chapter will begin by establishing lessons and learning objectives. The most efficient learning process involves distributed practice and the lessons provide these logical breaks. Mastering the learning objectives will increase confidence. Being relaxed and confident are keys to successful learning and examination preparation.

This all-new *Keeping Pace Plus* study guide prepares the student by providing various exercises designed to maximize learning. The study guide contains dozens of matching exercises, fill-in-the blanks, multiple-choice items, self-tests, and reviews tied to the learning objectives in the text. In the Exam Preparation Section the student is able to create simulated tests or exams.

In addition to teaching students to learn, *Keeping Pace Plus* challenges students to become *critical thinkers* by encouraging them to evaluate the research and generate personal meaning for the concepts presented in *Psychology*.

Keeping Pace Plus uses several techniques to optimize student learning:

1. Establishes clear learning objectives logically linked to the student text.

2. Provides a comprehensive and organized guide to the textbook.

3. Makes active use of the SQ3R *plus* model (survey, question, read, recite, review, *plus* write & reflect) for active study participation.

4. Provides various methods of learning in addition to the active reading material, including Applications, Crossword Puzzles, and Self-Tests.

5. Encourages students to establish schedules and goals for studying, to take breaks from studying, and to reward themselves for progress.

6. Encourages critical thinking about facts, issues, and methodologies.

7. Provides Enrichment Glossaries to clarify difficult words.

Plus a New Exam Preparation Section to simulate tests:

1. Flash Cards provide a proven method of learning key terms and concepts.

2. Crossword Puzzles provide a challenging way to test knowledge of key terms and definitions.

3. Practice Tests provide actual test questions that help students prepare for the real thing.

These added features are designed to enhance *Keeping Pace Plus* by providing structure for the *review* process as outlined in the SQ3R *plus* model and to relieve some of the anxiety of test taking by allowing the student to prepare and take course-specific simulated exams prior to test day.

I would like to thank the many students and faculty members from around the country who helped me by providing critiques of previous editions of *Keeping Pace*. This study guide was written in response to your suggestions. I am especially thankful to John "Trey" Mills, III, who probably never wants to see another crossword puzzle, and Marcia Gardner, who contributed many hours of typing, and was especially patient during times of stress. Most of all I want to express my gratitude to Suzanne Jackson for her tireless efforts in proofing and her willingness to accept this new challenge.

HOW TO STUDY AND HOW TO LEARN

What does it take to learn and remember?

Educational (or instructional) psychologists focus their attention on instruction and academic learning and know a lot about what it takes for a person to learn in school. The information in this section comes primarily from their research findings about teaching, thinking, and learning.

The three most important characteristics of effective study are:

♦ Being actively involved in the learning process.

♦ Making new information meaningful by linking your existing life experiences and knowledge (what you already know) to new information (what you are learning for the first time).

♦ Taking responsibility for your own learning.

These characteristics are important to learning for several reasons. The first characteristic, *active learning* or *active participation*, means that you interact with new information so that it becomes alive and challenging. Instead of passively yawning over lifeless facts that refuse to stay in mind long enough even to pass a test, an active learner makes the facts alive and important by wrestling and dancing with them and really getting to know them. By simply using your own thoughts, asking and answering your own questions, and organizing information in ways that make sense to you, you become an active learner. When you are an active learner, the facts become more than facts—they become meaningful and stay with you. This suggests the second characteristic of effective learning.

To *generate personal meaning* out of new material (so that it becomes relevant to your life and needs), you must find ways to connect yourself, your knowledge, and your life experiences to the material you are studying. People have a natural tendency to do this, but by knowing that learning and memory are enhanced when you create personal meaning, you will be more likely in the future to do it intentionally. When you can relate new information to your own life by connecting it to your past or present, to problems you need to solve, or to events in the world, you make it important, and you are much more likely to understand it, remember it, and use it.

The third characteristic of effective study, *taking responsibility for your own learning*, is essential, because no one can do your learning for you. We do not learn much just by being present in class and skimming over printed words on a page. To learn means to change, and to change we must experience things for ourselves. Teachers (and textbooks) can present ideas and try to make them interesting; but only you can learn those ideas for yourself, and only you can make them meaningful to your life. For this reason, it is important to take responsibility not only for how you go about learning, but also for how you will shape and mold the ideas that are presented to you.

DEVELOPING GOOD STUDY SKILLS

Remember trying to use a computer for the first time? You knew it could perform wonders, but you did not understand the new language required to operate it, or you tried the mouse and felt like you were suddenly totally uncoordinated. The first time you made a mistake or got a strange error message on the screen, you probably didn't feel so bad, but by the second or third time, you began to feel like maybe you were not cut out for computers. If you had friends who were becoming computer whizzes, you probably began to feel still more frustrated, maybe even dumb.

The point is this: lacking the appropriate skills makes any task harder than it should be. In Chapter 9 of the textbook you will learn that when people do not have the necessary skills or do not know what is expected of them, they experience failure, become frustrated, and lose their motivation to try. A lack of motivation is neither innate nor necessarily a fault in the individual; it may just mean that someone never learned the skills or values necessary to make the job worthwhile. When you have the necessary skills, your task, even though it may be difficult, will become easier and more rewarding. It may even be fun. This lesson is designed to teach efficient and effective study skills which, assuming that you use them, will help you with this and other courses as well.

Review Your Educational and Professional Goals

Each time you begin a new class, you will find it useful to think about why you are taking the class and decide how it fits in with your long-term educational and professional goals. For example, you are currently enrolled in introductory psychology. Will this class help you with your professional goals? With your personal life? Is it a class required for your major? If so, why? Decide what value this class has for you and try to keep it in mind throughout the term.

Knowing how the class is meaningful to you will help motivate you to study and master the material presented. If you cannot think of a personally or educationally meaningful reason for taking the class, perhaps you should talk to your teacher or a school counselor. Almost every class has value, but pinpointing the value may be difficult. In any case, a lack of interest in the class from the outset will probably lead you to struggle through, feel frustrated, and continually wish the semester would end. This attitude is not conducive to good study skills.

Scheduling Study Time

Once you have attended the first session of each of your classes, plan a study schedule based on the workload you expect to have for each class, your personal needs, your family's needs, and any other obligations you may have. Frequently people are not realistic about their time and think they can do more in a given period than they actually can. When planning your class and study schedule try hard to be reasonable: allow time for the unexpected, and remember you have obligations other than school. If you do not plan for these things and for "play" time, you will end up having to take time for them anyway, and be forced to break or readjust your educational commitments. Remember, your study schedule is just as important as your class schedule. If you commit yourself to a realistic study schedule, you should be able to fulfill all your obligations, including school, much more smoothly.

If you work full- or part-time, it is important to plan your class schedule so that you are enrolled in a few classes each semester that have little or no homework along with one or two classes that do. A student who works full-time should seriously consider being a part-time student since it is almost impossible to study four or five subjects well without a full-time commitment.

Some of my most successful students in my more than 10 years of teaching psychology have been the busiest students in class: students with jobs or family obligations and students carrying an extremely heavy courseload. What separated these students from the rest was their ability to organize. To be a well-organized student you begin each term by making a calendar of the due dates for every course. You should include all tests, papers, projects, personal dates to remember and most importantly, personal time. Personal time is time you set aside for yourself to relax and reward yourself for your hard work. This time does not have to be alone, just personal.

When planning your class and study schedule, try to mix your subjects. Also, when constructing your study sessions, plan to study several subjects at a time, each for about one hour, rather than one subject for several hours. Research indicates this is a much more efficient study tactic.

You will find it easier to fulfill your study schedule if you have a specific place to study. Select a quiet, well-illuminated place and always sit at a desk or table. If you study at home, be sure to move away from the television and family activities.

How to Deal with a Short Attention Span

The average college student can read for only twelve minutes before drifting away from a book and falling into a daydream. Since daydreaming interferes with learning, knowing how to control it helps. You will find that the active reading section of the study guide will, to some extent, automatically decrease the number of daydreams you have while reading *Psychology*. In addition, if you set small goals, take breaks from your study sessions, and reward yourself, you should learn more efficiently. Use these techniques over the next three or four years, gradually increasing your attention span so that you can study for a full hour without daydreaming.

READ ACTIVELY. When a study guide is not available, formulate and answer your own questions as you read.

SET SMALL GOALS. In the beginning do not expect yourself to read a complete chapter or finish an entire lesson in one study session. If you can do an entire lesson in one session, GREAT! But do not feel you have to. Set a goal of answering seven to ten questions and plan on taking a break when you have accomplished it. Over the next few years, gradually increase your goals.

TAKE BREAKS FROM YOUR STUDY SESSIONS. When you have answered or read the number of questions you set as a goal, break after each *Keeping Pace Plus* Lesson for 5-10 minute. If you notice you are daydreaming a lot before you reach your goal, perhaps it was too large a step, and you should start out with a smaller one the next time. If you should discover you are daydreaming more than you are studying, *answer one more question* and take a 10 minute break. When you go back to studying, review the questions you have answered and then continue. You should strive to study at least 30 minutes for every 10 minute break.

REWARD YOURSELF. You will discover in Chapter 5 of *Psychology* that research shows that behavior followed by reward tends to repeat itself. Of course earning a good grade, feeling proud of yourself, and having your teachers, family, and friends recognize your achievements are rewards, but why not go one step further? Make your hobbies, special activities, and favorite foods contingent (dependent) upon completion of your homework. The problem with self-reward is that it is easy to cheat. It is easy to watch a football game and plan to study afterward; but this can have a negative effect on your study habits. Instead, *always* plan your time so that reward comes *after* you study. This way you really will increase your studying and learning rates. The other way around (football and then study) only increases your procrastination rate!

Memorization versus Understanding

Meaningful learning is much more permanent than rote learning (memorization). So, whenever you can, try to apply the concepts you are studying to your own experiences, look up words you are not familiar with, pay attention to examples if necessary. It is your responsibility to make everything you are trying to learn meaningful. Others can help you, but you will have to take the initiative to ask about any concepts giving you trouble.

In some cases memorization is an efficient way to help you recall information. This is so when you have made the information meaningful and are trying to remember names or lists of words. An effective way to memorize lists of material is to us mnemonic (nuh-MON-ik) devices. Mnemonic devices allow you to organize meaningless material into meaningful stories or words. For example, if you wanted to remember the words cat, dish, punishment, nowhere, man, song, and gruesome you could create a story like this:

A *cat* was drinking milk from a *dish* when *punishment* fell upon him from *nowhere*. Turning his head the cat saw it was the *man* singing the *song* that had delivered the *gruesome* blow. Or if you wanted to remember the names Sabrina, Ulysses, Romeo, Pandora, Raina, Isis, Sebastian, and Ezekiel, you could simply remember the word SURPRISE. Mnemonic devices provide you with cues for recalling necessary information. You will learn more about mnemonics and other memory strategies in Chapter 6 of your *Psychology* text.

Active Reading without the Aid of a Study Guide

Frequently students who have used *Keeping Pace Plus* express frustration about not having similar study guides for their other classes. This need not be a problem, however, because you can be an active reader and use the SQ3R p*lus* method on your own, without the aid of a study guide. All you need to do is:

1. *Survey* the pages you plan to read.
2. *Read* the pages one paragraph at a time--stop reading at the end of each paragraph.
3. *Ask* one or two questions concerning a paragraph immediately after reading it. Ask questions similar to those you would expect your instructor to write for a short-answer essay test. *Write* your questions down, and after each question, *write* down the answer. You might try using two colors of ink or lead for this process, writing the questions in one color and the answers in another. Then read the next paragraph and again ask and answer questions.
4. *Recite* from memory all of the information you can remember in support of each of your questions following one of the two steps described in the paragraph explaining the Recite step of SQ3R *plus*. Rather than using learning objectives as your reciting stimulus, use your questions.
5. *Review*, concentrating on your weaker areas.
6. *Write* (in your words, not the instructor's) major points and key terms, and summarize all of the information.
7. *Reflect*. When you feel as if you have learned as much as you can, stop and reflect on the newly acquired information and try to relate it to your everyday life experiences.

In the next section, *"How to Use Keeping Pace Plus,"* you will learn how to use the SQ3R *plus* method for this course and any other course you may be taking this term or in the future.

DEVELOPING EFFECTIVE CLASSROOM BEHAVIORS

Active Listening

Although entertainment, socializing with your peers, and conforming to the norms of going to college may be among your reasons for attending classroom lectures, one would hope that your primary reasons are to listen and learn. As with reading, to be a successful learner through listening you must be an active participant. Here are some tips that might help:

1. Exercise control over your thoughts by consciously directing your attention toward what is being said.
2. Allow the speaker's lead-in statements to act as cues that important information is about to be given. Lead-in statements will begin with phrases like "The main idea ...," "There are four approaches ...," "Another viewpoint ...," "In conclusion ...," and so on.
3. Silently ask yourself questions about what is being said and, as the lecture proceeds, try to answer them.
4. Ask questions in class, when the lecturer is ready for them, to clarify anything you missed or did not understand.
5. Try to make connections between what is being said now and what you recall from previous lectures or text material.

Taking Notes

Listening and writing at the same time can be somewhat distracting. If you are listening actively and intently you may find it difficult to write down as much as you would like; if you are writing a lot down you may find yourself falling behind and missing parts of the lecture. For these reasons it is important to give some thought to your listening/note taking approach, and during the first few lectures of a course adapt your listening and note taking skills to the style and pace of the lecture.

As with reading and listening, note taking can become merely a passive activity. If your approach to note taking involves trying to write down, word for word, just about everything that the lecturer says, you will be more involved in getting words on paper than in focusing your attention and asking questions about what points are important. An effective approach for successful classroom learning is to be an active listener, take well-organized and brief yet explicit notes, making them complete enough to provide you with an overview of the entire lecture. Here are some ideas that may help you take good class lecture notes.

1. Use an 8 1/2" x 11" three-ring binder that allows you to add and remove pages. This will allow you to keep all of your notes in one place and in order.
2. Develop an outlining system that works well for you. Your outline of what is said in the lecture should reflect major ideas, minor points that follow those ideas, and the relationship between ideas. Complete sentences take time to write and, for the most part, are unnecessary. Try to catch the lecture ideas in short phrases that include key words.
3. Make some notation of all ideas brought out in the lecture, even those you have read about in the text or already know, so that you can be reminded of all the ideas the lecturer felt were important to the main lecture topic.
4. Use multiple color highlighters to reflect your outline. Try different colors for major and minor points.
5. If you are a "doodler," then turn your doodles into meaningful *icons* for emphasizing important material.

Some Final Comments

A student who does well in college is one who plans a study schedule, studies and listens as an active participant, makes use of organized study methods such as SQ3R *plus,* and feels confident and at ease with the learning process.

Being a good student does not come naturally or easily for most. It takes self-discipline, realistic scheduling, and a true desire to succeed. The important thing to remember is that almost anyone who wants to be a good student can be.

HOW TO USE KEEPING PACE *PLUS*

HOW TO USE THIS STUDY GUIDE

You may want to think of your study guide as a "How to Do It" manual or a carefully tested "recipe" that will help you succeed in your psychology class. As you work with it over the next few months and through practice come to understand its purpose, you will probably find yourself using the formula it provides in most of your other classes, too. *Keeping Pace Plus* is designed to compliment Lefton's *Psychology, Sixth Edition*. It will assist you in learning the essential terms, concepts, theories, and important research in the field of psychology. It is not meant as a substitute for *Psychology,* but rather as an adjunct to your learning process.

ACTIVE READING SECTION

CHAPTER OUTLINE

At the beginning of each study guide chapter you will find a convenient outline of the chapter with the text headings aligned with the learning objectives. Some chapters have been broken up into two, three, four or more short lessons. Research studies on learning and memory have shown it is much easier to learn small amounts (see "chunks" in Chapter 6) of material at a time than large amounts. If you try to learn too much all at once you may not be able to remember all that you could because of a phenomenon called interference. You will read more about interference in Chapter 6, Memory. Having the chapters broken into shorter lessons also provides you with good places for SQ3R *plus* study breaks.

THE LEARNING OBJECTIVES

"When you have mastered the material in this chapter you will be able to ...." The learning objectives serve four purposes: first, they tell you specifically what you should expect to know when you have completed studying the chapter; second, they give you an overview of what is in the chapter; third, they provide cues when you begin to review the chapter in order to prepare for a test; and fourth, they can be used as practice essay questions.

CHAPTER OVERVIEW

The overview is a brief description of what the chapter will cover. This should be read as part of your SQ3R *plus* "Survey" step and should begin to stir your interest in the topics covered in that chapter. You should also read the chapter overview again before you begin the active reading sections of the study guide and once more when you are in the SQ3R *plus* "Review" step.

MATCHING

People, terms, concepts, and other ideas will be presented in a matching format to test your skill at identifying new material. This exercise will be a good indicator of how quickly you are getting the information.

FILL-IN-THE-BLANKS

This exercise will provide you with a review of the chapter's concepts and help you determine the areas that need further study. Try to answer all of the items in a lesson before checking your answers.

APPLICATIONS

The application exercises in *Keeping Pace Plus* will allow you to test your understanding by applying the text's psychology concepts to new situations. If you can transfer your textbook knowledge successfully to these examples from everyday life, what you have learned is taking on meaning. Meaningful learning is much more permanent than simple memorization. Other ways that you can make the things you are learning meaningful include doing your best to apply the concepts you are studying to your own experiences, looking up unfamiliar words, and paying attention to examples given in your text.

THE SELF-TESTS

At the conclusion of each chapter you will be given a Self-Test. The self-tests will give you immediate feedback on how well you have studied. You will be using the self-test wisely if you wait until you have completed all steps of the SQ3R *plus* method before taking it. The answers are at the end of the study guide. If you miss more than one or two questions on the self-test you need to study the chapter lessons more thoroughly.

ENRICHMENT GLOSSARY

College students who speak English as a second language reviewed the textbook and circled words they did not understand. These words have been compiled and explained in the Language Enrichment Glossary at the end of each chapter.

EXAM PREPARATION SECTION

FLASH CARDS

This method of learning has been around for years, but has been revitalized in *Keeping Pace Plus*. By utilizing the prepared Flash Cards, you will have a better understanding of definitions, meanings, and concepts that may be new to the first time psychology student. Try combining the prepared cards with some of your own. You will be pleased with how well you learn the material with this proven study method.

PRACTICE TESTS

This feature has been requested by students from all types of courses and across the nation. Many students say they have a difficult time preparing for exams because they do not know what to expect, or they study for the wrong things. It has been my experience that providing students with a sample of what a test will be like in their course relieves much of the pre-test anxiety and allows them to concentrate on the material in a much more efficient manner. Students are encouraged to create their own practice exams by combining the material in the *Flash Cards* with multiple chapters of *Practice Tests* and simulate a virtual test before exam day. After scoring your own exam, you will have a chance to *reflect* on your answers and get help if needed.

CROSSWORD PUZZLES

This is one of the more challenging features of this edition of *Keeping Pace Plus*. Students often find it difficult to determine the correct answer to exam questions because they do not recall the information accurately when the topic is presented out of context. One way to prevent this from happening is to ask the student to determine the correct spelling and word from limited clues about the word. Crossword puzzles are the perfect practice for this type of learning. When added to the *Flash Cards* and *Practice Tests* as part of your exam preparation, you will gain more confidence in your ability to summon correct answers from a variety of methods.

EXAM SIMULATION

The *Exam Preparation Section* of the study guide will instruct you on how to prepare for your exams by teaching you to develop your own practice exams that simulate the real exam administered by your instructor. When exam time comes and you have completed the active reading section, then proceed to the exam preparation section to practice taking your next exam.

Following the Exam Preparation Section is the Answer Section. In this section are answers to all of the Active Reading Section items, solutions to the Crossword Puzzles and answers to the Practice Tests.

A METHOD OF ACTIVE PARTICIPATION

SQ3R *plus*: Studies show that passive approaches to learning things such as academic subjects are totally ineffective: effective learning requires the learner to actively participate. One strategy for becoming an active participant in the learning process is the SQ3R *plus* method. SQ3R *plus* is an acronym for Survey, Question, Read, Recite, Review, Write and Reflect, and *Keeping Pace Plus* is designed to familiarize you thoroughly with this method of study.

Survey: First, read the study guide learning objectives for the lesson and skim over the assigned pages in the text. As you skim through the text, look at the pictures and tables and read all of the captions. Also read the titles for the various sections of the chapter. Surveying the chapter before you begin to read will help you see how the chapter is organized, form an idea of what you will be studying, set a goal for how much you want to cover during the time you have allowed for your study session, and give you some direction for organizing your thoughts.

Question: Second, while surveying and reading the text ask some original questions about the information being presented, and in the margins write down your questions. Try to discover their answers in the text, and seek help from library resources or your professor when you cannot find the answers. Asking and answering your own questions will involve you in your own learning; and this will help you make meaningful connections to remember the information you study. You can formulate questions by looking at headings and subheadings in your text and asking yourself what they mean. For example, the heading "What is a Psychologist?" in Chapter 1 of your text could stimulate you to ask, "Are psychologists interested only in crazy people?" Or the heading "How Do Psychologists Study Behavior?" could prompt the question "Do psychologists study anything other than behavior?" The subheading "Naturalistic Observation" could lead you to ask "What does naturalistic mean?" You can also ask questions like "How does reinforcement apply to me?" "What do psychologists know about dreaming?" and so on. And of course, whenever you don't understand something, or understand but want to know more, write down your question.

Read: Reading without the goal of discovery and reading just to be able to say you did your homework are passive approaches and can lead to daydreaming instead of studying. Both are ineffective approaches and a waste of time. The reading section in your study guide is designed to encourage active reading. Read the learning objectives in the active reading section and all of the study questions pertaining to the objectives. These questions will help you discover the important points in the book that will allow you to master the material. Begin reading the text. As you discover answers to the questions, think about why the question has been asked and what the answer means; then, write the answer down in your study guide. The fill-in-the-blank questions will help you focus on key words. If during your reading you run across any words that you do not understand, refer to the enrichment glossary in your study guide or the glossary at the back of your text or look them up in a dictionary and write the definition down in the margin of your text. Continue this process, answering the questions put forth by the study guide and yourself until you have completed the lesson and then the chapter. The answers to the active reading section questions are at the back of your study guide.

Recite: When you have finished reading the text pages for a lesson, turn back to the lesson learning objectives in your study guide and repeat out loud or write down everything you can remember in support of each objective. There are at least three ways by which you can make this step an active process:

1. The fastest and most stimulating way requires the help of a friend, family member, or fellow student. Ask your friend to read the lesson learning objectives one-by-one to you. After he or she has read an objective, recite *out loud* everything you can remember in support of the objective. Ask your friend to make check marks next to the active reading questions that you have forgotten or remembered in error. (Later, when you review, concentrate on the areas where there are check marks.)

2. If a friend is not available or if you prefer to study alone, you can follow a procedure similar to the one described above. Read the learning objective and recite *out loud* or *write down* everything you can remember in support of the objective. It may seem silly to think of talking out loud to *yourself*, and you may have writer's cramp and feel like the last thing you want to do is write another word, but it is critical to the learning process that you do one of the *active rehearsal* steps. If you recite silently without writing, it is too easy to trick yourself into believing you have remembered more than you have--silent rehearsal is *passive*! Formulating ideas, in either spoken or written sentences, allows you to catch your weak areas and is an *active* process.

3. If you choose writing as your active reciting process, try visually outlining the information you recall. Reciting definitely leads to active involvement in the learning process, and it is a good way to practice for essay tests or class discussion situations.

Review: Finally, go back through the study guide lesson and reread your answers. Answer all of the questions you asked and concentrate on any areas where you showed weaknesses when reciting. The purpose of review is to double check your preparation, allowing you to be sure you have paid attention to all the important points in the lesson. As you can see, the SQ3R *plus* method is not the fastest way to cover the pages in your text; but covering pages quickly does not necessarily lead to learning. To be an active learner you must put yourself into the learning process, which is what the SQ3R *plus* method will help you to do. Also, once you get into it, you'll see the SQ3R *plus* does <u>not</u> take as long as it looks.

plus

Write: Write in your own words everything you can remember about the material you are studying. Summarize the main point, the minor points and see how rewriting your notes in a different format helps to encode the information into long term memory.

Reflect: Make your personal #1 Learning Objective for each chapter to be to ask and answer the question, "How can I utilize this new information in my future?" Apply this information in meaningful ways to you and your personal goals and objectives.

Keeping Pace Plus was written with the student in mind. The first task of *Keeping Pace Plus* is to assist students in general in learning Lefton's *Psychology sixth edition*, but the second goal is to provide students with general techniques students can apply to your other subjects. I welcome your comments, opinions, and suggestions for future editions. My address is Andrew H. Ryan, Jr. c/o Psychology Department, University of South Carolina, Columbia, SC 29208 or my E-Mail/internet address is Ryan@garnet.cla.sc.edu.

CHAPTER 1

What Is Psychology?

Psychology 6th Ed.		Keeping Pace Plus		
HEADINGS	**PAGE**	**LESSON**	**L.O.**	**LEARNING OBJECTIVES**
What Is This Science of Psychology?	4	1	1.1	Define psychology and identify the five aspects of human functioning that psychologists study.
Three Principles of Scientific Endeavor	5		1.2	Summarize the three principles that form the core of psychology.
The Scientific Method in Psychology	6		1.3	Identify and describe the five basic steps of the scientific method.
What Psychologists Do	7	2	1.4	Identify how psychologists are trained, possible career fields for psychologists, and two professional organizations to which many psychologists belong.
Differences among Practitioners	8		1.5	Compare the training and specialization of clinical psychologists, psychiatrists, and psychoanalysts.
Choosing Psychology as a Career	8		1.6	Discuss career opportunities in psychology and the impact of the increasing numbers of women and ethnic minorities who are entering the field.
Applied Research, Human Services, and Experimental Psychology	9		1.7	Describe applied research, human services, and experimental psychology and characterize the subfields of each.
DIVERSITY: Women and Ethnic Minorities Are Hidden no Longer	10			
The Research Process	13	3		
Correlation Is Not Causation	13		1.8	Compare cause-and-effect relationships to correlations.

Past and Present: Schools of Psychological Thought	25	5		
The Early Traditions	25		1.17	Define what it means to describe something as a school of psychological thought and then compare and contrast structuralism, functionalism, Gestalt psychology, and psychoanalytic theory.
Psychological Schools Grow Broader	28		1.18	Define behaviorism, humanistic psychology, cognitive psychology, and the biological perspective; discuss the similarities and differences between them and describe eclecticism.

Chapter 1 Overview

Students are introduced to the science of psychology. Since psychology is a science, adherence to the principles of scientific endeavor is critical. The scientific method is divided into five basic steps and each is outlined as it relates to research.

Psychologist/psychiatrist, what's the difference? The profession of psychology is diverse and has a number of educational requirements and specialty areas just as in medicine. Lefton describes the differences between psychologists, psychiatrists, and other professionals practicing psychology. The areas of applied research, human services, and experimental psychology are explained, and the subfields that encompass these exciting careers are examined.

This chapter covers a wide range of research techniques used by psychologists in the study of human behavior. Lefton begins with a discussion of how correlation differs from causation and expands the discussion by defining such terms as *variables*, *hypotheses*, *experimental* and *control groups*, *sample*, and what it means to say there is a significant difference. One of the skills that psychologists need is the ability to think critically. Lefton asks students to become critical thinkers to better understand and evaluate research and its findings.

Lefton also describes how to conduct a successful experiment by avoiding the pitfalls that could unwittingly influence the results of the experiment. In conducting effective research that will be generalizable, one must also attend to the many elements of a diverse society such as that of the United States

This chapter also covers many of the methods of psychological inquiry. The methods examined include experiments, questionnaires, interviews, naturalistic observation, and case studies. You will be exposed to these methods throughout the book, and it will serve you well to become very familiar with them in this early chapter.

The ethics of psychological research are discussed in relation to the necessity of animal research and the use of deception in human research.

Chapter 1 concludes with a look at the brief history of the science of psychology and its evolution over the past 100 plus years. An overview of how schools of psychological thought such as structuralism, functionalism, Gestalt psychology, and psychoanalysis, have expanded into the more modern schools of behaviorism, humanistic psychology, cognitive psychology, biological perspectives and the most common approach, known as eclecticism.

The science of psychology is as diverse as the behaviors and mental processes it seeks to understand. Chapter 1, like the discipline itself, is meant to give a broad understanding of this diversity and open your mind to the methods and procedures used by psychologist. Lefton provides a broad base from which the rest of the text will develop in taking you a this fascinating journey through *Psychology*.

SQ3R*plus*

SURVEY THE LESSON: Read learning objectives 1.1 through 1.18 and, in the text, examine the chapter headings, tables, and pictures on pages 4-32 in the text to *form an idea of what you should learn and to set goals for your study time*.

WRITE DOWN QUESTIONS: *While surveying and reading the text, write down questions* about the information being presented. *Write your questions* in the space below or on a separate piece of paper and try to find answers to these questions in the text.

ACTIVELY READ PAGES 4-32: The following exercise is designed to facilitate this process. Complete the following questions as you read, and when you are done, check your answers with those printed in the back of this study guide.

YOUR QUESTIONS:

Matching

Match the following terms or concepts from your textbook with the most appropriate description.

1. _____ accuracy
2. _____ correlation
3. _____ Counseling psychologist
4. _____ debriefing
5. _____ Educational Psychologist
6. _____ emotional response
7. _____ Engineering Psychologist
8. _____ Forensic Psychologist
9. _____ Health Psychologist
10. _____ hypothesis
11. _____ industrial/organizational
12. _____ objectivity
13. _____ overt actions
14. _____ psychology
15. _____ replication
16. _____ sample
17. _____ Sport Psychologist
18. _____ theory
19. _____ variables

a) science of behavior and mental processes
b) observable and measurable movements or results of movements
c) evaluating research based on its merit
d) feelings such as anger, depression, happiness
e) gathering of laboratory and real world data precisely
f) collection of interrelated ideas
g) educated guess
h) repeating an experiment to verify results
i) psychologist who focuses on how to use machines most efficiently
j) psychologist who focuses on how learning proceeds in the classroom, how intelligence affects performance, and the relationship between personality and learning
k) psychologist who focuses on legal issues and often evaluates whether an inmate is ready for parole, or whether a specific rehabilitation program is achieving its goals
l) psychologist who focuses on the way life-style changes can facilitate health improvement
m) emerging field that focuses on brain-behavior interactions
n) psychologist who works with people who have behavior problems; career planning; marriage and family problems; and parenting
o) psychologists concerned with the way employers evaluate employees; they focus on personnel selection, employee motivation, work behavior, and work appraisals
p) events not necessarily causally related
q) a condition or characteristic of a situation or person
r) group that is assumed to represent the population
s) information revealed following an experiment

True or False

1.	Psychology is the science of behavior and mental processes.	TRUE	FALSE
2.	Applied psychologists do research, then utilize research findings in everyday life.	TRUE	FALSE
3.	To say one is an experimental psychologist does not define the topic the psychologist studies; instead, it describes the techniques the psychologist uses.	TRUE	FALSE
4.	Psychologists only help people with problems.	TRUE	FALSE

5. A researcher who finds that subjects who are obese also have a high degree of anxiety can safely conclude that anxiety causes obesity.   TRUE   FALSE

6. In an experiment, the independent variable is manipulated, and the dependent variable is measured.   TRUE   FALSE

7 In a controlled experiment, the operational definition represents the primary question the study is trying to answer.   TRUE   FALSE

8. Interviews describe in detail a specific person's life history.   TRUE   FALSE

9. Psychologists often use more than one research method to find answers for a question they are trying to answer.   TRUE   FALSE

10. Students of psychology will succeed if they are able to think critically about research studies described in a variety of resources.   TRUE   FALSE

11. A critical thinker is able to find cause-and-effect conclusions from correlational studies.   TRUE   FALSE

12. Single-blind experiments are adequate to avoid self-fulfilling prophecy.   TRUE   FALSE

13. Humanistic psychologists see people as having free will and as being inherently good.   TRUE   FALSE

14. The American Psychological Association leaves ethical questions concerning animal research up to individual researchers.   TRUE   FALSE

15. Those who follow an eclectic approach reject all of the traditional approaches.   TRUE   FALSE

Fill-in-the-Blanks

1. A theory is a collection of interrelated ideas and facts put forward to _____ and _____ behavior.

2. Patients who see _____ often have both physical and emotional problems.

3. The goal of community psychologists is to help _____ and their neighborhoods grow, develop, and plan for the future.

4. Experimental psychology is a(n) _____, not a field of psychology.

5. Physiological psychologists are sometimes referred to as _____.

6. Events are _____ related when one event is contingent on the other.

7. Researchers manipulate _____ in order to determine relationships.

8. The control group is also called the _____ group.

9. A sample is supposed to represent the _____ under study.

10. One way of avoiding expectancy effect is not to reveal who is in the control and the experimental groups. This technique is referred to as a _____-_____.

11. Even when precautions are taken to avoid research pitfalls, participants sometimes behave differently due to the _____ effect.

12. When it comes to understanding diversity, we need to realize that there are usually more differences _____ a group than between groups.

13. Animal research is conducted in areas that it would be _____ to experiment on human beings.

14. If _____ is used in human research, then researchers must provide informed consent and a debriefing.

15. In applied psychology, _____ means to use combinations of approaches rather than to adhere to one school of psychological thought.

Applications

1. Identify the *independent and dependent variables* in each of the following experiments.

   A. A psychologist investigates the effects that level of background noise has on the time it takes subjects to complete a series of analytical problems.
      a) Independent _____
      b) Dependent _____

   B. A researcher conducts a study in which she measures academic performance among students who do not eat breakfast regularly.
      a) Independent _____
      b) Dependent _____

   C. Hospitalized schizophrenics are rewarded for cooperative behaviors, and a clinical psychologist observes to see if their rate of cooperation increases as a result.
      a) Independent _____
      b) Dependent _____

2. Identify the type of research method being employed in each of the following studies.

Experiment	*Naturalistic Observation*
Questionnaire	*Interview*
Case Study	

   A. _____ A researcher asks a number of people a series of standardized, open-ended questions concerning their awareness of substance abuse treatment centers. If the people give vague answers, she asks another question to clarify ideas. Her goal is to explore the issue in depth so that she can make recommendations to those treatment organizations.

   B. _____ A clinical psychologist who specializes in the treatment of people abusing alcohol or drugs keeps in-depth notes concerning his clients' life histories, emotional dispositions, and behavioral mannerisms. Based on these individual studies, he has identified life experiences and personality traits common among his clients.

C. _____ As part of a treatment program, substance abuse patients are asked to engage in structured group problem-solving activities. A psychologist watches their interactions from behind a mirrored one-way window (so she cannot be seen) and collects data concerning number and types of interactions that flow between individuals.

D. _____ In a well designed study that ensures that nobody actually gets hurt, a researcher tests her idea that substance abusers have a low tolerance for frustration and that this may be a factor in their addictions. She uses three groups of subjects and places one in a high frustration situation, one in low frustration situation, and the last group in a situation with no frustrating events. She then watches and collects data concerning the effects of the frustration.

E. _____ A researcher is interested in whether people in general know how to identify someone who is abusing drugs or alcohol. He mails a list of specific questions to a large number of households and asks them to complete and return the list. From this study he is able to gather a large amount of specific information in a short amount of time.

3. List the 5 research criteria that are helpful in being a critical thinker.

1. _____
2. _____
3. _____
4. _____
5. _____

4. List the strengths and weaknesses of each of the following research methods.

Research Approach	Strength(s)	Weakness(es)
Questionnaire		
Interview		
Naturalistic Observation		
Case Study		
Experiment		

5.   Fill-in-the-table.

School of Psychological Thought	Focus	Early Leader(s)
Structuralism		Wundt, Titchner
		James
Gestalt		
	unconscious mental processes	
Behaviorism		Watson, Skinner
	free will, desire for self-actualization & fulfillment	Maslow, Rogers
Cognitive		
Biological		

SQ3R*plus*

RECITE: When you have finished reading the assigned material in your text and you have completed the exercises in your study guide, turn back to the chapter outline. Read each learning objective and recite out loud everything you can remember in support of each objective.

REVIEW: Check to see if you have answered all the questions you wrote during the *Survey* stage. Complete all sections of your study guide and check your answers for accuracy. If you are having trouble with specific topics ask you instructor for help.

WRITE: Read the learning objective again and then, in your own words, write down everything you can remember about this chapter. Summarize the main points and the concepts introduced in this chapter.

REFLECT: After each study period, take a break and reflect on what you have just studied. Ask yourself how this newly acquired information can be used in the future.

CHAPTER ONE SELF-TEST

1. Behaviorism is primarily concerned with:
    A. focuses on describing and measuring only that which is observable.
    B. unconscious influences of early childhood experience.
    C. inherited characteristics.
    D. fulfillment of the human potential.

2. All of the following comparisons between clinical psychologists and psychiatrists are true *except*:
    A. Psychiatrists can prescribe medications while clinical psychologists cannot.
    B. Both see a similar mix of clients.
    C. Clinical psychologists generally have more extensive training in assessment than do psychiatrists.
    D. Both see abnormal behavior as a disease.

3. People who choose psychology as a career can expect:
   A. salaries ranging from $500,000 to $1,000,000 annually.
   B. to find a wide variety of job opportunities.
   C. some difficulty finding a job since employment opportunities have recently stabilized.
   D. all of the above

4. Which of the following would be considered an applied psychologist?
   A. forensic
   B. developmental
   C. social
   D. cognitive

5. One advantage of research with animals is:
   A. the ability to control the life history of the organism.
   B. it's easier to form hypotheses about animals.
   C. animals respond better to independent variables.
   D. you don't have to worry about operational definitions.

6. A correlation:
   A. exists when two events are regularly associated with one another.
   B. means a change in one variable causes a change in another variable.
   C. is found only through controlled laboratory experiments.
   D. is an experimental variable.

7. A tentative statement expressing a causal relationship between two events that will be evaluated in a research study is called:
   A. an operational definition.
   B. a theory.
   C. a hypothesis.
   D. a variable.

8. By increasing the sample size, the experimenter:
   A. can reasonably rule out chance as a cause and can increase generalizability of results.
   B. causes an unnecessary inconvenience for data collection.
   C. increases the likelihood that the experiment will not be replicated.
   D. all of the above

9. Researchers often do *not* collect data until their human subjects have adapted to the experimental situation in order to avoid problems that could arise from:
   A. the self-fulfilling prophecy.
   B. the Hawthorne effect.
   C. demand characteristics.
   D. some subjects dropping out of the experiment.

10. When psychologists consider factors such as ethnicity, gender, socioeconomic class, and religion, they are investigating:
    A. structuralism.
    B. dependent variables.
    C. random assignment of subjects.
    D. human diversity.

11. One disadvantage of naturalistic observation is
    A. many psychologists tend to discount the results.
    B. the behavior in question may not be exhibited.
    C. it requires travel to distant and remote places.
    D. there are not data available to justify conclusions made from the study.

Congratulations, you have completed Chapter 1. Now, proceed to the Exam Preparation Section in the back of your study guide for your final review, but don't forget to review the Enrichment Glossary for help understanding difficult words.

LANGUAGE ENRICHMENT GLOSSARY

Some students who reviewed the textbook listed the following words as difficult to understand. Use this list, your dictionary, and teachers and friends to learn the meaning of words you do not understand.

Page	Term	Explanation	Page	Term	Explanation
4	precise	exact	17	distort	give false information
4	underpinnings	a basis or foundation	17	concealing	hiding
6	gender	male or female	18	sorting through	thinking about the facts
7	debilitating	to make weak	18	glib	idea not well thought out
8	promoting human	improving the quality of people's lives	20	fuzzy	not clear or distinct
8	student affiliates	student members	21	SAT scores	test of college skills
8	emerged	been started	21	gathers	collects
8	rivalry	competition	21	weakness	what is bad about it
9	subfield	is a part of	21	exaggerated	made too large
10	equivalent	equal to	21	seemingly simple	look like a simple way
10	cornerstones	basis	23	grubby	dressed in dirty clothing
11	inmates	prisoner	23	flaws	problems or mistakes
11	parole	released from prison but still must report to work	25	orient	focus
11	work appraisals	evaluate quality of work	25	conscious	aware
11	absenteeism	not at work	26	evolving	changing for the better
11	coined the term	made up the term	27	perceptual	who we perceive
12	converging	coming together	27	interpret	understand
12	widespread desire	desires of diverse people	28	premise	belief
12	catastrophic	terrible or disastrous	28	maladjustment	problems
14	broken homes	divorced parents	28	eclipse	overshadow
14	contingent	dependent	28	brash	bold, disrespectful
14	causal inferences	explanations of cause	28	defiant	going against authority
15	justified	correct	29	assumptions	to guess or suppose
15	affirmed	supported	29	disordered	unhealthy behavior
15	ensure	make sure	29	inherently	basically
15	randomly	having no pattern	29	striving to fulfill	trying to be the best
16	Pitfalls	mistakes or errors	29	fraught with	troubled with
17	markedly	very much	30	threatening	dangerous
17	unwittingly create	cause something to happen without meaning to	30	engage in	do certain actions
17	prophesied	beliefs about the future	31	faulty	bad
17	elicit	produce	32	mainstay	most important part

CHAPTER 2

Biological Bases of Behavior

Psychology 6th Ed.		Keeping Pace Plus		
HEADINGS	**PAGE**	**LESSON**	**L.O.**	**LEARNING OBJECTIVES**
Nature versus Nurture	38	1	2.1	Make a distinction between the terms *nature* and *nurture*, and discuss how each affects the expression of human traits.
The Basics of Genetics	39		2.2	Describe how the field of behavioral genetics uses an understanding of basic biological mechanisms and their relationships to explain behavior.
Twins and the Nature versus Nurture Issue	41		2.3	Discuss how twin studies have revealed information about the contributions of nature and nurture to human behavior.
Communication in the Nervous System	42	2		
The Neuron	42		2.4	Review communication in the nervous system by specifying the three types of neurons, the parts of a neuron, and the electrochemical process.
Neurotransmitters and Behavior	47		2.5	Outline how the study of neurotransmitters has led scientists to a better understanding of the relationship between neurotransmitters and behavior.
Organization of the Peripheral and Central Nervous Systems	49	3		
The Peripheral Nervous System	49		2.6	Describe the peripheral nervous system and its subsystems.
The Central Nervous System	51		2.7	Identify and describe the structures of the central nervous system.

Chapter 2 Overview

You learned in Chapter 1 that psychology is the study of behavior and mental processes. All behavior as well as mental processes originate in the biological systems of our body. In Chapter 2, Lefton explains the importance of genetics and its contribution to behavior and mental processes. Studies of genetic defects and twins provide insight into the nature versus nurture controversy.

Communication in the nervous system is complex and difficult to grasp in its entirety at first. Therefore, Chapter 2 breaks the nervous system down into its basic units and begins by explaining how the electrochemical process works. Beginning with the neuron, Lefton describes the journey of a neural impulse from one neuron to another and explains how neurotransmitters may hold the key to understanding specific human behaviors such as drug addiction.

The nervous system is composed of two subsystems, the central nervous system (CNS) and the peripheral nervous system (PNS). Working concurrently, these two subsystems send, receive, process, interpret, and store neuronal information. The brain, which is a component of the CNS, is divided into three sections: hindbrain, midbrain, and forebrain. Several functions of these sections are described including how specific functions are linked to behavior.

Monitoring neuronal activity has progressed from measuring head size in the 18th century to using high-tech CAT, PET, and MRI technology to scan brain tissue and its processes more precisely and to provide valuable information about the workings of the brain and nervous system. Other important attributes such as brain specialization and plasticity are discussed to provide an understanding of the development of the brain in individuals. The idea that someday neurotransplants will be used as a therapeutic technique is implied.

In conclusion, Chapter 2 discusses the contribution of the endocrine system and its production of hormones to human behavior. Lefton refers to the pituitary gland as the master gland because of its role in regulating the adrenal gland and the pancreas in hormonal production. The question of gender differences being caused by brain structure or hormones is discussed.

Understanding the basics of biology and behavior will go a long way toward helping you in later chapters of *Psychology*. Chapter 2 provides the basics that Lefton will expand on in the rest of the text.

SQ3R*plus*

SURVEY THE LESSON: Read learning objectives 2.1 through 2.14 and, in the text, examine the chapter headings, tables, and pictures on pages 38-66 in the text to *form an idea of what you should learn and to set goals for your study time.*

WRITE DOWN QUESTIONS: *While surveying and reading the text, write down questions* about the information being presented. *Write your questions* in the space below or on a separate piece of paper and try to find answers to these questions in the text.

ACTIVELY READ PAGES 38-66: The following exercise is designed to facilitate this process. Complete the following questions as you read, and when you are done, check your answers with those printed in the back of this study guide.

YOUR QUESTIONS:

Matching

Match the following terms or concepts from your textbook with the appropriate description.

1. _____ agonists
2. _____ allele
3. _____ antagonist
4. _____ axon
5. _____ CNS
6. _____ dendrite
7. _____ EEG
8. _____ endocrine gland
9. _____ genetics
10. _____ hippocampus

11. _____ hormones
12. _____ hypoglycemia
13. _____ hypothalamus
14. _____ limbic system
15. _____ neuromodulator
16. _____ neuron
17. _____ PKU
18. _____ pons
19. _____ synapse
20. _____ thalamus

a) the study of heredity
b) each member of a pair of genes
c) phenylketonuria: genetic disorder that prevents amino acid processing
d) the basic unit of the nervous system
e) fibers extending from the neuron cell body that receive signals from neighboring cells
f) transmits signals from cell body through axon terminal to adjacent neurons
g) small space between neurons
h) chemical substance that functions to increase or decrease sensitivity to specific effects of neurotransmitters
i) chemical that mimics the actions of a neurotransmitter
j) chemical that opposes the actions of a neurotransmitter
k) ductless gland that secrets hormones directly to the bloodstream
l) brain and spinal cord
m) structure of the hindbrain involved in sleep
n) structure on the forebrain that acts to route information to other parts of the brain
o) connects the forebrain and the midbrain and affects eating, sleeping, and sexual behavior
p) made from the hippocampus and the amygdala
q) involved in memory, learning, and emotions
r) chemicals that regulate specific organs and cells
s) overproduction of insulin
t) record of electrical brain wave patterns

True or False

1. The effects of growing up on a farm is an example of nurture.　　TRUE　　FALSE

2. Experience provides the framework for the expression of genetic traits.　　TRUE　　FALSE

3. An allele is a gene on a chromosome that is exactly like its corresponding gene on another chromosome.　　TRUE　　FALSE

4. If a Y-sperm fertilizes an ovum, the result is a male.　　TRUE　　FALSE

5. Recent research suggests that genes may predispose people to mental retardation.   TRUE   FALSE

6. Efferent neurons send messages to the brain and spinal cord.   TRUE   FALSE

7. Glial cells are neurons that combine the activities of sensory and motor neurons.   TRUE   FALSE

8. In its resting state, a neuron is negatively charged inside the cell as compared to outside.   TRUE   FALSE

9. Neurons cannot usually fire more than 500 times per second   TRUE   FALSE

10. Neurons can only hold one neurotransmitter substance.   TRUE   FALSE

11. The autonomic nervous system is one subsystem of the peripheral nervous system.   TRUE   FALSE

12. Most somatic nervous system responses are involuntary.   TRUE   FALSE

13. In spite of the spinal reflex response, most signals eventually make their way to the brain.   TRUE   FALSE

14. Beta brain waves occur when people are not engaged in active thinking.   TRUE   FALSE

15. CT, MRI , and PET are techniques for examining the activity of the nervous system.   TRUE   FALSE

16. Structures in the hindbrain and midbrain are often assumed to be organizationally more primitive and are responsible for more basic reflexive actions.   TRUE   FALSE

17. The midbrain can cause the body to react immediately without the signal being relayed to more complex parts of the brain.   TRUE   FALSE

18. The hypothalamus acts primarily as a routing station.   TRUE   FALSE

19. The amygdala, part of the limbic system, has been associated with the expression of fear.   TRUE   FALSE

20. The basal ganglia controls movements and posture.   TRUE   FALSE

21. Studies of brain structure show that different areas are responsible for different functions.   TRUE   FALSE

22. The two primary methods of gathering information on lateralization are examining brain wave activity and observing split-brain patients.   TRUE   FALSE

23. Each cerebral hemisphere is neurologically connected to the opposite side of the body.   TRUE   FALSE

24. Most specific behaviors can be traced to a single, specific area of the brain.   TRUE   FALSE

25. Hormones influence behavior.   TRUE   FALSE

26. Human sexual behavior is totally under voluntary control.   TRUE   FALSE

27. Diabetes mellitus is a condition where there is an insufficient amount of insulin in the blood.   TRUE   FALSE

28. The adrenal gland is very involved in the body's reaction to stress.   TRUE   FALSE

29. Research shows that men and women do equally well at reading emotions from photographs.   TRUE   FALSE

Fill-in-the-blanks

1. A _____ is the basic unit of heredity transmission.

2. The _____ gene is the one whose characteristics will be expressed.

3. Down syndrome and phenylketonuria are examples of how _____ _____ _____ or _____ _____ result in dramatic changes in human development.

4. The basic unit of the nervous system is called a(n) _____.

5. _____ cells insulate the brain from toxins and also are the basis for a thin white myelinated covering that allows for signal conduction in neurons.

6. A long slim fiber that carries signals from the cell body is called the _____.

7. The resting state of a cell is maintained when the electrical charge is in a state of _____.

8. When neurons fire they generate action potentials in an all or none fashion, but they do not fire at all if the neuron does not reach _____.

9. The recovery period following neuronal firing is called the _____ _____ which lasts for a few thousandths of a second.

10. A change in the membrane potential of a neuron due to the release of neurotransmitters is called a _____ _____.

11. Chemicals known as _____ are involved in complex behaviors such as sleep, movement, anxiety, memory, learning, and sexual behavior.

12. _____ is the study of how drugs affect human behavior.

13. Chemicals can be administered to mimic the action of neurotransmitters. When an _____ is administered it blocks the cell's receptor site, while an _____ facilitates the cell's activity.

14. The part of the autonomic nervous system involved in emergency response is called the _____ nervous system.

15. The _____ _____ is part of the central nervous system and relays signals to the brain.

16. The _____ _____ is directly involved with a person's sleep, wake, and state of arousal.

17. The _____, which is sometimes called the "little brain", influences our ability to walk straight lines and to execute other coordinated movements such as dancing.

18. A thick group of cross hemisphere connections that when severed may prevent seizures is called the _____ _____.

19. The exterior of the brain is covered by the _____ which is convoluted to create more surface area.

20. Researchers suggest that within limits the brain is _____ from birth through adulthood, and therefore even brain injury may be corrected through treatment.

21. _____ were once thought to be impossible, but are now considered feasible especially in areas that are highly organized like the visual cortex.

22. Hormones are chemicals secreted directly into the bloodstream from the _____ gland.

23. The pea-sized gland that controls many of the endocrine glands is called the _____ gland.

24. The release of _____ by the adrenal gland causes heart rate to increase and is activated when one is threatened or becomes anxious.

25. The pancreas, one of the endocrine glands, is involved in the release of _____ which can result in low blood sugar and a feeling of being faint and lacking in energy.

Applications

1. Label each of the following statements as being primarily the product of nature, nurture, or both nature and nurture. Remember, all behavior is ultimately the product of both. However, the statements below *emphasize* (in some cases) nature or nurture. They are designed only to give you practice in discriminating between the two components of behavior. If you cannot determine a *primary* influence, "both" is probably the correct answer.

   A. _____ Unlike most babies, at the age of seven months, Mario said his first word in the language he had been exposed to by his parents.

   B. _____ Mary has blond hair and is very tall.

   C. _____ Having lived in China, France, and Italy, Kim can prepare Chinese, French, and Italian meals.

   D. _____ Donna's level of dopamine is so low that her body trembles most of the time.

   E. _____ By the age of twelve, Francis was mastering college-level academic material.

2. Complete the following table on the endocrine system.

ENDOCRINE GLAND	HORMONE	EFFECT
anterior lobe		
	antidiuretic (ADH)	acts on the kidneys
	oxytocin	
	prolactin	controls milk production
pancreas		
	epinephrinc (adrenaline)	

3. Identify the parts of the nervous system (central, somatic, parasympathetic, or sympathetic) that is most specifically illustrated by each of the following situations.

   A. _____ In an effort to shape up, John engages in a series of sit-ups and push-ups.

   B. _____ Mary, while walking to her psychology class, comes across a large dog who growls at her. Mary notices her heart beating faster and her breathing increased.

   C. _____ Jane just moved off-campus and must draw up a new budget. She carefully analyzes her assets, her bills, and how she would like to spend the excess after bills.

D. _____ An increase in the secretion of digestive juices and blood flowing to the gastrointestinal system causes the meal Simon just ate to break down into protein and carbohydrate molecules and nutrients that are eventually absorbed by his blood system.

SQ3R*plus*

RECITE: When you have finished reading the assigned material in your text and you have completed the exercises in your study guide, turn back to the chapter outline. Read each learning objective and recite out loud everything you can remember in support of each objective.

REVIEW: Check to see if you have answered all the questions you wrote during the *Survey* stage. Complete all sections of your study guide and check your answers for accuracy. If you are having trouble with specific topics ask you instructor for help.

WRITE: Read the learning objective again and then, in your own words, write down everything you can remember about this chapter. Summarize the main points and the concepts introduced in this chapter.

REFLECT: After each study period, take a break and reflect on what you have just studied. Ask yourself how this newly acquired information can be used in the future.

CHAPTER TWO SELF TEST

1. The term *nature* refers to:
   A. life experiences.
   B. heredity.
   C. personality.
   D. the environment.

2. In response to the nature verses nurture debate, most psychologists agree that:
   A. heredity is more important than environment.
   B. environment is more important than heredity.
   C. ultimately, all behavior is the result of the environment.
   D. both heredity and environment are important, but the question of which is more important has not been resolved.

3. Genes are:
   A. the units of heredity transmission consisting of DNA and protein.
   B. strands of genetic material.
   C. used to describe the development of twins.
   D. found only in ova and sperm sex cells.

4. A genetic disorder caused by the presence of a recessive gene is called:
   A. Huntington's disease.
   B. Mondrei Blue syndrome.
   C. Down syndrome.
   D. Phenylketonuria (PKU).

5. Twins make good subjects for studying the relative effects of nature-nurture because they:
   A. begin life in the same uterine environment.
   B. are easier to track over time.
   C. have the same life experiences.
   D. inherited chromosomes from their parents.

6. Twin and adoption studies have shown that intellectual abilities:
   A. depend entirely on nature.
   B. are primarily a result of nurture.
   C. are the result of an interaction of inherited traits and family environment.
   D. usually get better as a person matures.

7. The _____ of the neuron has thin branching fibers and receives information from neighboring neurons.
   A. cell body
   B. axon
   C. dendrites
   D. axon terminals

8. A neuron will fire when a rapid reversal of negative and positive ions stimulate the cell and reach a level of intensity that is above the cell's:
   A. potential.
   B. threshold.
   C. spikes.
   D. resting level.

9. Whether a neurotransmitter acts as an excitatory or an inhibitory PSP depends on:
   A. the type of neurotransmitter.
   B. the receptor cite onto which it binds.
   C. the permeability of the cell membrane.
   D. the strength of the action potential.

10. Endorphins:
    A. are narcotic drugs.
    B. excite synaptic transmission of pain.
    C. inhibit synaptic transmission of pain.
    D. are incomplete amino acids and ineffective as neurotransmitters.

11. By studying the effects of neurotransmitters, psychologists have determined that people with Parkinson's disease have a low level of:
    A. dopamine.
    B. serotonin.
    C. GABA.
    D. acetylcholine.

12. Your body assumes a "fight-or-flight" condition, preparing you for emergency situations, when the _____ nervous system is activated.
    A. central
    B. somatic
    C. sympathetic
    D. parasympathetic

13. Rapid changes in the autonomic nervous system are usually associated with:
    A. sleep.
    B. stress.
    C. increases in prolactin levels.
    D. the presence of alpha waves.

14. Which of the following is *not* a spinal reflex?
    A. knee jerk
    B. removing your hand from a hot object
    C. reaching for a candy bar
    D. pulling your foot from the cold water in a swimming pool

15. The technique for measuring neuronal activity that involves placing a microelectrode next to a neuron is called:
    A. electroencephalography.
    B. magnetic resonance imaging.
    C. computerized axial tomography.
    D. single unit recording.

16. The limbic system:
    A. is probably one of the most complex and least understood areas of the brain.
    B. is involved in memory, emotional behavior, and epilepsy.
    C. contains "pleasure centers."
    D. all of the above

17. The reticular formation that extends through the hindbrain, the midbrain, and forebrain is thought to be involved in:
    A. coordination of smooth muscle.
    B. experiencing pain.
    C. controlling heart beat.
    D. waking and sleeping.

18. In most people the right hemisphere of the brain:
    A.   controls speech and language.
    B.   specializes in logical thinking.
    C.   appears to be organized for the processing of spatial and artistic tasks.
    D.   is considered the dominant hemisphere.

19. Neurotransplants:
    A.   are done on a routine basis.
    B.   are successful 90 percent of the time.
    C.   cannot be done; they are purely science fiction.
    D.   have been successfully used to treat people with Parkinson's disease.

20. Hypoglycemia is a condition caused by:
    A.   too much thyroxin.
    B.   too little thyroxin.
    C.   too little insulin.
    D.   too much insulin.

21. When looking at gender differences, we find that:
    A.   hormones have no effect on behavior.
    B.   there are greater differences among women and among men than between women and men.
    C.   testosterone is a hormone found only in men.
    D.   structural differences in the brain are apparent at birth.

Congratulations, you have completed Chapter 2. Now, proceed to the Exam Preparation Section in the back of your study guide for your final review, but don't forget to review the Enrichment Glossary for help understanding difficult words.

LANGUAGE ENRICHMENT GLOSSARY

Some students who reviewed the textbook listed the following words as difficult to understand. Use this list, your dictionary, and teachers and friends to learn the meaning of words you do not understand.

Page	Term	Explanation	Page	Term	Explanation
38	proposition	idea	52	pinpointed	located exactly
38	inherited	qualities from parent	53	latticelike network	interlaced like a net
39	penchants	what he likes	53	Organizationally	to put in an order
39	abnormalities	problems	53	Cognitive	thinking
40	mapping	drawing a picture of it	53	arousal	becoming awake
40	irreparable	can not be fixed	53	waking	not being asleep
42	asserts	claims and states	54	radical	extreme
41	uterine	womb	55	convoluted	like closely placed hills and valleys
41	infancy	first 12 months of life	55	ravines	like valleys next to hills
41	adolescence	about 12 - 19 years old	55	abnormalities	not normal or average
41	IQ	measure of intelligence	55	ablation	cutting out
41	reared apart	grew up in different homes	57	synchronized	move together
41	unraveling	gaining understanding	57	erratic moves	with no pattern
	integrated	brought together	58	spatial tasks	activity involving space
42	initiating	starting	58	invaluable	extremely important
43	convey	send	60	protracted	long time
43	nourish	feed	60	fetal	baby before birth
43	toxins	poison	61	fostering	helping
45	generate	make	62	junk food	not healthy food
48	facilitate	make happen more easily	62	jumbled	mixed up, confused
47	virtually every	all most all	62	render	make
47	mimicked	copied	62	unaccountable	not responsible
48	precisely	exactly	62	mediated	controlled
50	dilation of pupils	black center of eyes grows larger	63	irreversible	can not be changed back
50	digestion	break down food in body	64	volatile	high energy
51	scrutinized	to inspect or look at	64	verbal fluency	ability to speak easily
52	elicited	make happen	65	sexually explicit	sexually bold
52	overstated	too much importance	66	alley	pathway between buildings
52	chief trunk line	main pathway	64	simultaneously	at the same time
53	stem	comes from	65	shrinking	getting smaller
55	tumors	extra growth of cells			

CHAPTER 3

Perception

Psychology 6th Ed.		Keeping Pace Plus		
HEADINGS	PAGE	LESSON	L.O.	LEARNING OBJECTIVES
The Perceptual Experience	72	1		
Sensation and Perception: Definitions	72		3.1	Outline why contemporary psychologists generally acknowledge that a strict distinction between sensation and perception is no longer necessary.
Psychophysics	73		3.2	Investigate psychophysics by contrasting the theories of perceptual threshold and signal-detection.
Subliminal Perception	74		3.3	Evaluate the research on subliminal perception, and discuss to what degree subliminal stimuli can influence behavior.
Selective Attention	75		3.4	Compare and contrast filter and attenuation theory as they relate to people's ability to attend selectively to multiple stimuli.
Restricted Environmental Stimulation	75		3.5	Discuss the known effects of a restricted environment, and give examples of recent applications for modifying human behavior.
The Visual System	76	2		
The Structure of the Eye	77		3.6	Identify and describe the parts of the eye and explain how each is related to the processing of visual stimuli.
The Electrical Connection	81		3.7	Describe the function of receptive fields, and discuss recent research and potential uses of these studies.

| Extrasensory Perception 109 | 3.24 Using critical thinking skills, evaluate extrasensory perception and how it fits into contemporary psychology. |

Chapter 3 Overview

Psychologists study perception primarily because what people sense and perceive determines how they interpret their environment. Psychophysics is the study of how physical stimuli are translated into psychological experience. Lefton describes the different types of thresholds thought to be necessary for perception, including a discussion of the possibility of subliminal perception. For some of you it is difficult to pat your head and rub your stomach at the same time. What about listening to two people talking to you at the same time? Although we can multitask some behaviors (walking and chewing gum), we must choose to attend to selected stimuli presented to the auditory and visual systems. Psychologists are interested in how we choose to selectively attend. Sensory restriction is being studied as a means of relaxing, with the possibility that it may be effective in altering such behaviors as smoking and insomnia.

The primary sensory processing system is the visual system. The structure and function of the eye is detailed in a discussion by Lefton of how nearsighted and farsighted vision are caused by differences in the shape of the eyeball. Photoreceptors such as rods and cones have implications for visual behavior such as dark adaptation, fine discrimination, and color vision. Researchers are using knowledge about the electrochemical process of stimulation to formulate theories about the visual process, associating receptive fields with body movements and recognition of common objects such as faces.

Your eyes are constantly in motion. Saccades are voluntary eye movements involved in reading, driving, and looking for objects. Eye movement research suggests that eye movements are cross-cultural and are involved in information processing. Color vision has three psychological properties--hue, brightness, and saturation--which correspond to the physical properties of wavelength, intensity, and purity. The trichromatic and opponent-process theories attempt to explain how we perceive color and why many males are color-blind.

Our perceptual systems are able to perceive constancy in size, shape, and depth by utilizing monocular and binocular cues. Illusions are described as breaks or differences in what is expected. Optical illusions are dependent on our culture and early experiences. The Gestalt laws of organization are an attempt to explain how the whole is more than the sum of its parts. Gestaltists claim the brain imposes organization on stimuli by proximity, similarity, continuity, closure, and common fate.

Chapter 3 presents the basic components of sound and the structure of the ear and explains the place and frequency theories of hearing. Lefton explains how the direction of sounds is determined by time and intensity differences. Hearing impairments are possible at all ages.

Taste and smell are characterized as chemical senses and the role of smell in communication is explored in animals and humans. The skin senses of touch and pain are examined. The gate control theory of pain and the body's use of endorphins are described as they relate to pain perception and management. Other perceptual senses such as kinesthesia, the vestibular sense, and extrasensory perception are also discussed.

Chapter 3 explains the complexity of our sensory systems and how each relies on the brain to interpret information after it has been perceived. Our sensory systems convert physical energy into neural signals in much the same way your computer converts code into meaningful data. Our early experiences and our culture influence how we perceive.

SQ3R*plus*

SURVEY THE LESSON: Read learning objectives 1.1 through 1.18 and, in the text, examine the chapter headings, tables, and pictures on pages 72-110 in the text to *form an idea of what you should learn and to set goals for your study time*.

WRITE DOWN QUESTIONS: *While surveying and reading the text, write down questions* about the information being presented. *Write your questions* in the space below or on a separate piece of paper and try to find answers to these questions in the text.

ACTIVELY READ PAGES 72-110: The following exercise is designed to facilitate this process. Complete the following questions as you read, and when you are done, check your answers with those printed in the back of this study guide.

YOUR QUESTIONS:

Matching
Match the following terms or concepts from your textbook with the appropriate description.

1. _____ absolute threshold
2. _____ accommodation
3. _____ amplitude
4. _____ convergence
5. _____ dichromats
6. _____ endorphin
7. _____ frequency
8. _____ illusion
9. _____ kinesthesis
10. _____ light
11. _____ monochromats
12. _____ myopic
13. _____ olfaction
14. _____ optic chiasm
15. _____ photoreceptors
16. _____ pitch
17. _____ psychophysics
18. _____ purity
19. _____ saccades
20. _____ sensation
21. _____ sound
22. _____ subliminal perception
23. _____ transduction
24. _____ trichromatic theory

a) the relationship between physical stimuli and conscious experience
b) sense organ receptor cells are stimulated
c) below threshold awareness
d) portion of electromagnetic spectrum visible to the eye
e) difficulty seeing things at a distance
f) light sensitive cells known as rod and cones
g) conversion or coding of perceptual stimuli into electrical impulses
h) the minimum level of stimulation required for perception
i) point on the optic nerves where fibers cross over and project to the opposite side
j) eye movements focusing on different points
k) depth of hue of reflected light, also called saturation
l) Young-Helmholtz theory of color being made by mixing red, green, and blue
m) people having reduced color vision due to a lack of cones on the retina
n) people who can only distinguish two of the three primary colors
o) as objects move closer or further away the lens of the eye changes
p) eye movements to keep information at corresponding points as objects move closer
q) a perception that differs from the expected or measurable reality
r) changes in air pressure that vary in frequency and amplitude
s) frequency of auditory stimulation
t) number of times air pressure change cycles in a unit of time
u) smell
v) an awareness of movement of joints, muscle and tendons
w) naturally produced painkillers
x) amount of energy in a sound wave which determines loudness

True or False

1. Normal perceptual development requires varied sensory experiences and interaction among the different perceptual systems.   TRUE   FALSE

2. Contemporary psychologists find it important to make a clear distinction between the concept of sensation and the process of perception.   TRUE   FALSE

3. Perceptual systems must operate independently of one another.   TRUE   FALSE

4. Lilly's early studies showing that sensory deprivation causes hallucinations and altered states has been well documented.   TRUE   FALSE

5. Light waves are part of the electromagnetic spectrum   TRUE   FALSE

6. Photoreceptors have individual pathways to visual centers in the brain   TRUE   FALSE

7. Cones are predominantly responsible for night vision.   TRUE   FALSE

8. Our eyes are always in some state of light or dark adaptation.   TRUE   FALSE

9. Our eyes are capable of instantly adapting to the dark.   TRUE   FALSE

10. Much of our knowledge of how the brain processes electrochemical signals comes from studies of the receptive field.   TRUE   FALSE

11. Specific cells on the retina that fire only when certain visual stimuli are present are called receptive fields.   TRUE   FALSE

12. Kittens who had their receptive fields oriented to horizontal lines bumped into the vertical legs of chairs.   TRUE   FALSE

13. The human eye makes approximately 250 saccades per second.   TRUE   FALSE

14. Eye movements are important to the way brain stores information, and there are individual differences among scan paths.   TRUE   FALSE

15. Color depends on the wavelength of light particles that stimulate the photoreceptors.   TRUE   FALSE

16. Unsaturated colors are produced by wider bands of light.   TRUE   FALSE

17. According to the trichromatic theory, the three basic colors involved in color vision are red, yellow, and blue.   TRUE   FALSE

18. The opponent-process theory explains how color information is transferred from the retina to the lateral geniculate nucleus.   TRUE   FALSE

19. Many color blind individuals have trouble with several colors.   TRUE   FALSE

20. People have difficulty judging the size of object when the size of the image on the retina changes.　　TRUE　FALSE

21. In Luger's study in all situations infants showed size constancy.　　TRUE　FALSE

22. Linear perspective is based on the principle that when an object blocks out part of another, the first appears closer.　　TRUE　FALSE

23. Convergence is controlled by muscles in the face that convey information to the brain.　　TRUE　FALSE

24. Misperception of stimulation is an illusion.　　TRUE　FALSE

25. Pitch is to loudness as amplitude is to intensity.　　TRUE　FALSE

26. The amplitude of a sound wave refers to its energy level.　　TRUE　FALSE

27. The eardrum is the boundary between the outer and middle ear.　　TRUE　FALSE

28. The cochlea is located in the middle ear.　　TRUE　FALSE

29. The place and frequency theories are to hearing as the trichromatic and opponent process theories are to color coding.　　TRUE　FALSE

30. Subliminal perception began in the 1950s as an advertising ploy.　　TRUE　FALSE

31. Research by Silverman showed that presenting aggressive or sexual messages subliminally will not generally affect behavior.　　TRUE　FALSE

32. Any learning that results from subliminal perception is influenced by non-perceptual variables such as motivation.　　TRUE　FALSE

33. Selective attention is confined to hearing.　　TRUE　FALSE

34. Sweet foods act almost as sedatives.　　TRUE　FALSE

35. The receptors for taste are made up of several taste cells.　　TRUE　FALSE

36. Both taste and smell are stimulated by chemicals.　　TRUE　FALSE

37. The pheromones emitted by a man may change a woman's menstrual cycle.　　TRUE　FALSE

38. Research proved that perfumes not only affect people, they can trigger specific behavior.　　TRUE　FALSE

39. The dermis consists primarily of dead cells.　　TRUE　FALSE

40. Athletes who are in competition often report not feeling pain from an injury until after an event has ended.　　TRUE　FALSE

41. Enkaphalins is a natural pain blocker.　　TRUE　FALSE

42. One result of kinesthesis is being able to tell how far away an object is.　　TRUE　FALSE

43. According to gate control theory, a closed gate results in increasing the perception of pain.　　TRUE　FALSE

Fill-in-the-Blanks

1. The interpretation of sensory information into meaning is called _____.

2. The smallest amount of change necessary for an observer to report stimulation is known as _____ _____.

3. Psychologists use the _____ _____ _____ to discover the range of perceptual thresholds.

4. _____ _____ theory suggests that there are no finite or absolute thresholds; each response is individual.

5. Nonperceptual variables such as motivation, experience, personality, learning, and culture may affect our being influenced by _____ _____.

6. The _____ theory states that humans are limited in capacity to attend, while the _____ theory states that we are not limited, rather we inhibit attention due to intervening factors.

7. _____ and _____ vision occurs because the image on the back of the eyeball is out of focus.

8. Full color vision is dependent on the _____, while night vision relies heavily on _____.

9. Receptive fields are known to be sensitive to specific features such as position, length, and color and are thought to be involved in the control of _____.

10. Saccadic movement of the eyes lead to _____ or delays which form representations of the visual world as when we read.

11. The color of an object is referred to as _____, the _____ is how light or dark hue is and the purity of the color is known as _____.

12. People possessing normal color vision are called _____.

13. While _____ cannot discriminate any colors, _____ may only have problems with one specific color recognition.

14. Our ability to maintain _____ _____ is determined by previous experience, distance, and presence of surrounding objects.

15. Monocular and binocular cues are important in _____ perception.

16. One type of binocular cue known as _____ _____ is helpful in determining distance.

17. The _____ _____ _____ suggests that we see things in terms of their relationship to surrounding elements, and we tend to group things as a whole which helps to define figure-ground relationships.

18. _____ is the psychological process that occurs as a result of changes in air pressure.

19. High pitched tones usually have _____ frequencies.

20. The middle ear is made up of _____ known as the hammer, anvil, and stirrup.

21. The interaural time and interaural intensity differences are analyzed by the brain to determine _____ _____.

22. Exposure to very high intensity sound for prolonged periods can lead to _____ deafness.

23. There are four basic taste groups: _____ _____ _____ _____.

24. The sense of smell is a chemical process known as _____.

25. _____ are chemical substances secreted as a means of communication in animals and possibly in humans.

26. Endogenous morphine or _____ are painkillers that are naturally produced by the pituitary gland.

27. The perception explained by the gate-control theory is the perception of _____.

28. The _____ _____ sense is our sense of bodily orientation or posture.

29. _____ is the ability to predict future events.

30. _____ is one's ability to move objects by mental powers.

Applications

1. Identify the independent variable and dependent variable involved in each of the following studies. (Refer to Chapter 1, Learning Objective 1.9 to review the concepts of independent and dependent variables.)

A. Hirsch and Spinelli (1971), and Blakemore and Cooper (1970), measured how kittens responded to horizontal and vertical objects after having been raised with goggles that oriented their receptive fields either horizontally or vertically.

1. Independent variable _____

2. Dependent variable _____

B. In a study investigating eye movement, Norton and Stark (1971), presented pictures in a learning period and subsequent testing period; they measure, the subject's fixations and scan paths in both phases of the experiment.

   1.   Independent variable _____

   2.   Dependent variable _____
   _____

2. Describe the following monocular depth cues.

   A.   Motion parallax _____

   B.   Kinetic depth effect _____

   C.   Linear perspective _____

   D.   Interposition _____

   E.   Texture _____

   F.   Highlighting _____

   G.   Atmospheric perspective _____

   H.   Accommodation _____
   _____

3. Describe the following binocular depth cues.

   A.   Retinal disparity _____

   B.   Convergence _____
   _____

4. Describe each of the following illusions and give an explanation of why each is thought to occur.

   A.   Muller-Lyer _____

         Explanation _____

   B.   Ponzo _____

         Explanation _____

   C.   Moon illusion _____

         Explanation _____

5. Match the following laws of organization to the appropriate description: proximity, similarlty, continuity, common fate, closure.
   A. _____ Items that move or change together are seen as a whole.
   B. _____ Parts of a figure that are left out will be filled in by the perceptual system.
   C. _____ Groups are formed by elements close to one another in space and time.
   D. _____ A string of items indicates where the next item will be found.
   E. _____ Similar items tend to be perceived in groups.

6. Match the following structures of the ear with the appropriate description: external ear, middle ear, inner ear.
   A. _____ The snaillike tube where pressure changes, received by the basilar membrane, stimulates hair cells and brings about the initial electrical coding of sound waves in the nervous system. This structure is also known as the cochlea.
   B. _____ The fleshy tissue on the outside of the head and the opening that leads to the eardrum.
   C. _____ The eardrum and tiny bones that amplify sound waves and stimulate the basilar membrane.

7. Identify the perceptual process that best explains why each of the following situations is perceived by the observer as described.

   monocular depth cue   *illusion*
   binocular depth cue   *Gestalt laws organization*

   A. _____ A basket of fruit and a bottle of wine are positioned in such a way that the basket blocks part of the image of the wine bottle; as a result the observer perceives the wine bottle as being closer.
   B. _____ As you move your new record album closer to your face so that you can read the song titles, a series of muscles attached to the crystalline lenses in your eyes change the shape of the lenses and keep the image on your retinas in focus.
   C. _____ As your lover moves closer to you to establish intimate eye contact, your eyes converge, moving toward one another and providing you with necessary depth dues.
   D. _____ An auditorium is filled with folding chairs that are either gray or blue. They are set up in sections by color beginning with ten rows of blue chairs, then rows of gray chairs, another ten rows of blue chairs and so on. As an observer, you perceive the chairs in groups by the similarity of their color.
   E. _____ As you look at your favorite painting you notice the darker objects seem to be farther away than the lighter objects.
   F. _____ You look at two lines, one of which appears to be longer. When you measure the two lines you find that they are the same length. Yet, when you look at them again one of the lines still appears to be longer.
   G. _____ The cowboy on a sign outside of "Joe's Place" appears to be waving at you because the light bulbs that make up the sign blink in a synchronized manner.

SQ3R*plus*

RECITE: When you have finished reading the assigned material in your text and you have completed the exercises in your study guide, turn back to the chapter outline. Read each learning objective and recite out loud everything you can remember in support of each objective.

REVIEW: Check to see if you have answered all the questions you wrote during the *Survey* stage. Complete all sections of your study guide and check your answers for accuracy. If you are having trouble with specific topics ask you instructor for help.

WRITE: Read the learning objective again and then, in your own words, write down everything you can remember about this chapter. Summarize the main points and the concepts introduced in this chapter.

REFLECT: After each study period, take a break and reflect on what you have just studied. Ask yourself how this newly acquired information can be used in the future.

CHAPTER THREE SELF-TEST

1. Perception:
   A. allows us to experience and adapt to our environment.
   B. is a complex process of receiving and interpreting stimuli.
   C. allows sensory input to acquire meaning.
   D. all of the above

2. The relationship between a person's conscious experience of a stimulus and the physical properties of a stimulus is the focus of:
   A. transduction.
   B. perception.
   C. sensation.
   D. psychophysics.

3. The human eye works very much like a:
   A. microscope.
   B. telescope.
   C. camera.
   D. prism.

4. The part of the eye that contains rods and cones is called the:
   A. retina.
   B. iris.
   C. cornea.
   D. bipolar layer.

5. Which of the following statements concerning duplicity theory is <u>false</u>? Duplicity theory:
   A. suggests that vision is controlled by two classes of cells.
   B. is supported by the uneven distribution of rods and cones in the retina.
   C. is supported by dark adaptation studies.
   D. originated in the 1980s when sophisticated computer data analysis became available.

6. The brain can process two sets of signals about a particular image and allows us to see form and depth because impulses cross to the opposite side of the brain when they reach the:
   A. optic chiasm.
   B. lateral geniculate nucleus.
   C. striate cortex.
   D. none of the above

7. We can discriminate between a circle and a triangle because each shape:
   A. is clearly different from any other shape.
   B. stimulates the cells of different receptive fields.
   C. passes through a different portion of the crystalline lens.
   D. is recognized by the primary visual cortex.

8. In Hirsch and Spinelli's study, the cats whose early visual experience was limited to horizontal lines:
   A. were able to see lines in all angles when the experimental goggles were removed.
   B. bumped into vertical objects, such as chair legs, after the goggles had been removed.
   C. became overwhelmed by too much visual stimulation when the goggles were removed.
   D. could see vertical lines, but ignored them since they had no experience with them.

9. Which of the following objects best illustrates the property of color called "saturation?"
   A. a pink carnation
   B. a blue sapphire
   C. a green olive
   D. a red brick

10. The ability to make all colors by mixing three basic colors--red, blue, and green--is part of the:
    A. opponent-process theory.
    B. Law of Similarity.
    C. Trichromatic theory.
    D. Law of Proximity.

11. The opponent process theory assumes that:
    A. there are three types of receptors, each maximally sensitive to one group of wavelengths.
    B. that three sets of receptors respond positively or negatively to different wavelengths.
    C. color coding occurs at the retina.
    D. A and C

12. Persons who are totally color blind would be considered:
    A. monochromats.
    B. trichromats.
    C. dichromats.
    D. anomolous trichromats.

13. You perceive a book as having the same shape whether you see it from the side or from the front because of a perceptual process known as:
    A. similarity.
    B. accommodation.
    C. interposition.
    D. constancy.

14. Retinal disparity:
    A. is most likely to occur when objects are far away.
    B. is greatest when images on the retina are the farthest apart.
    C. keeps information on corresponding points on the retina.
    D. is a monocular depth cue.

15. Two horizontal lines of same length surrounded by slanted lines is a:
    A. Ponzo Illusion.
    B. Moon Illusion.
    C. Muller-Lyer Illusion.
    D. none of the above

16. Which of the following statements concerning Gestalt principles is *false*?
    A. People will group together the elements of a visual stimulus that they see as being alike.
    B. At each level of organization people try to interpret the perceptual field as being made up of "wholes" rather than "parts."
    C. People try to impose organization on any units that are perceived as complete or "good."
    D. Gestalt principles clearly explain why we experience perceptual constancies and illusions.

17. Elements close to one another in space or time will be perceived as groups in the Law of:
    A. Common Fate Principles.
    B. Similarity.
    C. Proximity.
    D. Continuity.

18. Which of the following is the physical attribute of loudness?
    A.   frequency
    B.   amplitude
    C.   pitch
    D.   tone

19. The cochlea is:
    A.   part of the middle ear.
    B.   the fleshy tissue on the outside of the head that we usually refer to as the ear.
    C.   a snaillike tube where hair cells are stimulated by a change in sound pressure.
    D.   A and C

20. Which of the following statements is *true*?
    A.   Auditory cells are maximally sensitive to certain narrow ranges of frequencies.
    B.   Frequency theories seem to be much more accurate than place theories in providing an explanation for how we hear.
    C.   One Hertz (Hz) is equal to ten cycles per second.
    D.   Hair cells in the cochlea stimulate the basilar membrane.

21. Taste receptors are _____ found on the tongue.
    A.   the papillae
    B.   the "moats"
    C.   the taste buds
    D.   in the saliva

22 The olfactory epithelium:
    A.   is the technical name for the nose.
    B.   contains millions of olfactory rods.
    C.   is a nerve fiber that transmits information to the brain.
    D.   B and C

23. The _____ allows you to touch your finger to your nose with your eyes closed.
    A.   sense of touch
    B.   vestibular sense
    C.   kinesthesis sense
    D.   optical alignment sense

24. According to the Melzack-Wall gate control theory, pain is experienced when:
    A.   the chemical enkephalin is secreted in large doses.
    B.   endorphins in the brain are at a low level.
    C.   substance-P, released by sensory nerve fibers, transmits impulses across gates.
    D.   "gates" are closed.

25. An extrasensory process by which thought is transferred from one person to another without the use of normal communications is:
    A.   transference.
    B.   telepathy.
    C.   clairvoyance.
    D.   precognition.

26. Cutler and Preti's study suggest which of the following?
    A. The smell of other human beings affects the physiological processes in humans.
    B. Pheromones emitted by men may alter a woman's menstrual cycle.
    C. Pheromones are now recognized as initiators of sexual activity between men and women who live together.
    D. A and B

27. Adult human skin measures roughly _____ yards and is made up of _____ layers.
    A. 3-3
    B. 2-2
    C. 2-3
    D. 3-2

Congratulations, you have completed Chapter 3. Now, proceed to the Exam Preparation Section in the back of your study guide for your final review, but don't forget to review the Enrichment Glossary for help understanding difficult words.

LANGUAGE ENRICHMENT GLOSSARY

Some students who reviewed the textbook listed the following words as difficult to understand. Use this list, your dictionary, and teachers and friends to learn the meaning of words you do not understand

Page	Term	Explanation	Page	Term	Explanation
72	adhering to	attaching to, being part of	89	craggy rocks	rough rocks
72	austere	difficult and rigid	92	potent	powerful and important
72	meditating	focused deep thought	93	featureless	smooth
72	atriums	room made out of glass	94	oblique lines	slanted lines
72	wide array of	many different	93	assert	state or claim
74	subliminal	too small to sense	94	fragmented	separate
74	innovative	new and creative	96	investigations	research
74	noxious	harmful	96	intriguing	very interesting
75	extract	get	96	tuning fork	metal instrument used to produce a specific sound
76	translucent	able to see through	98	Ultimately	at the end
76	visors	something worn on the head to shade the eyes	101	fondness for	love
76	impaired	decreased	102	saliva	watery fluid in your mouth
76	fascinating	very interesting	103	texture	how something feels when it is touched
76	obesity	very fat	103	appealing	you would like to have it.
76	insomnia	not able to sleep	104	posit	to present as a fact
76	adversely	negatively	104	foul	a bad smell
76	frantically grope	a fast nervous touching	104	resinous	the smell of paints
76	fumble	a clumsy action such as not being able to hold it	104	burnt	smell when heated to much
77	pigmented iris	the colored part of the eye	104	silkworm	a worm that makes silks
88	casts	displays	104	hamsters	small animal like a mouse
79	predominantly	main	105	controversial	something argued over
80	illumination	how much light there is	105	binding	a covering

80	squint	close your eyelids so less light gets into your eyes	105	oil-producing	makes oil from the skin
80	dim test spot	a very low light beam	105	bumps	hits
80	gradually	something happens slowly	107	frostbite	skin damage from cold
83	gaze	looking	107	potent	strong
83	inferences	guesses	108	alleviated	to take away
83	discriminating	tell the difference between	108	trigger	start
87	precise	exact	108	abates	goes away
96	strikes	reaches or hits	108	cope	deal with
89	chopped	cut	108	strategies	plans

CHAPTER 4

States of Consciousness

Psychology 6th Ed.		Keeping Pace Plus		
HEADINGS	PAGE	LESSON	L.O.	LEARNING OBJECTIVES
Consciousness	116	1		
Defining Consciousness	116		4.1	Develop an understanding of the continuum of consciousness, from alertness through altered states of consciousness.
Theories of Consciousness	117		4.2	Examine the three theories of consciousness described by Jaynes, Ornstein, and Dennett.
Sleep	119	2		
The Sleep-Wakefulness Cycle: Circadian Rhythms	119		4.3	Develop an understanding of circadian rhythms and be able to give examples of how they affect human behavior.
Sleep: A Restorative Process	120		4.4	Examine four views of the restorative process of sleep and be able to discuss variations in the amount of sleep people need according to their age and activity level.
Sleep Cycles and Stages: REM and NREM Sleep	121		4.5	Characterize sleep by explaining sleep cycles and stages.
Sleep Deprivation: Doing without REM	123		4.6	Discuss how sleep deprivation affects behavior and subsequent sleep patterns.
Is There a Sleep Switch?	124			
Sleep Disorders	124		4.7	List and describe the major sleep disorders, and evaluate how nutritional supplements are being used to induce sleep without negative side effects.

Chapter 4 Overview

Consciousness refers to our awareness of our environment and our awareness of our own thoughts, feelings, and memories. Consciousness can be seen as a continuum from alertness to dreaming, hypnosis, or drug-induced states as levels from total awareness to unresponsiveness. In either case, psychologists study consciousness because of its obvious relationship with our awareness of our environment and its potential to affect behavior.

The most widely studied state or level of consciousness is sleep. Circadian rhythms regulate the sleep-wakefulness cycle, which can easily be altered by job duties, travel, and other interruptions to our daily routine. Sleep is a natural state of consciousness, but the reason for sleep remains unclear. Sleep may be physical restoration, brain restoration, or a form of hibernation. Whatever the case, our sleep cycles play an important role in this restoration process. One of the stages, called REM (rapid eye movement) appears to be critical for normal daily functioning. When we are deprived of REM sleep, we become anxious and irritable, have difficulty concentrating, and do worse on tests that involve attention and original responses. Sleep disorders are examined and the so-called wonder drug melatonin is discussed as a possible sleep aid that has few if any side effects.

Sigmund Freud described dreams as the royal road to the unconscious. Dreams have played an important role in psychology almost since the beginning. Dreams occur largely during REM sleep and may include vivid visual, auditory, or tactile imagery. The content of dreams remains a hot topic in psychology as well as in popular literature and the media, but recent research suggests that dreams may be a random collection of images and therefore have little or no importance.

Consciousness can be controlled and modified by biofeedback, hypnosis, or meditation. Each of these methods has had some success in treating problems such as headaches, high blood pressure, stress-related illness, pain management, and memory loss. However, each method is not without its critics.

In addition, conscious experience can be altered by drugs. Lefton points out that we live in a drug-using culture with numerous legal and illegal drugs readily available for all ages. Dependence and tolerance are defined and a description of a substance abuser is given. One of the most pervasive examples of drug abuse is alcoholism. Lefton outlines the effects of alcohol on individuals, society, and public safety. Treatment programs differ in philosophy, from complete abstinence to the more behavioral approach of unlearning a problem behavior. The risk factors for alcoholism and familial patterns are examined. Chapter 4 concludes with an listing of barbiturates, opiates, marijuana, amphetamines, and cocaine and their effects on behavior. Some insight into the widespread abuse of cocaine is provided.

Most students are aware of the effects that drugs can have on overt behavior. In this chapter, Lefton provides you with information about the potential harmful effects on your friends, family, and future society. Critical thinking skills will be helpful in this chapter.

SQ3R*plus*

SURVEY THE LESSON: Read learning objectives 1.1 through 1.18 and, in the text, examine the chapter headings, tables, and pictures on pages 116-144 in the text to *form an idea of what you should learn and to set goals for your study time*.

WRITE DOWN QUESTIONS: *While surveying and reading the text, write down questions* about the information being presented. *Write your questions* in the space below or on a separate piece of paper and try to find answers to these questions in the text.

ACTIVELY READ PAGES 116-144: The following exercise is designed to facilitate this process. Complete the following questions as you read, and when you are done, check your answers with those printed in the back of this study guide.

YOUR QUESTIONS:

Matching

Match the following terms or concepts from your textbook with the most appropriate description.

1. _____ addictive drug
2. _____ alcoholic
3. _____ biofeedback
4. _____ circadian rhythms
5. _____ consciousness
6. _____ dream
7. _____ drug
8. _____ electroencephalogram
9. _____ hypnosis
10. _____ insomnia

11. _____ lucid dream
12. _____ manifest content
13. _____ meditation
14. _____ opiates
15. _____ psychedelics
16. _____ psychostimulants
17. _____ REM
18. _____ sleep
19. _____ tolerance

a) a general state of being aware of and responsive to events in the environment
b) internally generated patterns of body functions which have an approximate 24 hour cycle
c) state of consciousness characterized by general unresponsiveness to the environment and general physical immobility
d) a record of an organism's electrical brain patterns
e) sleep stage characterized by high frequency, low voltage, brainwave activity, systematic eye movement, and dreams
f) prolonged inability to sleep
g) state of consciousness that occurs largely during REM sleep
h) dream in which the person is aware of dreaming while it is happening.
i) the overt storyline, characters, and setting of a dream
j) technique by which individuals can monitor and learn to control involuntary activity of some body organs and functions
k) altered state of consciousness brought about by procedures that induce trance
l) state of consciousness induced by a variety of techniques and characterized by concentration, restriction of incoming stimuli, and deep relaxation
m) any chemical substance that alters biological processes
n) drug that causes a compulsive physiological need and when withheld produces withdrawal
o) progressive insensitivity to repeated use of a specific drug
p) a problem drinker who has both physiological and psychological need to consume alcohol
q) drugs with pain relieving and sedative properties that are addictive and produce tolerance
r) consciousness altering drugs that effect mood, thoughts, memory, judgment, and perception
s) a drug that in low to moderate doses increases alertness, reduces fatigue, and elevates mood

True or False

1. Today, cognitive psychologists assert that people are aware of all mental processes.   TRUE   FALSE

2. Both Jaynes and Ornstein suggest that evolution of the human brain helps us to explain states of consciousness.   TRUE   FALSE

3.   Biological clocks run on about a 24-hour per day cycle.   TRUE   FALSE

4.   Optional sleep fills the time from the end of core sleep until   TRUE   FALSE
     waking.

5.   Newborns spend about 50% of their time in REM sleep.   TRUE   FALSE

6.   The sleep disorder that might be involved in Sudden Infant   TRUE   FALSE
     Death Syndrome is called sleep apnea.

7.   Dreams are mostly visual, and they occur mostly in color.   TRUE   FALSE

8.   The way a therapist interprets the meaning of a person's dream   TRUE   FALSE
     depends upon his/her theoretical orientation.

9.   Hobson and McCarley have suggested that dreams serve the   TRUE   FALSE
     function of getting rid of conflicting psychological messages.

10. Biofeedback techniques began when Neal Miller trained rats to   TRUE   FALSE
     control glandular responses.

11. The primary goal of biofeedback is to record the activity of   TRUE   FALSE
     facial muscles.

12. Barbers' approach of giving task-motivating instructions instead   TRUE   FALSE
     of using hypnotic induction is called the cognitive-behavioral
     viewpoint.

13. Salzberg and DePiano found that task-motivating instructions   TRUE   FALSE
     are less effective than hypnosis.

14   Psychologists are seeing a growing number of people addicted   TRUE   FALSE
     to legal drugs (i.e., diet pills).

15   Only a few psychoactive drugs are considered consciousness-   TRUE   FALSE
     altering.

16. Showing evidence of substance abuse and withdrawal symptoms   TRUE   FALSE
     or tolerance is called pathological use.

17. Few substance abusers have similar abuse patterns.   TRUE   FALSE

18   All addictive drugs affect the brain in the same way.   TRUE   FALSE

19   Alcohol consumption in the U.S. has been at an all-time high for   TRUE   FALSE
     more than a decade.

20   Most Americans consider some alcohol consumption   TRUE   FALSE
     appropriate.

21	All problem drinkers are alcoholics.	TRUE	FALSE
22	Abstinence is the goal of all alcohol treatment programs.	TRUE	FALSE
23	Children of alcoholics are more likely to be alcoholics.	TRUE	FALSE
24	Barbiturates and tranquilizers have been widely abused by all segments of society because of their availability.	TRUE	FALSE
25	A lethal dose of heroin is much larger than any heavy user would inject.	TRUE	FALSE
26	Methadone maintenance alone is often successful in treating the heroin addict.	TRUE	FALSE
27	50% of high school seniors have used cocaine at least once.	TRUE	FALSE
28	Crashing refers to the unpleasant feelings a person experiences when the effects of cocaine wear off.	TRUE	FALSE

Fill-in-the Blanks

1. When someone is aware of and responsive to events in the environment, they are in a state of being known as _____.

2. An _____ _____ is the dramatically different state of consciousness different from ordinary awareness and responsiveness.

3. Internally generated patterns of body functions such as hormones, sleep, and blood pressure are known as _____ _____.

4. _____ is defined as a nonwaking state of consciousness. When one is immobile and unresponsive.

5. The two major types of sleep are: _____ and _____.

6. Various stages in sleep can be characterized through _____ or records of electrical brain patterns.

7. The first four stages within the cycle of sleep are known as _____.

8. The fifth stage of sleep that is characterized by high frequency, low voltage brain wave activity, rapid and systematic eye movements, and dreams is termed _____.

9. A rhythmic burst of brain waves is called a _____ _____.

10. A higher amplitude burst of activity in stage two is called a _____.

11. In the deepest stage of sleep, stage 4, even high amplitude brain wave traces are called _____ _____.

12. People who suffer from _____ fall asleep suddenly.

13. When a person experiences _____ _____, the airflow stops for at least 15 seconds, causing the person to stop breathing.

14. A person's inability to sleep is known as _____.

15. _____ _____ are panic attacks that occur within a few hours after the person falls asleep.

16. When a person suffers from the disorder of _____, they appear both awake and asleep.

17. The state of consciousness that occurs mostly during REM sleep that is accompanied by vivid imagery is called a _____.

18. A _____ dream is the type of dream when a person realizes that they are dreaming.

19. A dream consists of an overt story line, characters, setting, and the events of the dream or the _____ _____ of the dream.

20. The _____ _____ of a dream has deeper meaning and is usually filled with symbolism, hidden content, and repressed ideas.

21. The inherited primitive ideas and images that a person has are known as the
_____ _____.

22. _____ is the technique people use to monitor and control the involuntary activity and function of the body.

23. The altered state of consciousness brought about by procedures that induce a trance is called _____.

24. The person's willingness to follow the instructions of the hypnotist is called suggestibility or _____ _____.

25. Often hypnotized people claim they can describe an event that took place years earlier. This effect of hypnosis is known as _____ _____.

26. Hypnosis is helpful in reducing pain or the _____ pain that amputees feel in body parts that no longer exist.

27. Barber's approach of changing people's behavior during hypnosis is referred to as the
_____ _____.

28. The state of consciousness that is induced by techniques to produce a sense of detachment is known as _____.

29. There are two types of meditation: _____ and
_____.

30. Any chemical substance that alters normal biological processes is called a _____.

31. A drug that alters biochemical reactions in the nervous system, thereby affecting consciousness is called a _____ drug.

32. A drug that causes a compulsive psychological need is known as an _____
_____.

33. People who abuse or overuse substances are called _____
_____.

34. _____ _____ refers to one's overwhelming desire to use a drug and the inability to inhibit that desire.

35. When a dependent person ceases to use a drug, he/she may experience _____
_____.

36. The progressive insensitivity to the repeated use of a drug is called _____.

37. A _____ abuser is an abuser that takes several drugs at one time.

38. Drugs that relax and often induce sleep are referred to as _____
drugs.

39. A person who has a physiological and psychological need to consume alcohol is termed an _____.

40. One sedative-hypnotic drug that decreases the excitability of neurons throughout the nervous system is a _____.

41. Drugs that calm and sedate people are _____.

42. _____ are a class of drugs that reduce pain, calm, are addictive, and produce tolerance.

43. Drugs that are taken to affect moods, thoughts, memory, judgment and perception are called _____.

44. A _____ is any drug that increases alertness, reduces fatigue, and elevates mood.

Applications

1. Characterize the two modes of consciousness described by Ornstein.
   A. Active mode
      1. Descriptive terms _____
      2. Evolution has made it _____
      3. Humans use this mode in order to _____
      _____

   B. Receptive mode
      1. Descriptive terms _____
      2. This mode expands _____
      3. People use this mode when _____

2. Match the following sleep disorders with the appropriate description.
      narcolepsy   sleep apnea   insomnia   night terrors
   A. _____ People with this disorder stop breathing for at least fifteen seconds up to as many as 100 times a night. During the day they are very sleepy, and may have memory losses, work related accidents, and severe headaches.
   B. _____ This disorder is especially common in children between the ages of 3 and 8. The symptoms involve sitting up abruptly in a state of shear fright, screaming, and breathing quickly.

C. _____ This is a common disorder often caused by anxiety or depression where a person has a prolonged inability to fall asleep.

D. _____ People with this disorder could have difficulty on the job or when driving a car because they suddenly and unexpectedly fall asleep.

3. Discuss the following researchers' positions on dreaming.
   A. Freud _____
      1. Manifest content _____
      2. Latent content _____
   B. Jung _____
   _____
   C. Hobson and McCarley _____
   _____
   _____

4. Match the following terms to the appropriate definition.
   dependence   *tolerance*   *withdrawal symptoms*
   A. _____ Reliance on regular use of a drug, without which the individual suffers a psychological and/or physiological reaction.
   B. _____ A variety of physiological reactions that occur when a person who has developed a physiological dependence to a drug no longer takes the drug.
   C. _____ A progressive insensitivity to repeated use of a drug in the same dose. A user must have increasingly greater amounts of the drug to achieve the desired high.

5. Describe the following treatment techniques used for alcoholics and their families.
   A. Alcoholics Anonymous
      1. Goal _____
      2. Assumption _____
   B. Alternative approach
      1. Goal _____
      2. Assumption _____
   C. Family therapy _____
   D. Multimodal _____

6. List physiological effects from the use of heroin and give two reasons why herion addicts die.
   A. Physiological effects
      1. _____
      2. _____
   B. Herion addicts die because
      1. _____
      2. _____

7. Describe the drug known as Methadone and its effects on heroin users.
   A. Methadone _____
   _____
   B. Effects _____
   _____

8. Explain (A) the effects that amphetamines and cocaine have on the central nervous system and (B) discuss the long term use effects they have on individuals.
    A. Effects
        1. Amphetamines _____

        2. Cocaine _____

    B. Long-term use
        1. Amphetamines _____

        2. Cocaine _____

SQ3R*plus*

RECITE: When you have finished reading the assigned material in your text and you have completed the exercises in your study guide, turn back to the chapter outline. Read each learning objective and recite out loud everything you can remember in support of each objective.

REVIEW: Check to see if you have answered all the questions you wrote during the *Survey* stage. Complete all sections of your study guide and check your answers for accuracy. If you are having trouble with specific topics ask you instructor for help.

WRITE: Read the learning objective again and then, in your own words, write down everything you can remember about this chapter. Summarize the main points and the concepts introduced in this chapter.

REFLECT: After each study period, take a break and reflect on what you have just studied. Ask yourself how this newly acquired information can be used in the future.

CHAPTER FOUR SELF-TEST

1. When describing the consciousness of a person who has been drinking alcohol, a "states" interpretation would emphasizes:
    A. that a deeper level of consciousness exists--that of intoxication.
    B. the general state of being aware and responsive to alcohol.
    C. concerns for emotional disturbances.
    D. that distinctly different behaviors and attention patterns exist; the drinker is in a totally different condition.

2. According to Daniel Dennett, the brain:
    A. creates multiple drafts of experience which are constantly being reanalyzed.
    B. is busy deleting extraneous information and experience from storage.
    C. operates out of the active and receptive modes proposed by Ornstein.
    D. all of the above

3.   Circadian rhythms control all *except:*
     A.   yawning.
     B.   bodily rhythms.
     C.   body temperature.
     D.   sleep patterns.

4.   The amount of sleep people need is more clearly related to _____ than it is to
     _____.
     A.   sex; age
     B.   activity level; sex
     C.   age; activity level
     D.   activity level; age

5.   A K complex is:
     A.   a rhythmic burst of brain waves that wax and wane over a period of one or two seconds.
     B.   observed in the last third of stage 2 sleep.
     C.   a unique "sawtooth" wave characteristic of REM sleep.
     D.   a low-amplitude burst of activity.

6.   In one study where subjects were deprived of sleep for eight-and-a-half days, it was found that on subsequent nights when subjects were finally permitted to sleep they:
     A.   had trouble falling asleep.
     B.   slept almost twice as long as they normally slept in one night on the first night and gradually worked their way back to a normal night's sleep.
     C.   spent a larger percentage of time than usual in REM and stage 4 sleep.
     D.   went right to sleep, had a normal night's sleep, and woke up at their usual time.

7.   Autonomic nervous system disturbance, lowered arousal, and perhaps neurochemical problems are characteristic of:
     A.   sleep apnea.
     B.   insomnia.
     C.   night terrors.
     D.   narcolepsy.

8.   In order to determine the effectiveness of biofeedback researchers need to answer all of the following questions *except:*
     A.   under what conditions is biofeedback effective.
     B.   what kind of physical and psychological problems can be treated.
     C.   what types of clients successfully respond to biofeedback.
     D.   does biofeedback give subjects accurate data concerning their biological states.

9.   People most likely to be susceptible to hypnosis are:
     A.   adults.
     B.   children age seven to fourteen years.
     C.   old people.
     D.   females of any age.

10. Studies have shown that meditation can alter which of the following psychological responses?
    A.   sleep patterns
    B.   brain wave activity
    C.   oxygen consumption
    D.   all of the above

11. Which of the following has been used to provide an explanation for substance use and abuse?
    A.   societal factors
    B.   individual family situations
    C.   genetic heritage and medical problems
    D.   all of the above

12. When we say a person has gained a tolerance to a drug, we mean that the person:
    A.   can take a drug without suffering from any negative side effects.
    B.   can take a minimum amount of a drug without experiencing withdrawal symptoms.
    C.   no longer experiences the desired effect from that particular amount of a drug.
    D.   has become addicted to a drug.

13. Which of the following is thought to be a reason for why people develop substance abuse problems?
    A.   stress, poverty, boredom, or loneliness
    B.   wanting to feel confident or to lose weight
    C.   having materialistic values, poor self esteem or stressful life changes
    D.   all of the above

14. Alcohol is classified as a _____ drug.
    A.   sedative-hypnotic
    B.   narcotic
    C.   psychostimulant
    D.   psychedelic

15. Biomedical researchers who have looked at the effects of alcohol on the body have found all of the following *except:*
    A.   loss of brain tissue.
    B.   liver malfunctions.
    C.   decreased levels of glucose.
    D.   impaired cognitive and motor abilities.

16. Which of the following statements concerning alcoholism is false?
    A.   Most researchers believe that controlled drinking is a reliable answer to most alcoholics.
    B.   Alcoholics have a physiological and usually a psychological dependence on alcohol.
    C.   Alcoholics develop a tolerance.
    D.   Alcoholics are addicted to alcohol.

17. The conclusion made by Finn and Pihl concerning people who should be assigned a high-risk label for alcoholism is:
    A.   anyone having one or more alcoholic relatives is at high-risk.
    B.   people with high intelligence are at high-risk.
    C.   people with deadened taste buds are at high-risk.
    D.   multi-generational alcoholism vs. one-generational alcoholism criterion may be needed to assign risk potential.

18. Which of the following drugs would be classified as *minor* tranquilizers?
    A.   Prozac and Paxil
    B.   Valium and Librium
    C.   Codeine and Morphine
    D.   Thorazine and Phenobarbital

19. Many researchers assert that _____ keeps people addicted to heroin and other addictive drugs.
    A.   the biological reinforcing quality of the drug
    B.   a lack of will power
    C.   social pressure
    D.   poor nutrition

20. The major physiological effect of heroin use is:
    A.   decreased functioning of the respiratory system.
    B.   loss of appetite.
    C.   increased blood pressure.
    D.   stomach cramps.

21. Which of the following drugs alters consciousness, affects moods, thoughts, memory and perception, and is considered a *psychedelic*?
    A.   cocaine
    B.   crack
    C.   marijuana
    D.   crank

Congratulations, you have completed Chapter 4. Now, proceed to the Exam Preparation Section in the back of your study guide for your final review, but don't forget to review the Enrichment Glossary for help understanding difficult words.

Some students who reviewed the textbook listed the following words as difficult to understand. Use this list, your dictionary, and teachers and friends to learn the meaning of words you do not understand

Page	Term	Explanation	Page	Term	Explanation
116	probed	deep examination	126	scrutiny	examination
116	diagrammed	drawn out	126	tactile	touch
116	tide has clearly	Belief has become accepted	126	auditory	hearing
117	drug-induced state	condition produced by drugs	127	aggressive incidents	violent actions
117	continuum	continuous level	128	omen	statement about future
117	intoxication	drunk, not sober	128	siesta time	afternoon nap, sleep
117	modes	ways or conditions	128	frivolous	a waste of time
118	evolution	ongoing change	128	discernible	understandable
118	alternating fashion	in different ways	128	emotional disturbance	mentally upset
118	inhibited	blocked or not working	129	uncensored	not judged
118	intuitive activities	actions taken because of feeling they are right	129	spontaneously	by chance, accidentally
118	underlies	is important to	130	excitation	how awake you feel
118	skeptical	in disbelief, not sure	130	stuttering	a speech disorder
119	deviant	bad, not normal	131	arousal	alertness
119	sluggishly	slowly	131	time distortion	change in how time is understood
119	rejuvenate	renew, refresh	132	searing migraines	very bad headache
120	arbitrary	changeable	133	detachment	separation
120	thrown off	interfered with	134	tranquilizer	drug that reflexes people
120	dilemma	a problem	134	delineated	outlined, defined
120	chat	talk	134	illicit	not legal
120	restorative process	to rebuild, make new again	134	hazardous	dangerous
120	holdover	something left over	135	alcohol binge	drinking too much alcohol
120	hibernation	a very long sleep, like what bears do in winter	135	dosage	amount
120	overload	feeling very stressed	136	alcohol consumption	the drinking of alcohol
121	wax and wane	gradually comes and goes	136	staggering	walking unevenly
121	vague	not specific	136	deterioration	getting in bad condition
123	fragmentation	splitting up	137	mood swings	feeling happy then sad
123	deprived	not allowed to have it	138	predispose	tendency toward something
123	lethargic	no energy	138	aversive	negative or bad
125	Insomniacs	someone that cannot sleep	138	criterion	rule
126	surreal	not organized	139	transmission	task or job
			141	euphoria	extremely happy

CHAPTER 5

Learning

Chapter 5 Overview

Humans differentiate themselves from animals by their ability to learn complex behaviors. Lefton defines and describes the three basic learning processes of classical conditioning, operant conditioning, and cognitive learning. Pavlov's accidental discovery of the process of classical conditioning has led researchers to uncover many human behaviors that are learned. Behaviors such as emotions can be learned through association. Reflexive behaviors can be paired with other behaviors to create a chain of higher order learning. Complex behaviors can be extinguished as well, using the principles of classical conditioning. Also, the effectiveness of classical conditioning may depend on factors such as timing and the strength of the unconditioned stimulus.

"As a result of..." This phrase summarizes what B. F. Skinner thought about learning. According to Skinner, behaviors are acquired and maintained *as a result of* some consequence following the behavior. This process is termed *operant conditioning* and relies on the principles of reinforcement and punishment. Put simply, behaviors will increase when reinforced and decrease when punishment is the consequence. Like classical conditioning, operant conditioning is influenced by many variables, such as the nature of reinforcers, schedules of reinforcement and stimulus discrimination and generalization. Intrinsically motivated behaviors and their resistance to conditioning are discussed. Practical applications for behavioral regulation are also presented.

All behaviors cannot be explained by association or consequences. Cognitive variables like insight, latent learning, and generative learning focus on the thinking process and thoughts that establish and maintain behaviors. Lefton describes a learning-to-learn model that provides an interesting approach to study habits. Finally, observational learning theory illustrates how we learn by watching models. As in other learning models, the effectiveness of observational learning depends on several important elements surrounding the model as well as the observer.

The remaining chapters of *Psychology* rely on your understanding the concepts of learning. If you spend a little extra time on this chapter, you will benefit from your efforts.

SQ3R*plus*

SURVEY THE LESSON: Read learning objectives 5.1 through 5.27 and, in the text, examine the chapter headings, tables, and pictures on pages 150-188 in the text to *form an idea of what you should learn and to set goals for your study time*.

WRITE DOWN QUESTIONS: *While surveying and reading the text, write down questions* about the information being presented. *Write your questions* in the space below or on a separate piece of paper and try to find answers to these questions in the text.

ACTIVELY READ PAGES 150-188: The following exercise is designed to facilitate this process. Complete the following questions as you read, and when you are done, check your answers with those printed in the back of this study guide.

YOUR QUESTIONS:

Matching

Match the following terms or concepts from your textbook with the most appropriate description.

1. _____ conditioned response
2. _____ conditioned stimulus
3. _____ conditioning
4. _____ extinction
5. _____ fixed interval schedule
6. _____ fixed ratio
7. _____ latent learning
8. _____ learning
9. _____ negative reinforcement
10. _____ punishment
11. _____ reflex
12. _____ reinforcer
13. _____ shaping
14. _____ spontaneous recovery
15. _____ stimulus generalization
16. _____ superstitious behavior
17. _____ unconditioned response
18. _____ unconditioned stimulus
19. _____ variable interval
20. _____ variable ratio

a) a relatively permanent change in an organism that occurs as a result of experiences in the environment
b) systematic procedure to which associations and responses are learned
c) involuntary automatic behavior which occurs without prior learning
d) a stimulus that normally produces an involuntary response
e) the unlearned or involuntary response to an UCS
f) a neutral stimulus that through repeated association with an UCS begins to elicit a CR
g) the response elicited by a CS
h) a process in classical and operant conditioning by which the probability of a response is reduced
i) a recurrence of an extinguished response following a rest period
j) occurrence of a conditioned response to a stimulus similar but not identical to the original conditioned stimulus
k) a gradual training of an organism to give the proper responses through selected reinforcement
l) event that increases the probability of a recurrence of a response
m) the removal of an aversive stimulus after a response
n) behavior learned through coincidental association
o) presentation of an undesirable or noxious stimulus or removal of a desirable stimulus
p) reinforcement schedule from which the reinforcement is delivered after a specified time
q) reinforcement schedule in which the reinforcer is delivered after a predetermined but varying interval of time
r) reinforcement schedule in which a reinforcer is delivered after a specified number of responses
s) a reinforcement schedule in which the reinforcer is delivered after a predetermined, but variable number of responses
t) learning that occurs in the absence of any direct reinforcement

True or False

1. Classically conditioned responses are like reflexes in that they occur involuntarily to specific stimuli.   TRUE   FALSE

2. Prior to conditioning an unconditioned stimulus is called a neutral stimulus.   TRUE   FALSE

3. Classical conditioning is sometimes called Pavlovian conditioning.   TRUE   FALSE

4. If a bright light or a puff of air is delivered to your eye and you blink, your blink is considered a conditioned response.   TRUE   FALSE

5. Neutral stimuli must physically resemble the conditioned stimuli for them to elicit conditioned responses.   TRUE   FALSE

6. Fear can be classically conditioned.   TRUE   FALSE

7. The timing of an unconditioned stimulus does not influence conditioning.   TRUE   FALSE

8. The more consistent the pairings of the unconditioned stimulus to the neutral stimulus, the more quickly the conditioned response will be learned.   TRUE   FALSE

9. Spontaneous recovery shows that the extinction leads to permanently forgotten behaviors.   TRUE   FALSE

10. The behavior of humans can become limited when they have difficulty discriminating between two stimuli.   TRUE   FALSE

11. A crucial component of operant conditioning is the kind of consequence that follows a behavior.   TRUE   FALSE

12. The process of reinforcing behavior that approximates a desired response is called shaping.   TRUE   FALSE

13. The organism's needs, desires, and general physiological state play an important role in determining what consequences will act as reinforcers.   TRUE   FALSE

14. Negative reinforcement occurs when the stimulus for a behavior is aversive.   TRUE   FALSE

15. An avoidance response stops a stimulus that is present and causing pain.   TRUE   FALSE

16. Frowning at a child who has misbehaved is an example of a primary punisher.   TRUE   FALSE

17. In time-out a pleasant stimulus, such as the key to the family car, is taken away.   TRUE   FALSE

18. Punishment suppresses existing behaviors but it does not eliminate them.   TRUE   FALSE

19. Punishment can be used to establish new desired behaviors in children.   TRUE   FALSE

20. Parents who use physical punishers provide their children with a model for physically aggressive behaviors.   TRUE   FALSE

21. A closeness in time (contiguity) between the behavior and the delivery of a consequence is usually critical in operant conditioning.   TRUE   FALSE

22. The overall response rate of an organism that has been trained on a fixed-interval schedule is better than one trained on a variable-ratio schedule.   TRUE   FALSE

23. Stimulus discrimination has occurred when an organism makes a particular response only in the presence of a specific stimulus.   TRUE   FALSE

24. A response will be more likely to resist extinction if, previous to the extinction procedure, it was reinforced on a consistent and frequent schedule.   TRUE   FALSE

25. Spontaneous recovery no longer occurs after a number of rest periods when reinforcement has consistently been withheld.   TRUE   FALSE

26. With latent learning an organism must have motivation to demonstrate learning has occurred.   TRUE   FALSE

27. Observational learning is sometimes called social learning.   TRUE   FALSE

28. Laboratory studies have shown that people can learn classically conditioned responses merely by observing the conditioning process.   TRUE   FALSE

29. Psychologists have found that children who observe aggression immediately display aggressive behavior   TRUE   FALSE

Fill-in-the-Blanks

1. Permanent change that results because of experiences within the environment is known as _____.

2. The three important aspects of learning are: _____, _____, _____.

3. Another word for learning is _____.

4. The systematic procedure through which a person learns to associate and react to various stimuli is called _____.

5. When a response to a stimulus occurs without any prior learning, we call the automatic behavior a _____.

6. The Russian psychologist, _____, uncovered the basic principle of _____ _____.

7. _____ _____, or Pavlovian conditioning, is a situation in which an originally neutral stimulus, when repeatedly paired with a stimulus that naturally brings about a response, comes to bring about the same response.

8. The stimulus that normally produces the response is called the _____ stimulus.

9. The response to the unconditioned stimulus is the _____.

10. The bell in Pavlov's experiment which caused the dogs to salivate as a result of learning was the _____ stimulus.

11. The salivation, which was the learned response from the bell, was termed the _____ response.

12. The process of repeating trials to get the neutral stimulus to yield a conditioned response is called the _____ process.

13. The process of _____ _____ takes place when a neutral stimulus, paired with another conditioned stimulus, takes on conditioned properties.

14. The two determining factors of higher-order conditioning are: 1) the _____ between the higher-order stimulus and the original conditioned stimulus and 2) the _____ and consistency with which the conditioned stimuli are paired.

15. The three most important variables in classical conditioning are the _____ _____ _____ of the unconditioned stimulus.

16. The _____ of the association of the unconditioned and conditioned stimuli is key in determining whether conditioning will occur.

17. John Garcia studied taste aversion as a conditioned response, sometimes known as the _____ _____.

18. The process of withholding the unconditioned stimulus to reduce the probability of the conditioned response is called _____.

19. Once the probability of the response has been extinguished, it can recur after a rest period. This event is called _____ _____

20. When we develop a conditioned response to a stimulus that is similar to another original conditioned response, we call that _____ _____.

21. When we learn to respond only to a specific reinforced stimulus, we are completing the process of _____ _____.

22. B.F. Skinner wrote _____ _____ _____.

23. Conditioning for a response to occur by either increasing or decreasing a response as a consequence of the behavior is called _____ _____.

24. Operant conditioning is also known as _____ _____.

25. As in classical conditioning, a reward acts as a _____.

26. A _____ decreases the chances of the behavior occurring.

27. B.F. Skinner designed a box called the _____ _____ which had a mechanism inside it which delivered a consequence.

28. Psychologists developed a _____ to measure responses.

29. When a psychologist reinforces a behavior that is close to the desired behavior, he is said to be _____.

30. Another term for shaping is the _____ _____.

31. Any event that increases the chances of the same response to recur is called a _____.

32. Rewarding a person with _____ _____ will increase the likelihood that the response will recur.

33. On the other hand, _____ _____ increases the probability of the response by removing an unpleasant stimulus.

34. Unpleasant stimuli are often used in studying animals in experiments focusing on _____ and _____ conditioning.

35. Behaviors that are likely to happen are called _____ _____.

36. A reinforcer that is based on the survival of an organism is called a _____ _____.

37. When a primary reinforcer is linked with a _____ _____, the reinforcer can become rewarding.

38. When one coincidentally associates behavior with a reinforcer, he/she may develop _____ _____.

39. In order to decrease the likelihood of a response, one should _____ _____ _____ or present a noxious stimulus.

40. A stimulus that is naturally painful to an organism is called a _____ _____.

41. A neutral stimulus that takes on negative qualities is known as a _____ _____.

42. If a punishment is not delivered in an effective and consistent manner, it may lead to _____ _____, in which a person feels little control.

43. The frequency with which an organism is reinforced depends on the pattern of presentation of the reinforcer or the _____ _____ _____.

44. _____ _____ is the simplest reinforcement pattern.

45. Reinforcement follows two basic schedules: _____ and _____ schedules.

46. When the reward follows the first required response, the experiment is said to be on a _____.

47. When an experiment is on a _____ _____ schedule, the reinforcer is delivered after varying amounts of time.

48. When an organism's conditioned response is reduced because reinforcement no longer follows, the process is referred to as _____.

49. The measure of how many trials it takes to achieve extinction is known as _____ _____ _____.

50. Motivation can be labeled as _____ or _____.

51. When you are able to recognize relationships and connections between a series of events, you have _____.

52. When learning occurs but is not demonstrated, it is known as _____ _____.

53. The process by which a learner makes connections and constructs meaning between familiar and unfamiliar events is called _____ _____.

54. _____ is thinking about thinking.

55. _____ _____ takes place when one organism observes a behavior and then imitates it.

Applications

1. Identify the stimuli and responses that are involved in each of the following examples of classically conditioned behavior:

unconditioned stimulus (UCS)   *unconditioned response (UCR)*
conditioned response (CR)   *neutral stimulus that becomes the conditioned stimulus (NS/CS)*

A. On several occasions Sybil's teacher gave her permission to draw on the blackboard. On each occasion, just as Sybil picked up the chalk, the recess bell that hung directly above where she was standing blasted a loud ring and startled her. Now whenever Sybil is asked to write on the blackboard, she feels apprehensive about having to touch the chalk.
   1. UCS _____
   2. UCR _____
   3. NS/CS _____
   4. CR _____

B. When Jake first adopted his pet cat, Tiger, he was able to use his electric can opener without any interference. However, after using the can opener many times just before giving Tiger his canned food, Jake finds that when he tries to use the appliance Tiger makes a nuisance of himself by standing underfoot and making anticipatory eating responses.
   1. UCS _____
   2. UCR _____
   3. NS/CS _____
   4. CR _____

2. Fill-in-the-boxes:

stimulus or cue

behavior

consequence

When teaching a child to say **"thank you"**, a parent frequently says **"Say thank you."** When the child says "thank you", the parent responds with **"Good"**. In the figure above, identify the cue, the behavior, and consequence involved in this teaching situation involving operant conditioning.

3. Define the following types of punishment and punishers; give an example of each.
  A. Punishment _____

     Example _____
  B. Removal of a pleasant stimulus _____

     Example _____
  C. Time-out _____

     Example _____
  D. Primary punisher _____

     Example _____
  E. Secondary punisher _____

     Example _____

	Desired stimulus	Noxious stimulus
Stimulus is presented after a particular behavior	Positive reinforcement	Punishment
Stimulus is removed after a particular behavior	Punishment	Negative reinforcement

4. In each of the four boxes in the table above, draw an arrow pointing either up (for increase) or down (for decrease) to indicate how the behavior will be affected by the consequence.

5. Describe the following types of reinforcement schedules and tell what kind of response output can be expected from each.

   A. Fixed-interval _____

   _____

   Response output _____

   _____

   B. Variable interval _____

   _____

   Response output _____

   _____

   C. Fixed-ratio _____

   _____

   Response output _____

   _____

   D. Variable-ratio _____

   _____

   Response output _____

   _____

6. Identify the operant conditioning principle involved in controlling the italicized behavior in each of the following situations.

   positive reinforcement   *negative reinforcement*   *punishment*   *extinction*
   spontaneous recovery   *shaping*   *time-out*

   A. _____ Shawna's behavior of teasing her older sister has begun to decrease because now, whenever Shawna teases, her sister *acts as if she does not notice or hear* the tease instead of chasing after Shawna as she used to.

   B. _____ Raul experiences the discomforting feeling of anxiety whenever his wife Marcey probes him to share his inner feelings about their relationship. To eliminate the discomfort of anxiety he *terminates the conversation by coming up with something else he must do at the moment*, like make a call or watch the news.

   C. _____ Because Nancy's behavior of leaving unclean dishes on the kitchen counter annoys Sue, Sue has decided to change the situation by telling Nancy, when she sees her rinsing and putting the dishes in the dishwasher, how much she appreciates the help in keeping their apartment neat. Lately Sue has noticed that *Nancy consistently puts her dishes in the dishwasher* as soon as she is done eating.

   D. _____ In an attempt to curb Peter's aggressive behavior when he started a fight on the playground, he was sent back to the classroom where he had *to sit quietly at his desk* while the other children continued to play their outdoor game.

   E. _____ Jason's teacher is trying to help him *improve the neatness of his handwriting*. When Jason writes more neatly than she has seen from him in the past, she gives him a special privilege. When he does not show improvement, she says nothing.

F. _____ Lisa's parents were pleased that their efforts to ignore her bedtime tantrums had been fairly effective and that for four nights in a row she had gone to bed with almost no complaint. Then, on the fifth night, Lisa surprised them with *another bedtime tantrum*.

G. _____ Every time Rusty shows up late for school a tardy slip is mailed to his parents, and he is required to help the school ground's keeper for an hour after school. Recently school officials have noticed that *Rusty's tardiness* is declining.

7. Identify the schedule of reinforcement that is illustrated in each of the following situations.

   fixed-ratio   fixed-interval   variable-interval   variable-ratio

   A. _____ Sam collects aluminum cans and drops them off at the local grocery store for cash. He works hard gathering cans because he earns twenty-four cents for each pound of cans he collects.

   B. _____ Lynn goes door-to-door selling Girl Scout cookies. Sometimes people buy a box, other times they do not. Lynn knows that the more doors she knocks on the higher her total sales will be.

   C. _____ Because Ginger's psychology teacher tends to given unannounced pop quizzes, she studies more frequently and consistently for her psychology class than she does for any other class.

   D. _____ Miguel's job allows a lot of freedom. He can work hard or not so hard and either way he gets his usual paycheck at the end of the week.

8. Identify the type of learning process that would be involved in establishing the italicized behaviors in each of the following situations.

   classical conditioning   operant conditioning   observational learning

   A. _____ On several occasions during lightning storms, when Terry switched on the kitchen light she received a shock that caused severe pain. Now, even when the sky is clear, she feels *frightened as she touches the kitchen light switch*.

   B. _____ Randy used an aerosol product to soothe his painful sunburn. The product eliminated the pain and now whenever Randy is sunburned, *he uses the product*.

   C. _____ Lee's cat Belle purrs when its scalp is scratched. When Lee gets home from work she usually does two things in this sequence: she plays Beethoven's Ninth Symphony on her stereo, and she scratches Belle's head while she listens. One day Lee played the Ninth Symphony, but she did not have time to scratch the cat's head. She noticed with surprise that when the music began, *Belle began to purr*.

   D. _____ Daryl, who has never eaten a Chinese meal before, watched his friends eat for several minutes and then he too *positioned his chopsticks in his hand* and began to eat.

SQ3R*plus*

RECITE: When you have finished reading the assigned material in your text and you have completed the exercises in your study guide, turn back to the chapter outline. Read each learning objective and recite out loud everything you can remember in support of each objective.

REVIEW: Check to see if you have answered all the questions you wrote during the *Survey* stage. Complete all sections of your study guide and check your answers for accuracy. If you are having trouble with specific topics ask you instructor for help.

WRITE: Read the learning objective again and then, in your own words, write down everything you can remember about this chapter. Summarize the main points and the concepts introduced in this chapter.

REFLECT: After each study period, take a break and reflect on what you have just studied. Ask yourself how this newly acquired information can be used in the future.

CHAPTER FIVE SELF-TEST

1. Psychologists define learning as:
   A. a process that increases the intelligence and creativity of an individual.
   B. the acquisition of new knowledge.
   C. the ability to think rationally.
   D. a relatively permanent change in behavior that occurs as a result of experience.

2. Conditioning is defined in your text as:
   A. modifying reflexive behavior.
   B. being prepared to respond to stimuli.
   C. being able to tell the difference between stimuli.
   D. a systematic procedure through which associations and responses to specific stimuli are learned.

3. Karen's father had several accidents while she was a passenger in his car. By the time she was eighteen, riding in a car as a passenger was so frightening for Karen that she could not go anywhere if someone else was going to drive. In this case, the unconditioned stimulus was:
   A. the accidents.
   B. fear.
   C. the car.
   D. her father.

4. In classical conditioning, the conditioned response is:
   A. a unique and original response.
   B. a "carbon copy" of the unconditioned response.
   C. somewhat stronger than the unconditioned response.
   D. somewhat weaker than the unconditioned response.

5. Which of the following statements is *false*?
   A. Emotional responses can be learned through classical conditioning.
   B. Emotional responses occur only in response to unconditioned stimuli.
   C. Through higher-order conditioning a conditioned response to a variety of different stimuli can occur.
   D. Classical conditioning can be used to help people develop new, more adaptive behaviors.

6. In Pavlov's classical conditioning experiment the _____ acted as an unconditioned stimulus.
   A. food
   B. bell
   C. dog trainer
   D. salivation

7. Extinction is the term used to describe:
   A. a process where the unconditioned stimulus is no longer paired with the conditioned stimulus.
   B. a conditioned response that is no longer elicited by the conditioned stimulus.
   C. a situation where the reinforcer is withheld.
   D. all of the above

8. Spontaneous recovery is:
   A. the recurrence of a conditioned response following a rest period after extinction.
   B. the sudden responsiveness to the conditioning process by an organism who previously had been unresponsive.
   C. the immediate elimination of a maladaptive conditioned response.
   D. a term used to describe a response that suddenly reaches maximum strength.

9. Randy taps her foot and gets involved in the tune whenever she hears a country song. However, if the music is not country, she does not even know it's playing. Randy's response to country music illustrates:
   A. formation of a conditioned stimulus.
   B. instrumental conditioning.
   C. stimulus discrimination.
   D. stimulus generalization.

10. Whether or not conditioning takes place depends on the predictability of the association between the:
    A. NS and CS.
    B. UCS and CS.
    C. UCS and CR.
    D. NS and UCR.

11. The Garcia effect is:
    A. organisms learning to avoid foods that make them sick.
    B. pairing pills with nausea such that an aversion is produced in animals.
    C. cancer patients avoiding certain foods following their chemotherapy.
    D. all of the above

12. Physical responses to the world such as _____ can be classically conditioned.
    A. pulse
    B. blood pressure
    C. allergic reactions
    D. all of the above

13. Psychologists call behavior that receives feedback in the form of a reinforcing or punishing consequence _____ behavior.
    A. respondent
    B. classical
    C. operant
    D. involuntary

14. A device that allows researchers to control when an organism will receive reinforcement or punishment is called a:
    A. cumulative recorder.
    B. Skinner box.
    C. maze.
    D. differential apparatus.

15. When lever pressing is being conditioned and we see the rat consistently turning its head prior to pressing the lever, we would say that superstitious behavior had occurred as a result of the head turn being:
    A. deliberately reinforced.
    B. accidentally rewarded.
    C. placed on extinction.
    D. tested for spontaneous recovery.

16. In order for a consequence to act as a reinforcer, the organism must:
    A. know that it has made the correct response.
    B. feel positive about the response it has made.
    C. understand the value of the consequence.
    D. need or want the consequence.

17. If using punishment to discipline a particular behavior, a parent should:
    A. positively reinforce desired behaviors that are incompatible with the undesired behavior.
    B. use a very mild punisher.
    C. punish the behavior on a variable-interval schedule.
    D. all of the above

18. Ratio schedules of consequences are based on:
    A. time passing between responses.
    B. time passing between a response and a consequence.
    C. the frequency of responses (i.e., work output).
    D. the number of consequences that are given for one response.

19. On several occasions Julie found and bought her favorite dresses at Cecilia's Discount Clothing store. Now, whenever she does shopping for clothes, she heads for the nearest discount store. Julie's habit of shopping at any discount store illustrates:
    A. higher-order conditioning.
    B. latent learning.
    C. generalization.
    D. discrimination.

20. When provided with hypothalamic stimulation, rats will:
    A. attack members of their own species.
    B. fall asleep.
    C. stop responding.
    D. frequently choose brain stimulation over food.

Congratulations, you have completed Chapter 5. Now, proceed to the Exam Preparation Section in the back of your study guide for your final review, but don't forget to review the Enrichment Glossary for help understanding difficult words.

LANGUAGE ENRICHMENT GLOSSARY

Some students who reviewed the textbook listed the following words as difficult to understand. Use this list, your dictionary, and teachers and friends to learn the meaning of words you do not understand

Page	Term	Explanation	Page	Term	Explanation
149	argyle	a certain style of clothing	165	pat on the head	pet or stroke animal
150	knob	a handle	166	noxious	harmful
150	jerks back	pull away	166	boredom	dull, nothing to do
150	loafers	shoes with no laces	167	rodent's	an animal like a rat
150	deviant behavior	wrong behavior	167	intrinsic value	value in itself
150	organism	animal or person	167	sedans	large car
150	heritage	background born with	167	nods	move head up and down
150	underlie	are the basis, make up	168	curfew	the time when a child must be home at night
150	jerks	pull back quickly	168	grounded	they must stay in the house for punishment
150	elicited	caused	170	imitate	copy
151	salivate	watery fluid in mouth	170	strike out	to hit
154	puffs of air	small forced amount of air	170	class bullies	person who hurts a smaller person
154	frolicking	playing joyfully	171	lawns	grass covered yard
154	cozy	warm, close feeling	171	moderation	amount in the middle
154	remote	distant	172	targeted behavior	behavior focused on
155	speeding tickets	fine for driving too fast	172	intermittently	on, off, on, off
155	inconspicuously	without being seen	172	work output	work completed or done
155	stretch of road	a part or piece of a road	172	scalloped	up and down pattern
155	sinister	evil or bad person	172	best bet	best choice
155	scary	frightening	172	gamblers	people who bet money
156	contiguous	close in time	172	slot machines	a machine for gambling
156	interval	time period	172	a jackpot	money won gambling
156	contextual cues	environmental information	173	rotten attitude	bad attitude or outlook
156	aversions	to hate something, disgust	174	widget	general term for product
157	nausea	upset stomach	174	discriminate	tell difference between
157	chemotherapy	drugs that kill cancer cell	175	apparent	observed or seen
159	scratch	small or slight cut	175	depicting	picturing or showing
159	gunfire	sound of gun going off	176	ordeals	stressful
160	ellipse	oval	178	diabetes	disease in which sugar cannot be used
160	stereotyped	not natural	179	regimen	routine
160	scope	range	179	urge	desire
160	pollen	yellow powder from plants	179	grueling	very hard or difficult
160	mold	small growth in wet places	179	rampant	common, many
163	cash bonuses	money rewards	184	disoriented	confused, lost
163	morale	employee attitude	184	parlor	restaurant
163	paws	animal's feet	185	collage	grouping
164	grid on the floor	a metal rack	187	high esteem	a lot of respect
164	stumbles	accidentally falls	187	stutter	trouble talking
164	pellet of food	small piece of food	188	peers	people their own age
165	sloppy	not neat			

CHAPTER 6

Memory

Psychology 6th Ed.		Keeping Pace Plus		
HEADINGS	**PAGE**	**LESSON**	**L.O.**	**LEARNING OBJECTIVES**
Approaches to Memory	194	**1**		
The Information Processing Approach	195		6.1	Outline the information-processing model by describing sensory memory, short-term memory, and long-term memory.
Three Key Processes: Encoding, Storage, and Retrieval	195		6.2	Detail how encoding, storage, and retrieval are involved in memory processes.
Levels of Processing	196		6.3	Describe how the levels-of-processing approach to memory differs from those earlier linear models.
Parallel Distributed Processing	197		6.4	Summarize the theory of parallel distributed processing in memory.
The Neuroscience Approach	198		6.5	Describe the neuroscience approach to memory.
Sensory Memory: Focus on Encoding	198	**2**	6.6	Describe the two types of encoding that take place in sensory memory.
Short-Term Memory: Focus on Storage	200	**3**	6.7	Understand how short-term memory differs from sensory memory, by focusing on rehearsal, an active processing of information. Also, relate how duration and capacity are involved in short-term memory.
The Discovery of Short-Term Memory	200			
Short-Term Memory as Working Memory	202		6.8	Discuss the concept of working memory and explain how it differs from traditional thoughts about sensory, short-term, and long-term memory.

Chapter 6 Overview

Chapter 6 begins with a description of four different approaches to how memories are processed. The information-processing approach looks at the process involved in memory and outlines three stages of memory: encoding, storage, and retrieval. The levels of processing approach breaks from the linear model suggested by the information processing approach and states that memory is processed at varying levels or depths depending on the cues provided. The parallel distributed processing approach focuses on the neural network similar to computer networks which allow for simultaneous processing of different information. The neuroscience approach refers to the electrochemical process and proposes that memories are stored in multiple locations throughout the nervous system.

Memory is divided into sensory memory, short-term memory, and long-term memory. Sensory memory focuses on the encoding process and is temporary and fragile. Short-term memory focuses on storage. Memories can be stored for longer periods of time if techniques like rehearsal are used. Long-term memory focuses on the retrieval process and is thought to have a limitless capacity. Two types of information can be stored in long-term memory, procedural and declarative. Declarative memory is further divided into episodic and semantic memory, episodic memory being based on the chronological sequence of events, objects, or situations, and semantic memory on memory for ideas, rules, and general concepts. Memory for distinctive events is termed <u>flashbulb memory</u>.

The process of retrieval has generated hundreds of research studies, most of which focus on the accuracy of recall and methods to improve recall. Lefton discusses primacy and recency effects, imagery techniques, and extraordinary memory, and provides some practical suggestions for improving your memory.

Forgetting can be caused by a number of factors including improper rehearsal or not using memory for an extended period. To prevent forgetting information, one must develop an understanding of how information is retrieved. Specific measures of retention are described, including recall, recognition, reconstruction, and pictorial memory. Each of these measures helps explain how we remember or forget information. Decay and interference can cause forgetting, and information can be lost from both short- and long-term memory. Although some suggest that memories are retained, but sometimes not readily available, this usually is due to improper encoding or some other secondary cause. Lefton examines memory in the context of state-dependent learning, motivated forgetting and eyewitness testimony.

Amnesia is the inability to remember information because of some physiological trauma. Retrograde amnesia is the inability to remember events that preceded the trauma, and anterograde amnesia is the inability to remember events following the trauma. Consolidation theory supports the neuroscience approach to memory by postulating that memories are processed and later distributed to thousands of neurons in the brain. This biochemical approach may hold the key to a better understanding of how and why we remember or forget.

It may never be clear where remembering ends and forgetting starts, but if you use your knowledge of memory, you will begin to enhance your own memories.

SQ3R*plus*

SURVEY THE LESSON: Read learning objectives 6.1 through 6.22 and, in the text, examine the chapter headings, tables, and pictures on pages 194-225 in the text to *form an idea of what you should learn and to set goals for your study time*.

WRITE DOWN QUESTIONS: *While surveying and reading the text, write down questions* about the information being presented. *Write your questions* in the space below or on a separate piece of paper and try to find answers to these questions in the text.

ACTIVELY READ PAGES 194-225: The following exercise is designed to facilitate this process. Complete the following questions as you read, and when you are done, check your answers with those printed in the back of this study guide.

YOUR QUESTIONS:

Matching
Match the following terms or concepts from your textbook with the most appropriate description.

1. _____ amnesia
2. _____ chunks
3. _____ consolidation
4. _____ decay
5. _____ declarative memory
6. _____ elaborative rehearsal
7. _____ encoding
8. _____ episodic memory
9. _____ imagery
10. _____ implicit
11. _____ interference
12. _____ long term memory (LTM)
13. _____ maintenance rehearsal
14. _____ memory
15. _____ primacy effect
16. _____ procedural memory
17. _____ recency effect
18. _____ rehearsal
19. _____ retrieval
20. _____ schema
21. _____ semantic memory
22. _____ sensory memory
23. _____ short term memory (STM)
24. _____ state defendant learning
25. _____ storage

a) the storage system that allows for retention and retrieval of previously learned information
b) the process by which information is put into memory
c) the process of maintaining information in memory
d) the process by which stored information is recovered from memory
e) also known as sensory register
f) memory storage system that temporarily holds current or recently attended to information
g) the process of repeatedly verbalizing, thinking about, or otherwise acting on information in order to kept information in memory
h) manageable and meaningful units of information
i) repetitive review of information with little or no interpretation
j) repetition in which the stimulus may be associated with other events
k) system that keeps relatively permanent record of information
l) memory for perceptual for motor and cognitive skills
m) memory for specific facts
n) memory for specific events, objects, and situations
o) memory for ideas, rules, and general concepts
p) memory for previously experienced events, and is a passive process
q) the more accurate recall of items presented first

r) the accurate recall of items presented last
s) cognitive process in which a mental picture is created
t) conceptual framework that organizes information
u) the loss of information as a result of the passage of time
v) the suppression or confusion of one bit of information with another that was received earlier or later
w) the tendency to recall information learned in a particular physiological state
x) the inability to remember information
y) the evolution of a temporary neural circuit into a more permanent circuit

True or False

1. Organizing information so that the nervous system can process it is called storage. TRUE FALSE

2. Encoding is the first step in establishing memory. TRUE FALSE

3. Although some researchers have challenged the existence of the sensory register and its physiological basis, most researchers still hold that it is the first stage of coding. TRUE FALSE

4. Baddeley's introduction of a working memory expanded the concept of short-term memory, focusing on its complexity and how single tasks analyze single components of a multistage system. TRUE FALSE

5. Repetitive review with little or no interpretation is called maintenance rehearsal. TRUE FALSE

6. Encoding information into long term memory involves only rehearsal or repetition. TRUE FALSE

7. Specific memories, in which a person can recall when and where an event happened and the circumstances surrounding it, are examples of procedural memory. TRUE FALSE

8. A phenomenon called the primacy effect states that recall is higher for words at the end of a list. TRUE FALSE

9. Flashbulb memory occurs when people vividly remember the circumstances in which they learned of major personal and public events. TRUE FALSE

10. With long delays both emotion and rehearsal are required to generate flashbulb memories. TRUE FALSE

11. People's imagery systems can be activated by visual, auditory, or olfactory stimuli or by other images. TRUE FALSE

12. Paivio's studies found that when using imagery as a memory aid, adjectives evoked better imagery than did nouns.　　TRUE　FALSE

13. State-dependent learning argues that people's memory/recall is greater when they are in the same physiological state they were in when they originally learned the information.　　TRUE　FALSE

14. Our limited capacity of memory makes us susceptible to interference or confusion with other learned items.　　TRUE　FALSE

15. A person that can acquire knowledge can recall it at will.　　TRUE　FALSE

16. Ebbinghaus tried to quantify how quickly subjects could learn, relearn, and forget information.　　TRUE　FALSE

17. The saving method implies that once something is initially learned it is not totally forgotten.　　TRUE　FALSE

18. Distributed practice is especially effective in perceptual motor skills where hand-eye coordination is important.　　TRUE　FALSE

19. Recognition involves remembering the details of a situation or idea and placing them in a meaningful framework.　　TRUE　FALSE

20. Retroactive inhibition is the increase in accurate recall of an item as a result of later presentation of other items.　　TRUE　FALSE

21. Repression of unpleasant thoughts often occurs with retrograde amnesia.　　TRUE　FALSE

22. Anterograde amnesia is the inability to remember events that preceded a traumatizing event.　　TRUE　FALSE

23. There is clear evidence that certain protein synthesis occurs just after learning and that long-term memory depends on this protein synthesis.　　TRUE　FALSE

24. Penfield's studies determined exactly where memories are stored in the brain.　　TRUE　FALSE

25. It is possible that when a neuron is stimulated over and over again, it is enriched and may branch out and become more easily accessible.　　TRUE　FALSE

26. Milner's data provide neurological support for a distinction between short and long-term memory.　　TRUE　FALSE

27. Some research contends that hormones may affect the way memories are stored.　　TRUE　FALSE

Fill-in-the-Blanks

1. The storage system that allows us to recall past events, images, ideas, or previously learned skills is called _____.

2. When we organize information so the nervous system can process it, we are _____ the information.

3. Maintaining information or keeping information in memory is called _____.

4. When we recover or _____ information, we are pulling the information from memory.

5. The theory that many operations within the brain take place at the same time is called the concept of _____ _____ _____.

6. The memory storage system that holds recently acquired information needed short term use is called _____ _____.

7. When one repeats information aloud, thinks about, or otherwise acts on the information to keep it in memory, one is completing the process of _____.

8. The _____ _____ which usually contains one or two single chunks, is the limited number of items that can easily be called up or reproduced.

9. The manageable or meaningful _____ of information can be numbers, words, or sentences.

10. The repetitive review of information that involves the physical stimulus, not its meaning, is called _____ _____.

11. _____ _____ involves repetition in which one makes associations with other events.

12. The more complex storage system of memory, called _____ _____, is the process of information maintenance while it is being processed.

13. Information can be found in permanent form in _____ _____.

14. The necessary memory to operate a car, wash dishes, or swim involves _____ memory.

15. The memory of specific facts is called _____ memory.

16. When one orders events chronologically, it is _____ memory.

17. Memory that deals with ideas, structures, rules, and events is known as _____ memory.

18. _____ memory tasks force one to recollect events or information; however, _____ memory tasks indirectly ask one to connect the event with knowledge of a previously experienced event.

19. The _____ effect is the phenomenon termed to describe why recall is higher for words at the beginning of a list, as opposed to words in the middle.

20. Words at the end of a list are easily recalled. This is explained in the _____ effect phenomenon.

21. The mental pictures that people create are our _____ systems.

22. In order to organize information, people create _____ or conceptual frameworks.

23. _____ or loss of information occurs over periods of time of disuse.

24. When one confuses information with other chunks of information, _____ has taken place.

25. When previous information interferes with recall, a decrease in accurate recall of information results called _____ _____.

26. _____ _____ occurs when there is a decrease in accurate recall as a result of the subsequent presentation of information.

27. The _____ _____ _____ asserts that information retrieval cues depend on the connections made with the information when it was initially encoded.

28. _____ _____ is based on the knowledge that information learned is most accurately recalled when the person is again in the same physiological state.

29. The inability to remember events is called _____.

30. The inability to remember events and experiences that preceded a traumatic event is called _____ _____; however, _____ _____ is described as the inability to remember events after the traumatic event.

31. When a temporary neural circuit changes to a more permanent circuit, this evolution is known as _____.

Applications

1. Define the following terms:
   A. Schema _____
   B. Leveling _____
   C. Sharpening _____
   D. Assimilation _____

2. Define the following terms.
   A. Interference _____
   B. Proactive inhibition _____

   C. Retroactive inhibition _____

   D. Retrograde amnesia _____
   E. Anterograde amnesia _____

   _____

3. Identify the concept that explains why remembering or forgetting occurs in each of the following situations.

decay   retrograde amnesia
retroactive inhibition   anterograde amnesia
proactive inhibition   primacy effect
motivated forgetting   recency effect

A. _____ Joyce could not remember her grandfather's version of the family's traditional Thanksgiving blessing after having recited a different one at a church social gathering.

B. _____ When Sam arrived at the company party he was introduced to twelve other guests. Sam can remember the names of the first three people he met.

C. _____ As a result of a serious head injury Jennifer suffered some brain damage. She remembers things like her name, where she grew up, and what she was doing before the accident. However, she cannot remember who her doctor is, what she ate for breakfast, or that her mother visited her yesterday.

D. _____ For years, as a child, Dale dialed his friend Leon's phone number from memory. Ten years later while visiting his hometown, Dale decided to phone Leon's parents to see if they could help him get in touch with his old friend. When Dale went to dial the number he realized that he could not remember it.

E. _____ Doug studied his psychology vocabulary words and then his sociology vocabulary words. His accuracy in recalling the sociology vocabulary words was poor.

F. _____ Somehow Claire lost her grocery list on the way to the store. Although she had read over the list just before leaving home, when she began to shop she realized that all she could remember were the last few items on the list.

G. _____ When David was five years old he lost his puppy, which upset him very much. When his mother related the story later she said she thought it strange that he did not remember the event, because the puppy had been so important to him and the loss was so traumatic. David's mother suggested that perhaps he did not want to remember.

H. _____ While climbing a mountain Frank fell and received a serious blow to his head. When he regained consciousness, he did not know who he was, where he came from, or when he was born.

SQ3R*plus*

RECITE: When you have finished reading the assigned material in your text and you have completed the exercises in your study guide, turn back to the chapter outline. Read each learning objective and recite out loud everything you can remember in support of each objective.

REVIEW: Check to see if you have answered all the questions you wrote during the *Survey* stage. Complete all sections of your study guide and check your answers for accuracy. If you are having trouble with specific topics ask you instructor for help.

WRITE: Read the learning objective again and then, in your own words, write down everything you can remember about this chapter. Summarize the main points and the concepts introduced in this chapter.

REFLECT: After each study period, take a break and reflect on what you have just studied. Ask yourself how this newly acquired information can be used in the future.

CHAPTER SIX SELF-TEST

1. Even though something is learned it may not always be remembered because:
   A. learning is a relatively permanent change.
   B. learning and memory are two separate processes.
   C. memory is the ability to remember past events, information, or skills.
   D. A and C

2. The information processing approach talks about 3 stages, _____, _____, _____ in learning and memory.
   A. encoding, storage, retrieval
   B. learning, memory, recall
   C. code, analyze, store
   D. sensory-memory, short-term memory, long-term memory

3. The sensory register provides:
   A. coding and storage for about 30 seconds.
   B. coding and permanent storage.
   C. initial encoding of information and brief, temporary storage.
   D. encoding, storage, and retrieval.

4. A chunk:
   A. can be a letter, a group of words and numbers, or sentences organized in a familiar way.
   B. is a manageable and meaningful unit of information.
   C. a brief and limited number of items that can be easily reproduced after presentation.
   D. A and B

5. Procedural memory:
   A. is memory for specific facts.
   B. is storage for the perceptual, motor, and cognitive skills necessary to complete a task.
   C. covers specific events, objects, and situations.
   D. covers the memory of ideas, rules, and general concepts about the world.

6. Recall of words at the end of a list is an example of:
   A. recency effect.
   B. extraordinary memory.
   C. primacy effect.
   D. rehearsal of information.

7. According to Bohannon, simple emotional responses without rehearsal produce:
   A. long-term memory.
   B. sensory registration.
   C. flash-bulb memory.
   D. short-term recall

8. Paivio and other researchers argue that imagery, verbal coding mechanisms, and semantic memory operate together to:
   A. code information.
   B. retrieve information.
   C. form conceptual memory.
   D. both A and B

9. Remembering two items of information by associating them with a third item that ties them together is:
   A. using mediation and memory.
   B. using mnemonics.
   C. using the SQ3R method.
   D. reviewing in different contexts and modalities.

10. Relearning a skill or information easily is an example of:
    A. recall.
    B. retrieval.
    C. saving method.
    D. retention.

11. Contemporary explanations of reconstructive memory have focused on:
    A. schema.
    B. leveling.
    C. sharpening.
    D. assimilation.

12. The decay hypothesis is not as widely accepted today, because many early studies did not take into consideration variables such as:
    A. interference and crowding.
    B. proactive and retroactive inhibition.
    C. rate and mode of stimulus presentation.
    D. coding and chunking.

13. Retroactive inhibition is:
    A. retrieval failure.
    B. the decrease in accurate recall of an item as a result of later presentation of other items.
    C. the increase in accurate recall of an item as a result of later presentation of other items.
    D. the decrease in accurate recall as a result of previous events interfering with a to-be remembered one.

14. Burying unpleasant ideas in the unconscious where they remain inaccessible is an example of:
    A. motivated forgetting.
    B. amnesia.
    C. retrograde amnesia.
    D. anterograde amnesia.

15. An example of state dependent learning would be:
    A. learning information while sober and recalling while intoxicated.
    B. learning and recalling information while sober.
    C. the tendency to recall information learned in a particular psychological state more accurately when one is again in that psychological state.
    D. learning information while intoxicated and recalling while sober.

16. The hippocampus region of the brain is responsible for:
    A. remembering old information, but not new information.
    B. the ability to remember remote events.
    C. the transfer of new information to permanent memory.
    D. the ability to remember new information, but not old information.

17. Enhancement of memories over time is an example of:
    A. constructed testimony.
    B. episode impairment.
    C. rehearsal.
    D. Bartlett's theory of assimilation.

18. Yuille and Curshall's study of eyewitness testimony showed that people's recall of events after 5 months was:
    A. very inaccurate.
    B. very accurate.
    C. frozen into crystalline clarity.
    D. none of the above

19. Hebb argues that _____ serves as the basis of short-term memory and permits _____ of information into long-term memory.
    A. coding, consolidation
    B. consolidation, coding
    C. neural activity, circuits
    D. circuits, neural activity

20. Many psychologists believe that the _____ provides the key to understanding learning and memory.
    A. coding process
    B. neural stimulation process
    C. consolidation process
    D. rehearsal process

21. Alkon argues that the spread of _____ and _____ activity from one site to another -- without activity or firing of the neurons -- seem to be critical for memory storage.
    A. electrical, chemical
    B. dendrite, synoptic
    C. synoptic, chemical
    D. synoptic, electrical

22. Penfield's studies indicated that stimulation of the _____ triggered memory retrievals.
    A. cortex
    B. cortical neurons
    C. temporal lobe
    D. frontal lobe

23. Other studies indicated that only when structures deep within the brain, in the _____, were also stimulated were experiences reported.
    A. visual areas
    B. limbic system
    C. cortex
    D. both A and C

24. Penfield's conclusion that the temporal lobe holds the memory trace has been contested because:
    A. destruction of tissue at these locations did not destroy the memory.
    B. nearly half the reported visual images occurred when stimulation spread from the cortex to other areas of the brain.
    C. structures in other parts of the brain, especially the limbic system, seem to be involved in producing mental images.
    D. all of the above

Congratulations, you have completed Chapter 6. Now, proceed to the Exam Preparation Section in the back of your study guide for your final review, but don't forget to review the Enrichment Glossary for help understanding difficult words.

LANGUAGE ENRICHMENT GLOSSARY

Some students who reviewed the textbook listed the following words as difficult to understand. Use this list, your dictionary, and teachers and friends to learn the meaning of words you do not understand

Page	Term	Explanation	Page	Term	Explanation
193	honeymoon	vacation after wedding	212	extensive	a lot of
193	studio	small apartment	210	cram	push
193	crammed	filled	210	drawn-out	spread out
193	stuffy	hot and little air	211	mnemonics	techniques that help memory
193	verbatim	exact words that were said	211	format	structure
194	organism	a plant or animal	211	jingle	song
194	retention	remembering information	211	treble-clef	top half of written music
194	trigger	to begin action	211	bizarre	very strange
194	gist	the main idea	211	clutter	messiness
195	rock band	type of musical group	211	jot	write
197	equate	see as the same	214	touch-type	use typing machine without looking at keys
197	enamored	liked	214	massed	all at the same time
197	elaborated	explain more details	214	space craft	space ship
197	sophisticated	advanced	215	Walter Cronkite's	famous man that reports the news
197	simultaneously	at the same time	216	bias	prejudice
198	analogy	to compare	216	grudge	resentment
198	deteriorate	break down, fall apart	216	stake	benefit from what happens
199	fragile	easily destroyed	216	clarity	clearness
200	decay	break down	216	ambiguity	not being clear
200	chef	cook	216	hazy	not clear
200	crucial	very important	216	echoed	repeated
202	interfere with	stop	216	prominent	important
201	accuracy	correctness	218	potent	strong
201	rehearsal	go over and over it	218	Retrieval	remembering
202	shallow	not deep	218	misshelved	put in the wrong place
202	scratch pad	paper to write on	220	intoxicated	drinking too much alcohol
204	etched	put into permanently	222	soap operas	television dramas
204	Springsteen	popular musician	222	epileptic attacks	seizures
206	categorized	put into groups	223	reverberating	to come back
206	synthesized	put together	223	consolidation	to make something solid
206	vividness	strength	223	infancy	very early stage
206	phenomenon	happening	224	elicited	brought out
206	facilitated	helped	224	intact	able to be used
209	olfactory	sense of smell	224	anatomical	spot in the brain
211	Extraordinary	much better than average	224	locations	where something is

CHAPTER 7

Cognition: Thought and Language

Chapter 7 Overview

The chapters on consciousness, learning, and memory were concerned with how we attend to, acquire, store, and retrieve information. In Chapter 7 Lefton blends the previous concepts into the application of thought and language. Cognitive psychologists are interested in a variety of thought-oriented issues, and many overlap other topics in psychology. In this chapter, the focus is on concept formation, decision making, problem solving, and language.

People organize their world by organizing their thoughts into concepts. Concept formation is thought to be the structure behind how each of us makes sense of the world. Concept formation is relatively easy to study in the laboratory; the two most common methods are the reception and selection methods. Each derives the formation of concepts, but the selection method is less structured. The problem with concept formation is that many concepts are termed fuzzy concepts, so that operational definitions are difficult.

Cognitive psychologists are interested in the thinking process. Lefton examines in detail syllogisms, logical decision making, and estimating probabilities. Problem solving is considered one of the highest cognitive processes. However, problem solving can be hindered by obstacles such as functional fixedness and psychological set. Both can limit the available responses to problems. Critical thinking and creative problem solving are ways to expand on the possible solutions to problems. In the second Applications box, Lefton suggests some ways to improve your problem solving skills. Computers also have the ability to problem solve by the use of algorithms and heuristics. Although computers can be programmed to simulate human problem solving, they lack (for now) ingenuity and imagination. Researchers are developing artificial neural networks which are interconnected units that serve as neural models. These models may someday answer many of the unanswered questions about human information processing.

People come from diverse cultures and experience life in many different contexts, but in all societies we have language. The study of psycholinguistics and the major areas of phonology (the study of the sounds of language), semantics (the study of the meaning of language), and syntax (the study of the relationships of words) are examined. Chomsky suggests that all sentences have structure of words and structure of meaning. Chomsky's transformational grammar includes surface and deep structures. The deep structure is far more important to understanding what is being communicated through language. Lefton concludes this chapter with the nature versus nurture debate of language acquisition. Learning theorists contend that language is acquired through imitation and reinforcement, and biologists contend that humans are born with an innate predisposition. Chimpanzee studies are presented to critically evaluate these arguments.

SQ3R*plus*

SURVEY THE LESSON: Read learning objectives 7.1 through 7.20 and, in the text, examine the chapter headings, tables, and pictures on pages 232-260 in the text to *form an idea of what you should learn and to set goals for your study time*.

WRITE DOWN QUESTIONS: *While surveying and reading the text, write down questions* about the information being presented. *Write your questions* in the space below or on a separate piece of paper and try to find answers to these questions in the text.

ACTIVELY READ PAGES 232-260: The following exercise is designed to facilitate this process. Complete the following questions as you read, and when you are done, check your answers with those printed in the back of this study guide.

YOUR QUESTIONS:

Matching

1. _____ algorithms
2. _____ brainstorming
3. _____ concept
4. _____ creativity
5. _____ decision making
6. _____ deep structure
7. _____ functional fixedness
8. _____ grammar
9. _____ heuristics
10. _____ linguistics
11. _____ logic
12. _____ morpheme
13. _____ phoneme
14. _____ problem solving
15. _____ psycholinguistics
16. _____ reasoning
17. _____ semantics
18. _____ subdural analysis
19. _____ surface structure
20. _____ syllogism
21. _____ syntax

a) mental category used to classify events or objects
b) the process by which people generate logical and coherent ideas
c) procedure used to reach a valid conclusion
d) a sequence of statements or premises followed by a conclusion
e) assessing and choosing among alternatives
f) the behavior of individuals when confronted with a situation or task that requires some insight or some unknown elements
g) inability to see that an object can have a function other than its stated or usual one
h) a problem solving technique that involves considering all possible solutions
i) a quality of thoughts and problem solving generally considered to include originality, novelty, and appropriateness
j) simple, specific, exhaustive problem solving procedure
k) set of strategies not strict rules that act as guidelines for problem solving
l) heuristic procedure in which a task is broken down into smaller parts
m) the study of language
n) the study of how language is acquired, perceived, understood, and produced
o) basic unit of sound
p) basic unit of meaning
q) analysis of the meaning of language components
r) the way words and groups of words are related to form phrases and sentences
s) the linguistic description of how language functions
t) the organization of a sentence that is closest to its written or spoken form
u) the organization of a sentence that is closest to its underlying meaning

True or False

1. Cognitive psychologists study thought, reasoning, and the interplay between humans and their environment.   TRUE   FALSE

2. The study of concept formation is the examination of how people organize and classify events and objects.   TRUE   FALSE

3. Green is a positive instance of a pine tree.   TRUE   FALSE

4.	Red is a dimension of the attribute color.	TRUE	FALSE
5.	The reception method presents all stimuli at once.	TRUE	FALSE
6.	Ethical systems, religious beliefs, and political views affect decision making.	TRUE	FALSE
7.	Eliminating possibilities one by one is an example of logical decision-making skills.	TRUE	FALSE
8.	A decision-making approach in which some variables take on more importance than others is called a compensatory model.	TRUE	FALSE
9.	Previous events often have little effect on how people estimate probabilities.	TRUE	FALSE
10.	Human beings have great difficulty in problem solving tasks.	TRUE	FALSE
11.	People can be taught to be more effective problem solvers.	TRUE	FALSE
12.	All human beings have functional fixedness.	TRUE	FALSE
13.	Functional fixedness limits problem-solving abilities.	TRUE	FALSE
14.	Brainstorming allows people to break away from the fear that their ideas may be silly.	TRUE	FALSE
15.	If an idea is original, novel, and appropriate, it is creative.	TRUE	FALSE
16.	Representing a problem physically can help enhance creative solutions.	TRUE	FALSE
17.	Algorithms involve looking at only one solution to a problem.	TRUE	FALSE
18.	Heuristics have strict rules and guidelines that must be followed in problem solving.	TRUE	FALSE
19.	Once language emerges, all children attach semantic meanings to words.	TRUE	FALSE
20.	"Mama" is a child's phoneme.	TRUE	FALSE
21.	The basic structure of words is semantics.	TRUE	FALSE
22.	The meaning of a sentence is equivalent to the definitions of the individual words in the sentence added together.	TRUE	FALSE

23. The surface structure of a sentence can be transformed into more than one deep structure. TRUE FALSE

24. According to learning theorists, words and grammatical rules are learned through reinforcement. TRUE FALSE

25. The conditioning approach to language acquisition stresses the importance of language experiences during the formative years. TRUE FALSE

26. Linguists promoting the biological approach to language acknowledge the role that learning experiences play in language acquisition. TRUE FALSE

27. Lenneberg's claim that brain lateralization is not complete until age thirteen has been challenged. TRUE FALSE

28. Biological theories state that humans are born with a predisposition toward language and that the blueprint for language is preprinted. TRUE FALSE

Fill-in-the-Blanks

1. The study of the different fields of learning like perception and memory is called _____ _____.

2. We use _____ when we classify events and objects according to common properties.

3. According to the _____ _____ _____, people form ideas about concepts, test those hypotheses, and make inferences about stimuli.

4. An inefficient method of eliminating possible solutions is called _____ _____.

5. When we generate ideas about a situation, evaluate the situation and reach a conclusion, we are _____.

6. We use _____ as the procedure to reach a valid conclusion.

7. _____ _____ involves assessing various alternatives and choosing the best one.

8. Asking participants to contemplate _____, thinking about statements or premises, followed by a conclusion, helps psychologists trace people's cognitive processes.

9. When one organizes thoughts in order to attack a problem, they are working on _____ _____.

10. When one experiences the inability to see another use for a familiar object, they are experiencing _____ _____.

11. When people _____, they generate ideas and consider all possible solutions without making judgments about the worth of the ideas and solutions.

12. _____ is the ability to generate new, original, and novel ideas to a problem.

13. When answering a question, if one narrows down choices and alternatives to find the answer, _____ _____ is taking place.

14. _____ _____ is allowing the mind to expand and consider a range of possibilities and options for the solution to the problem.

15. _____ are usually very precise and involve using a set of rules to implement particular steps over and over again until the problem is solved.

16. As opposed to strict rules, _____ use flexible guidelines for discovery-oriented problem solving.

17. When a problem is broken down into smaller steps, each of which has a subgoal, the heuristics approach used is _____ _____.

18. When one compares the current situation with the desired end in order to determine the most efficient means of reaching the desired end, he/she is implementing

_____ _____.

19. A _____ _____ involves starting from the goal or end solution and working backward to analyze the problem and define the needed steps.

20. The study of language is _____.

21. _____ is the study of how humans acquire, perceive, understand, and produce language.

22. _____ are the basic units of sound that make up words.

23. Different from the basic units of sound, _____ are the basic units of meaning in a language.

24. When one analyzes the meaning of language, focusing on the individual words, the relationship between words, and the significance of words, he/she is studying the _____ of a language.

25. The way groups of words come together to form language is called

_____.

26. The function of a language is called _____.

27. Noam Chomsky described a new type of grammar termed _____ _____ that said that each sentence contained both a surface structure and a deep structure.

28. The organization of the sentence is called _____ _____.

29. The underlying meaning of the sentence in transformation grammar is called the

_____ _____.

30. Chimps do not spontaneously develop communication skills, such as _____ _____, or spontaneously learning to name and point to objects.

Applications

1. Define the following.
   A. Reasoning _____
   B. Logic _____
   C. Decision making _____

2. Define algorithms. _____
   _____

3. Define heuristics. _____
   _____

4. Ashcraft has suggested 8 ways for people to improve their problem-solving abilities; list them:

   1. _____   5. _____
   2. _____   6. _____
   3. _____   7. _____
   4. _____   8. _____

5. Identify the type of problem solving strategy involved in each of the following situations.

   brainstorming   *conservative focusing*
   hypothesis checking   *global focusing*
   dimension checking

   A. _____ Maureen responds to Jack's tease, "Bet you can't guess how big my new television is?" with "Is it bigger than a breadbox?" Jack says, "Yes," and Maureen asks, "Is it bigger than a swamp cooler?" Maureen continues her questioning until she can determine the size of Jack's television.

   B. _____ Jack teases Maureen saying, "Bet you can't guess what I bought you for your birthday?" Maureen responds with a series of questions that go something like this: "A car?"; "A microwave oven?"; "A dress?"; "A puppy?" Maureen gives up before she is able to guess.

   C. _____ Mother's Day is nearing, and Jack teases Maureen once again. "Bet you can't guess what I got you for your special day?" Maureen begins by asking, "Is it something for the kitchen?" Jack says, "No." Maureen asks, *"Can I wear it?"* "Yes," says Jack. "Is it jewelry?" "Yes." "Is it a necklace?" Jack mumbles, "Maybe," and quickly changes the subject. Maureen figures that she was getting real close.

D. _____ Jack and Maureen were having trouble figuring out the ultimate gift to buy for Freddie's fiftieth birthday. Every idea either one of them had seemed boring, or Freddie "already had one." At dinner, they decided to get wild-and-crazy with their ideas and began writing down every gift idea that came to mind. When Jack blurted out, "How about a picnic basket!" they grinned at one another, both knowing that it was a super idea.

E. _____ To afford all these gifts, Jack realizes that he must budget and invest his earnings wisely. He studies the various plans provided by his financial counselor and asks himself "if-then" questions about each plan. After considering all of the possibilities, he selected the "J" plan, which is a combination of the plans provided to him plus his own new plan. He tells Maureen it probably is time for her to start looking for the job she has been wanting to have for so long.

6. Match the following terms with the appropriate definition.

psycholinguistics   *syntax*
grammar   *phonemes*
phonology   *morpheme*
semantics

A. _____ The study of the basic units of sound found in a language.

B. _____ The basic unit of meaning in a language; a word or meaningful part of a word.

C. _____ The basic units of sound in a language.

D. _____ The study of how language is acquired, perceived, understood, and produced.

E. _____ The linguistic description of how a language functions.

F. _____ The relation between groups of words and how those words are arranged in phrases and sentences.

G. _____ The study of meanings of words and sentences, and the analysis of how thought is generated by the placement of words in a particular context.

7. Define transformational grammar, surface structure, and deep structure, and give an example that shows the surface structure and deep structure of two sentences.

A. Transformational grammar _____

_____

B. Surface structure _____

_____

C. Deep structure _____

_____

SQ3R*plus*

RECITE: When you have finished reading the assigned material in your text and you have completed the exercises in your study guide, turn back to the chapter outline. Read each learning objective and recite out loud everything you can remember in support of each objective.

REVIEW: Check to see if you have answered all the questions you wrote during the *Survey* stage. Complete all sections of your study guide and check your answers for accuracy. If you are having trouble with specific topics ask you instructor for help.

WRITE: Read the learning objective again and then, in your own words, write down everything you can remember about this chapter. Summarize the main points and the concepts introduced in this chapter.

REFLECT: After each study period, take a break and reflect on what you have just studied. Ask yourself how this newly acquired information can be used in the future.

CHAPTER SEVEN SELF-TEST

1. Cognitive researchers are interested in processes that are:
    A. declarative compared to procedural.
    B. automatic compared to controlled.
    C. attention compared to representative knowledge.
    D. ideas and perceptions gathered from others.

2. The hypothesis-testing strategy called hypothesis checking:
    A. is the most efficient strategy identified by Levine.
    B. involves testing the hypothesis of one dimension at a time.
    C. requires a person to keep all possible hypotheses in mind at one time while focusing on one at a time.
    D. involves people testing one hypothesis at a time.

3. In syllogisms, the truth of the premises is _____ to the validity of the syllogism.
    A. logically true
    B. irrelevant
    C. relevant
    D. traced

4. Errors in probability judgments may be attributed to:
    A. ethical systems or religious beliefs.
    B. ignoring key pieces of data.
    C. an individual's political view.
    D. all of the above

5. Functional fixedness increases when:
    A. an object has no name or label to describe it.
    B. an object has no specific function.
    C. a person has had previous experience with an object.
    D. all of the above

6. Brainstorming:
    A. decreases functional fixedness.
    B. promotes creativity.
    C. produces a higher quality of ideas.
    D. all of the above

7. Computers have been programmed to simulate human thought processes such as:
    A. information processing.
    B. ingenuity.
    C. creativity.
    D. A & C

8. SQ3R *plus* approach to problem-solving is an example of:
    A. drawing inferences and developing subgoals.
    B. following a plan.
    C. searching for contradictions and relations.
    D. practice.

9. Language and thought are:
    A. related, but separate processes.
    B. both influenced by one's experience with the environment.
    C. both influenced by genetic factors.
    D. all of the above

10. Rosch's studies showed that:
    A. language is not adaptive.
    B. language does not determine thought.
    C. language does not respond to specific environment, events, and cultures.
    D. thoughts do not help shape language.

11. A phoneme is the basic unit of _____ in a language.
    A. sound
    B. meaning
    C. inflection
    D. grammar

12. Syntax is:
    A. the analysis of the meaning of individual words.
    B. the study of language.
    C. the study of how words and word groups combine to form phrases, sentences, clauses.
    D. the underlying pattern of words that help convey meaning.

13. A person who is concerned with what the word *love* means in the sentence, "I love roses," is concerned with:
    A. grammar.
    B. semantics.
    C. syntax.
    D. phonology.

14. "That is an enormous turkey" and "That turkey is enormous" are two sentences that:
    A. have the same surface structure.
    B. have a different deep structure.
    C. represent transformational grammar.
    D. all of the above

15. If language is based on biology:
    A. many aspects should be evident early in life.
    B. regardless of culture or language, all children should develop grammar in a similar way.
    C. the role of learning should be permanent.
    D. A and B

16. Kanzi, the pigmy chimp learned:
    A. languages steadily.
    B. to understand human speech and syntax.
    C. languages only after intense training.
    D. A and B

17. Lenneberg's view derives in part from:
    A. observing that maturation at about 18-24 months permits children to acquire grammar.
    B. observations that most children learn grammar at a very early age.
    C. a lack of maturity in certain structures limits infants' ability to speak.
    D. seeing that language does not depend on maturation of certain neurological capacities.

18. Lana, the chimpanzee, learned to communicate:
    A. with geometric forms and a computer.
    B. by using sign language.
    C. by humming phonetic sounds.
    D. by arranging symbols on a magnetized board.

Congratulations, you have completed Chapter 7. Now, proceed to the Exam Preparation Section in the back of your study guide for your final review, but don't forget to review the Enrichment Glossary for help understanding difficult words.

LANGUAGE ENRICHMENT GLOSSARY

Some students who reviewed the textbook listed the following words as difficult to understand. Use this list, your dictionary, and teachers and friends to learn the meaning of words you do not understand

Page	Term	Explanation	Page	Term	Explanation
231	blindfolded	eyes covered by cloth	247	optimize	make the most of
232	trace	follow	247	implicitly	mainly
232	domestic	house	247	buffers	protective space
232	omelet	food made out of eggs	247	permutation	change
232	drew mental images	picture in your mind	248	integral	important part of
232	felines	cats	248	hampered	interfered with
232	history	background	248	ingenuity	creativity
232	mainstream	most common	249	clusters	groups
234	pilot episode	first show	249	been corrupted	developed a problem
234	stereotypes	overgeneralized label	249	simultaneously	at the same time
234	incongruity	contrasts	250	crash	stop completely
235	embedded	a part of	250	ablated	cut out or hurt
237	discarding	to throw out	250	swim trunks	men's clothes for swimming
238	valid	true	250	surfer	a person who rides a surfboard
238	trivial	small and not important	250	grab	take hold of
238	warranted	correct and logical	250	surfboard	board to stand on and ride a wave in the ocean
238	devised	make up	252	millennia	thousands of years
239	compensate	make up for	252	hemlock	poison
241	regime	routine or schedule	252	constituencies	people they serve
241	mitigating	lessening	252	astonishingly adept	surprising good at
242	minuscule	very small	253	cooing	sounds baby makes
242	hindrances	things that hold us back	253	utterances	sounds the child makes
243	preconceived	thought out earlier	253	misconstrue	not understand
243	rigid	not flexible	253	fired	discharged from work
244	predisposition	make person like certain thing	255	unique	special unusual quality
244	biasing effect	causing person to like or hate something	255	transformational-grammar	how words are used when a person gets older
244	innovation	thinking new ideas	256	verbatim	using the exact words
245	not headstrong	flexible	256	wind velocities	how fast the wind is blowing
244	Einstein	famous math scientist	256	precipitation	rain
244	Picasso	famous artist, painter	256	preeminent	stand out, be important
244	nonstereotyped ways	you think your own thoughts freely	257	innate	born with
245	illuminate	discover	259	concrete	real
246	entrepreneurs	people who start a business			

CHAPTER 8

Intelligence

Psychology 6th Ed.
Keeping Pace Plus

Chapter 8 Overview

Are you intelligent? Before you can answer that question you must be able to define intelligence. Psychologists have debated for more than 75 years over the definition of intelligence, without agreeing. Various theories have been proposed and probably thousands of intelligence tests have been created. Several people have suggested theories of intelligence, including Piaget, Spearman, Thurstone, Guilford, Jensen, Wechsler, and Sternberg. One of the most widely accepted theories is that of David Wechsler. Wechsler's theory defines intelligence as the aggregate or global capacity of an individual to act purposefully, to think rationally, and to deal effectively with the environment. Sternberg's new theory of intelligence challenges the older theories and most intelligence tests. He suggests that a new "practical intelligence" needs to be assessed and tested in our schools. Lefton reports on Goleman's recent publication, Emotional Intelligence, which is said to include self-awareness, impulse control, persistence, self-motivation, ability to recognize emotions in others, and social agility.

Developing a test is a long and complicated process. Proper test development involves standardization and the establishment of test norms. All professional tests must be reliable and valid. Lefton examines three important intelligence tests: the Stanford-Binet Intelligence Scale, the Wechsler Scales, and the Kaufman Assessment Battery for Children.

Intelligence testing is not without controversy. In the beginning of this chapter, Lefton introduces the recent book by Hernstein and Murray, *The Bell Curve*. Their book argues that in the United States there exists a cognitive class that is determined by genetic intelligence and is unlikely to change. Critics of intelligence tests have argued for years that the tests are biased and flawed by misinterpretation of the scores. This debate brings back the old nature versus nurture issue and focuses on inherited intelligence. Environmental factors need to be considered as well as cultural differences in the interpretation of intelligence scores. Fortunately, the differences between racial groups is eroding. Other issues such as family structure and childrearing practices, score stability, and gender differences, need further study. The chapter concludes with a look at giftedness and mental retardation. Lefton includes a discussion of how the law and education have interacted to provide appropriate education to all children.

SQ3R*plus*

SURVEY THE LESSON: Read learning objectives 8.1 through 8.19 and, in the text, examine the chapter headings, tables, and pictures on pages 266-294 in the text to *form an idea of what you should learn and to set goals for your study time*.

WRITE DOWN QUESTIONS: *While surveying and reading the text, write down questions* about the information being presented. *Write your questions* in the space below or on a separate piece of paper and try to find answers to these questions in the text.

ACTIVELY READ PAGES 266-294: The following exercise is designed to facilitate this process. Complete the following questions as you read, and when you are done, check your answers with those printed in the back of this study guide.

YOUR QUESTIONS:

Matching

Match the following terms or concepts from your textbook with the most appropriate description.

1. _____ halo effect
2. _____ intelligence
3. _____ IQ
4. _____ mainstreaming
5. _____ mental retardation
6. _____ norms
7. _____ percentile score
8. _____ raw score
9. _____ reliability
10. _____ standard score (SS)
11. _____ standardization
12. _____ validity

a) the aggregate or global capacity of the individual to act purposefully, to think rationally, and to deal effectively with the environment

b) the process of developing uniformed procedures for administering and scoring a test

c) scores and corresponding percentile rank of a large and representative sample of individuals from the population

d) an examinee's test score that has not been transformed or converted

e) score that expresses an individual's position relative to the mean

f) a score indicating what percentage of the test population would obtain a lower score

g) a standard deviation test score for which the mean and standard deviation remain constant at all ages

h) a test's ability to yield the same score for the same individual through repeated testing

i) the ability of a test to measure what it is suppose to measure

j) the tendency for one of an individual's characteristics to influence the evaluation of other characteristics

k) below average intellectual functioning accompanied by substantial limitations in functioning that originates before age 18

l) the administrative practice of placing special needs children in regular classroom settings

True or False

1. In 1986, twenty-five respected researchers agreed upon a scientific definition of intelligence.   TRUE   FALSE

2. Factor theories use statistical procedures to discover the elements of intelligence.   TRUE   FALSE

3. Factor theories are based on the idea that elements of intelligence are highly correlated, suggesting that some underlying attribute (such as verbal abilities) determine a person's score on several dimensions of intelligence.   TRUE   FALSE

4.	Guilford believes that three factors are necessary to prove a correct assessment of an individual's abilities.	TRUE	FALSE
5.	Sternberg is not as concerned about how much intelligence people have but rather with how they use it.	TRUE	FALSE
6.	Binet referred to the age level at which a child is functioning cognitively as intelligence.	TRUE	FALSE
7.	Norms serve as a reference point to which individual test scores can be compared.	TRUE	FALSE
8.	A percentile score indicates the percentage of other students taking the test who obtain a *higher* score.	TRUE	FALSE
9.	Reliability on intelligence tests is important so that meaningful comparisons can be made.	TRUE	FALSE
10.	Because it was biased by verbal questions and was not standardized, the original Binet-Simon Scale was revised by Terman at Stanford University.	TRUE	FALSE
11.	Researchers have found that the criticism suggesting IQ tests *systematically* discriminate in terms of race is *not* true.	TRUE	FALSE
12.	Psychologists are eliminating cultural biases by using better test construction and scoring techniques.	TRUE	FALSE
13.	According to Angoff, if cognitive training begins early in life and is carried out in a continuously supportive and motivating atmosphere, children from impoverished homes can achieve high scores on standardized tests.	TRUE	FALSE
14.	Differences among individuals of particular racial or ethnic groups are greater than differences among the various groups.	TRUE	FALSE
15.	IQ tests only measure innate intellectual ability.	TRUE	FALSE
16.	Based on many studies, research indicates that genetics and environment contribute equally to IQ scores.	TRUE	FALSE
17.	If genetics were the sole factor for determining IQ test scores, then the correlation for identical twins should be 1.0 whether they were raised together or apart.	TRUE	FALSE

18. According to Zajonc and Markus, when the first child is born the average level of intellectual ability in the home *increases from 20 units to 30 units*.　　TRUE　　FALSE

19. Based on Hyde and Linn's findings, mathematical test scores are the most reliable when selecting and placing students in academic programs.　　TRUE　　FALSE

20. Studies indicate IQ scores remain relatively stable once people reach adulthood.　　TRUE　　FALSE

21. Because of their exceptional abilities gifted children generally do not require special schooling to achieve their potential.　　TRUE　　FALSE

22. Mental retardation is characterized by significantly sub average intellectual functioning, with limitations in two or more adaptive skill areas.　　TRUE　　FALSE

23. McDonald's and other restaurants have reported that many of their mentally retarded employees have a higher rate of being late and calling in sick than other employees.　　TRUE　　FALSE

24. Public Law 94-142 significantly decreased the amount of testing in the public school systems.　　TRUE　　FALSE

Fill-in-the-Blanks

1. _____ is the ability to think rationally, to act purposefully, and to deal effectively with the environment.

2. The father of contemporary behaviorism is _____ _____.

3. When using statistics to discover mutually independent elements, one is using _____ _____.

4. Spearman's basic approach to intelligence is the _____ _____ _____ _____ _____.

5. The process of developing a uniform procedure for giving a test, scoring the test, and establishing norms is called _____.

6. A _____ is a score corresponding to a percentile of a large group that represents a sample of individuals from the population for which the test was designed.

7. A sample of individuals who have similar characteristics to the population with whom they are compared is called a _____ _____.

8. A bell shaped graph illustrating data to show the number of the population under the "bell" is the _____ _____.

9. The simplest score on a test that has not be altered is the _____ _____.

10. A score that illustrates the percentage of the population that would score lower is called the _____ _____ _____.

11. _____ _____ is the standard IQ test score in which the mean and the standard deviation never changes.

12. The ability for a test to yield the same score for the same person if they take it more than once is called _____.

13. _____ is the ability of a test to measure specifically what it is designed to measure and to predict what it is supposed to predict.

14. The _____ _____ is dangerous for teachers because this effect causes one to judge a particular characteristic about a student based on tests of other characteristics.

15. _____ _____ organized the Wechsler Bellevue Intelligence Scale to test the IQ of adults.

16. The genetic heritage established before birth is called _____; however, the life experiences or _____ of a person play an important role in intelligence.

17. Children that are _____ have higher cognitive, leadership, or performing arts abilities.

18. Limitations in present functioning are called _____ _____.

19. The two ways to classify the causes of mental retardation: _____ and _____.

20. Ninety percent of those classified as mentally retarded are people with _____ _____.

21. A person with _____ retardation has the intellectual level equivalent to a 5 or 6 year old.

22. Integrating children with special needs into a regular classroom is called _____.

23. Bringing the support staff to the classroom of a needy child, instead of removing the child from the classroom is called _____.

Applications

1. Match the following researchers with the appropriate explanation of their theories of intelligence.

Piaget's theory	*Thurstone's factor-theory*	*Sternberg's triarchic view*
Wechsler's theory	*Guilford's intellect model*	*Gardner and Hatch's view*
Spearman's two-factor theory	*Jensen's two-level theory*	

A. _____ Claimed that associative and cognitive abilities are inherited.

B. _____ Proposed that there are seven multiple types of intelligence.

C. _____ Focused on invariant stages of intellectual development and the interaction of biological readiness and learning.

D. _____ Believed intelligence consists of general factors (affecting all performance) and specific factors (affecting specific tasks).

E. _____ Argued that tests involving spatial relations and verbal comprehension reveal little about overall intelligence because intelligence is the broad ability to deal with the world.

F. _____ Has criticized most widely used intelligence tests stating that they are too narrow and don't account for intelligence in the everyday world; believes in multiple types of intelligence.

G. _____ Developed a three dimensional theory describing 150 factors that seem appropriate in describing intelligence.

H. _____ Developed a computational scheme which described seven factors of intelligence such as word fluency, number facility, perceptual speed, reasoning, and spatial visualization.

2. Match the following terms to the appropriate definitions.

standardization	*normal curve*	*percentile score*
norms	*raw score*	*deviation IQ*
representative sample	*standard score*	*intelligence quotient*

A. _____ A large group of individuals who match the target population (the group for whom the test is being designed) with regard to important variables such as socioeconomic status and age.

B. _____ Necessary for standardization, these scores and corresponding percentile ranks are obtained by administering the test to the individuals in the representative sample. When the test is released for general use, the scores of those who take the test will be compared to these scores.

C. _____ The process of developing a uniform procedure for administering and scoring the test. The test is given to a large sample of people who are matched with regard to important variables so that norms can be determined for the basis of comparison. In addition, time limits for testing and specific guidelines for test administration are established.

D. _____ The number of correct answers an individual receives on the test. To be meaningful this score must be converted, taking into account the individual's age, sex, and grade level.

E. _____ A bell-shaped curve that provides a graphic illustration of representative test scores. The data are arranged so that those with low scores fall on the left side of the curve; those with middle range scores fall in the middle of the curve (most people achieve scores in the middle ranges); and those with high scores fall on the right side of the curve.

F. _____ A standard score that indicates what percentage of people in the population under consideration would achieve a lower score.

G. _____ A simple formula to measure intelligence calculated by dividing a person's mental age by the person's chronological age and multiplying the result by 100.

H. _____ A standard score that has the same mean and standard deviation at all ages. Thus, a child of nine and a child of sixteen, each with an IQ of 115, occupy the same position (they have the same percentile score) relative to others who have taken the same IQ test.

I. _____ A score that expresses an individual's position relative to the mean based on the standard deviation. It is often derived by converting a raw score to one that can be interpreted on the basis of a population variable such as age or grade. Two examples of this type of score are a percentile score and a deviation IQ.

3. Match the following types of mental retardation with the appropriate description.

Mild   Moderate   Severe   Profound

A. _____ People in this category have the intellectual ability of a ten-year-old. They need some supervision, but can acquire certain academic and occupational skills. The Wechsler IQ range is 55-69 and approximately 90% are classified in this category.

B. _____ People in this category show great motor, speech, and intellectual impairment and are almost totally dependent on others to take care of their basic needs. The retardation is often a result of a birth disorder or traumatic injury to the brain. The Wechsler IQ range is 25-39 and approximately 3% are classified in this category.

C. _____ People in this category are usually institutionalized or dependent on their families. They are somewhat clumsy in motor coordination, posture, and social skills. Their intellectual abilities are comparable to those of a 5 to 6 year-olds. The Wechsler IQ range is 40-54 and approximately 6% are classified in this category.

D. _____ People in this category are institutionalized and need constant supervision. They are unable to master simple skills and have minimal intellectual and motor skills. Frequently they have physical deformities and congenital defects such as blindness, deafness, and seizures. The Wechsler IQ is below 25 and only 1% are classified in this category.

4. Discuss three ways of determining whether a test is reliable.
   1. Test-retest _____
      _____
   2. Alternative form _____
      _____
   3. Split-half _____
      _____

5. Define the following types of validity.
   A. Content validity _____
      _____
   B. Predictive validity _____
      _____
   C. Face validity _____
      _____
   D. Construct validity _____
      _____

6. Complete the following boxes associated with the major criticisms, the validity of intelligence tests and testing and give the rebuttal commonly offered in response to these criticisms.

Criticism	Response (Rebuttal)
1. Intelligence cannot be measured because no clear, agreed-upon measure of intelligence exits.	
2. IQ tests consist of learned information and reflect the quality of a child's schooling rather than actual intelligence.	
3. Because of the Halo effect, a test administrator can develop positive or negative feelings about individuals, classes, or groups of students that can influence test scores.	
4.	Items on IQ tests are unfamiliar even to experienced test takers and the effects of practice are seldom or never evident.
5. IQ scores often depend on motivation to succeed; minority groups often do not have the same motivation to succeed as do members of the majority.	

7. Identify the intelligence test being administered to seven-year-old children in each of the following testing situations.

                    Stanford-Binet   *WISC-III*   *K-ABC*

A. _____ By the time the test has been completed, Trystan will have responded to eleven subtests, each of which contains a series of tasks related to a particular content area. One of the subtests, "Comprehension," requires Trystan to verbally answer questions with common sense answers. Another subtest "Picture Completion" requires that he point to the area in a picture that is missing; he does not have to verbally explain what is wrong with the picture. The data gathered from Trystan's responses to the subtests will produce three deviation IQ scores.

B. _____ Sarah is given a variety of tasks that do not call upon her language skills or acquired knowledge, but rather require her to process new information and solve novel problems by organizing, sequencing, and integrating the new stimuli that she is being shown. Toward the end of the test she does have to call upon her verbal ability to answer some questions concerning reading comprehension, word identification, and computation.

C. _____ Aaron is given a variety of tasks that are presented according to his chronological age; the score achieved determines the level at which all other subtests will begin. The content of these subtests varies considerably according to the mental age he is able to achieve. Some of the tasks require verbal responses, others require that he take stimuli presented in the test and call upon his memory, recall, and arranging abilities. When the test is completed, the psychologist will use the data to determine Aaron's mental age.

8. Identify the most probable cause for each of the following cases of mental retardation.

      deprived environment   *physical trauma*
      infectious disease   *genetic abnormality*

A. _____ Neil was born into an impoverished family. During infancy and early childhood his family provided for his physical needs the best they could, but because of their own intellectual abilities and values, they were unable to provide him with an environment that was intellectually stimulating. When Neil started school, he was classified as mildly retarded.

B. _____ Tina's mother is an alcoholic. While carrying Tina, she drank almost constantly, and her diet was poor. Tina was born with brain damage and has since been diagnosed as severely retarded.

C. _____ Joe has been classified as moderately retarded. He was born with Down syndrome, a condition that is caused by three chromosomes on the twenty-first pair of chromosomes. Joe's subnormal intelligence is a direct result of this condition. In addition, physically Joe shows signs of the condition; his head is small, his eyes slant upward, his ears are low-set, and his tongue protrudes from his mouth.

D. _____ Jill's mother had a serious case of the German measles while she was pregnant with Jill. Jill was born blind, deaf, and with apparent brain damage. She has been classified as profoundly retarded.

SQ3R*plus*

RECITE: When you have finished reading the assigned material in your text and you have completed the exercises in your study guide, turn back to the chapter outline. Read each learning objective and recite out loud everything you can remember in support of each objective.

REVIEW: Check to see if you have answered all the questions you wrote during the *Survey* stage. Complete all sections of your study guide and check your answers for accuracy. If you are having trouble with specific topics ask you instructor for help.

WRITE: Read the learning objective again and then, in your own words, write down everything you can remember about this chapter. Summarize the main points and the concepts introduced in this chapter.

REFLECT: After each study period, take a break and reflect on what you have just studied. Ask yourself how this newly acquired information can be used in the future.

CHAPTER EIGHT SELF-TEST

1. Which of the following statements is *false*?
   A. Today's researchers have been successful finding specific brainwave patterns and locations in the brain associated with specific types of intelligent behavior.
   B. Intelligence tests provide a complete measure of a person's intelligence
   C. Psychologists use a variety of tests and other data to make predictions about a person's intellectual abilities.
   D. Intelligence is hard to define.

2. "Intelligence is the aggregate or global capacity of the individual to act purposefully, to think rationally, and to deal effectively with the environment." Whose definition is this?
   A. Quinn McNemar
   B. Jean Piaget
   C. J.P. Guilford
   D. David Wechsler

3. Jean Piaget believed that intelligence is:
   A. genetically determined.
   B. an acquired academic skill.
   C. a reflection of a person's ability to adapt to the environment.
   D. "a quality the other guy lacks!"

4. According to Jensen's two-level theory, the intellectual abilities that deal with reasoning and problem solving are called:
   A. associative abilities.
   B. cognitive abilities.
   C. interpersonal abilities.
   D. logical-mathematical abilities.

5. Gardner and Hatch would say that a person who is sensitive to the sounds, rhythms, and meaning of words has a _____ type of intelligence and might choose to be a _____.
   A. musical; composer
   B. spatial; sculptor
   C. interpersonal; therapist
   D. linguistic; poet

6. When Simon and Binet developed their first intelligence test their goal was to:
   A. determine the cause of intelligence.
   B. determine the future of children with high intelligence.
   C. separate children of normal intelligence from those who showed signs of retarded intellectual development.
   D. all of the above

7. The first thing a psychologist must decide about a test is:
   A. the mental age of the test subject.
   B. what the test is suppose to measure.
   C. the population for whom a test will be designed.
   D. a uniform procedure for administering and scoring the test.

8. Heather's teacher informed her that 92 percent of her classmates scored lower than she did on an intelligence test. The number 92 represents:
   A. an intelligence quotient.
   B. a standard deviation.
   C. a percentile score.
   D. a raw score.

9. A test intended to measure musical ability should contain items that measure only this ability. In other words, the test should measure what it was intended to measure. This is called:
   A. content validity.
   B. predictive validity.
   C. face validity.
   D. construct validity.

10. Which of the following statements concerning intelligence scales is *false*?
    A.   The most recent version of the Stanford-Binet contains items that minimize gender and racial biases.
    B.   The WISC-III is administered to adults.
    C.   The K-ABC assesses an individual's unique problem solving styles by minimizing the role of language and acquired skills.
    D.   Many psychologists consider the K-ABC to be child-oriented and easy to administer.

11. The Wechsler intelligence scales have been found to be valid with:
    A.   cross-cultural population.
    B.   special education and learning disabled students.
    C.   people institutionalized for clinical, mental health problems.
    D.   all of the above

12. An intelligence test is considered culturally biased if:
    A.   ethnic and racial questions are excluded from the test.
    B.   when all factors are held constant, the content of the test is more difficult for one group than it is for another group.
    C.   it is administered by someone who is prejudiced.
    D.   someone with a culturally impoverished background is required to take it.

13. In determining IQ scores which of the following also needs to be considered?
    A.   home environment
    B.   personality and socioeconomic status
    C.   special abilities
    D.   all of the above

14. If a behavior or characteristic is genetic:
    A.   it will be fully manifested at some time in a person's life.
    B.   it is fixed and therefore cannot be changed.
    C.   it establishes a range of possible reactions which will be manifested if the person's environment influences the genetic component.
    D.   a standardized test will provide a perfectly reliable and valid score.

15. According to Zajonc, all of the following are true except:
    A.   the statistical family size model does not hold true for all individuals in all families.
    B.   Factors such as increased spacing between birth of children can minimize negative effects.
    C.   Large families contribute to individual growth by nurturing social competence, moral responsibility, and ego strength.
    D.   The overall level of intellectual performance is likely to increase for each new member of the family.

16. Intelligence test scores:
    A.   begin to gradually decrease beginning around age 40.
    B.   generally reach their peak when a child learns to talk.
    C.   tend to increase with age and level off in adulthood.
    D.   of 10 year-old chimpanzees correlate well to those of average 3 year-old humans.

17. Most students are usually classified and labeled as to their projected future development based on standardized test scores by the end of the:
    A.   first grade.
    B.   fourth grade.
    C.   eighth grade.
    D.   tenth grade.

18. A diagnosis of mental retardation is given:
    A.   if the symptoms are apparent before the age of 18.
    B.   when a person is mute.
    C.   when IQ's are below 100.
    D.   to a student who is held back twice in grade school.

19. A diagnosis of mental retardation requires:
    A.   an IQ score below a 70.
    B.   difficulty adapting to the environment.
    C.   symptoms of hyperactivity.
    D.   both A and B are correct.

20. Employed individuals who are mildly mentally retarded:
    A.   often times experience greater stress in their personal lives because of the demands placed on them at their job.
    B.   do not pay any federal and state taxes.
    C.   do better in their lives outside of their jobs than they did before.
    D.   both A and B are correct.

21. When a child is placed in a mainstreaming educational system the child typically:
    A.   stays in a regular classroom setting for at least half of the school day.
    B.   is placed in school with other children who are mentally retarded.
    C.   is labeled according to his or her mental age level and level of retardation.
    D.   has only one teacher and learns on a one-to-one basis.

Congratulations, you have completed Chapter 8. Now, proceed to the Exam Preparation Section in the back of your study guide for your final review, but don't forget to review the Enrichment Glossary for help understanding difficult words.

LANGUAGE ENRICHMENT GLOSSARY

Some students who reviewed the textbook listed the following words as difficult to understand. Use this list, your dictionary, and teachers and friends to learn the meaning of words you do not understand

Page	Term	Explanation	Page	Term	Explanation
266	gifted	very smart	280	arithmetic	mathematics
266	mentally retarded	low intelligence	281	geared toward	made for
266	academically	courses at school	281	tap	apply to, relate to
267	guy lacks	person does not have	281	remediation	to fix or correct
267	aggregate	gathered together	281	synonymous	the same as
267	exhibit	show or demonstrate	281	alternative	another choice
267	emerged	came up, we are aware	289	assumptions	guessing something true
267	invariant	constant or not changing	281	barring	stopping or preventing
267	calculus	very advanced math	284	disproportionate	not having correct number relationship
267	predominates	greater or more important	284	desegregation	combining different cultural groups
267	perspective	point of view, thought of	284	minorities	smaller cultural groups
268	postulating	thinking of an idea without being sure	284	fosters	helps, or assists
268	scheme	system, organized plan	284	minimize	make smaller
268	asserts	states or says	284	strikingly	very, extremely
268	optimally	the ideal, the best	284	adept	expert, aware
268	composite	combined	284	astute	smart, clever
270	far-ranging	many possibilities from many places	285	persuasive	can talk others into it
271	competencies	things they do well	283	unravel	take it apart to understand
271	subtasks	small work from one larger project	283	adopted	not raised by biological parents
272	nontrivial	important	286	myth	believe that is not true
273	alternative modes	other ways	286	estimate	guess
273	curriculum	material learned in school	287	predicted	told the future
273	rendered	given back	289	diminishing	becoming less
273	inadequacies	faults, mistakes, problems	289	consensus	what everyone believes
273	collaboration	working together	289	Ample	enough, a good amount
273	commissioned	given important job to do	289	fluctuation	changing
274	pitfalls	problems; a trap	290	impairments	problems
274	elaborate	detailed, careful planned	290	theoretical	educated guess
274	norms	typical or average pattern	291	mild	slight, a little
274	ensures	make sure or certain	291	addressed	looked at and discussed
275	indicator of	things you see that tell you about a person's skills	292	institutionalize	put in special hospitals for mental problems
277	aptitude	test for, discover	292	clumsy	awkward, not good
277	assess	test for, discover	292	traumatic	severe, bad
277	inexpertly	not by a qualified person	293	Physical deformities	parts of the body are not normally shaped
278	revised	do again with changes	294	mandates	requires or makes you
279	converted	changed over	294	stigmatization	thought of as abnormal
279	potent	strong, very good	295	derived	taken from or come from
279	correlates well	compares in many ways			

CHAPTER 9

Motivation and Emotion

9.16 Explain how differences in language and cultural practices make it difficult for psychologists to develop a global theory about human emotions.

9.17 Distinguish between James-Lange and Cannon-Bard physiological theories of emotion.

9.18 Explain how measurements of physiological changes in the autonomic nervous system indicate whether someone is lying.

9.19 Describe the Schachter-Singer, Valins, Shaver, and Frijda cognitive explanations of emotion.

9.20 Describe how behavioral expressions are used to display emotions and explain how gender and social context influence behavioral expressions.

9.21 Describe the self-regulation view of emotion, including how thought, arousal, culture, and expectations influence the expression of emotion.

Chapter 9 Overview

Psychologists and people in general are always asking the question: Why? To answer the question we must try to understand the interacting forces behind specific behaviors and accept that no one theory or explanation will fit all situations. Motivation is an internal condition that exhibits itself as goal-directed behavior. Several theories exist to explain people's motivation. Drive theory assumes that an organism is motivated by some internal need to survive. Arousal theory assumes that we have a need to maintain an optimal level of central nervous system arousal. Expectancy theory states that we are driven by our thoughts and expectations for success. Cognitive theory also endorses the contribution of thoughts, but adds that people are actively involved in determining their goals and means to achieve them. This approach focuses on the decision making process and begins to move away from the mechanistic theories of physiological needs toward an understanding of intrinsic and extrinsic motivations. Humanistic theory focuses on human dignity, individual choice, and self-worth. Humanists are looking at the big picture, stating that people strive toward a lifelong goal of self-actualization.

Hunger is certainly a true physiological need. Or is it? We all know the feeling of being hungry you may get stomach pangs, begin to feel weak, or even become lightheaded. Your body is sending signals that it is time to eat. The glucostatic approach to explaining hunger argues that food deprivation leads to low blood sugar and results in a chemical imbalance that is cured by eating. The goal of eating is to maintain a balance. The problem with the balance approach is it does not fully explain problem eating, obesity, or eating disorders such as anorexia nervosa and bulimia nervosa. Lefton describes the relationship between hunger and obesity by first looking at the genetic contribution and then examining the findings of Schacter's research on the role of external cues in overeating. Anorexia nervosa and bulimia nervosa are examples of major disturbances in eating behaviors which are described in this section.

Sexual behavior in animals is relatively straightforward. Animals' sexual behavior is driven by their hormones. However, it is not so simple in humans. Many factors contribute to sexual behavior in humans; sights, sounds, smells, thoughts, feelings, and even fantasy have the potential to initiate or satisfy sexual motivation. Lefton looks at classic research on human sexual behavior starting with the Kinsey studies in the 40s and 50s, and continuing to the more contemporary works of Hunt, Masters and Johnson, and Laumann. These studies surveyed a variety of sexual behaviors including sexual orientation. Lefton also examines the need for achievement (social need) and how these achievement motives are measured.

Emotions by definition are subjective responses accompanied by a physiological change. Many psychologists claim that emotions consist of three basic elements: feelings, physiological responses, and behaviors. Others describe emotions in terms of types, levels or additional elements. Few take all of these elements into account in their research, so we must examine emotions by their components. The *limbic system* is thought to contribute to emotions by integrating information at the neuronal level resulting in an emotional response. The two physiological theories of emotion, James-Lange and Cannon-Bard, describe this process in terms of the physiological and emotional response. They differ as to which comes first. Physiological expression of emotion can be monitored by use of a polygraph, which is based on the premise that autonomic nervous system responses are involuntary.

Cognitive theories of emotion focus on the interpretation as well as the physiological response. For example, the Schachter-Singer approach looked at incorporating both the James-Lange and Canon-Bard theories, stating that the context of the situation must be considered. Other researchers, such as Valins, Reisenzein, Shaver, Ekman, and Frijda, express their points of view on this complex topic. In closing, Lefton looks at the universality of behavioral expressions and whether we have the ability to control our emotions.

SQ3R*plus*

SURVEY THE LESSON: Read learning objectives 9.1 through 9.21 and, in the text, examine the chapter headings, tables, and pictures on pages 300-334 in the text to *form an idea of what you should learn and to set goals for your study time.*

WRITE DOWN QUESTIONS: *While surveying and reading the text, write down questions* about the information being presented. *Write your questions* in the space below or on a separate piece of paper and try to find answers to these questions in the text.

ACTIVELY READ PAGES 300-334: The following exercise is designed to facilitate this process. Complete the following questions as you read, and when you are done, check your answers with those printed in the back of this study guide.

YOUR QUESTIONS:

Matching

Match the following terms or concepts from your textbook with the most appropriate description.

1. _____ anorexia nervosa
2. _____ arousal
3. _____ bulimia nervosa
4. _____ drive
5. _____ emotion
6. _____ extrinsic rewards
7. _____ learned helplessness
8. _____ motivation
9. _____ motive
10. _____ need
11. _____ organism phase
12. _____ plateau phase
13. _____ resolution phase
14. _____ self actualization
15. _____ social need
16. _____ vasocongestion

a) internal condition that appears by inference to initiate, activate, or maintain goal directed behavior
b) internal aroused condition that directs and organism to satisfy a physiological need
c) state of physiological imbalance accompanied by arousal
d) activation of the central nervous autonomic nervous system, muscles, and glands
e) a specific condition usually involving some sort of arousal and goal directive behavior
f) an aroused condition that directs people toward establishing feelings about themselves and others, and toward establishing relationships
g) rewards that come from the external environment
h) the process of achieving everything that one is capable of achieving
i) eating disorder characterized by an intense fear of becoming obese
j) eating disorder characterized by repeated episodes of binge eating followed by purging
k) increased blood flow particularly in the genital area
l) second phase of the sexual response cycle and preparation for organism
m) third phase of the sexual response cycle, during which autonomic nervous system activity reaches its peak, and muscle contractions occur throughout the body
n) fourth phase of the sexual response cycle during which the body naturally returns to its resting state after organism
o) behavior of giving up or not responding believed to be a result of organism's response not effecting the future
p) subjective response usually accompanied by a physiological change which is interpreted by an individual

True or False

1. Drive theories focus on the role of human choice and personal expression.   TRUE   FALSE

2. A drive is an external condition of arousal that directs an organism to satisfy physiological needs.   TRUE   FALSE

3. When obese people successfully diet, they decrease the number of fat cells in their bodies.   TRUE   FALSE

4. Eating can serve as a rationale for social interaction, a means to reward good behavior, and a way to fend off unhappy thoughts.   TRUE   FALSE

5. An obstinate and willful refusal to eat is a primary characteristic of bulimia.   TRUE   FALSE

6. As many as fifty percent of patients with anorexia suffer relapses within a year.   TRUE   FALSE

7. Thirst is not a result of a dry mouth or throat.   TRUE   FALSE

8. The sexual behavior of humans is primarily under physiological control.   TRUE   FALSE

9. A key characteristic of the excitement phase is vasocongestion.   TRUE   FALSE

10. In humans, lack of sensory experience results in a psychological imbalance.   TRUE   FALSE

11. Arousal is generally thought of as activation of the central nervous system, autonomic nervous system, and the muscles and glands.   TRUE   FALSE

12. The higher the arousal level an organism experiences the more performance will improve.   TRUE   FALSE

13. According to Hebb, arousal energizes behavior, but does not direct it.   TRUE   FALSE

14. Social motives and needs that a person develops are not physiological in origin.   TRUE   FALSE

15. A motive is a specific external condition that usually involves some sort of arousal that directs or impels a person toward a goal.   TRUE   FALSE

16. Canavan-Gumpert's study showed that while praise had a significant impact on motivation, criticism had little, if any, effect, positive or negative.   TRUE   FALSE

17. Cognitive theorists assume that individuals set their goals and decide how to achieve them.   TRUE   FALSE

18. Verbal extrinsic rewards are more likely to interfere with intrinsic motivation.   TRUE   FALSE

19. The highest need according to Maslow is the need for self-actualization.   TRUE   FALSE

20. Emotions in humans are controlled, in a large part, by the limbic system.   TRUE   FALSE

21. James-Lange theory states that the body responds physically to emotional states.   TRUE   FALSE

22. Cannon argued that when a person is emotional, two areas of the brain, the thalamus and the hypothalamus, are stimulated simultaneously.   TRUE   FALSE

23. Schachter-Singer argue that the label attached to the emotion depends on the person's situation.   TRUE   FALSE

24. Facial expressions are generally an accurate index of a person's emotional state.   TRUE   FALSE

25. Many physiological changes are due to an increase in the autonomic nervous system activity.   TRUE   FALSE

26. Most states accept the lie detector as valid in court.   TRUE   FALSE

27. Research has shown that arousal is not an essential component in emotion.   TRUE   FALSE

28. Learning to manage motivational and emotional responses can have a positive impact on people's lives.   TRUE   FALSE

Fill-in-the-Blanks

1. A condition that influences one to initiate, activate, or maintain an organism is called _____ .

2. The four components of motivation are: _____ _____
_____ _____ .

3. _____ _____ explains behavior that an organism is motivated to act because of a need to maintain the organism or the species.

4. An internal feeling or condition that encourages an organism to satisfy physiological needs is a _____ .

5. All motivation systems involve _____, or the activation of the central nervous system, the autonomic nervous system, and the muscles and glands.

6. When one expects success in reaching a goal and the need for achievement serves as an energizing factor, this behavior is explained through _____ _____ .

7. The need for establishing feelings about oneself, others, and relationships is noted through the aroused condition of a _____ _____ .

8. The _____ _____, in the study of motivation, explains one's behavior of actively and regularly determining one's goals and achieving them.

9. _____ _____ _____ are behaviors engaged in only for pleasure, with no expected reward.

10. Rewards that come from the outside or the external environment are called _____ _____ .

11. Behaviors that emphasize the big picture of life rather than the individual components of behavior are called humanistic behaviors which are explained through the _____ _____ .

12. _____ _____ is the process one goes through in which he/she is naturally motivated to realize their human potential.

13. A balanced diet of food and fluid intake necessary to maintain functioning is called _____ .

14. A low blood sugar level which comes with food deprivation creates a chemical imbalance which is explained by the _____ approach.

15. Psychological disorders that are characterized by gross disturbances in eating behavior and in the way people respond to food are called _____ _____ .

16. The eating disorder of _____ _____ is characterized by a stubborn refusal to eat; a starvation disease that affects 40 out of every 10,000 young women in the U.S.

17. Binge eating and purging is an eating disorder labeled as _____
_____ .

18. The stages of sexual arousal are known as the _____ _____
_____.

19. The first stage of sexual arousal is called the _____ _____ which
is characterized by an initial increase in heart rate, blood pressure, and respiration.

20. Because of the increased blood flow in stage one, _____ or an engorgement
of blood vessels takes place particularly in the genital area.

21. The second phase of sexual arousal is the _____ _____ during which
sexual partners are preparing for orgasm.

22. When the autonomic nervous system activity reaches its peak and muscle contractions
occur throughout the body in spasms, one is in the third phase or the _____
_____.

23. After orgasm, when the body returns to its resting state, the _____
phase is complete.

24. The social need for people to strive for excellence and success is the _____
_____ _____.

25. _____ _____ is the behavior of giving up or not responding
to stimuli because one has been exposed to punishment that they cannot control.

26. An _____ is a feeling that is usually accompanied by a physiological change.

Applications

1. List the four basic parts of motivation.
   1. _____
   2. _____
   3. _____
   4. _____

2. List the four stages of the sexual response cycle.
   1. _____
   2. _____
   3. _____
   4. _____

3. Identify the phase involving the sexual response cycle.

   Excitement   Plateau   Orgasm   Resolution.

   A. _____ The stage of the sexual response cycle in which both men
   and women are preparing for orgasm.

   B. _____ The stage of the sexual response cycle in which the body
   naturally returns to its resting or normal state.

   C. _____ The stage of the sexual response cycle in which there are
   initial increases in heart rate, blood pressure, and respiration.

D. _____ The stage of the sexual response cycle in which the autonomic nervous system activity reaches its peak, and muscle contractions occur throughout the body in spasms.

4. Identify the theory that most adequately explains why the particular emotion in the following situations is experienced.

self-regulation	*Cannon-Bard*
James-Lange	*Schachter-Singer*

A. _____ Barry lacks his usual energy level, does not have any appetite though he has not eaten for some time, and has trouble concentrating and going to sleep. Based on this feedback from his body, Barry is aware that he is *depressed*.

B. _____ While discussing a pay raise with her boss, Tanya feels an awkward and odd feeling inside but is not certain what she is feeling or why. When she recounts the conversation, she realizes that her boss had subtly accused her of being lazy on the job. Based on this information she told herself she is feeling *embarrassed*.

C. _____ Having just been insulted by a student, Professor Sunn notices his adrenaline level and feelings of anger rising. He quickly reminds himself that the student is immature and probably feeling badly over a flunked test. With these thoughts, Professor Sunn notices that his adrenaline level and feelings of anger dissipate and that he feels *secure*.

D. _____ Olga sits in her hot tub and as her muscles begin to relax, she begins to feel *peacefully content*.

SQ3R*plus*

RECITE: When you have finished reading the assigned material in your text and you have completed the exercises in your study guide, turn back to the chapter outline. Read each learning objective and recite out loud everything you can remember in support of each objective.

REVIEW: Check to see if you have answered all the questions you wrote during the *Survey* stage. Complete all sections of your study guide and check your answers for accuracy. If you are having trouble with specific topics ask you instructor for help.

WRITE: Read the learning objective again and then, in your own words, write down everything you can remember about this chapter. Summarize the main points and the concepts introduced in this chapter.

REFLECT: After each study period, take a break and reflect on what you have just studied. Ask yourself how this newly acquired information can be used in the future.

CHAPTER NINE SELF-TEST

1. Which of the following is not one of the four basic parts of motivation?
   A. observed by inference
   B. goal directed behavior
   C. external condition
   D. initiation, activation, or maintenance

2. That organisms are motivated by needs is a statement of:
   A. drive theory.
   B. mechanistic theory.
   C. a drive.
   D. drive state.

3. After food is consumed, it takes approximately _____ minutes for it to be converted into sugar.
   A. 20 minutes
   B. 30 minutes
   C. 40 minutes
   D. 50 minutes

4. Schacter's work on obesity focused on:
   A. external cues.
   B. set point theory.
   C. fat cell theory.
   D. metabolism.

5. One physiological explanation for anorexia may be that people with this eating disorder lack a hormone to induce:
   A. a feeling of hunger.
   B. a feeling of fullness.
   C. the "stop eating" center of the hypothalamus.
   D. the "start eating" center of the hypothalamus.

6. Bulimia tends to occur in:
   A. over-weight women.
   B. under-weight women.
   C. normal-weight women.
   D. women who also have a history of anorexia.

7. Researchers who explain motivation in terms of an optimal level of arousal assume that individuals seek an optimal level of arousal; thus, people who show a _____ anxiety level and arousal tend to produce the most and do best.
   A. high
   B. moderate
   C. low
   D. A and C

8. Hebb's idea focused on _____ in determining behavior.
   A. people's response
   B. stimuli
   C. drives
   D. needs

9. Which of the following is <u>not</u> true about motives?
   A. They have no psychological origin.
   B. They have no urgent physiological need.
   C. They are a specific internal conditions that involve some sort of arousal.
   D. People learn them through interactions with their environment.

10. A social need is an aroused condition involving all but feelings about:
    A. relationships.
    B. goals.
    C. self.
    D. others.

11. The goals people set and the amount of risk they are willing to take are also affected by all of the following except:
    A. the kinds of needs that motivate them.
    B. their past experiences.
    C. their moods.
    D. their need for feeling good about themselves.

12. Cognitive theory focuses on _____ as initiators and determiners of behavior.
    A. sensory stimulation
    B. external cues
    C. thoughts
    D. arousal

13. Creating objects in your spare time because it gives you a sense of pleasure and accomplishment is probably motivated by:
    A. extrinsic reward.
    B. intrinsic motivation.
    C. a need for achievement.
    D. a Type B personality.

14. According to Maslow's pyramid of needs, the very first needs that must be met are _____ needs.
    A. love and recognition
    B. recognition and approval
    C. physiological and safety
    D. cognitive and aesthetic

15. Maslow's humanistic theory of motivation:
    A. rejects drive theories.
    B. is an expectancy theory.
    C. is a unique theory that has nothing in common with the other theories discussed in the chapter.
    D. incorporates the best elements of drive, expectancy, and cognitive theories.

16. Which of the following is *not* included in the definition of emotion? Emotions:
    A. have motivating properties that impel and direct behavior.
    B. have a private, personal, unique, and subjective component.
    C. are the result of irrational thoughts.
    D. are generally accompanied by physiological changes.

17. The aspect of emotion that is considered unquantifiable because it cannot be easily measured or observed is the:
    A. subjective response.
    B. physiological response.
    C. behavioral component.
    D. emotional component.

18. Whose theory states that people do not experience emotion until after their bodies become aroused?
    A. Cannon's
    B. James-Lange
    C. Schachter-Singer
    D. Shaver's

19. Neither the James-Lange nor the Cannon-Bard approach considered the idea that a person's _____ might alter their reaction/response to a situation.
    A. motivation
    B. arousal
    C. emotional state
    D. thoughts

20. In the study conducted by Valins where male subjects were shown slides of nude women, those subjects who thought they were hearing their own heartbeat found the nude women to be more attractive than those subjects who were not aware of a heartbeat, apparently because they:
    A. experienced a higher level of physiological arousal.
    B. felt personally attracted to the women in the slides.
    C. interpreted the attractiveness of the women in terms of the specific context (the heartbeat cues) in which the slides were seen.
    D. were unable to deny the physiological arousal that was induced by the slides.

21. Which of the following is not one of the six emotions that Shaver showed most people will describe?
    A. anger
    B. fear
    C. happiness
    D. joy

22. In humans, emotions:
    A. develop over time.
    B. are learned behaviors.
    C. are influenced by inborn qualities.
    D. all of the above

23. Lie detectors record:
    A. voluntary physiological changes.
    B. emotional states.
    C. autonomic nervous system activity.
    D. involuntary physiological changes.

Congratulations, you have completed Chapter 9. Now, proceed to the Exam Preparation Section in the back of your study guide for your final review, but don't forget to review the Enrichment Glossary for help understanding difficult words.

LANGUAGE ENRICHMENT GLOSSARY

Some students who reviewed the textbook listed the following words as difficult to understand. Use this list, your dictionary, and teachers and friends to learn the meaning of words you do not understand

Page	Term	Explanation	Page	Term	Explanation
300	munching	eating	315	aesthetic	beautiful appearance
302	Kittens	baby cats	315	obstinate	refuse to cooperate
302	embrace	favor very much	315	relentlessly	without giving up
303	shift	change	315	emaciation	underweight too much
303	subtle	slight	316	sustain	keep or maintain
304	affiliation	bonding with others	316	purge	get rid of already eaten food
305	brilliant	very smart	316	vomiting	throwing up
305	overt	easily seen	316	laxatives	a chemical which loosens the bowels
305	commentary	talk or discussion	316	diuretics	a drug which causes an increased flow of urine
306	lego	model toy cities	317	disharmonious	family members are not close
306	jigsaw puzzles	pictures cut into many parts to make a game	318	erotic	sexual desire
308	innate	natural tendency	319	expel	pass out
308	inclination	work toward	321	startled	scare
308	strive	try hard	322	vague	not clear
309	acquire	obtain or hold	322	captions	statements that explain the picture
310	global	world wide	322	discern	decide
310	dizzy	not feeling steady	324	praise	nice things that are said
310	delicate	gentle	324	hurl	throw
310	dehydration	absence of fluid	324	lash out	yell
311	converted	changed	324	electrify	make you more powerful
312	pancreas	organ that secret digestive juices and insulin	324	umbrella term	a term that covers a broad area
312	triggers	make something happen	325	deceiving	not what they look like
312	armamentarium	protective system	325	convey	show, send
312	stigmatized	give a negative identity	325	bewilderment	confusion
312	perverse	bad	326	hiss	a sharp slight sound
312	determinants	qualities	326	sham	not real
313	rampant	filled with	329	innocent	not guilty
313	merriment	fun and happiness	330	butterflies in the-stomach	an uneasy uncomfortable feeling
313	coax	make someone think a certain way	330	stooges	people paid to act a certain way
314	junk food	snack foods of low nutritional value	331	suffice	be enough
314	infer	believe	331	nostalgia	warm thoughts of the past
314	prominence	importance	332	commonalties	things that are similar
315	pronounced	obvious, seen the most	333	smock	loose fitting shirt

CHAPTER 10

Child Development

Chapter 10 Overview

In this chapter we return to the question of nature versus nature by looking at child development. Twin studies provide interesting and intriguing information about the contributions of genetics and the environment. Three theories considered by developmental psychologists are the *reductionistic* view, which suggests that all behavior can be reduced to its essential elements and that because organisms are acted upon by the environment so individual differences come from differing experiences. The *organismic* view suggests a more active role by the organism. Behaviors develop via qualitatively different stages in which behaviors may emerge. The third point of view combines the *reductionistic* and *organismic* views into the *contextual* view which states that the context of the behavior must be included along with the child's elements and experiences. Researchers use two methods to study child development. In cross-sectional research many individuals at a variety of ages are investigated simultaneously. In longitudinal research the same individuals are followed over a period of time. Each provides valuable information.

The prenatal period is the first developmental stage and extends from conception to birth. During this critical period, development may be affected by environmental variables. Factors such as diet, infection, radiation, and drugs have the potential to affect the mother and the child. Substances known as teratogens can cause birth defects and may lead to early infant death. Many substances like alcohol, cigarettes, certain foods, and drugs can have teratogenic effects. Therefore, both parents should take cautions to avoid any potential harm. The prenatal period ends with the birth process.

The period of infancy (birth to 18 months) is a time of dramatic growth and change. Newborns can hear, see, smell, and respond to the environment immediately after leaving the birth canal. Newborns exhibit several reflexive behaviors at birth which are indicative of sound neurological development and, in just a few short months, develop complex perceptual skills such as pattern recognition and depth perception.

The physical development of children is dramatic and exciting. Cognitive development is equally dramatic and exhilarating. In the first two years of life a child learns to assimilate and accommodate information into a developmental process that lasts, for a lifetime. Piaget describes child development in four stages. The *sensorimotor* stage (birth ≈ 2 years) is considered by Piaget to be the most significant. In just two years the child develops from a reflexive organism into a fully responsive individual, exhibiting independence of movement and early language. The *preoperational* stage (from 2 ≈ 7) is the time when a child begins to be less self-centered through a process called decentration. The third stage of *concrete* operations (from 6 or 7 ≈ 11 or 12) is highlighted by the development of conservation skills. The final stage of Piaget's cognitive development is called formal operations (age 12 and beyond). In this stage, children begin to engage in abstract thought processes and eventually develop into adults. Piaget has had a tremendous effect on the way we look at early child development. He has influenced many of the methods used by educators and parents alike. However, his theory is a stage theory and many critics argue that his stages are not universal. Vygotsky's view is that children may not have the innate ability to develop complex cognitive skills without the help of their society (usually parents). You should use your critical thinking skills to form your own opinions.

Children also develop a sense of morality primarily from their parents, teachers, and society. Children will begin with a black-and-white view of morality and develop into more complex situational views as described by Kohlberg's stages of moral development. Kohlberg outlines three stages of moral development, including preconventional, conventional, and postconventional levels. Gilligan also suggests that we consider gender as we look at moral development.

Attachment and bonding are examined by Lefton as components of a child's emotional development. He also describes how verbal exchanges between children and their caregivers help them learn socialization skills. One emotion that appears to be longlasting is temperament. Research indicates that there are four broad categories of temperament easy, difficult, slow-to-warm-up, and unique.

This chapter concludes with a discussion of some very important issues in the social development of a child. The child's early interactive learning plays an important role in a developing personality. Parents have great influence in determining the child's gender-based interests. Erikson's psychosocial stage theory is presented in part to show how the child searches for self-identity. Finally child care is considered in a contemporary context.

SQ3R*plus*

SURVEY THE LESSON: Read learning objectives 10.1 through 10.18 and, in the text, examine the chapter headings, tables, and pictures on pages 340-374 in the text to *form an idea of what you should learn and to set goals for your study time.*

WRITE DOWN QUESTIONS: *While surveying and reading the text, write down questions* about the information being presented. *Write your questions* in the space below or on a separate piece of paper and try to find answers to these questions in the text.

ACTIVELY READ PAGES 340-374: The following exercise is designed to facilitate this process. Complete the following questions as you read, and when you are done, check your answers with those printed in the back of this study guide.

YOUR QUESTIONS:

Matching
Match the following terms or concepts from your textbook with the most appropriate description.

1. _____ accommodation
2. _____ assimilation
3. _____ attachment
4. _____ Babinski reflex
5. _____ bonding
6. _____ concrete operational
7. _____ conservation
8. _____ decentration
9. _____ egocentrism
10. _____ embryo
11. _____ fetus
12. _____ formal operational
13. _____ grasping reflex
14. _____ labor
15. _____ morality
16. _____ moro reflex
17. _____ placenta
18. _____ preoperational stage
19. _____ rooting reflex
20. _____ sensorimotor stage
21. _____ sucking reflex
22. _____ temperament
23. _____ teratogen
24. _____ zygote

a) a fertilized egg.
b) human organism from the 5th to 49th day
c) human organism after the 49th day
d) mass of tissue in the uterus serving as a mechanism for the exchange of nutrients and waste produces
e) substance that produce developmental malformation in a fetus
f) process in which the uterus contracts and the cervix opens so that the fetus can decent through the birth canal
g) infant reflex when soles of feet are touched
h) infant reflex in which arms and legs are stretched and the infant cries due to a loud noise or abrupt change
i) the reflex in which newborn turns its head toward a mild stimulus applied to the lips or cheeks
j) infant reflex when presented with a stimulus to the lips
k) vigorously grasping any object touching its palms or fingers
l) process of incorporating new concepts into existing mental framework
m) process by which new concepts modify existing cognitive structures
n) the first two years of life during which memory may be established
o) age 2 through 7, during which symbolic thought is developed
p) inability to perceive a situation or event except in relation to oneself
q) process of changing from a total self-oriented point of view to one that recognizes other's feelings, ideas, and view points
r) third stage of development, ages 6 or 7 to 11 or 12, during which the ability to understand constant factors, rules, and higher order symbolism develops
s) the ability to recognize that something has changed in some way, but maintains the weight, substance, or volume
t) fourth development stage, beginning at about 12, during which individuals can think hypothetically and become capable of deductive logic
u) a system of learned attitudes about social practices, institutions, and individual behavior
v) strong emotional tie that a person feels toward another special person

w) special process of emotional attachment between parents and babies
x) long lasting individual differences in the intensity and especially the quality of emotional reactions

True or False

1. An organismic view holds that if we can reduce an organism's behavior to its essential elements, we can explain behavior. TRUE FALSE

2. The contextual view looks at behavior from the standpoint of the stage of the organism's life and the context in which the behavior occurs. It blends the reductionistic and organismic view with a third element, social context. TRUE FALSE

3. From the forty-ninth day after conception until birth, the organism is a fetus. TRUE FALSE

4. By the end of the third month, the mother can feel movement. TRUE FALSE

5. The influence of drugs is especially important during the embryonic stage of development when the mother may not realize that she is pregnant. TRUE FALSE

6. An expectant mother usually enters the hospital in the transition stage of labor. TRUE FALSE

7. At birth, infants can hear, see, smell, and respond to the environment in adaptive ways. TRUE FALSE

8. A sudden change in the environment is apt to trigger the Moro reflex in infants. TRUE FALSE

9. Infants prefer simple visual fields. TRUE FALSE

10. Jean Piaget believed that fundamental development of all intellectual abilities takes place during the first two years of life. TRUE FALSE

11. Piaget's theories focus on what people think. TRUE FALSE

12. Two stages of Piaget's theory are assimilation and accommodation. TRUE FALSE

13. According to Piaget each stage of intellectual development builds upon the previous stage. TRUE FALSE

14. All normal children enter the stage of preoperations at the age of two. TRUE FALSE

15. Children develop object permanence during the concrete operations stage.   TRUE   FALSE

16. Egocentrism is particularly obvious during the sensorimotor and formal operations stages.   TRUE   FALSE

17. Pushing children beyond their current stage of intellectual development can have harmful effects.   TRUE   FALSE

18. Research showed that Head Start closed the social and educational gap of disadvantaged preschoolers.   TRUE   FALSE

19. Zigler et al. argue their data should be seen as a mandate for enhancing the Head Start program.   TRUE   FALSE

20. Altering rules or conventions because of situational factors is moral relativity.   TRUE   FALSE

21. Some researchers assert that Gilligan's focus on gender differences fosters a continuation of sex-role stereotyping. TRUE   FALSE

22. People judge physically attractive babies as more competent, likable, and healthier than average or unattractive babies. TRUE   FALSE

23. Adoptive parents cannot form the same type of secure, close attachment as biological parents can.   TRUE   FALSE

24. Any specific temperament, like shyness, can be changed.   TRUE   FALSE

25. Research shows that children often share spontaneously.   TRUE   FALSE

26. Very young children understand the concept of sharing.   TRUE   FALSE

27. The quality and quantity of time that men spend with their children can be analyzed in simple terms.   TRUE   FALSE

28. Evidence exists to show that children who are raised in single parent homes are worse off than kids raised in two parent homes. TRUE   FALSE

29. Most Americans believe that when children are reared by people other than their parents, their development is less than optimal. TRUE   FALSE

30. Wives determine the amount of time fathers spend with their children.   TRUE   FALSE

Fill-in-the-Blanks

1. According to the _____ _____ view, theorists believe that if they are able to reduce behavior to essential elements, they can explain the behavior.

2. The _____ view asserts that people's behavior goes through stages that are qualitatively different and cannot be reduced to elements.

3. According to the _____ view of development, all events are interrelated.

4. A fertilized egg is called a _____.

5. From the time when an ovum and a sperm join until the 49th day after conception, the organism is called an _____.

6. From the 8th week until birth, the organism is referred to as a _____.

7. The mass of tissue that provides oxygen, food, and antibodies to the fetus and eliminates waste is called the _____.

8. _____ are the substances that can produce birth defects in the fetus.

9. _____ is the process in which the uterus contracts to open the cervix so the fetus can be born.

10. When one touches the sole of the foot of an infant, which causes the toes to turn upward and out, the _____ reflex is exhibited.

11. The _____ reflex is an outstretching of the arms and legs and crying in response to a loud noise.

12. The _____ reflex, or the turning of an infants head toward a mild stimulus, occurs when the infants lips or cheek is touched.

13. The _____ reflex occurs from placing a finger in the mouth of an infant.

14. The _____ reflex occurs from touching the palm of an infant's hand.

15. The _____ _____ _____ was established to test the depth perception of an infant.

16. _____ is the process by which people learn new ideas, incorporate them in thought processes, and use them.

17. When one modifies the cognitive structures and behaviors to adapt them to a new concept, the process is termed _____.

18. The _____ stage occurs from birth to about age 2 and is important for the foundation of cognitive development.

19. The stage in which children present the world symbolically, the _____ stage, lasts from about age 2 to age 7.

20. The inability to perceive a situation except in relation to oneself is called _____.

21. _____ is the process after Piaget's preoperational stage in which children differentiate between feelings, ideas, and interests.

22. The _____ _____ stage is the stage from about 6 to 12 in which a child develops an understanding for rules, constant factors in the environment, and higher-order symbolism.

23. _____ is the ability to see that objects may be transformed, yet may still be the same amount of weight, substance, or volume.

24. When an individual is able to think hypothetically and logically, he or she is in the _____ _____ stage.

25. _____ is the ability to evaluate situations and behaviors as right or wrong.

26. Differences between males and females are known as _____ _____.

27. The strong emotional tie one feels toward another person is called _____.

28. The process of emotional attachment is called _____.

29. _____ refers to the lasting individual differences in the intensity and quality of a person's emotional reactions.

30. The behavior patterns that are expected because of one's gender are known as _____ _____.

Applications

1. Define the following terms
   A. Zygote _____

   B. Embryo _____

   C. Fetus _____

2. Define placenta. _____
   _____
   _____

3. Define labor. _____
   _____

4. Match the following stages of labor with the appropriate description:

   early labor   active labor   transition

   A. _____ Characterized by infrequent contractions of the uterus, "labor pains." The cervix dilates to about three centimeters. The contractions occur at regular intervals from five to thirty minutes apart and last about thirty seconds.

   B. _____ The cervix dilates from three to seven centimeters; contractions are intense and occur every three to five minutes. The woman is generally hospitalized during this stage.

C. _____ The cervix dilates to a full ten centimeters. Contractions become stronger and last longer. If a woman is to experience major discomfort, it will be during this stage.

5. Define the following terms and describe how the two processes become a learning cycle.
   A. Assimilation _____

   _____

   Example _____
   B. Accommodation _____

   _____

   Example _____

6. List Piaget's four stages of intellectual development, the age range that each state encompasses, and the major intellectual accomplishment associated with each stage.

	Stage	Age	Major Accomplishment
1.	_____	_____	_____
			_____
			_____
2.	_____	_____	_____
			_____
			_____
3.	_____	_____	_____
			_____
			_____
4.	_____	_____	_____
			_____
			_____

7. Describe the following accomplishments that are made by children during the sensory-motor stage.
   A. Memory _____

   _____
   B. "Making interesting sights last" _____

   _____
   C. Object permanence _____

   _____
   D. Other skills _____

   _____
   E. Language _____

   _____

8. Describe egocentrism, the initial "self-image" of a child in the sensory-motor stage, and decentration, the process that gradually brings about a change in this "self-image."

   A. Egocentrism _____

   _____

   B. Decentration _____

   _____

9. Kohlberg believed that moral development proceeds through a series of three levels, each of which is divided into two stages. Discuss

   A. Level I _____

   _____

   B. Level II _____

   _____

   C. Level III _____

   _____

10. Identify the concept of intellectual development that is illustrated in each of the following situations.

   assimilation   *egocentrism*
   intentionality   *accommodation*
   decentration   *conservation*

   A. _____ After playing with her cousin Mary's doll all afternoon, Tammy became very upset when her mother reminded her that the doll was Mary's and that she would have to leave it at Mary's house. Tammy was upset because she was unable to understand why she could not keep the doll.

   B. _____ Billy's parents gave him a bicycle for his birthday. Billy had mastered the skills of riding a tricycle, but when he got on his new bike it was apparent that his previously learned skills would have to be modified before he could ride the bicycle with ease.

   C. _____ Several weeks after receiving his bicycle, Billy incorporated into his behavioral repertoire the new skills he needed to ride it easily.

   D. _____ Walter gives his sons, Jason and Kirk, equal-size balls of modeling clay. Jason takes a few moments to think about what to do with his clay, while Kirk quickly rolls his out into a long snakelike shape. When Jason sees Kirk's snake, he fusses and complains that his brother has received more clay. We can conclude that Jason lacks what ability?

   E. _____ Although Pia would like the red balloon rather than the yellow one, she relinquishes her wishes to her younger brother because she knows he would be disappointed if he could not have the red balloon. Pia is able to recognize her brother's feelings because she has gone through what process?

SQ3R*plus*

RECITE: When you have finished reading the assigned material in your text and you have completed the exercises in your study guide, turn back to the chapter outline. Read each learning objective and recite out loud everything you can remember in support of each objective.

REVIEW: Check to see if you have answered all the questions you wrote during the *Survey* stage. Complete all sections of your study guide and check your answers for accuracy. If you are having trouble with specific topics ask you instructor for help.

WRITE: Read the learning objective again and then, in your own words, write down everything you can remember about this chapter. Summarize the main points and the concepts introduced in this chapter.

REFLECT: After each study period, take a break and reflect on what you have just studied. Ask yourself how this newly acquired information can be used in the future.

CHAPTER TEN SELF-TEST

1. The disadvantages of longitudinal studies are:
   A. subjects' backgrounds differ.
   B. subjects may move, withdraw, or even die.
   C. behavior or performance of a task or ability may reflect their subjects' predisposition, i.e., liking of the task.
   D. individual differences are impossible to assess.

2. An individual's basic characteristics, such as eye color and sex, are determined _____ fertilization.
   A. prior to
   B. within minutes after
   C. about ten hours after
   D. four to eight weeks after

3. The heartbeat of the growing human organism can be heard with a stethoscope for the first time:
   A. about the twenty-fifth day after conception.
   B. during the second month of prenatal development.
   C. during the third month of prenatal development.
   D. during the second trimester.

4. Environmental factors such as _____ affect both the mother and the fetus.
   A. diet, infection, radiation, drugs
   B. diet, infection, drugs
   C. diet, infection, radiation
   D. diet, drugs, radiation

5. The second stage of labor is called:
   A. early labor.
   B. active labor.
   C. dilation stage.
   D. transition stage.

6. Only during the past _____ years have women in developed countries given birth in hospitals.
   A. sixty
   B. fifty
   C. eighty
   D. seventy

7. Newborn babies prefer to stare at:
   A. random patterns.
   B. simple patterns.
   C. human faces.
   D. breasts.

8. If an infant's lips or cheeks are touched, it will turn its head toward the stimulus because of the _____ reflex.
   A. sucking
   B. rooting
   C. Babinski
   D. Moro

9. Infancy is defined as ending and childhood as beginning when the child:
   A. is 18-24 months old
   B. can stand without support.
   C. begins to represent the world abstractly through language.
   D. drops the rooting reflex and uses learned behaviors in its place.

10. The nervous systems of newborns:
    A. will be further developed by experience.
    B. are complete at birth.
    C. are well formed, but still developing.
    D. none of the above

11. During the _____ trimester, the fetus consumes a good deal of food, oxygen, and water through the placenta, increasing in weight and strength.
    A. first
    B. second
    C. third

12. Assimilation and accommodation occur in which stages of Piaget's theory of development?
    A. 1 and 2
    B. 2 and 3
    C. 3 and 4
    D. A and C

13. The preoperational stage occurs from:
    A. birth to age two.
    B. age seven to age eleven.
    C. age two to age six.
    D. age eleven on.

14. Decentration is:
    A. the ability to recognize that objects may be transformed visually or physically, yet represent the same amount of weight or volume.
    B. the ability to understand the difference between their interests and those of others.
    C. the belief that the world exists solely to satisfy the needs and interests of the child.
    D. the ability to recognize that objects continue to exist even when they are out of sight.

15. Piaget's theory focuses on:
    A. thought processes.
    B. content.
    C. cognitive development.
    D. social development.

16. Egocentrism is first found in what stage of Piaget's theory?
    A. sensorimotor
    B. preoperational
    C. concrete operator
    D. formal operator

17. What kinds of stimulation does Piaget stress?
    A. intellectual and social
    B. physical and cognitive
    C. physical and social
    D. sensory and cognitive

18. Piaget stressed that children should:
    A. be pushed to accelerate development.
    B. not be pushed to accelerate development.
    C. be provided with intellectual stimulation that is appropriate to their current level of development.
    D. B and C

19. Some researchers claim that Piaget may have overestimated the extent of
     _____ in young children.
     A. egocentrism
     B. maturity
     C. cognitive development
     D. age

20. Fischer and Silvern argue that Piaget's theory reduces the role of
     _____ in development.
     A. language
     B. age
     C. the environment
     D. cognition

21. The analysis of Head Start data indicates that Head Start children do not do as well as:
     A. children who did not attend preschool.
     B. children who attended another preschool program.
     C. children from advantaged homes.
     D. Both A and B

22. Kolhberg viewed the stages of morality as _____, and Piaget viewed them as
     _____.
     A. discrete/overlapping
     B. systematizing/discrete
     C. overlapping/discrete
     D. discrete/systematizing

23. Carol Gilligan found that people use the concepts of _____ when reasoning moral
     conflicts.
     A. justice
     B. caring, relationships, and connections with other people
     C. justice, caring and responsibility, and relationships with other people
     D. justice, caring, relationships, and connections to other people

24. Close and warm parent-child relationships make:
     A. children who require less discipline.
     B. attachments that are fairly permanent.
     C. enduring adult relationships.
     D. later cognitive and emotional development easier.

25. Many researchers contend that certain personality traits, including shyness, are:
     A. environmental.
     B. biological.
     C. long lasting.
     D. all the above

26. Children who were given social toys were more likely to:
    A. share.
    B. play with other children.
    C. play alone.
    D. both A and B

27. The quality of the time a father spends with his children is enhanced if the father is high in feelings of:
    A. autonomy
    B. self-worth
    C. competence
    D. adjustment

Congratulations, you have completed Chapter 10. Now, proceed to the Exam Preparation Section in the back of your study guide for your final review, but don't forget to review the Enrichment Glossary for help understanding difficult words.

LANGUAGE ENRICHMENT GLOSSARY

Some students who reviewed the textbook listed the following words as difficult to understand. Use this list, your dictionary, and teachers and friends to learn the meaning of words you do not understand

Page	Term	Explanation	Page	Term	Explanation
341	phobia	fear	354	hallmark	main part
341	obsessively	excessively, too much	354	squat	short and wide
341	suffers from the fact	is not correct because	355	Abundant	much
341	predisposition	tendency or bias	355	phenomenon	something that can be seen
343	stethoscope	instrument used to listen to sounds in the body	356	glorious	wonderful
343	prematurely	before the usual time	356	empirical	from experience and observation
344	despondency	depression	356	naive	believing in something that is not true
344	benevolent perspective	a kind and friendly view	356	ensuring	making sure
345	mental retardation	poor thinking ability	357	variation	difference
345	hyperactivity	overly active, too much energy	357	strict view	only one way to look at it
345	teratogenic	damaging to an unborn baby	357	cognitively deficient	without some thinking skills
345	contraction	muscle movements	357	milestone	an important program
346	ingenious	very smart and creative	357	inoculate	prevent
347	palm	inside of hand	360	Conscientious objection	refuse based on moral belief
347	genetic transmission	passing of traits from parent to child	360	capital punishment	death as punishment
347	avalanche	great amount	361	discrete	particular
350	controversial	not everyone agrees	362	gravitate	move toward
350	checkerboard	alternating light and dark colored squares	364	heightened	great or intense
351	gadgets	devices or special locks	364	deepens	becomes greater
351	skeptical	not willing to believe	364	affectionate	loving
353	manipulate	move things	365	enduring	long lasting
353	acquisition	learning	365	dialogues	communication
353	obstacles	things that get in the way	365	exert control	take charge of
353	doggy	child's word for dog	366	soothing	calm and gentle
353	Big Bird	a television character who is not real	366	cuddled	hold close in a loving way
354	pester	bother, annoy	366	reticence	quiet and cautious
354	vacillates	goes back and forth	366	painstakingly	with great effort
354	charming	pleasant	367	shyness	quiet, not comfortable around others
354	awful	mean, not nice	367	deliberative	on purpose
354	constancy	things not changing			

CHAPTER 11

Adolescence and Adulthood

Chapter 11 Overview

This chapter discusses the developmental changes that occur following childhood through adulthood. The discussion begins with adolescence, the period between childhood and adulthood. Adolescence is first considered as a concept used to describe the transitional period from child to adult. Lefton cautions that we must first consider the social and cultural context from which the adolescent develops and that the research findings may not be universal. Adolescence is marked by the significant physical and cognitive changes associated with puberty and the social implications for the adolescent. Ethnic differences are considered in the *Diversity* box. Adolescents self-images influenced by early childhood experiences as well as by involvement in sports, parents, and peers. Additionally, a person's gender identity and sex roles develop during adolescence. Sexual behavior among American adolescents is changing. Parental discipline, relaxed attitudes, and other trends affecting adolescents' sexual behavior are discussed. One-parent families are also discussed.

Erikson's views of adult development are presented. Each stage presents a crisis and each crisis may be resolved in a positive or negative fashion. Levinson offers a differing view of adult development. He suggests that as people grow older they adapt; that four eras present adults with different life structures specific to the individual, and therefore that adaptation is also unique. As all theories are challenged, so is Levinson's. Some contend that he needs to consider more seriously the gender differences in adult development. An adult's physical change is less dramatic than that of the earlier stages of childhood and adolescence. However, the changes that occur are just as significant. Adult physical fitness, sensory changes, sexual drives, and cognitive processes all go through the aging process. Theories are offered to explain these transitions. Personality seems to be one of the most stable components of development.

There are numerous myths and stereotypes about older people. Lefton discusses the realities of this final developmental stage. A description of the impact of Alzheimer's disease on the individual and the family, is given.

Death is the end of a lifespan, so preparing for and accepting death is also a transition. Kubler-Ross's theory of death and dying is presented, as well as the benefits of hospice care.

SQ3R*plus*

SURVEY THE LESSON: Read learning objectives 11.1 through 11.18 and, in the text, examine the chapter headings, tables, and pictures on pages 380-404 in the text to *form an idea of what you should learn and to set goals for your study time*.

WRITE DOWN QUESTIONS: *While surveying and reading the text, write down questions* about the information being presented. *Write your questions* in the space below or on a separate piece of paper and try to find answers to these questions in the text.

ACTIVELY READ PAGES 380-404: The following exercise is designed to facilitate this process. Complete the following questions as you read, and when you are done, check your answers with those printed in the back of this study guide.

YOUR QUESTIONS:

Matching
Match the following terms or concepts from your textbook with the most appropriate description.

1. _____ adolescence
2. _____ ageism
3. _____ Alzheimer's
4. _____ androgynous
5. _____ dementia
6. _____ gender identity
7. _____ gender role
8. _____ puberty
9. _____ thanatology

a) the period extending from the onset of puberty until early adulthood.
b) the period during which the reproductive system matures at the end of the childhood period.
c) a person's sense of being male or female.
d) the full range of behaviors generally associated with one's gender, also known as sex role.
e) having both typically male and female characteristics.
f) prejudice against the elderly and the discrimination that follows.
g) impairment of mental functioning and global cognitive abilities.
h) a chronic disorder of the brain that is a major cause of degenerative dementia.
i) the study of psychological and medical aspects of death and dying.

True or False

1. Some experts link the "invention" of adolescent life-stage with social and historical events.   TRUE   FALSE

2. Most research that has been done on adolescents cuts across ethnic, cultural, and economic backgrounds.   TRUE   FALSE

3. The words adolescence and puberty can be used interchangeably.   TRUE   FALSE

4. Secondary sex characteristics are the physical features of a person's gender identity, directly involved with reproduction.   TRUE   FALSE

5. Early childhood interactions influences an adolescent's social development and self-image.   TRUE   FALSE

6. Young children use gender as a social category.   TRUE   FALSE

7. Today in the workplace, gender role stereotypes have a minimal impact on wages and promotions.   TRUE   FALSE

8. American adolescents now view sexual intimacy as an important and normal part of growing up.   TRUE   FALSE

9. Close relationships with parents and feelings of family support have been associated with later first intercourse.   TRUE   FALSE

10. Gender identity remains a part of the transition to adulthood.   TRUE   FALSE

11. A transition suggests people have reached a time of life when old ways of coping no longer work.   TRUE   FALSE

12. In general, strength, muscle tone, and overall fitness deteriorate from age thirty on.   TRUE   FALSE

13. By age seventy, most people can no longer hear high-frequency sounds.   TRUE   FALSE

14. Most people between thirty-five and forty-five will have a "life crisis."   TRUE   FALSE

15. Levinson sees life as a journey toward some specific goal or objective.   TRUE   FALSE

16.	During adolescence people begin to make their first major life choices.	TRUE	FALSE
17.	People in their early sixties learn to assess their lives in terms of happiness, meaningfulness, and cohesiveness.	TRUE	FALSE
18.	The developmental courses of women, especially transitions, are similar to men, but often occur at later ages and in more irregular sequences.	TRUE	FALSE
19.	Economically, women often see a decrease in their standard of living after a divorce.	TRUE	FALSE
20.	Being over sixty-five brings with it new developmental tasks.	TRUE	FALSE
21.	At birth women's life expectancy is four years greater than men's.	TRUE	FALSE
22.	The term elder suggests that an individual is past his prime.	TRUE	FALSE
23.	Multiple infarct dementia is usually caused by small strokes.	TRUE	FALSE
24.	In Alzheimer's disease initial memory losses are often overlooked.	TRUE	FALSE
25.	Some researchers contend that there may be many types of Alzheimer's.	TRUE	FALSE
26.	Deficits in intellectual functioning that occur with age are often devastating.	TRUE	FALSE
27.	Psychologists dealing with death complicated by fears and misunderstandings.	TRUE	FALSE
28.	People fear death in middle age more than at any other time in the life cycle.	TRUE	FALSE

Fill-in-the-Blanks

1. A person's actual age in years is known as their _____ _____.

2. The way a person actually performs is known as their _____
_____.

3. The time period in a person's life from puberty to adulthood is called
    _____.

4. _____ is the time period during which one's reproductive system matures.

5. The physical characteristics of a person's gender identity that separate and distinguish
    men from women are called _____ _____ _____.

6. Adolescents can think abstractly, develop hypotheses, and learn cognitive strategies
    because they are in the _____ _____.

7. A _____ _____, which can be influential, is a group of people that
    identify with and compare themselves to each other.

8. An important element of identity, a sense of being either male or female, is called
    _____ _____.

9. As a way of classifying, understanding, and accepting the world, children and adolescents
    use _____ _____ _____ to form their perceptions of the
    world.

10. The specific roles or behaviors associated with one's gender are _____
    _____.

11. A _____ _____ _____ is a belief about a gender-based
    behavior that is expected by society.

12. Behaviors that are shared by both men and women are called _____
    behaviors.

13. Sexual behaviors occur at a later age for adolescents who see their parents as being
    _____ and who feel a strong sense of family.

14. Erik Erikson's stage theories 1-4 focus on early childhood, while stage 5 focuses on
    _____ _____ _____ _____.

15. The patterns of behavior and interaction in one's life can be called _____
    _____.

16. People learn to accept responsibility, make major life choices for the first time, and move
    toward greater independence in _____ adulthood.

17. During _____ adulthood, people are usually well established in their
    careers and family.

18. The time of enjoying one's lifelong hard work and family comes during _____
    adulthood.

19. A _____ suggests that a person has reached a point in life when old
    ways are giving way to new ways, goals have been reached, and new methods of life are
    surfacing.

20. A _____ occurs when old ways of doing things become ineffective,
    leaving one feeling helpless.

21. Normal aging that occurs in humans that is irreversible, progressive, and universal is called _____ _____.

22. _____ _____ is aging due to extrinsic factors.

23. Prejudice and discrimination against elderly people is called _____.

24. _____ are impairments in mental functioning that cause memory loss and other symptoms.

25. The most common degenerative dementia is _____ _____ which is a chronic and progressive disorder of the brain.

26. The study of death and dying is _____.

27. A _____ is a specially designed facility to provide efficient and humane care to terminally ill patients.

Applications

1. Complete the table below.

Erikson's Psychosocial Stage Theory

Stage	Age	Successful Completion	Result of Conflict
Basic Trust vs. Mistrust	1		Sees the world as a hostile, unloving environment
Autonomy vs. Shame and Doubt	2-3		Unable to achieve control over elimination and/or is punished for such behavior; develops fear, shame, and doubt
Initiative vs. Guilt	4-5	Successfully achieves things on his or her own and identifies with the parent of the same sex	
Industry vs. Inferiority	6-11		Failure and feelings of incompetence and inferiority
Identity vs. Role Confusion	12-18		Unable to develop an identity or life goal
Intimacy vs. Isolation	16-25	Establishes warm, close, loving relationship	
Generativity vs. Stagnation	20-40	Contributes warmth, love, and information to a variety of people, especially children	
Ego Integrity vs. Despair	40-		Sees his life as a waste or lacking productivity

2. Identify the approximate age span and the changes that take place as an individual passes through the following stages.

   A.   Adolescence (ages _____) _____

   B.   Early adulthood (ages _____) _____

_____

C. Middle adulthood (ages _____) _____
_____

D. Late adulthood (ages _____) _____
_____
_____

E. Creativity/destructiveness (ages _____) _____
_____

3. Briefly describe each of the following stages.
   A. Denial _____
   _____

   B. Anger _____
   _____

   C. Bargaining _____
   _____

   D. Depression _____
   _____

   E. Acceptance _____

SQ3R*plus*

RECITE: When you have finished reading the assigned material in your text and you have completed the exercises in your study guide, turn back to the chapter outline. Read each learning objective and recite out loud everything you can remember in support of each objective.

REVIEW: Check to see if you have answered all the questions you wrote during the *Survey* stage. Complete all sections of your study guide and check your answers for accuracy. If you are having trouble with specific topics ask you instructor for help.

WRITE: Read the learning objective again and then, in your own words, write down everything you can remember about this chapter. Summarize the main points and the concepts introduced in this chapter.

REFLECT: After each study period, take a break and reflect on what you have just studied. Ask yourself how this newly acquired information can be used in the future.

CHAPTER ELEVEN SELF-TEST

1. Adolescence may be a challenging life period but few than _____ percent of adolescents have serious difficulty.
   A. ten
   B. twenty
   C. thirty
   D. five

2. Most research on adolescence has been conducted on:
   A. white teenagers.
   B. black teenagers.
   C. middle class teenagers.
   D. both A and C

3. Just before the onset of puberty, boys and girls experience significant growth spurts, gaining as many as _____ inches in a year.
   A. four
   B. five
   C. six
   D. three

4. The development of a teenager's personality is affected by:
   A. biological factors.
   B. environmental factors.
   C. both A and B
   D. neither A or B

5. Peer groups consist of people of the same:
   A. age.
   B. gender.
   C. race.
   D. all of the above

6. Gender schema:
   A. is a person's sense of being male or female.
   B. is a social category.
   C. asserts children use gender as an organizing theme to help them understand their world perceptions.
   D. states that the way a person is raised and taught has a profound impact on behavior and seems to have a gender related component.

7. Behaviors that are shared by both genders are:
   A. gender based.
   B. androgynous.
   C. role based.
   D. stereotypical.

8. Factors associated with delayed age of first intercourse are:
   A. strict parents.
   B. moderately strict parents.
   C. parents seen as not being strict.
   D. close parental relationships and family support.

9. Which of the following is <u>not</u> a reason suggested by Dreyer for early expression of sexual behavior?
    A. Low levels of self-esteem and feelings of powerlessness and alienation.
    B. Adults' sexual attitudes and behavior are changing.
    C. Teens consider sexual behavior normal in an intimate relationship.
    D. Adolescents are reaching sexual maturity at younger ages than before.

10. Identity versus role confusion is the _____ stage of Erikson's theory.
    A. fifth
    B. fourth
    C. seventh
    D. sixth

11. _____ of the sixty-two million family households in the U.S. are headed by single parents.
    A. 15 percent
    B. 25 percent
    C. 20 percent
    D. 12 percent

12. Physically, human beings are at their peak of agility, speed, and strength between ages:
    A. 11-17.
    B. 20-30.
    C. 18-30.
    D. 18-25.

13. By age _____, most people can no longer hear high-frequency sounds.
    A. 50
    B. 60
    C. 65
    D. 70

14. New dilemmas, challenges, and responsibilities that require reassessment, reappraisal, and development of new skills are:
    A   transitions.
    B. mid-life crises.
    C. transition-crises.
    D. none of the above

15. People reorient their career and family choices at about age:
    A. 20.
    B. 30.
    C. 40.
    D. 50.

16. According to Levinson, life structures are:
    A. unique patterns of behavior and ways of interacting with the world.
    B. unique new life conditions, challenges, and dilemmas.
    C. a person's distinctive qualities and different life problems.
    D. the development of skills to reach common goals.

17. According to Levinson's theory, we can think of a person's life as:
    A. the development of stable life structures to get them through life.
    B. made up of several stages.
    C. a period during which individuals work out various developmental tasks.
    D. alternating between stable periods and transitional periods.

18. During which era does Levinson claim a person often reaches his/her peak in creativity and achievement?
    A. adolescence
    B. early adulthood
    C. middle adulthood
    D. late adulthood

19. Research shows that a person's _____ may be sensitive to the unique experiences of the individual.
    A. stability
    B. personality
    C. security
    D. development

20. Which of the following is <u>not</u> one of the traditionally held myths about the elderly? They are:
    A. inflexible.
    B. financially secure.
    C. incompetent.
    D. less intelligent.

21. Ageism is exceptionally prevalent in:
    A. the media.
    B. health care.
    C. housing.
    D. Both A & B

22. The genetic component to aging is found in which theory?
    A. external
    B. heredity
    C. homeostatic
    D. wear and tear

23. Elderly people do poorly on intelligence measuring tests because:
    A. they see poorly.
    B. they are not as motivated to do well.
    C. intelligence decreases with age.
    D. memory skills are decreased.

24. Reversible dementias are caused by all except of the following.
    A. toxins.
    B. alcoholism.
    C. strokes.
    D. malnutrition.

25. Terminal drop is:
    A. the year before death.
    B. rapid physical decline.
    C. rapid intellectual decline.
    D. Both A & C

26. Which of the following may contribute to the development of Alzheimer's Disease?
    A. depletion of enzymes necessary for formation of neurotransmitters
    B. accumulation of toxins
    C. blood supply problems
    D. all of the above

27. The cost of caring for Alzheimer's patients may reach as high as:
    A. $41 billion.
    B. $41 million.
    C. $14 million.
    D. $14 billion.

28. During the bargaining stage, most bargains are made with:
    A. God.
    B. doctors.
    C. oneself.
    D. all of the above

29. A hospice:
    A. is a traditional hospital that admits only terminally ill patients.
    B. attempts to care for a patient's emotional, spiritual, social, and physical needs.
    C. focuses upon prevention rather than dying.
    D. makes use of paternalistic techniques when interacting with the patient and family.

Congratulations, you have completed Chapter 11. Now, proceed to the Exam Preparation Section in the back of your study guide for your final review, but don't forget to review the Enrichment Glossary for help understanding difficult words.

LANGUAGE ENRICHMENT GLOSSARY

Some students who reviewed the textbook listed the following words as difficult to understand. Use this list, your dictionary, and teachers and friends to learn the meaning of words you do not understand

Page	Term	Explanation	Page	Term	Explanation
379	matured	grown up	389	"identity crisis"	when you are not sure of who you are
379	gallery	place where art is displayed	390	stagnate	not going forward
379	arthritis	a disease with joint pain	390	cohesive	fits together, makes sense
380	frame of mind	what you think	391	offspring	children
380	unsettling	uneasy feeling	391	mellowing	more calm, quiet
380	jolt	shock or surprise	391	cohesive	held together well
380	storm and stress	a lot of emotions	391	disputes	disagreeing
380	turmoil	problems	391	junctures	times in life when changes occur
381	roamed	walked	392	misnomer	not named correctly
381	pickpockets	people who steal wallets	392	catastrophe	disaster, failure
381	purse snatchers	people who steal purses	393	surge	big increase
381	wits	ability to think well	393	custody	care for the children
381	growth spurts	time of fast growth	393	juggle	manage many things
382	facial hair	hair on face	393	visible	seen or observed
382	ova	egg	393	peak of agility	time of best physical skill
382	prowess	skill or good ability	393	deteriorate	decline or decrease
384	buffer	protection	394	erections	penis in upward position and hard
384	cajole	gently try to get someone to change her mind	394	cessation	stopping
384	shoplifting	stealing	394	discriminations	observations
384	profound	important	394	testosterone	male sex hormone
385	submissively	lead by others	394	vigor	high energy
385	appropriate	correct or right	394	extravagant	trying very hard
386	stoic	not emotional	394	concoct	mix together
387	its permanency	that it will always be that way	394	elixir	medicine
387	contraception	birth control, prevent pregnancy	394	quacks	bad doctors
388	public assistance	welfare, financial help from the government	399	allude	refer to, make you think about
388	vastly	very	401	gnarled	not formed correctly
388	despair	sadness, depression	401	unrelenting	never giving up

CHAPTER 12

Personality and Its Assessment

Psychology 6th Ed.		Keeping Pace Plus		
HEADINGS	**PAGE**	**LESSON**	**L.O.**	**LEARNING OBJECTIVES**
Psychoanalytic Theory	411	1	12.1	Define the term *personality*, and cite the five key questions that personality theorists ask in describing personality.
Three Key Concepts	411		12.2	Distinguish between psychodynamic theory and psychoanalysis and discuss the key concepts behind Freud's theory, including the libido and the source of anxiety.
Structure of Consciousness and the Mind	412		12.3	Describe Freud's three levels of consciousness and the mental forces he said explained causes of behavior.
Development of Personality	413		12.4	Describe Freud's psychosexual stage theory of personality development.
Unresolved Conflicts	416		12.5	Explain how fixations affect development; identify the major defense mechanisms and explain how people use these to reduce anxiety.
Freud Today	417		12.6	Explain how Freud's theory has been a major influence on psychology and Western culture.
Cultural Determinants of Personality	418		12.7	Discuss why personality theories must be considered in a cultural context and give examples of how cultures differ in shaping personality.
Neo-Freudians-- Dissent and Revision	419		12.8	Specify the views of the neo-Freudians and explain how they differ from those of traditional psychoanalysts.

Chapter 12 Overview

What do you think of when you hear your friends describing someone you've never met? Personality is a set of relatively enduring behavioral characteristics and internal predispositions that describe how a person reacts to the environment. Theories of personality and personality development abound. Theories attempt to explain the role of nature and nurture, the presence of unconscious processes, and the stability and consistencies of these behaviors.

Sigmund Freud's psychoanalytic theory offers a perspective on how the unconscious is involved in our behavior; his ideas continue to influence modern theories. The three key concepts of Freud's theory are psychic determinism, unconscious motivation, and conflict. There are three levels of consciousness described as the conscious, the preconscious, and the unconscious. Freud also believed that the *id, ego,* and *superego* are the structures of the personality and that conflict arises among these components. Freud claims that personality develops through a series of five stages: oral, anal, phallic, latency, and genital. Unresolved conflicts that occur during these stages may develop into fixations if the individual inappropriately uses defense mechanisms to attempt to resolve the conflict. Freud's theory must be considered in the context from which it came. Lefton offers an interesting insight into the development of Freud's theory. The original theory influenced many later theorists, one group of whom is called the neo-Freudians. Carl Jung proposed that we all have a collective unconscious that is a shared storehouse of inherited images and ideas. Adler suggested that we all strive to overcome inferiority in order to fulfill ourselves; the social nature of individuals was more important to Adler than Freud proposed.

Humanistic theories were developed in response to Freud's theory. Humanists like Maslow and Rogers emphasize the importance of people's interpretation of the world. Maslow's theory of self-actualization focuses on what one might achieve. Rogers' key concepts center around the ideal self and the real self. He stressed the importance of agreement between one's view of the ideal and real self. Appropriate self-concept is a result of this agreement.

Lefton examines the trait and type theories of Allport, Cattell, and Eysenck. Allport decided that traits could be divided into three categories. The *cardinal* traits, those that determine one's direction in life, the *central* traits, the basic units of one's personality; and the *secondary* traits, those which are situation specific. Cattell used factor analysis to cluster traits into what he termed *surface* traits and *source* traits. Eysenck focused at a higher level. He determined that traits were organize into types and that there were three basic dimensions of this organization, emotional stability, introversion-extroversion, and psychoticism. Finally, the "*Big Five*" theory attempts to blend the trait and type theories into five supertraits. This theory proposes that personality can be described by looking at five broad categories: extroversion-introversion, agreeableness-antagonism, conscientiousness-undirectedness, neuroticism-stability, and openness to experience.

Behavioral approaches to personality are based on learning, and on the idea that our personality is a result of learning from our environment. They focus on overt behaviors rather than covert mechanisms. The approach relies heavily on precise definitions of behaviors and practical approaches to changing or relearning different responses. Classical conditioning, operant conditioning, and observational learning are obvious contributors to the behavioral approach to personality.

The cognitive approach accepts the behavioral premise and adds a new dimension. Cognitive psychologists emphasize the interactive role of thought process and behavior. One of the conceptual frameworks used to describe the cognitive approach is that of *self-schemata* or global themes that we use to describe ourselves. Rotter's *locus of control* is another view of how individuals with an internal locus of control differ from those with an external locus-of-control in personality. Bandura submits that a person's belief or expectancy for success determines the types of behavior undertaken. Mischel also believed thought was important, but added that through a process called *self-regulation* people learned to interact with their environment in flexible ways. This chapter also considers the stability of shyness and the changes in women's personality through the lifespan.

The last section in this chapter looks at personality assessment. Psychologists may use objective instruments such as the popular MMPI/MMPI-2, which are self report types of tests, or they may use projective tests like the Rorschach inkblots which attempt to reveal unconscious motives, or they may use the behavioral assessment method of recording overt behaviors. Most psychologists will use some combination of these techniques to assess individual personalities and determine treatment plans.

SQ3R*plus*

SURVEY THE LESSON: Read learning objectives 12.1 through 12.30 and, in the text, examine the chapter headings, tables, and pictures on pages 410-444 in the text to *form an idea of what you should learn and to set goals for your study time*.

WRITE DOWN QUESTIONS: *While surveying and reading the text, write down questions* about the information being presented. *Write your questions* in the space below or on a separate piece of paper and try to find answers to these questions in the text.

ACTIVELY READ PAGES 410-440: The following exercise is designed to facilitate this process. Complete the following questions as you read, and when you are done, check your answers with those printed in the back of this study guide.

YOUR QUESTIONS:

Matching
Match the following terms or concepts from your textbook with the most appropriate description.

1. _____ anal stage
2. _____ archetypes
3. _____ assessment
4. _____ conscious
5. _____ defense mechanism
6. _____ denial
7. _____ ego
8. _____ fixation
9. _____ fulfillment
10. _____ genital stage
11. _____ id
12. _____ ideal self
13. _____ latency stage
14. _____ libio
15. _____ Oedipus complex
16. _____ oral stage
17. _____ personality

18. _____ phallic stage
19. _____ preconscious
20. _____ projection
21. _____ projective tests
22. _____ rationalization
23. _____ reaction formation
24. _____ repression
25. _____ self
26. _____ self actualization
27. _____ self monitoring
28. _____ self-efficacy
29. _____ shyness
30. _____ sublimation
31. _____ super ego
32. _____ trait
33. _____ types
34. _____ unconscious

a) a set of relatively enduring behavioral characteristics and internal predispositions
b) Freud's instinctual life force that energizes the id
c) Freud's first level of awareness consisting of thoughts, feelings, and actions
d) Freud's second level of awareness consisting of mental activities of which people can gain awareness by attending to them
e) Freud's third level of awareness consisting of mental activities beyond people's normal awareness
f) Freud's source of instinctual energy
g) the part of personality that seeks to satisfy the id and super ego in accordance with reality
h) the moral aspect of mental functioning
i) from birth to about age 2, during which ratification is primarily gained through the mouth
j) from age 2 to about 3, during which children learn to control the immediate gratification obtained through deification and become responsive to societal demands
k) from about age 4 through 7, during which children gain gratification primarily from the genital area
l) feelings of rivalry with the parent of the same sex and love of parent of the opposite sex
m) fourth stage of personality development from age seven until puberty during which sexual urges are inactive
n) from the onset of puberty to adulthood, during which the sexual conflicts of childhood resurface and are often resolved during adolescence
o) excessive attachment to some person or object
p) unconscious way of reducing anxiety by distorting perceptions of reality
q) anxiety provoking feelings are pushed into the interconscious

r) people attribute their own undesirable traits to other people or objects

s) people refuse to recognize the true source of their anxiety

t) people behave in a mannor opposite of their true anxiety provoking feelings

u) people redirect socially unacceptable impulses into the acceptable ones

v) people reinterpret undesirable feelings or behaviors in terms that make them appear acceptable

w) emotionally charged ideas and images that have rich meaning and symbolism and exist within the collective unconscious

x) an inborn tendency directing people toward actualizing their essential nature and thus obtaining more potential

y) perceptions individuals have of themselves and their relationships to other people

z) the self a person would ideally like to be

aa) process of growth in the realization of human potential

bb) any readily identifiable stable quality or behavior that characterizes individual differences

cc) categories of personality in which broad traits are loosely interrelated

dd) extreme anxiety in individuals who are socially reticent and often leading to avoidance of social situations

ee) a person's belief about whether he or she can successfully engage and execute a specific behavior

ff) the process of evaluating individual differences

gg) personality assessing devices or instruments in which examinees are asked to respond to a standard set of ambiguous stimuli

hh) as assessment procedure in which a person systematically counts and records the frequency and duration of specific behaviors

True or False

1. Each theory of personality is incomplete yet important because each addresses some key element of personality.   TRUE   FALSE

2. The term "life energy" was used by Freud to describe the super ego.   TRUE   FALSE

3. The superego works according to the reality principle.   TRUE   FALSE

4. According to Freud an erogenous zone lies somewhere between the conscious and unconscious mind.   TRUE   FALSE

5. When people attribute their own undesirable traits to others, they are using the defense mechanism called reaction formation.   TRUE   FALSE

6. A neo-Freudian is a modern day psychologist who closely follows Freud's original conception of personality development.   TRUE   FALSE

7. Carl Jung's theory is called the psychoanalytic approach.   TRUE   FALSE

8. Adler emphasized that an innate social need motivates people toward perfectionism.   TRUE   FALSE

9. Humanistic psychology focuses on healthy people and how they can improve characteristics such as self esteem.   TRUE   FALSE

10. As a personality theorist Maslow focused on what was missing in a person's personality or life.   TRUE   FALSE

11. Trait and type theories are popular because they make intuitive sense.   TRUE   FALSE

12. Secondary traits, as describe by Allport, are difficult to change.   TRUE   FALSE

13. Psychologists believe that the trait categories known as the *Big Five* have provided them with a complete theoretical description of personality.   TRUE   FALSE

14. Even major events that occur in a person's life cannot alter a person's "type" of personality.   TRUE   FALSE

15. According to behaviorists, personality is equivalent to the sum of a series of responses.   TRUE   FALSE

16. Cognitive approaches to personality developed as a reaction to strict behavioral models and added a new dimension of personality.   TRUE   FALSE

17. The cognitive theory that describes how people identify the causes of successes or failures in their lives is called social learning theory.   TRUE   FALSE

18. At least 40 million adults find their shyness to be a serious problem.   TRUE   FALSE

19. According to Bandura, people's expectations of mastery and their convictions about their own effectiveness determine the amount of risk they will take.   TRUE   FALSE

20. Mischel says, that when we change our responses on the basis of past experience and our current assessment of a present situation, we are using a process called *competencies*.   TRUE   FALSE

21. The process of evaluating individual differences by using interviews, observations, tests, and recordings of physiological processes is the definition of *assessment*.   TRUE   FALSE

22. One personality characteristic that is measured by the MMPI-2   TRUE   FALSE
is psychopathic deviation.

23. Projective tests are designed to measure a person's unconscious   TRUE   FALSE
motives.

24. Naturalistic observation is an example of a behavioral   TRUE   FALSE
assessment technique.

25. Self-monitoring is appealing because it is inexpensive, easy to   TRUE   FALSE
do, and applicable to a variety of problems.

Fill-in-the-Blanks

1. An enduring behavioral characteristic and an internal disposition is called a
   _____.

2. _____ _____ is the assumption that all feelings, thoughts,
   and actions have a purpose and are determined by something that happened in the past.

3. When one is motivated by desires and goals of which an individual is unaware, he or she
   is experiencing _____ _____.

4. The _____ is a level in which people are aware of thoughts, feelings, and
   actions.

5. The _____ is a level in which people are aware of what is going on if they
   pay close attention.

6. The _____ is a level in which people are unaware of mental activities.

7. The source of a person's instinctual energy is called the _____.

8. The _____ is the part of the personality which seeks to satisfy the person's
   instinctual needs.

9. Freud's moral aspect of mental functioning is called the _____.

10. The concept of the _____ stage focuses on the mouth which is the primary
    pleasure-seeking center.

11. The _____ stage focuses on children's ability to have control of their bodily
    functions, thereby learning control and orderliness as adults.

12. Gratification of the genital area in children occurs during the _____ stage.

13. The _____ _____ deals with feelings of rivalry between the same sex
    parent.

14. During the _____ _____, children develop physically but have
    inactive sexual urges.

15. During the _____ _____, the feelings of sexuality, fear, and
    repressed feelings of earlier stages come out.

16. When one has an attachment to some person or object which is developmentally inappropriate, this is called _____.

17. When one distorts reality in order to reduce anxiety, he/she is employing a _____ _____.

18. _____, a defense mechanism, allows anxiety provoking thoughts to be pushed into the unconscious.

19. Placing your own undesirable traits on another person is called _____.

20. Refusing to accept reality is called _____.

21. _____ _____ is a mechanism in which people defend themselves against anxiety by behaving in a way that is opposite to their true feelings.

22. Directing an inappropriate impulse into an acceptable impulse is called _____.

23. Interpreting undesired feelings in a way which makes them appear acceptable is called _____.

24. _____ are theorists who have developed new ideas based on Freud.

25. The images and ideas that are stored in the unconscious that we inherit are called the _____ _____.

26. The person one would ideally like to be is called the _____ _____.

27. People maximize their self concept through _____ _____.

28. The qualities that characterize people and distinguish them from others are called _____.

29. _____ is a behavior problem that inhibits a person's social, personal, and professional growth.

30. _____ _____ is a person's belief that they can participate in and execute a behavior successfully.

Applications

1. Match the following levels of consciousness with the appropriate definition.

   Preconscious   Unconscious   Conscious

   A. _____ The thoughts, feelings, and actions a person is *aware* of. This is the first level of consciousness and is very easy to study and understand.

   B. _____ Mental activity (thoughts and feelings) that a person can become aware of if they closely pay attention to them. This is the second level of consciousness; it takes a little time and effort to study and understand it.

   C. _____ Thoughts and feelings beyond normal awareness. This is the third level of consciousness; so deeply repressed, it can be studied and understood only by spending a lot of time and effort using a technique like psychoanalysis, according to Freud.

2. Match the following defense mechanisms to the appropriate definition.

   repression   *projection*   *denial*   *reaction formation*   *rationalization*
   sublimation

   A. _____ Making unreasonable feelings and behaviors seem reasonable by reinterpreting them.

   B. _____ Refusing to accept reality and the true source of anxiety.

   C. _____ Attributing one's own undesirable traits to others.

   D. _____ Behaving in a manner that is opposite to one's true, but anxiety-producing, feelings.

   E. _____ Anxiety-producing feelings are blocked from conscious awareness and pushed into the unconscious. For Freud this defense mechanism was the most important to understand.

   F. _____ Energy from an impulse that might be considered taboo is channeled or redirected into a socially acceptable form.

3. Match the following neo-Freudians with a key idea put forth by each.

   Alfred Adler   *Erich*   *Karen Horney*   *Harry Sullivan*   *Carl Jung*
                     Fromm

   A. _____ Emphasized the influence of cultural and interpersonal factors.

   B. _____ Argued that people are not driven solely by sexual instincts.

   C. _____ Focused on the central role of anxiety in shaping personality and maladjustment.

   D. _____ Argued that the ego has more of a role than Freud thought in controlling behavior.

   E. _____ His is one example of a theory that is optimistic and future oriented.

4. Describe Freud's primary structural elements of personality: the *id, ego,* and *superego.*
   A. Id
      1. It is a source of _____
      2. Pleasure principle _____
      3. Characteristics of the id _____
   B. Ego
      1. It grows out of _____
      2. It seeks to _____
      3. Characteristics of the ego _____
   C. Superego
      1. It can be thought of as _____
      2. It tells the id and ego _____
      3. It helps the ego to control the id by _____

5. Describe Allport's cardinal, central, and secondary *traits* and give an example of each.
   A. Cardinal traits _____
       Example _____
   B. Central traits _____
       Example _____
   C. Secondary traits _____
       Example _____

6. Complete the table to describe the trait categories that have come to known as the *Big Five* by modern day psychologists.

Trait Categories	Description
Extroversion-introversion	
	The extent to which people are good-natured or irritable, courteous or rude, flexible or stubborn, lenient or critical.
Conscientiousness-undirectedness	
Neuroticism-stability	
	The extent to which people are open to experience or closed, original or conventional, independent or conforming, creative or uncreative, daring or timid.

7. Briefly describe the following assessment tests.
   A. Intelligence tests _____
       _____
   B. CPI _____
       _____
   C. MMPI-2 _____
       _____
   D. Rorschach _____
       _____
   E. TAT _____
       _____

8. Briefly describe each of the following behavioral assessment techniques.
   A. Behavioral assessment interviews _____

   B. Naturalistic observation _____

   C. Self-monitoring _____

9. Which of the following defense mechanisms is being used by the person in the situations described below?

   repression   reaction formation   rationalization   projection   denial

   A. _____ Deep inside Karmara holds strong feelings of anger towards her father and other men who are similar to him. She protects herself from these angry feelings (which are accompanied by fears of rejection) by playing the role of the benevolent angel willing to comfort men for any distress they might have.

   B. _____ (In this case, a defense mechanism that normally protects Duane fails. What is it?) Duane has always been a reserved, shy person, so when he accidentally blurted out "Where's the sex-pack?" instead of "Where's the six-pack?" everyone at the picnic laughed. Duane was mortified. His friend, Don realized that Duane had made what some people call a "Freudian slip." Because they cause Duane such pain, thoughts about sex normally reside deep in his unconscious.

   C. _____ Roni tells her husband Bob that she can no longer live comfortably in their marriage and wants a divorce. Bob gives Roni a hug and reminds her of their upcoming vacation and picks her up and takes her to the bedroom. What defense mechanism is Bob using?

   D. _____ Elton knew that it was not in his best interest to go to Joe's party. He knew that he should really spend the evening studying for his psychology final, but he quickly dismissed that thought and told himself that he could study for a few minutes in the morning and that the final would probably be easy anyway. When he found out that he had failed his final, Elton said to himself, "Oh well, nobody's perfect!"

   E. _____ Gordon is a manipulative and controlling kind of person. He has to have everything go his way and does all he can to ensure that it will. When Gordon is unsuccessful and senses he is not getting what he wants, he accuses the other person of being manipulative and controlling.

SQ3R*plus*

RECITE: When you have finished reading the assigned material in your text and you have completed the exercises in your study guide, turn back to the chapter outline. Read each learning objective and recite out loud everything you can remember in support of each objective.

REVIEW: Check to see if you have answered all the questions you wrote during the *Survey* stage. Complete all sections of your study guide and check your answers for accuracy. If you are having trouble with specific topics ask you instructor for help.

WRITE: Read the learning objective again and then, in your own words, write down everything you can remember about this chapter. Summarize the main points and the concepts introduced in this chapter.

REFLECT: After each study period, take a break and reflect on what you have just studied. Ask yourself how this newly acquired information can be used in the future.

CHAPTER TWELVE SELF-TEST

1. Which of the following *best* defines personality?
   A. A collection of all behaviors an individual has ever emitted.
   B. The behaviors a person emits when he or she is with other people.
   C. Behavior characteristics that describe how a person reacts to the environment.
   D. Behaviors that make a person stand out in a crowd.

2. Freud theorized that people are energized and act the way they do because of two basic instinctual drives. They are:
   A. sex and aggression.
   B. instinctual gratification and minimizing punishment.
   C. release of anxiety and tension.
   D. life and death.

3. The ego:
   A. is a preconscious behavior.
   B. acts like a manager.
   C. acts like the moral branch for the id.
   D. works on the pleasure principle.

4. Georgia is very controlled in everything she does. Her desk must be neat at all times; she apologizes for the slightest hedging on someone's privacy; she cannot be spontaneous. In understanding Freud's psychosexual stages we could predict that Georgia is fixated in the _____ stage.
   A. oral
   B. anal
   C. phallic
   D. genital

5. Clyde has a number of extremely hostile unconscious feelings. Unknowingly, he reduces the anxiety that these feelings produce by getting involved in highly aggressive sports, such as rugby. He is using the defense mechanism known as:
   A.   sublimation.
   B.   denial.
   C.   reaction formation
   D.   projection.

6. Many modern psychologists agree that Freud's psychoanalytic theory:
   A   is useful for people with minor adjustment problems, but not for those with extreme mental disorders.
   B.   makes specific predictions about an individuals behavior almost impossible.
   C.   closely resembles the theory of behaviorism.
   D.   should be thrown out the window, and all of the books he wrote should be burned.

7. Neo-Freudians differ from traditional psychoanalysts in that neo-Freudians:
   A.   begin analysis by focusing on unconscious material in the id.
   B.   place little importance on cultural factors.
   C.   argue that behavior is driven solely by sexual instincts.
   D.   focus on helping people to develop stronger control of their ego in the initial stages of therapy.

8. Compared to Freud, a major difference in Jung's conception of the structure of consciousness was:
   A.   that there is a collective unconscious that stores primitive ideas inherited from our ancestors.
   B.   that unconscious processes determine behavior.
   C.   people store past events in the unconscious.
   D.   that dreams have little importance in helping people understand unconscious thought.

9. Fictional finalism refers to:
   A.   distorting or denying what one is truly experiencing.
   B.   a goal that motivates a person even though it probably won't be achieved.
   C.   lifestyles that interfere with actual growth.
   D.   fulfillment through achieving specific goals.

10. Phenomenological approaches focus on all of the following except:
    A.   an individuals unique experiences with interpreting the events in the world.
    B.   examining immediate experiences rather than experiences from the past.
    C.   how people carve their own destinies through self-determination.
    D.   the therapists perception and interpretation of the clients needs.

11. The process of self-actualization according to Maslow is:
    A.   the process of growth.
    B.   achieving full potential.
    C.   the process of realizing potential and of growing.
    D.   both A and B

12. People with healthy self-concepts:
    A. can allow new experiences in their lives.
    B. move in a positive direction.
    C. come closer to the goal of self-actualization.
    D. all of the above

13. All of the following statements represent the humanistic perspective *except:*
    A. Their orientation emphasizes free-will.
    B. They believed behavior is determined by biological drives.
    C. They believe humans can use decision processes to guide behavior.
    D. They show an abiding concern for individual development.

14. Which of the following is an example of a "type?"
    A. energetic
    B. apprehensive
    C. prejudice
    D. introverted, shy, withdrawn

15. According to Allport many people do *not* have:
    A. central traits.
    B. source traits.
    C. cardinal traits.
    D. secondary traits.

16. Many modern day psychologists use the *Big Five* model to understand personality because:
    A. they can identify over 100,000 different traits.
    B. it provides them with a concise description of "super traits" which describes the dispositions that characterize most people.
    C. it's based on Einstein's theory of relativity.
    D. they can avoid placing personality labels on individuals.

17. Trait and type theories are appealing to psychologists because they:
    A. arrange lists of important behaviors into a hierarchy.
    B. can predict how a person will behave in a particular situation.
    C. provide simple explanations for how individuals behave.
    D. explain which personality characteristics will change as a person ages.

18. Jason beats his head against the walls of his room whenever his father yells at him for not completing a household chore. From a behavioral point of view Jason's self-destructive personality is the result of:
    A. early childhood experiences.
    B. a death wish.
    C. a response that has been reinforced.
    D. an overly strong libido.

19. Behavioral psychologists working in the Florida public schools, used a procedure called time-out and successfully decreased the child's undesirable behavior of:
    A. using as many as 150 obscene words in an hour.
    B. kicking other children during recess.
    C. picking his nose during math class.
    D. falling asleep during class.

20. One of the first psychologists to assert the cognitive view that people make rational choices in trying to predict and manage events in the world is:
    A. Carl Jung.
    B. George Kelly.
    C. Sigmund Freud.
    D. Carl Rogers.

21. People with an external locus of control are more likely to _____ than people with an internal locus of control.
    A. blame others for their mistakes
    B. engage in preventative health measures
    C. profit from psychotherapy
    D. lose weight when they go on a diet

22. Which of the following symptoms might be exhibited by shy people?
    A. being overly concerned with how others perceive them
    B. having physical symptoms such as clammy hands, trembling, blushing, and needing to go the bathroom
    C. showing extreme anxiety in social situations
    D. all of the above

23. A person's belief about whether he or she can successfully engage in and execute a specific behavior is known as:
    A. self-regulation.
    B. self-worth.
    C. self-esteem.
    D. self-efficacy.

24. In order to determine if Helson and Moane's findings are still valid researchers need to:
    A. account for changing political, social, and moral values.
    B. examine social economic, lifestyle, educational, and work issues.
    C. conduct a longitudinal study of the current generation of college women over the next 20 years.
    D. all of the above

25. When might a psychologist refer a client to a neuropsychologist to gather more information for an accurate evaluation?
    A. when the client spits on the psychologist's shoes
    B. when obscene gestures, inappropriate facial tics, and other symptoms associated with Tourette syndrome are apparent
    C. when the client complains about arguing with his or her spouse
    D. when the psychologist has no idea of what the client's problem is

Congratulations, you have completed Chapter 12. Now, proceed to the Exam Preparation Section in the back of your study guide for your final review, but don't forget to review the Enrichment Glossary for help understanding difficult words.

LANGUAGE ENRICHMENT GLOSSARY

Some students who reviewed the textbook listed the following words as difficult to understand. Use this list, your dictionary, and teachers and friends to learn the meaning of words you do not understand

Page	Term	Explanation	Page	Term	Explanation
410	conflicts	struggles, concerns	419	intolerant	does not want to put up with or talk with others
410	impel	make up do something	420	ancestors	our parents, their parents
410	Contemporary	current times, today	420	wizards	person who does magic
410	manageable	in a way you can do it	420	prominence	fame, important position
411	heretical	going against others who are respected	420	inferiority	feeling less than others
411	conceptualize	form certain ideas	420	denounced	put down, criticized
411	frown	make a sad or angry face	420	irreconcilable	cannot fix or restore
411	prominently	important	420	advocates	helpers
411	preoccupied	thought mostly of	420	executives	important person in a business
411	paints a picture	makes a statement	422	warding off	pushing away
412	gratification	reward	422	decent	good
412	therapeutic	treatment	422	destinies	fate, future
412	reside	live in	422	hierarchy	different levels of human needs
412	raw impulses	basic desires	422	uniqueness	special and different qualities
412	shivering	shaking from cold	422	fuzzy	unclear
413	internalizing	keeping it inside	422	romantic	with emotional appeal
413	transgressions	wrong doings	423	uninterrupted	steady, no stops
413	elaborate	very large; has many parts	423	analogy	similar story or idea
414	bitter	harsh and distasteful	423	devoted	loyal, loving
415	urination	liquid waste from genitals	423	discrepancies	disagreements, differences
415	defecation	waste material coming out of anus	423	nuisance	gets in the way
415	compulsive	very strong feelings that you must do something	423	threatening	you think it can hurt you
415	repressed	held back or held in	423	religious observances	things you do for church
415	castration	genital being cut off	424	denies	refuses to believe
415	subservient to	less than, servants of	424	distorts	think of it as different than it really is
416	exhibited	show up, displayed	424	broadening	going further out
416	shakes off	lets go of	424	abiding	long lasting, enduring
416	conventional	traditional, same as always	425	preponderance	a lot
416	overindulgent	giving too much to a child	425	counterparts	people who were like them
416	disturbed	upset, have problems	425	aggressiveness	angry physical behavior
416	distorting	changed from what is really true	425	intuitive sense	seem reasonable, correct
417	reinterpret	explain again	425	interrelated	connected together
417	maladaptive	doesn't work well	425	characterize	personal qualities
417	absurd	very wrong or incorrect	425	apprehensive	fearful
417	idolize	look up to	425	keen	intense or strong
417	speculations	theories, guesses	426	nurturance	caring for others
418	matrons	mature proper women	426	stilted	formal, serious
418	implication	what it appears to mean	427	gregarious	outgoing
419	attributed	assign or give a cause	434	obstacles	things that get in the way

CHAPTER 13

Stress and Health Psychology

Psychology 6th Ed.		Keeping Pace Plus		
HEADINGS	**PAGE**	**LESSON**	**L.O.**	**LEARNING OBJECTIVES**
Coping	462	**2**		
What Is Coping?	462		13.8	Define what is meant by the term *coping* and outline the relationship among resilience, coping skills, social support, and ability to cope.
Resilience, Coping Skills, and Social Support	463			
Defense-Oriented and Task-Oriented Coping Strategies	463		13.9	Distinguish between defense-oriented and task-oriented coping strategies, and outline a plan for developing a stress reduction program.
APPLICATIONS: *Coping, Health, and a Positive Attitude*	466		13.10	Assess how positive and negative attitudes influence coping abilities and the immune system, and state steps one can take to develop effective coping strategies.
Health Psychology	466	**3**	13.11	Describe the fields of health psychology and behavioral medicine and explain what contemporary psychologists mean by the term *health*.
Variables That Affect Health and Illness	468		13.12	Discuss how personality, cognitions, social environment, gender, and sociocultural variables are related to health.
APPLICATIONS: *AIDS (Acquired Immune Deficiency Syndrome)*	470		13.13	Describe how health psychologists involved in AIDS prevention are educating the public about high-risk behaviors.
The Psychology of Being Sick	469		13.14	Explain what is meant by the psychology of being sick, focusing on when people seek medical care and adopt a sick role and under what circumstances they may comply with medical advice.

Health Psychology and Adaptive Behavior	471	13.15 Explain how behavioral interventions, pain management, and stress management try to develop adaptive behaviors that will improve people's lives.

Chapter 13 Overview

This chapter presents a contemporary view of stress, coping, and the field of health psychology. It begins by defining stress and stressors. A stressor is an environmental stimulus that has the potential to affect an organism in a harmful way by producing anxiety or tension. Stress is the end result of that stimulus. The key is the interpretation of the stressor as being stressful. Sources of stress include frustration, conflict, and pressure. Frustration results when goal-directed behavior is blocked, conflict results when people are required to make difficult decisions, and pressure usually comes from work, time pressures or life events. Responses to stress include emotional, physical, and behavioral reactions. While a moderate amount of stress is thought to be adaptive, too much may lead to burnout, a state of physical and emotional exhaustion, which contribute to serious health problems such as heart disease and cancer by affecting the body's immune system.

Hans Selye developed a model describing physiological changes resulting from stress. He called this model the general adaptation syndrome. The syndrome consists of three stages: the alarm stage, the resistance stage, and finally exhaustion. Holmes and Rahe developed a scale to assess the potential for a stress-induced illness following a series of life events. Lefton examines cultural differences in responding to stress in Native American Indians and Hispanics. Work-site stress, Type A behavior, and physiological reactivity are examined for their relationships to heart disease. Victims of war, crime, natural disasters, and man-made disasters have the potential to suffer from posttraumatic stress disorder (PTSD). Although most of the research on PTSD is with war veterans, many organizations and practitioners are using this knowledge to mitigate the effects of PTSD through early intervention techniques with other populations of victims.

Deal with it! This is one way of defining coping. Our ability to cope depends on a number of factors including our resilience, current coping skills, and social supports. We may choose defense-oriented or task-oriented coping strategies. Defense-oriented strategies isolate the stress, but do not provide long term solutions. Task-oriented strategies clearly identify the source of stress, develop a plan of action, and through implementation and monitoring usually results in effective change. In the Application box Lefton outlines positive thinking as a task-oriented strategy and lists several coping strategies such as proper nutrition, sleeping, and learning to relax.

Health psychology is an emerging field that looks to incorporate the principles of health enhancement, prevention, diagnosis, and rehabilitation into a more holistic approach. Our personality, thoughts, social environment, and sociocultural variables all contribute to good health. Lefton examines how psychologists are addressing the AIDS issue from a behavioral perspective. Psychologists are looking more closely at the "psychology of being sick" and how education and prevention can be used to help people become and remain healthy.

SQ3R*plus*

SURVEY THE LESSON: Read learning objectives 13.1 through 13.15 and, in the text, examine the chapter headings, tables, and pictures on pages 450-472 in the text to *form an idea of what you should learn and to set goals for your study time*.

WRITE DOWN QUESTIONS: *While surveying and reading the text, write down questions* about the information being presented. *Write your questions* in the space below or on a separate piece of paper and try to find answers to these questions in the text.

ACTIVELY READ PAGES 450-472: The following exercise is designed to facilitate this process. Complete the following questions as you read, and when you are done, check your answers with those printed in the back of this study guide.

YOUR QUESTIONS:

Matching

Match the following terms or concepts from your textbook with the most appropriate description.

1. _____ anxiety
2. _____ burnout
3. _____ conflict
4. _____ coping
5. _____ coping skills
6. _____ frustration
7. _____ health psychology
8. _____ pressure
9. _____ psychoneuroimmunology
10. _____ PTSD
11. _____ resilience
12. _____ stress
13. _____ stress inoculation
14. _____ stressor

a) an environmental stimulus that effects an organism in physically or psychologically injurious ways

b) a generalized feeling or fear and apprehension accompanied by increased psychological arousal

c) a nonspecific often global response to real or imagined demands

d) emotional state or condition that results when a goal is blocked

e) emotional state or condition in which a person has to make difficult decisions about two or more competing motives, behaviors, or impulses

f) emotional state or condition resulting from others' expectations of specific behaviors

g) state of emotional and physical exhaustion, lowered productivity, and feelings of isolation

h) mental disorder that may become evident after the person has undergone extreme stress caused by some type of trauma or disaster

i) process by which the person takes some action to manage environmental or internal demands that cause stress

j) the extent to which people or flexible, less easily impaired, and respond adaptively to internal or external demands

k) the technique people use to deal with stress and changing situations

l) procedure of giving realistic warnings, recommendations, and reassurances to help people prepare and cope with impending danger or losses

m) study of how psychological processes and the nervous system effect the immune system

n) subfield concerned with the use of psychological ideas and principles and health enhancement, prevention, diagnosis, treatment, and rehabilitation processes

True or False

1. Physiological arousal is often the first change that appears when a person experiences a stressor. TRUE   FALSE

2. Conflict arises from the inability to achieve certain goals. TRUE   FALSE

3.   When people face conflict situations, stress, anxiety, and even   TRUE   FALSE
      symptoms of maladjustment can occur.

4.   A moderate amount of stress is necessary because it keeps us   TRUE   FALSE
      active and involved.

5.   Children are especially likely to experience stress because they   TRUE   FALSE
      are usually unable to change or control the circumstances in
      which they find themselves.

6.   A response like the fight or flight syndrome occurs during the   TRUE   FALSE
      alarm stage of Selye's general Adaptation Syndrome.

7.   According to Holmes and Rahe a person who scores above three   TRUE   FALSE
      hundred on their scale will likely suffer stress-induced physical
      illness.

8.   In the study comparing Hispanic and non-Hispanic subjects, the   TRUE   FALSE
      researchers found major differences in the life events (i.e. divorce
      and unemployment) experienced by the two groups.

9.   Current research shows that there is a direct relationship between   TRUE   FALSE
      Type A behavior pattern and heart disease.

10.   Most Vietnam veterans suffer Posttraumatic Stress Syndrome.   TRUE   FALSE

11.   Coping begins at the psychological level.   TRUE   FALSE

12.   Saying you never really liked a person who dumped you is a   TRUE   FALSE
      defense-oriented coping skill called reaction formation.

13.   The first step in task-oriented coping strategies is choosing the   TRUE   FALSE
      action for reducing stress.

14.   Research shows that people can help themselves cope with stress   TRUE   FALSE
      by talking to themselves.

15.   Stress has little, if any, impact on the immune system.   TRUE   FALSE

16.   Today's physicians and psychologists define health as the absence   TRUE   FALSE
      of disease.

17.   AIDS destroys the body's ability to fight off infections.   TRUE   FALSE

18.   Men may be less willing to seek medical attention because they   TRUE   FALSE
      see illness as a sign of weakness.

Fill-in-the-Blanks

1. An environmental stimulus that affects an organism by producing anxiety, tension, or
    physiological arousal is a _____.

2. A general feeling of fear and apprehension that is accompanied by increased physiological
    arousal is _____.

3. _____ is an emotional response to real or imagined demands.

4. When one feels _____, it is because a personal goal has been blocked by an obstacle.

5. A _____ is a condition in which people must make difficult decisions about two or more motives, behaviors, or impulses.

6. The conflict that occurs when one has to choose between two equally attractive options is called _____ _____ _____.

7. The conflict that occurs when one has to choose between two equally unattractive options is called _____ _____ _____.

8. The conflict that occurs when one has to choose an option that has both attractive and unattractive aspects is called _____ _____ _____.

9. People feel _____ because of real or imagined expectations of others for results.

10. Psychologists divide stress reaction into three categories: _____, _____, and _____.

11. The state of physical and emotional exhaustion because of stress is called _____.

12. According to Hans Selye, people's response to a stressor occurs in three stages: _____ _____, _____, _____.

13. Events in a person's life on a day-to-day basis that necessitate change are called _____ _____ _____.

14. Stress is effected by the extent that a person controls the speed, flow, and level of work or the degree of _____.

15. Competitive, hostile, and constantly striving individuals are labeled as _____ _____ _____.

16. Calm, patient, and less hurried people are labeled as _____ _____ _____.

17. _____ is a third possible factor that relates to heart disease in conjunction with stress.

18. The mental disorder that occurs when people endure the severe stress caused by some type of disaster is called _____ _____.

19. _____ is dealing with a situation.

20. The extent to which people are flexible in coping with their problems is called _____.

21. The techniques that people use to deal with stress are called _____ _____.

22. _____ _____ is the availability of friends and family to encourage, recognize, and approve.

23. Techniques that do not reduce stress but protect people from its effects are called

_____ _____ _____ _____.

24. Reinterpreting reality to make it make more sense is called _____.

25. Expressing a feeling that is opposite to the true feeling is called _____

_____.

26. The procedure of giving people realistic warnings, recommendations, and reassurances to help them cope with impending danger is called _____ _____.

27. _____ is the study of how psychological processes and the nervous system are affected by the immune system.

28. People cope better when they increase their _____ _____.

29. _____ _____ is the subfield that studies the use of psychological ideas and principles in the study of health.

30. _____ _____ _____ is the role adopted by people who are doing what they think will get them well.

Applications

1. Beyond cognitive appraisal, list three things that determine whether a particular event is stressful.
    1. _____
    2. _____
    3. _____

2. List and describe three types of situations that involve conflict because of competing demands.
    1. _____ :

    _____
    2. _____ :

    _____
    3. _____ :

    _____

3. List the principles Miller developed to predict how a person will behave in a conflict situation.
    1. _____
    2. _____
    3. _____

4. List and describe the three components of the stress reaction.

   A. _____ : _____

   B. _____ : _____
   _____

   C. _____ : _____
   _____

5. Explain the causes, symptoms, and impact of posttraumatic stress disorder.

   A. Causes _____
   _____

   B. Symptoms _____
   _____

   C. Impact _____
   _____

6. List the five components involved in the coping process.

   1. _____
   2. _____
   3. _____
   4. _____
   5. _____

7. Explain how the following conditions affect a person's vulnerability to stress.

   A. Coping skills _____
   _____

   B. Learned helplessness _____
   _____

   C. Social support _____
   _____

8. Briefly describe the following coping techniques.

   A. Relaxation techniques _____
   B. Cognitive coping strategies _____
   C. Self-talk procedures _____

SQ3R*plus*

RECITE: When you have finished reading the assigned material in your text and you have completed the exercises in your study guide, turn back to the chapter outline. Read each learning objective and recite out loud everything you can remember in support of each objective.

REVIEW: Check to see if you have answered all the questions you wrote during the *Survey* stage. Complete all sections of your study guide and check your answers for accuracy. If you are having trouble with specific topics ask you instructor for help.

WRITE: Read the learning objective again and then, in your own words, write down everything you can remember about this chapter. Summarize the main points and the concepts introduced in this chapter.

REFLECT: After each study period, take a break and reflect on what you have just studied. Ask yourself how this newly acquired information can be used in the future.

CHAPTER THIRTEEN SELF-TEST

1. An environmental stimulus that affects an organism in physically or psychologically injurious ways is called:
    A.   a stressor.
    B.   stress.
    C.   anxiety.
    D.   arousal.

2. Children often show their stress response:
    A.   by laughing.
    B.   by telling their teachers and parents about their discomfort.
    C.   with symptoms of physical illness.
    D.   by playing a game of charades.

3. Which of the following would be classified as a high stress job?
    A.   air traffic controllers
    B.   inner-city high school teacher
    C.   customer service agent
    D.   all of the above

4. A physiological response to stress is characterized by arousal of the _____ nervous system.
    A.   central
    B.   somatic
    C.   autonomic
    D.   bilateral

5. Cosmos has very high standards in accomplishing the tasks at his job. However, because of extreme work related pressures, he has been experiencing emotional and physical exhaustion and lower productivity, and has felt isolated from the other employees. Cosmos is experiencing:
    A   reality.
    B.   burnout.
    C.   anxiety.
    D.   resistance

6. At this stage of Selye's GAS, physiological and behavioral responses become more moderate and sustained.
   A. alarm
   B. acceptance
   C. resistance
   D. exhaustion

7. According to Holmes and Rahe, stressful life events are:
   A. every day hassles in a person's day-to-day experiences.
   B. a combination of every day hassles and irritations.
   C. the build up of every day hassles and irritations.
   D. prominent events in a person's life that necessitate change.

8. In their research comparing Hispanic-American and non-Hispanic whites, Golding, Potts, Aneshensel found no significant differences *except* for:
   A. economic strain affected Hispanics more than non-Hispanic whites.
   B. uneducated white were more likely to have marriage problems.
   C. uneducated Hispanics were likely to suffer from unemployment.
   D. Hispanic immigrants were more likely to be burglarized.

9. Which of the following events contribute to posttraumatic stress disorder?
   A. victims of violence
   B. natural disasters
   C. man-made disasters
   D. all of the above

10. The availability of comfort, recognition, approval, and encouragement from other people is called _____ and is extremely helpful when people are trying to cope.
    A. psychological manipulation
    B. social support
    C. friendship
    D. mentoring

11. A stress coping strategy that is especially useful before painful medical procedures such as chemotherapy or a root canal is:
    A. rationalization.
    B. hypnotherapy.
    C. self-talk.
    D. acupuncture.

12. Stress inoculation includes all of the following *except*:
    A. fostering coping skills.
    B. preparing one for pressure through gradual exposure to increasingly higher stress levels.
    C. encouraging confidence about successful outcomes.
    D. building a commitment to personal action and responsibility for an adaptive course of action.

13. People can develop a positive attitude by _____ resources.
  A.   conserving
  B.   developing
  C.   designing
  D.   replacing

14. The immune system responds to which of the following?
  A.   moods
  B.   stress
  C.   basic attitudes about life
  D.   all of the above

15. Today at least _____ of all premature deaths in the U.S. are the result of unhealthy life-styles.
  A.   one-fourth
  B.   one-half
  C.   two-thirds
  D.   three-quarters

16. Illness among the elderly is affected by which of the following?
  A.   loneliness
  B.   loss of a spouse
  C.   isolation
  D.   all of the above

17. Most people with AIDS are _____ years old.
  A.   25-35
  B.   20-40
  C.   20-49
  D.   30-49

18. People seek medical treatment when:
  A.   they think attention will provide a cure.
  B.   the symptoms are visible and persist.
  C.   they are sure the problem is physical.
  D.   all of the above

19. People are *less* likely to comply when:
  A.   advice is for wellness or prevention.
  B.   when family and friends pressure the patient.
  C.   an illness is chronic.
  D.   they have no fears of the possible diagnosis.

20. Pain which is long-lasting and ever-present is:
  A.   chronic pain.
  B.   periodic pain.
  C.   progressive pain.
  D.   acute pain.

21. Biofeedback is often used to:
    A. detect tumors.
    B. manage pain
    C. cure stress.
    D. alter egos.

Congratulations, you have completed Chapter 13. Now, proceed to the Exam Preparation Section in the back of your study guide for your final review, but don't forget to review the Enrichment Glossary for help understanding difficult words.

LANGUAGE ENRICHMENT GLOSSARY

Some students who reviewed the textbook listed the following words as difficult to understand. Use this list, your dictionary, and teachers and friends to learn the meaning of words you do not understand

Page	Term	Explanation	Page	Term	Explanation
449	juggling	trying to do many things at one time	462	vehemently	strongly
450	hassles	small problems	462	whisked home	taken home quickly
450	Herein	this is where	462	reacclimate	readjust
450	appraise	evaluate, figure out	462	assessed	evaluated
450	detrimental	harmful, damaging	463	resilient	able to deal with problems
451	choral	singing, vocal music	463	contingent	depend on
451	dizzy	difficult to stand	463	thereby	they result in
451	hindered	kept from, blocked	463	palatable	agreeable
451	thwarted	to keep from taking place	463	dumps	gets rid of
451	alleviate	let go of	463	raves	says many nice things
452	draftees	non-volunteer soldiers	463	untangling	to understand
452	flee	run away	465	antibiotic	medicine
452	distasteful	something you don't like	465	ward off	push away
452	suffering	hurting	466	optimism	think good thoughts
452	absenteeism	not coming to work	466	pessimistic	to think bad thoughts
453	allocate	spend, use	466	harness	hold together
454	modest	small, slight	466	lethargic	low energy, very tired
454	annoyed	upset, bothered	467	bolster	build up
454	dilation	enlarging	467	half-hearted	only in part
455	susceptibility	ability, vulnerability	467	Wearing rose colored glasses	looking only for the good
455	ailments	diseases, problems	467	corner	place, side
455	dominated	was the focus of	469	affluent	rich, a lot of money
456	traumatized	harmed, hurt	469	dread	do not want it
456	diverted	sent to another place	469	impairs	blocks
456	pale	no pink in the skin	470	shun	ignore, push away
459	burglarized	have home robbed	470	moral stigma	labeled as bad
459	striking	very strong	470	mental acuity	clear, accurate thinking
460	upbeat	feeling happy	470	fades	slowly goes away
460	reactivity	how you react	470	ailing	sick
460	prevalence	frequency	470	complying	going along with
460	striving	trying, attempting	470	severity	how bad it is
460	triggering process	begin to do things	471	adhere to	follow, obey
461	waged war	fought	471	prolong	extend, make longer
461	lapses	loss	471	workshops	short classes
462	alienation	feeling alone and shut out	472	out of hand	out of control
462	vicious cycle	keeps repeating itself	472	twinge	a small feeling
462	alleviate	make it go away	472	peer	someone your own age

CHAPTER 14

Psychological Disorders

Psychology 6th Ed.   Keeping Pace Plus

HEADINGS	PAGE	LESSON	L.O.	LEARNING OBJECTIVES
What Is Abnormal Behavior?	478	1		
A Definition	478		14.1	List and describe five distinguishing characteristics of abnormal behavior and explain why psychologists prefer the term *maladjustment* to *abnormality*.
Perspectives on Abnormality	479		14.2	Distinguish among the medical, psychodynamic, humanistic, behavioral, cognitive, sociocultural, legal, and interactionists models of abnormal behavior.
Diagnosing Maladjustment: The DSM-IV	482		14.3	Outline the goals of DSM-IV, list the five axes of the multiaxial system, and tell what each axis is intended to describe; also discuss some of psychologists' criticism and resistance to fully implementing the DSM-IV.
Anxiety, Somatoform, and Dissociative Disorders	484	2		
Defining Anxiety	484		14.4	Contrast the differing views of anxiety of Horney and Freud.
Generalized Anxiety Disorders	485		14.5	Describe generalized anxiety disorder and list the three areas of impaired functioning.
Phobic Disorders	485		14.6	Define *phobic disorder* and characterize the differences between agoraphobia, social phobia, and specific phobia.

14.7   Discuss the different levels of anxiety disorders in African Americans and white Americans and list the five problems associated with conducting multicultural research.

14.8   Describe obsessive-compulsive disorder and name some typical ritualistic behaviors performed by persons with this disorder.

14.9   Characterize three types of somatoform disorders: somatization disorder, conversion disorder, and hypochondriasis.

14.10   Differentiate between dissociative amnesia and dissociative identity disorder.

14.11   Name several of the sexual disorders known as paraphilias, or sexual deviations, and describe some of the behaviors that characterize these deviations.

14.12   List and describe five specific personality disorders and discuss the contributions of nature and nurture to antisocial personality disorder.

14.13   Explain what is meant by the phrase *child abuse* and cite statistics concerning the rate of child abuse in the United States.

14.14   Define rape give some statistics concerning its rate of occurrence, and characterize the typical rapist.

14.15   Identify the two phases of bipolar disorder, its prevalence in men and women, the typical age of onset, and success rate of treatment.

Chapter 14 Overview

Abnormal behavior today is characterized as atypical, socially unacceptable, distressing, maladaptive, and the result of distorted cognitions. As treatments have changed and different behaviors have become acceptable, this definition has changed. Before treatment plans are implemented, mental health professionals want to know something about the maladaptive behavior. To do this, they have used several models to outline the reasons for the maladjustment and to define treatment plans. The medical-biological model assumes a physical or biological basis for the disorder and therefore focuses on medical interventions. The psychodynamic model suggests that unresolved conflict and anxiety are at the root of the problem, and treatment focuses on resolving the conflicts. The humanistic model assumes that inner psychic forces are at work and focuses on the individual's uniqueness and decision making processes for treatment. The behavioral model asserts that faulty learning or conditioning lead to abnormal behavior and therefore that these behaviors can be unlearned or replaced. The cognitive model maintains that false assumptions and unrealistic coping strategies lead to abnormal behavior, and intervention focuses on changing these thought patterns. The sociocultural model contends that abnormal behavior occurs in the context of the family, community, or society. Finally, the legal model simply attaches guilt or innocence to the behavior based on the law. As can be seen from the number of models, explaining abnormal human behavior with a strict model is difficult; therefore, most psychologists subscribe to an interactionist model drawing from each perspective.

The Diagnostic and Statistical Manual of Mental Disorders, Fourth Edition, is the most recent diagnostic manual. It consists of 16 major categories of maladjustment and more than 200 subcategories. The DSM-IV uses a multiaxial system for precise diagnosis. The goal of the DSM-IV and previous editions is to provide reliable diagnosis and assure that diagnosis is consistent with the research.

Anxiety disorders are discussed first. Generalized anxiety disorders are marked by chronic and persistent levels of anxiety in one of three areas of functioning: motor, autonomic, or vigilance. In phobic disorders irrational fears lead to avoidance behaviors that interfere with normal functioning. Obsessive-compulsive disorders (OCD) involve ritualistic behaviors to decrease anxiety. Somatoform disorders are characterized by real physical symptoms. Somatization, conversion disorder, and hypochondriasis are examples of somatoform disorders. The dissociative disorders include dissociative amnesia and dissociative identity disorder. Each of the dissociative disorders is rare and usually sudden and temporary.

Sexual disorders include sexual deviations such as fetishism, transvestic fetishism, voyeurism, exhibitionism, pedophilia, sadism, and masochism. Most psychologists agree that sexual disorders are learned behaviors and treatment seeks to change the reinforcement system.

Personality disorders are usually long-standing maladaptive behaviors that begin in childhood or adolescence and continue through adulthood. These disorders are divided into three broad categories: odd or eccentric; fearful or anxious; or dramatic, emotional, and erratic. Lefton examines five specific personality disorders: the paranoid personality, the dependent personality, the histrionic personality, the narcissistic personality, and the antisocial personality disorders. The antisocial personality receives a lot of notoriety when criminals are diagnosed as being antisocial. Although child abuse is not classified as a personality disorder, many abusers suffer from other forms of personality disorder. Lefton also describes the violent act of rape as the behavior of a maladjusted person.

Mood disorders which include bipolar disorders and depressive disorders may develop slowly or may be initiated by some traumatic event. Bipolar (manic-depressive) disorder is illustrated by extreme swings from mania to depression. Depressive disorders, including major depressive disorder, do not represent the vacillation between mania and depression. Major depression is thought to be caused by a combination of biological, learning, and cognitive factors. Treatment should incorporate components of each model. When people suffer from major depression, they are at risk for suicide, which accounts for 30,000 deaths per year and is the second leading cause of death among adolescents. A distinction is made between the attempters and the completers, as there are strong gender differences. The causes of suicide are not fully understood, but there is no dearth of attempts to explain why someone would resort to a fatal problem-solving technique.

Schizophrenia is one of the most perplexing, frustrating, and devastating mental disorders. Schizophrenics show significant deficits in cognitive functioning, perception, mood, and overall behavior. They can become delusional, experience hallucinations, display inappropriate affect, become depressed, and appear withdrawn or excited. There appears to be a strong biological basis, and most treatments include pharmaceutical intervention. Some environmental factors have been suggested, but the focus remains on genetic predisposition being the major contributor, according to studies of high-risk children.

SQ3R*plus*

SURVEY THE LESSON: Read learning objectives 14.1 through 14.22 and, in the text, examine the chapter headings, tables, and pictures on pages 478-512 in the text to *form an idea of what you should learn and to set goals for your study time*.

WRITE DOWN QUESTIONS: *While surveying and reading the text, write down questions* about the information being presented. *Write your questions* in the space below or on a separate piece of paper and try to find answers to these questions in the text.

ACTIVELY READ PAGES 478-512: The following exercise is designed to facilitate this process. Complete the following questions as you read, and when you are done, check your answers with those printed in the back of this study guide.

YOUR QUESTIONS:

Matching

Match the following terms or concepts from your textbook with the most appropriate description.

1. _____ affect
2. _____ agoraphobia
3. _____ anxiety
4. _____ bipolar disorders
5. _____ child abuse
6. _____ concordance rate
7. _____ conversion disorders
8. _____ delusions
9. _____ depressive disorders
10. _____ dissociative disorder
11. _____ double bind
12. _____ free floating anxiety
13. _____ hallucinations
14. _____ hypochondriasis
15. _____ model
16. _____ obsessive/compulsive disorder
17. _____ personality disorders
18. _____ phobic disorder
19. _____ prevalence
20. _____ psychotic
21. _____ rape
22. _____ schizophrenia
23. _____ social phobia
24. _____ somatization disorder
25. _____ somatoform disorder
26. _____ vulnerability

a) a prospective approach derived from data used to help describe data in another field
b) the percentage of a population displaying a disorder during any specific period
c) a generalized feeling of fear and apprehension often accompanied by increased physiological arousal
d) persistent anxiety not clearly related to any specific object or situation
e) anxiety disorder characterized by unreasonable fears and avoidance of specific objects or situations
f) anxiety disorder characterized by fear and avoidance of being alone or in public places from which escape might be difficult
g) anxiety disorder characterized by fear of and desire to avoid situations in which the person might be exposed to scrutiny
h) anxiety disorder characterized by persistent and uncontrollable thoughts and irrational beliefs that cause the performance of compulsive rituals
i) disorders characterized by real physical symptoms not under voluntary control and for which no physical cause exists
j) disorder characterized by recurrent and multiple physical complaints over several years

k) disorders characterized by the loss of or alterations in physical functioning for no apparent physiological reason

l) disorder characterized by an inordinate preoccupation with health and illness

m) disorder characterized by sudden but temporary alteration in consciousness, identity, sensory, motive, behavior, or memory

n) disorders characterized by inflexible and long standing maladaptive ways of dealing with the environment

o) physical, emotional, or sexual mistreatment of children

p) forcible sexual assault on an unwilling partner

q) disorders characterized by vacillation between two extremes--mania and depression

r) general category of disorders in which people show extreme and persistent sadness, despair, and loss of interest in usual activities

s) false beliefs inconsistent with reality

t) gross impairment in reality testing that interferes with the ability to meet ordinary demands

u) compelling perceptual experiences without a real, physical stimulus

v) a person's emotional responses

w) disorders characterized by lack of reality testing and by deterioration of social and intellectual functioning with significant changes in thought, mood, perception, and behavior

x) percentage of occasions when two groups of individuals show the same trait

y) situation in which an individual is given two different and inconsistent messages

z) person's diminished ability to deal with demanding life events

True or False

1. Recent data suggests that in any one month about 15% of the population over 18 years old meet the criteria for a mental disorder.   TRUE   FALSE

2. An eclectic approach to abnormal behavior requires an interactionist perspective as to the models of cause.   TRUE   FALSE

3. The goal of the DSM-IV is to support the behavioral model of abnormal disorders by linking diagnoses to observable behavior.   TRUE   FALSE

4. For a diagnosis of generalized anxiety disorder, DSM-IV requires persistent anxiety to be of at least one month's duration.   TRUE   FALSE

5. Fear alone does not distinguish a phobia.   TRUE   FALSE

6. Agoraphobia is generally caused by fear of maternal abandonment as a child.   TRUE   FALSE

7. Obsessive-compulsive disorders are relatively common.   TRUE   FALSE

8. Conversion disorders are more common in women.   TRUE   FALSE

9. The existence of multiple personalities is not completely accepted by all psychologists.   TRUE   FALSE

10.	A narcissistic personality disorder has an extreme sense of self-importance.	TRUE	FALSE
11.	Antisocial personality disorders occur 6 times more often in men than women.	TRUE	FALSE
12.	Many abusive parents were abused by their parents.	TRUE	FALSE
13.	Most rapists are unable to understand cues and messages from women who say no.	TRUE	FALSE
14.	Most psychologists agree that sexual disorders are learned.	TRUE	FALSE
15.	Learned helplessness states that a person learns not to respond because his behavior makes no difference.	TRUE	FALSE
16.	Social and occupational behaviors are impaired by major depression.	TRUE	FALSE
17.	Bipolar disorders do not respond well to drug therapy.	TRUE	FALSE
18.	Stressful life events are generally good predictors of depression.	TRUE	FALSE
19.	Lewinsohn's approach is that depressed people lack the social skills needed to obtain reinforcement.	TRUE	FALSE
20.	The onset of a schizophrenic disorder is usually rapidly apparent.	TRUE	FALSE
21.	Delusions of grandeur preclude delusions of persecution.	TRUE	FALSE
22.	To be diagnosed as having a schizophrenic disorder, a patient must show symptoms for at least six months with onset after age 45.	TRUE	FALSE
23.	Sometimes catatonics use their immobility to maintain control over their environment.	TRUE	FALSE
24.	Freud believed that all people diagnosed as schizophrenic had not yet developed an ego.	TRUE	FALSE
25.	Stressful events will tend to produce schizophrenia in genetically predisposed individuals.	TRUE	FALSE

Fill-in-the-Blanks

1. Behavior characterized as: 1) atypical, 2) socially unacceptable, 3) distressing, or 4) maladaptive and/or the result of distorted cognitions is called _____ _____.

2. A _____ is a perspective that helps scientists discover connections among data.

3. The branch of psychology that is concerned with maladaptive behavior is called _____ _____.

4. The percentage of the population affected by each disorder during a specific period of time is called _____.

5. Feelings of fear and apprehension are known as _____.

6. When one experiences _____ _____ _____, he or she feels persistent anxiety more often than not for 6 months.

7. A persistent feeling of anxiety that is not clearly related to anything in particular is called _____ _____ _____.

8. When one feels excessive, irrational, and unreasonable fear of an object or situation, they may suffer from a _____ _____.

9. The fear of being alone in a large public place without being able to escape is _____.

10. A _____ _____ is an anxiety disorder which is characterized by a fear of being embarrassed or scrutinized in a humiliating way.

11. A phobia in which one is frightened by a specific object or situation is called a _____ phobia.

12. An _____ _____ is an anxiety disorder that is characterized by persistent thoughts and uncontrollable behavior that causes breaks in daily performance.

13. A _____ disorder is a disorder that has real physical symptoms but no known cause.

14. A somatoform disorder that continues for years for which medical attention has been ineffective is called a _____ _____.

15. The loss of physical functioning for no apparent physiological reason in a somatoform disorder is called a _____ _____.

16. A somatoform disorder characterized by a preoccupation with health and illness is called _____.

17. A _____ _____ is a disorder that is characterized by a temporary loss of consciousness.

18. The inability to recall important information is called _____ _____.

19. The disorder of multiple personality is called _____ _____ _____.

20. A _____ _____ is a sexual practice that is directed toward an object, a nonconsenting partner, or an encounter involving humiliation.

21. A person with a _____ _____ has an inability to cope with the environment, thereby causing stress.

22. The personality disorder characterized by egocentrism is called _____ _____ _____.

23. The physical, emotional, or sexual mistreatment of a child is called _____ _____.

24. A forced sexual assault on a unconsenting partner is called _____ .

25. The disorder in which a person's behavior swings between mania and depression is a _____ disorder.

26. _____ _____ are a category of mood disorders in which a person feels persistent sadness, despair, or loss of interest in life.

27. A loss of interest in all of life's usual activities is a symptom of _____ _____ _____ .

28. Depressed people often have false beliefs or _____ .

29. The behavior of giving up or not responding is called _____ _____ .

30. _____ _____ are characterized by a lack of reality testing and by a deterioration of intellectual functioning.

Applications

1. Define each of the following
   A. Phobic disorder _____
   _____

   B. Agoraphobia _____
   _____

   C. Social Phobia _____
   _____

   D. Specific Phobia _____
   _____

2. Define each of the following.
   A. Somatoform Disorder _____
   _____

   B. Somatization Disorder _____
   _____

   C. Conversion Disorder _____
   _____

   D. Dissociative disorders _____
   _____

   E. Dissociative amnesia _____
   _____

   F. Dissociative identity _____
   _____

3. Describe each of the following personality disorders.
   A. Paranoid _____
   _____

   B. Dependent _____
   _____

C.   Histrionic _____

_____

D.   Antisocial _____

4. Define Paraphillias. _____

_____

A.   Fetishism _____

B.   Transvestic Fetishism _____

C.   Voyeurism _____

D.   Exhibitionist _____

E.   Pedophilia _____

F.   Sexual Masochism _____

G.   Sexual Sadism _____

_____

5.   Match the following subcategories of Schizophrenic Disorder with the appropriate description.

Disorganized Type, Paranoid Type, Catatonic Type, Residual Type, Undifferentiated Type

A.   _____ _____: Characterized by stupor in which individuals are mute, negative, and basically unresponsive. Characteristics can also include displays of excited or violent motor activity. Individuals can switch from the *withdrawn* to the *excited* state.

B.   _____ _____: Characterized by frequent incoherence, absence of systematized delusions, and blunted, inappropriate, or silly affect.

C.   _____ _____: Characterized by prominent delusions, hallucinations, incoherence, or grossly disorganized behavior and does not meet the criteria for any other type or meets the criteria for more than one other type.

D.   _____ _____: Characterized by delusions and hallucinations of persecution and/or grandeur; irrational jealousy is sometimes evident.

E.   _____ _____: Characterized by a history of at least one previous episode of schizophrenia with prominent psychotic symptoms, a current state of being in touch with reality, and signs of inappropriate affect, illogical thinking, social withdrawal, or eccentric behavior.

6. Identify the type of disorder that is illustrated in each of the following situations.

Generalized anxiety disorder   Specific phobia
Obsessive-compulsive disorder   Somatization disorder
Agoraphobia   Conversion disorder
Social phobia   Dissociative disorder

A. _____ Clay was outwardly shocked and experienced a severe depression when he heard that his best friend had been murdered. Interestingly, when he was arrested for the murder several weeks later, Clay was again shocked. Although he could not recall where he had been at the time of the murder, he had no awareness of committing a crime and was certain he could not have done such a thing. Weeks later, the psychologist assigned to the case discovered that Clay had a second distinct personality. His other personality was that of a woman and a jealous lover. It was this personality that had killed his friend.

B. _____ Cathy made eighteen appointments with her gynecologist and other physicians in one year. Each time she complained of severe pain in her lower abdomen, but even with extensive medical tests, her physicians were unable to determine a physical cause for her complaints.

C. _____ For the past several months Burt has been feeling upset with himself. There is nothing really happening in his life that should upset him to such an extreme degree, but he cannot seem to get control over his feelings. He finds himself worrying constantly, feels a desperate fear that something terrible is about to happen, and is so worried that he cannot sleep.

D. _____ When she visits her mother, rather than walking the half block to her mother's house, Ginger insists on driving her car from her garage to her mother's garage. She drives to avoid encountering and having to speak to anyone who might be walking down the street. Even the thought of having inescapable eye contact with a stranger makes Ginger suffer severe anxiety.

E. _____ One of Jeff's first calls as a volunteer firefighter involved battling a major forest fire. The situation was life threatening. Consciously Jeff wanted to do all that he could to help, but unconsciously he was so frightened that he needed to escape from the situation. Jeff was evacuated from the area and taken to the hospital because his left leg became paralyzed. The paralysis lasted for weeks but physicians were unable to determine any cause.

F. _____ Glenda has a great fear of closed spaces and will climb dozens of flights of stairs in order to avoid riding an elevator.

G. _____ When Karl was working in the pharmacy, he became convinced that he had to shake liquid prescriptions 600 times before he could safely sell them to his customers. When his boss demanded that he stop shaking the medication and hand it over to the customer, Karl became terribly worried and anxious. Because of his anxiety, Karl was unable to follow his boss's directive and eventually was fired.

H. _____ Julia cannot participate in any dancing or athletic activities because she is afraid that others will evaluate her an uncoordinated "klutz." Her fear is so great that she consistently turns down party and picnic invitations even though she would like to interact with her friends.

SQ3R*plus*

RECITE: When you have finished reading the assigned material in your text and you have completed the exercises in your study guide, turn back to the chapter outline. Read each learning objective and recite out loud everything you can remember in support of each objective.

REVIEW: Check to see if you have answered all the questions you wrote during the *Survey* stage. Complete all sections of your study guide and check your answers for accuracy. If you are having trouble with specific topics ask you instructor for help.

WRITE: Read the learning objective again and then, in your own words, write down everything you can remember about this chapter. Summarize the main points and the concepts introduced in this chapter.

REFLECT: After each study period, take a break and reflect on what you have just studied. Ask yourself how this newly acquired information can be used in the future.

CHAPTER FOURTEEN SELF-TEST

1. The use of the term maladjustment rather than abnormal to describe behavior is important because:
    A. it implies that the behavior is treatable.
    B. it does not carry social stigma.
    C. it is less vague and makes diagnosis easier.
    D. none of the above

2. Practitioners who treat maladjusted behavior by teaching people how to develop new thought processes that instill new values is an example of the _____ model of abnormal behavior.
    A. behavioral
    B. biological
    C. humanistic
    D. cognitive

3. The primary purpose of revising the Diagnostic and Statistical Manual is to:
    A. reduce reliance on Freudian theory.
    B. increase influence of behavior theory.
    C. increase reliability of diagnosis.
    D. all of the above

4. A generalized anxiety disorder may be the result of:
    A. free-floating anxiety, where anxiety is not obviously tied to a specific source.
    B. a specific anxiety producing source that has generalized.
    C. insomnia and other sleep disturbances.
    D. A or B

5. A Specific phobia is:
   A. any phobia of a specific object or situation, along with a compelling desire to avoid it.
   B. the normal everyday hesitations that we all experience.
   C. easy to diagnose but very difficult to modify.
   D. a fear of having to put forth effort or commitment.

6. Which of the following illustrates an obsessive-compulsive disorder?
   A. Mary's desk is always neat because she spends fifteen minutes each day before leaving work putting things in order.
   B. Sam makes a point of checking to see that he has unplugged the coffee pot before going to work because he worries about small appliances causing fires.
   C. Mark loves sports and watches every television sports show he can.
   D. Elida mops the kitchen floor three times before preparing a meal because she fears it is infested with mites, and she cannot feel comfortable exposing food until she has finished her mopping.

7. A disorder that begins before the age of thirty, is characterized by recurrent and multiple physical complaints for several years, and which has not been helped by medical attention, is diagnosed as a:
   A. somatization disorder.
   B. conversion disorder.
   C. anxiety disorder.
   D. dissociative disorder.

8. Somatoform disorders involve:
   A. a feeling of impending doom.
   B. a deliberate and conscious attempt to get attention.
   C. an inability to sleep.
   D. real physical *symptoms* not under voluntary control.

9. The words "smooth operator" and "superficial charm" would be used to describe:
   A. an exhibitionist.
   B. antisocial personality.
   C. histrionic personality.
   D. narcissistic personality.

10. People diagnosed as having antisocial personalities:
    A. constantly blame themselves for their own problems.
    B. do not fear or learn from punishment.
    C. conform only so that they may avoid feelings of shame and guilt.
    D. have insight into how their behavior affects others.

11. Which of the following is NOT a characteristic of a rapist according to current research?
    A. poor
    B. uneducated
    C. middle-aged
    D. high-level of aggressiveness

12. Paraphilia refers to:
    A.   a sexual deviation stemming from psychological causes.
    B.   a gender identity disorder.
    C.   a man who molests children for gratification.
    D.   a person who receives sexual gratification with objects rather than people.

13. A diagnosis of pedophilia implies that the individual:
    A.   achieves sexual gratification through cross-dressing.
    B.   has a homosexual or lesbian orientation.
    C.   feels trapped in the body of the wrong sex.
    D.   derives gratification from children.

14. If a psychologist says that a depressed patient is showing delusions, we can assume that
    the psychologist means the patient:
    A.   is displaying false beliefs.
    B.   will talk excessively.
    C.   is evaluating the consequences of suicide.
    D.   has had a recurrence of a depressive episode.

15. People who exhibit symptoms of major depressive disorder:
    A.   are usually unable to explain why their response is prolonged.
    B.   may need to be hospitalized.
    C.   usually blame their loved ones for their problems.
    D.   are too depressed to consider suicide.

16. The neurotransmitter thought to contribute to major depressions is:
    A.   dopamine.
    B.   phenothiazine.
    C.   norepinephrine.
    D.   lithium carbonate.

17. Which of the following is *not* an explanation offered by learning theorists about the cause
    of major depressions? Depressed people:
    A.   lack prosocial behaviors and are avoided or punished because of the behaviors they
          do emit.
    B.   have negative views and expectations about the human condition.
    C.   experience an imbalance in certain body chemicals when they are involved in stress
          inducing situations.
    D.   feel they have no control over the consequences of their behavior.

18. Schizophrenia affects _____ individuals.
    A.   1 out of 10
    B.   1 out of 100
    C.   1 out of 1,000
    D.   1 out of 10,000

19. A delusion is:
    A. a thought disorder.
    B. a perceptual malfunction that causes a person to hear voices of people who are not present.
    C. a perceptual disorder.
    D. A & C

20. A prominent characteristic in catatonic type schizophrenia is:
    A. the presence of delusions of persecution and grandeur.
    B. extreme overt behavior that involves either excessive motor and verbal activity or a severe decline in motor and verbal activity.
    C. the lack of good personal hygiene.
    D. the absence of systematized delusions.

21. People who show symptoms attributable to a schizophrenic disorder but who remain in touch with reality are diagnosed as _____ type.
    A. disorganized
    B. undifferentiated
    C. residual
    D. B and C

22. Those psychologists who explain the development of schizophrenic disorders as a combination of nature and nurture would suggest that:
    A. if one twin has schizophrenia, the other twin also will develop the disorder.
    B. contentious parents who minimize closeness and warmth will produce schizophrenic offspring.
    C. brain impairment left undiagnosed will produce schizophrenia.
    D. a genetic predisposition triggered by environmental stressors may lead to a behavioral pattern of schizophrenia.

23. Freud's view that schizophrenic patients make judgments based on the pleasure principle of the id is supported by the fact that schizophrenic behavior:
    A. is self-centered and egocentric.
    B. is withdrawn and allows for few social contacts.
    C. is based on the pleasure principle and not the reality principle.
    D. all of the above

24. The assumption that underlies the vulnerability-stress hypothesis is:
    A. when stressors appear, schizophrenia may appear.
    B. the more stressors, the greater the likelihood of schizophrenia.
    C. some people have a low tolerance for stress.
    D. all of the above.

Congratulations, you have completed Chapter 14. Now, proceed to the Exam Preparation Section in the back of your study guide for your final review, but don't forget to review the Enrichment Glossary for help understanding difficult words.

LANGUAGE ENRICHMENT GLOSSARY

Some students who reviewed the textbook listed the following words as difficult to understand. Use this list, your dictionary, and teachers and friends to learn the meaning of words you do not understand

Page	Term	Explanation	Page	Term	Explanation
477	huddling	bend over holding herself	493	humble	does not need much for himself
477	incoherent	did not make sense	493	protectors	people who guard over you
477	passerby	people walking by	493	excessively	overly, too much
477	inaccessibility	can not get to them	493	shame	feeling bad about oneself
478	eccentric	an unusual thing to do	493	humiliation	feeling bad in front of others
478	state of flux	change	493	reckless	not careful
478	unrelenting	keeps going, never give up	494	render	leave
479	atypical	not normal	494	strained	difficult
480	Proponents	people who agree with it	494	child abuse	hurting children
481	irrational	makes no sense	494	prominent	important, high position
481	prevalent	most common	494	aversive control	changing behavior through punishment
481	decade	10 years	494	blaming	tell someone they caused something bad to happen
481	assassinate	kill an important person	494	scapegoating	blaming other
483	ethnicity	race	494	threats	saying they will hurt someone
484	renowned	well-known, famous	494	verbal degradation	saying very hurtful words
484	pervade	go into	495	interactive process	including many factors
485	quirk	slight difference	496	equivocal	same
485	palpitation	heart beating fast	495	assault	physically hurting someone
485	dizziness	feeling faint	495	meticulous	thought out thoroughly
485	apprehension	scared	495	spur-of-the-moment	you suddenly want to do it
485	insomnia	cannot sleep	495	obscures	blocks
485	jumpiness	nervous	495	assailants	someone who attacks
485	restlessness	can not be still	495	"mere"	only or simply
485	pulse rate	heart beat	495	on a whim	do without planning
485	petrified	very scared	496	overwhelmed	feeling like you have too much to do
485	shudders	becomes very afraid	496	boundless energy	make less important
485	derives	gets, obtains	497	trivializes	sad
486	hyperventilation	very fast breathing	498	gloomy	falling apart
486	incapacitating	keeps you from doing what you want	498	disintegrating	feeling sad
487	orderliness	neatness	498	diminished	less
488	fatality	death	499	dejected	rejected
489	dismiss	think something is not important	500	accentuate	make greater
491	eavesdrop	listen to someone else without him knowing	500	prosocial behaviors	doing good things for others
491	vivid	very real	500	universally wretched	thought of as bad everywhere
492	"peeping Toms"	people who secretly watch other people undress	500	harsher	critical, not easy
492	haywire	far away from normal	501	contingent	depends on
493	criticism	judgments that are negative	501	long-standing	for a long time planning against
			503	potential	ability

CHAPTER 15

Approaches to Treatment

Chapter 15 Overview

There are two broad categories of therapy: biologically based therapies and psychotherapy. Biologically based therapies, sometimes called somatic therapies, treat psychological disorders with medical and pharmaceutical strategies. Psychotherapies, on the other hand, treat psychological disorders through psychological techniques. There is no *magic bullet;* treatment of psychological disorders requires proper diagnosis, an understanding of the contributing factors, and the right treatment strategy. Research on the effectiveness of psychotherapy concludes that it is effective with a wide variety of disorders. Is one therapy more effective that another? There are more than 200 types of psychotherapeutic approaches, some focus on individuals, some on families, and some on communities. In determining the effectiveness of a therapeutic approach, one must also consider the dynamics of the individual, the therapist, and the culture from which the client comes. In general, the therapist and client must work together for treatment to be effective.

Psychoanalysis (Freudian therapy) is an insight therapy and attempts to discover relationships between unconscious motives and behavior. Psychoanalysis use techniques such as free association, dream analysis, and interpretation. Additionally, resistance and transference are seen as central processes essential for effective treatment. Some of Freud's followers differ in their beliefs concerning the contributions of the ego. These ego-analysts assume people have voluntary control over their urges and therefore can be helped if they learn to master their egos. Criticisms of psychodynamically based therapies are discussed.

Uniqueness and free will are the focus of humanistic therapies. Roger's client-centered approach is nondirective. The client determines the direction of therapy while the therapist remains somewhat passive. The therapist must be warm and accepting of the client and show unconditional positive regard. Gestalt therapy examines the here-and-now of the client and tries to put him or her in touch with feelings. Hypnosis is used as an adjunct to many therapeutic approaches.

Behavior therapy (behavior modification) sees maladaptive behavior as learned behavior. Behaviorists assume that people are not abnormal, but are having trouble with a life situation, and they can learn to cope with the situation, and the maladaptive behavior will cease. Operant conditioning, counterconditioning, and modeling are three major behavioral techniques. Operant conditioning is useful with a wide variety of behaviors in a variety of settings. Counterconditioning teaches new, more adaptive responses to familiar stimuli. Modeling is effective with new behaviors, fear reduction, and enhancing existing behaviors.

Cognitive therapists offer three basic propositions: (1) thought affects behavior, (2) thoughts can be monitored, and (3) behavior will change through thought change. Rational emotive therapy (RET) emphasizes the role of logical, rational thoughts. Maladaptive behavior is the result of irrational beliefs and faulty thinking. Beck also supports the role of irrational thoughts, and the goal is to develop more positive, realistic perceptions of the self and the world. Meichenbaum believes that people are what they say to themselves and restating (self-instruction) the event will result in more adaptive behaviors. Brief intermittent therapy is discussed as a newer cognitive approach.

Group therapy may follow any approach and involves putting together a group of people, usually with similar problems, to support each other in resolving their problems. Family therapy involves changing family systems by changing some of the family interactions. Lefton reviews the family problem of codependence.

Biologically based therapies may be used in conjunction with other psychological treatment approaches. These approaches may involve medication, hospitalization, and the involvement of physicians. Psychosurgery, electroconvulsive shock, and drug therapy are examples of biologically based psychotherapy. Recent research with depression indicates that psychotherapy is especially effective for treating depression, and that drug therapy is not necessary.

SQ3R*plus*

SURVEY THE LESSON: Read learning objectives 15.1 through 15.25 and, in the text, examine the chapter headings, tables, and pictures on pages 518-550 in the text to *form an idea of what you should learn and to set goals for your study time*.

WRITE DOWN QUESTIONS: *While surveying and reading the text, write down questions* about the information being presented. *Write your questions* in the space below or on a separate piece of paper and try to find answers to these questions in the text.

ACTIVELY READ PAGES 518-550: The following exercise is designed to facilitate this process. Complete the following questions as you read, and when you are done, check your answers with those printed in the back of this study guide.

YOUR QUESTIONS:

Matching

Match the following terms or concepts from your textbook with the most appropriate description.

1. _____ behavior therapy
2. _____ brief therapy
3. _____ client centered therapy
4. _____ counter conditioning
5. _____ ECT
6. _____ encounter group
7. _____ free association
8. _____ Gestalt therapy
9. _____ insight therapy
10. _____ interpretation
11. _____ placebo effect
12. _____ psychoanalysis
13. _____ psychodrama
14. _____ psychotherapy
15. _____ resistance
16. _____ RET
17. _____ symptom substitution
18. _____ time out
19. _____ token economy
20. _____ transference

a) treatment of emotional or behavioral problems through psychological techniques
b) a non-specific therapeutic change that occurs as a result of a person's expectations
c) a lengthy therapy aimed at uncovering conflicts and unconscious impulses through free association, dream analysis, and transference
d) therapy that attempts to discover relationships between unconscious motivations and current abnormal behavior
e) technique in which a person reports his or her thoughts and feelings as they occur
f) technique of providing a context meaning or cause of a specific idea, feeling, or set of behaviors
g) a reluctance to provide the therapist with information, or to help the therapist understand or interpret a situation
h) phenomenon in which a therapist becomes the object of a patient's emotional attitudes
i) therapy that seeks to help people evaluate the world and themselves from their own perspective by providing unconditional positive regard
j) therapy that emphasizes the importance of a person's being aware of current feelings and situations
k) therapy that focuses on changing overt behaviors; also known as behavior modification
l) the appearance of one overt symptom to replace another
m) procedure in which individuals who engage in appropriate behavior receive reinforcement
n) procedure in which a person is physically removed from a desired or reinforcing situation
o) the process in which a person is taught a new more adaptive response to a familiar stimulus
p) therapy that emphasizes the importance of logical rational thought processing

q) approach that focuses on identifying the client's current problem
r) procedure in which members act out their situations, feelings, and roles
s) process by which people meet to learn more about their feelings, behaviors, and interactions
t) brief application of electric shock to treat severe mental illness by causing a generalized seizure

True or False

1.	Placebo effects are very likely to fade away with time.	TRUE	FALSE
2.	Most psychologists are convinced that psychotherapy is effective.	TRUE	FALSE
3.	Insight therapies treat the cause of abnormal behavior rather than the actual behaviors themselves.	TRUE	FALSE
4.	To succeed in psychoanalysis a patient must be willing to change his/her lifestyle.	TRUE	FALSE
5.	Insight therapists try to help people see life from a different perspective.	TRUE	FALSE
6.	Ego-analysts believe that people control how, when, and if their biological urges will be expressed.	TRUE	FALSE
7.	In nondirective therapy the therapist is determining the direction of therapy.	TRUE	FALSE
8.	Behavior therapists believe that maladjustments disappear once people are taught effective ways of coping.	TRUE	FALSE
9.	The goal of behavior therapy is to restructure personality.	TRUE	FALSE
10.	Symptom substitution is a technique used by behavior therapists that allows maladaptive behavior to be replaced (substituted) by adaptive behavior.	TRUE	FALSE
11.	Operant conditioning procedures are used in a variety of settings with a wide range of behaviors.	TRUE	FALSE
12.	The advantage of modeling is that people consistently model worthwhile, desired behaviors.	TRUE	FALSE
13.	Ellis believes that if people have rational thoughts they will also have adaptive behaviors.	TRUE	FALSE
14.	Alcoholics Anonymous makes use of group therapy.	TRUE	FALSE
15.	Codependence is a form of family therapy.	TRUE	FALSE

Fill-in-the-Blanks

1. When an emotional or behavioral problem is treated with a psychological technique, the treatment is called _____.

2. A _____ _____ is when a person thinks that a change happens because of treatment when in fact the nonspecific therapeutic change occurs because of the person's expectations.

3. Freud's lengthy insight analysis therapy is called _____.

4. Psychologists refer to their therapies as _____ _____ therapies.

5. _____ _____ is therapy that attempts to discover relationships between unconscious motivations and behavior.

6. Saying whatever comes to mind is known as _____ _____.

7. _____ _____ allows patients to describe their dreams, interpret them, and connect the interpretations to unconscious motivations.

8. Analyzing the context, meaning, or cause of a specific feeling or set of behaviors is called _____.

9. A patient's unwillingness to cooperate is called _____.

10. When a therapist becomes the object of a patient's emotional attitude, this phenomenon is called _____.

11. The process of _____ _____ is the entire process of interpretation, resistance, and transference.

12. Psychoanalytic practitioners who assume that ego has greater control over behavior than Freud suggested are called _____ _____.

13. Insight therapy that seeks to help people evaluate themselves and the world from their own perspective is called _____ _____.

14. _____ _____ allows the therapist to be permissive and passive, while the client determines the direction of therapy.

15. Therapy that encourages one to be aware of current feelings and situations is called _____ _____.

16. Applying learning principles to human behavior is called _____ _____.

17. _____ _____ is when a patient substitutes one symptom to replace another that has been eliminated by treatment.

18. One type of operant conditioning is _____ _____ in which a person receives tokens for appropriate behavior that they can exchange for desirable items.

19. _____ _____ is the physical removal of a person from sources of reinforcement to decrease undesired behavior.

20. When one is taught to recondition himself/herself to adapt a new response to a familiar stimulus, one is practicing the behavior therapy of _____.

21. _____ _____ teaches people to relax when presented with a stimuli that formerly elicited anxiety.

22. _____ _____ pairs an undesired stimulus with a stimulus that creates negative behavior so the client will adopt worthwhile behavior.

23. Therapy that emphasizes rational, logical thought is called _____ _____.

24. _____ _____ _____ focuses on the client's problem, treats it efficiently, and gets the client back on their own as quickly as possible.

25. _____ _____ is when several people meet to receive psychological help together.

26. Groups in the 1960s and 1970s that came together to discuss feelings, behaviors, and interactions were called _____ _____.

27. When two or more people are committed to working on each other's well being, they are practicing _____ _____.

28. The adjustment problems families face when one family member has a problem is called _____.

29. _____ _____ is a treatment for severe mental illness in which a shock of electricity is applied to the head.

30. Drugs used to relieve mental problems are termed _____ _____.

Applications

1. Match the following therapeutic techniques and patient responses with the appropriate description:

   free association, dream analysis, interpretation, resistance, transference

   A. _____ The therapist becomes the object of the patients emotional attitudes about a person in the patient's life.

   B. _____ Patients are asked to describe in detail, used to gain insight into unconscious motivations.

   C. _____ A common occurrence in psychoanalysis, where the patient shows through some kind of behavior an unwillingness to cooperate with the therapist.

   D. _____ A major part of free association and dream analysis. The analyst tries to discern common threads in the patient's behavior and thoughts.

   E. _____ Patient is asked to report whatever comes to mind. The purpose is to recognize connections and allow the unconscious to express itself uncensored.

2.   Explain how extinction, punishment, and time-out are used to decrease undesired behaviors.

    A.   Extinction _____

        _____

    B.   Punishment _____

        _____

    C.   Time-out _____

        _____

3.   Name the four classes of drugs used to treat mental problems, state their effects, and list what disorder each may be used to treat.

    1.   Drug _____
        Effect _____
        Disorder treated _____
    2.   Drug _____
        Effect _____
        Disorder treated _____
    3.   Drug _____
        Effect _____
        Disorder treated _____
    4.   Drug _____
        Effect _____
        Disorder treated _____

SQ3R*plus*

RECITE: When you have finished reading the assigned material in your text and you have completed the exercises in your study guide, turn back to the chapter outline. Read each learning objective and recite out loud everything you can remember in support of each objective.

REVIEW: Check to see if you have answered all the questions you wrote during the *Survey* stage. Complete all sections of your study guide and check your answers for accuracy. If you are having trouble with specific topics ask you instructor for help.

WRITE: Read the learning objective again and then, in your own words, write down everything you can remember about this chapter. Summarize the main points and the concepts introduced in this chapter.

REFLECT: After each study period, take a break and reflect on what you have just studied. Ask yourself how this newly acquired information can be used in the future.

CHAPTER FIFTEEN SELF-TEST

1. Psychotherapy typically refers to treatment that involves:
   A. the manipulation of diet and physical exercise.
   B. the use of electroconvulsive shock and prescriptions for tranquilizers and antipsychotic drugs.
   C. techniques based upon psychological techniques.
   D. all of the above

2. Clinical psychologists who use therapeutic techniques that are rooted in Freudian theories:
   A. usually have been specifically trained in psychoanalysis.
   B. refer to their therapies as psychodynamic therapy.
   C. focus on the treatment of actual behavior problems rather than on the causes of the behavior problem.
   D. all of the above

3. The purpose of techniques such as dream analysis and free association is to:
   A. encourage the patient to talk about events in the "here and now."
   B. observe the frequency of thoughts that arise from the reality principle.
   C. clarify the patient's point of view concerning his or her behavior.
   D. gain access to thoughts in the unconscious.

4. The therapist is empathic, understanding, and very attentive, and yet the patient continues to respond to him as if he is not going to hear, care about, or accept what she has to say. After many months of therapy, both the therapist and patient realize that as a child the patient was constantly exposed to the attitude "children should be seen and not heard." Her behavior toward the therapist illustrates:
   A. interpretation.
   B. resistance.
   C. transference.
   D. reaction formation.

5. Ego-analysis assumes that:
   A. because it is such a lengthy process, psychoanalysis is not the most appropriate method for treatment.
   B. uprooting unconscious material in the id and superego should be the focus of treatment.
   C. increasing the patient's ego control will result in behavior control.
   D. therapy should focus on developing the part of the personality that responds realistically to the demands of the environment.

6. When looking at the effectiveness of psychotherapy, in general and in psychoanalysis, in particular, research suggests that they are:
   A. always more effective than no therapy at all.
   B. effective within a narrow range of situations.
   C. selectively effective; the effectiveness varies with the disorder being treated.
   D. ineffective.

7. The assumption that people are innately good and effective in dealing with the environment is made by:
   A. Carl Rogers.
   B. Sigmund Freud.
   C. Frederick Perls.
   D. all insight therapists.

8. The primary tenet used in client-centered therapy is:
   A. counterconditioning.
   B. interpretation.
   C. direct suggestion.
   D. empathetic, warm, and accepting therapist, who shows unconditional positive regard.

9. Gestalt therapists focus on the patients':
   A. current understanding and awareness of events in their lives.
   B. traumatic experiences from early childhood.
   C. fears and worries about the future, particularly about death.
   D. self-concept.

10. Gestalt techniques are designed to help patients:
    A. become more aware of their surroundings.
    B. get in touch with their true feelings.
    C. channel internalized anxiety into prosocial and productive behavior.
    D. all of the above

11. Behavior therapists are dissatisfied with insight therapies for all of the following reasons *except*:
    A. They find many of the terms used by insight therapists to be difficult to define and measure.
    B. They disagree with insight therapist's belief that most maladjustments must be changed by the person with the behavior problem.
    C. They feel that the labels used by insight therapists can themselves cause maladaptive behavior.
    D. They question the effectiveness of insight therapies.

12. A behavior therapist knows that treatment has been effective when:
    A. symptom substitution can be noticeably measured.
    B. the client says he has learned new coping skills.
    C. follow-up observations show that the new behavior is still occurring.
    D. all of the above

13. In a token economy the number of tokens a person receives is usually dependent on:
    A. a variable-interval schedule of reinforcement.
    B. the time of day or the day of the week.
    C. the number of privileges the person desires.
    D. the level of difficulty of the behavior emitted.

14. If Robin's parents ignore her every time she makes irritating noises in hopes of getting their attention, behavior therapists would say they are:
    A.   using a technique called extinction.
    B.   neglecting the child's cries for help.
    C.   punishing the child for a socially unacceptable behavior.
    D.   trying to control the child's behavior through counterconditioning.

15. When aversive counterconditioning is used, the patient:
    A.   is forced into a high anxiety state until he or she sees that the problem behavior is unreasonable.
    B.   gradually becomes less emotional.
    C.   learns a new behavior in response to a stimulus that needs to be avoided.
    D.   learns to challenge fear-producing stimuli.

16. Behavior therapists would say a child's fear of dogs diminishes when she observes other children playing with dogs because of _____ therapy.
    A.   operant conditioning
    B.   modeling
    C.   cognitive restructuring
    D.   play

17. Rational-emotive therapists:
    A.   assume that abnormal behavior is caused by faulty and irrational beliefs.
    B.   assume that abnormal behavior is caused by faulty and irrational thinking patterns.
    C.   assume that abnormal behavior causes irrational thoughts.
    D.   A & B

18. From a family therapist's point of view, the patient in family therapy is:
    A.   the family member who is used as a scapegoat.
    B.   the family member or members who do the scapegoating.
    C.   the parents.
    D.   the family structure and organization.

19. The specific composition of a group involved in group therapy usually:
    A.   occurs by chance.
    B.   is the result of one avid member who solicits others to join the group.
    C.   depends on legal and medical referrals.
    D.   is controlled by the therapist's selection of who can gain from and offer to the group's purpose.

20. The primary goal of encounter and sensitivity groups is to:
    A.   have fun.
    B.   self-actualize.
    C.   meet new people.
    D.   get a quick cure.

Congratulations, you have completed Chapter 15. Now, proceed to the Exam Preparation Section in the back of your study guide for your final review, but don't forget to review the Enrichment Glossary for help understanding difficult words.

LANGUAGE ENRICHMENT GLOSSARY

Some students who reviewed the textbook listed the following words as difficult to understand. Use this list, your dictionary, and teachers and friends to learn the meaning of words you do not understand

Page	Term	Explanation	Page	Term	Explanation
518	peer pressure	friends trying to get you to do something	529	representation	speaking for someone
518	coping	dealing with, handling	531	interventions	actions taken in therapy
520	Analyses	figure	532	aggravated	made worse
520	regardless	it doesn't matter which one	532	capabilities	skills and abilities
521	determine	cause, create	533	verbalization	talking
521	effectiveness	how well it works	534	maintaining	keeping the same
522	commonalities	keen	534	personal hygiene	keeping your body clean
522	maturity	how grown up you act	534	extinction	doing away with certain behavior
523	purposefully	well, effectively	535	tantrums	acting out with anger
524	unresolved	never been taken care of	535	misbehaved	did not follow the rules
524	illustrate	create a picture in your mind with words	536	undergoes	experiences
524	diminishing	becoming less and less	536	billowing	large of amount of
524	exploration	looking into something	536	administer	give
525	arrangement	way of doing something	536	imitating	doing the same as
525	censoring	removing, taking away	537	unwomanly	not feminine or lady like
525	unconscious	not awake	539	unrealistic	not real, false
525	current	present, happening now	539	illogical	does not make sense
525	symbolism	when something represents or takes the place of something else	539	adopts	begins to do
525	minimize	make less	540	overgeneralizations	grouping too many ideas together
525	thoroughly	completely	540	insufficient	not enough, too little
526	modified	somewhat changed	540	speech impediments	problems with talking
526	principle	important idea	542	established	set, created
526	unscientific	not proven by the study of experts	542	popularity	liked by many people
526	untestable	not able to be tested	545	plagued	made sick
526	anxiety disorders	problems with fear	545	wrapped up	involved with
527	articulate	able to speak well	546	alleviate	take away
527	components	parts	546	docile	peaceful and cooperative
527	comprehensive	complete	546	routinely	normally, almost always
527	emphasize	give importance to	546	overzealous	to believe in something too much
527	outgrowth	they came from it	547	warranted	deserved, should be given
528	approach	way of doing something	547	tranquilizers	drugs that calm you
528	reinforcement	reward	548	overreliance	depend on too much
528	assumptions	ideas believed true	549	optimistic	positive
529	acclaimed	thought by many to be good	549	warding off	keeping away
			550	altering	changing

CHAPTER 16

Social Psychology

Psychology 6th Ed.		Keeping Pace Plus		
HEADINGS	**PAGE**	**LESSON**	**L.O.**	**LEARNING OBJECTIVES**
Attitudes	556	1	16.1	Characterize the field of social psychology; then describe the three dimensions of an attitude and explain how attitudes and convictions can guide behavior.
Dimensions and Functions of Attitudes	556			
Forming Attitudes	557		16.2	Explain how the three learning theories describe how attitudes are formed.
Predicting Behavior from Attitudes	558		16.3	List and describe the four attitudinal variables that are said to predict behavior.
Changing Attitudes	558		16.4	Identify the four components of attitude change and describe the elaboration-likelihood model used to explain the cognitions of individuals whose attitudes are being changed.
APPLICATIONS: Techniques to Induce Attitude Change	562		16.5	Describe six techniques to induce attitude change.
Searching for Cognitive Consistency	561		16.6	Explain why people seek to maintain consistency between their attitudes and their behavior, and describe how they try to maintain consistency according to cognitive dissonance, self-perception, and reactance theories.
Social Cognition	565	2	16.7	Describe the thought process of social cognition, and its relation to impression formation.

16.13 Explain how social influence arises from conformity and obedience and evaluate the methods, results, and important conclusions of the classic studies by Asch and Milgram.

16.14 Characterize aggression and discuss recent shifts away from biological explanations and toward social and cognitive theories of how stimuli in the environment may elicit aggressive behaviors.

16.15 Discuss the influence television has on aggressive and prosocial behaviors.

16.16 Summarize the findings as to gender differences in aggression and review the current information on domestic assault.

16.17 Review the sociobiological explanations of prosocial behaviors such as altruism.

16.18 Discuss how proximity, physical attractiveness, and shared attitudes contribute to interpersonal attraction and list some common elements found in love relationships.

16.19 Define *social facilitation*; then describe the concepts of social loafing, group polarization, groupthink, and deindividuation and their effects on behavior in groups.

Chapter 16 Overview

Social psychologists are interested in how individuals influence and are influenced by the thoughts, feelings, and behavior of others. Attitudes are expressed through either cognitive, emotional, or behavioral dimensions. Attitudes may be formed early in life through classical conditioning, operant conditioning, or observational learning. Although behavior is not always predicted by attitudes, the presence of four variables increase the likelihood of this occurring. The four variables are attitude strength, vested interest, specificity of the attitude, and accessibility of attitudes.

Changing people's attitudes requires four components: the communicator must project integrity, credibility, and trustworthiness; the communication should be clear, convincing, and logical; the medium usually requires face-to-face communication; and the audience is susceptible to change. Petty and Cacioppo offer the elaboration-likelihood model for attitude change, which consists of two routes for changing attitudes. The central route relies on effective, authoritative, and logical communication, and the peripheral route is more indirect and relies more on the delivery and the communicator. Lefton outlines several techniques to induce attitude change. Attitudes change throughout life primarily because we generally search for cognitive consistency. Cognitive dissonance, self-perception theory, and reactance theory offer explanations of how we strive for these consistencies.

Many personal interactions rely on social cognition which attempts to understand other people's communications to form impressions of them. This process can be verbal or nonverbal, and we tend to create mental shortcuts to facilitate impression formation. A modest amount of eye contact leaves the most lasting impression and conveys a surprising amount of information.

Making an attribution involves inferring someone's motives and intentions by observing their behavior and determining whether that behavior is dispositional or situational. We rely on consensus, consistency, and distinctiveness to determine whether the causes of the behavior are internal or external. The two most common attribution errors are the fundamental attribution error and the actor-observer effect. Errors in self attribution can lead to self-serving bias. The Diversity box provides an interesting look at the self-perception of African-American women.

The next section in the text explores prejudice and how it can be prevented. When prejudice translates into behavior it is called discrimination. Four theories are considered in explaining prejudice: social learning theory, motivational theory, cognitive theory, and personality theory. To reduce and eliminate prejudice we must begin to think of people as individuals, not as members of a group.

The next section of the text looks at social influence and focuses on conformity and obedience. Asch's studies on conformity found that people adopt a group standard when even when they are not pressured to do so. Four variables interact to produce conformity. They are social conformity, attribution, risks of independence, and expediency. Additionally, Milgram's studies of obedience provide understanding into when people will conform and obey.

The old theory that people are innately aggressive is wrong. We now know that aggression can be learned and is usually displayed when we feel unable to control situations. Exposure to violence is also shown to weaken inhibitions, suggest techniques, stimulate aggressive ideas, and reduce a person's overall emotional sensitivity to violence. Men are more physically aggressive, but both men and women use psychological aggression. Lefton concludes this section with a look at domestic violence.

Is prosocial behavior like altruism learned or inherited? Behaviorists contend that prosocial behavior is self-reinforcing and therefore can become a powerful initiator of prosocial behavior. On the other hand, sociobiologists suggest that prosocial behavior is simply an inherited tendency to survive. Latane' and Darley offer an explanation for bystander apathy.

Attraction to others and the formation of relationships depend on several factors. Proximity, physical attractiveness, and shared interests and attitudes contribute to relationships. Friendship is a two-way interaction, and equity plays an important role in friendships. Intimacy and love are discussed as special relationships. The central components of love appear to be intimacy, commitment, and passion.

Our behavior in groups differs somewhat from our independent behaviors. Social facilitation theory asserts that our behavior is affected not only by membership in a group but also by the presence of a group. Social loafing suggests that individual performance and effort decline when working in a group. We make decisions that may be riskier when we are subject to group influence. This is called group polarization. In another light, people in a group seeking concurrence with one another tend to make premature decisions in the interest of getting along, by a method called groupthink. Finally, unrestricted group behavior such as mob violence is examined from the perspective of deindividuation.

SQ3R*plus*

SURVEY THE LESSON: Read learning objectives 16.1 through 16.19 and, in the text, examine the chapter headings, tables, and pictures on pages 556-596 in the text to *form an idea of what you should learn and to set goals for your study time*.

WRITE DOWN QUESTIONS: *While surveying and reading the text, write down questions* about the information being presented. *Write your questions* in the space below or on a separate piece of paper and try to find answers to these questions in the text.

ACTIVELY READ PAGES 556-596: The following exercise is designed to facilitate this process. Complete the following questions as you read, and when you are done, check your answers with those printed in the back of this study guide.

YOUR QUESTIONS:

Matching
Match the following terms or concepts from your textbook with the appropriate description.

1. _____ aggression
2. _____ altruism
3. _____ attitudes
4. _____ attribution
5. _____ cognitive dissonance
6. _____ conformity
7. _____ debriefing
8. _____ deindividuation
9. _____ discrimination
10. _____ elaboration likelihood model
11. _____ equity theory
12. _____ fundamental attribution error
13. _____ group
14. _____ group polarization
15. _____ group think
16. _____ impression information
17. _____ interpersonal attraction
18. _____ intimacy
19. _____ prejudice
20. _____ prosocial behavior
21. _____ reactance
22. _____ self perception theory
23. _____ social cognition
24. _____ social facilitation
25. _____ social loafing
26. _____ social psychology
27. _____ sociobiology
28. _____ Solomon Asch

a) study of how individuals influence and are influenced by the thoughts, feelings, and behaviors of others

b) long lasting patterns of feelings and beliefs about other people, ideas, or objects that are based in our past experiences and shape our future

c) a view of attitude change suggesting there are two routes to attitude change: central and peripheral

d) state of discomfort that results when a discrepancy exists between two or more of a person's beliefs and overt behavior

e) an approach to attitude formation in which people are assumed not to know what their attitudes are until they stop and examine their own behavior

f) the inconsistency that lies between our images of ourselves as free to choose and our realization that someone is trying to force us to choose a particular alternative

g) thought process involved in making sense of events, other people, ourselves, and the world in general through analyzing and interpreting them

h) process by which people use the behavior and appearance of others to infer their internal states and intentions

i) process by which we infer other people's motives and intentions through observing their behavior and deciding whether the causes of the behavior are dispositional or situational

j) assumption that other people's behavior is caused by internal dispositions and the tendency to underestimate situational influences

k) negative evaluation of an entire group of people that is typically based on unfavorable ideas or stereotypes about the group

l) prejudice translated into behavior

m) people going along with the behaviors and attitudes of their peers or family groups

n) procedure to inform participants about the true nature of the experiment after its completion

o) any behavior designed to harm another person or thing

p) behavior that benefits someone else or society, but that generally offers no obvious benefits to the person performing it

q) behaviors that benefit other people for which there is no extrinsic reward

r) idea that we are genetically predisposed toward certain behaviors

s) tendency of one person to evaluate another person in a positive way

t) states that people attempt to maintain stable, consistent interpersonal relationships in which the ratio of both members' contributions are balanced

u) willingness to self-disclose and to express important feelings and information to another person

v) a large number of people working toward a common purpose or a small number of people who are loosely related and have common goals

w) a change in performance that occurs when people believe they are in the presence of other people

x) a decrease in an individual's effort and productivity as a result of working in a group

y) shifts or exaggerations that take place among group members after group discussions

z) tendency of people in a group to seek concurrence with one another when reaching a decision

aa) process by which individuals lose their self-awareness and distinctive personalities in the context of a group

bb) psychologist who found that people are likely to conform to the standard of the group

True or False

1. A person's willingness to act on beliefs is a good predictor of their strength of attitude.   TRUE   FALSE

2. Social psychologists can predict people's behavior by knowing only the strength of an attitude and the accessibility of the attitude.   TRUE   FALSE

3. It is important for a communicator to have perceived power in order to effect attitude changes.   TRUE   FALSE

4. It is best to use a logical argument when trying to change attitudes about an emotional issue.   TRUE   FALSE

5. Mass communication through television and writing has more impact than face-to-face communication.	TRUE	FALSE
6. To maintain a sense of control over our own environment, we choose to engage in the process of attribution.	TRUE	FALSE
7. Prejudice is one of the building blocks of discrimination.	TRUE	FALSE
8. Obedience is sensitive to both authority and peer behavior.	TRUE	FALSE
9. Love is a state, an act, and a series of behaviors.	TRUE	FALSE
10. Eye contact is an important indicator of his or her sexual attraction.	TRUE	FALSE
11. People decide how they will react towards others through the process of attribution.	TRUE	FALSE
12. Job applicants are rated more favorably when they make moderate amounts of eye contact.	TRUE	FALSE
13. By making errors in attribution, people can maintain their sense of their world.	TRUE	FALSE
14. Self-serving biases that boost self-esteem can be adaptive.	TRUE	FALSE
15. Most people are very realistic when it comes to evaluating themselves.	TRUE	FALSE
16. When people feel a conflict exists between their attitudes and their behaviors, they are motivated to change either their attitudes or their behavior.	TRUE	FALSE
17. People change their attitudes because of internal states such as dissonance.	TRUE	FALSE
18. People define their emotional states from situations and physical states.	TRUE	FALSE
19. According to the reactance theory, the extent of reactance is directly correlated to the extent of the restriction of freedom of choice.	TRUE	FALSE
20. It is not helpful to organize your world using mental shortcuts because we are unable to fully assess other's verbal and non verbal communications.	TRUE	FALSE
21. Body language differs according to culture and gender.	TRUE	FALSE
22. People are unable to mask true emotion with a smile.	TRUE	FALSE
23. External attribution is the belief that a person's behavior is caused by outside events.	TRUE	FALSE
24. African-American women were more than twice as likely to characterize themselves as androgynous and less likely than white women to characterize themselves as feminine.	TRUE	FALSE

25. A person's self-perception is affected by parenting, education, and ethnicity.   TRUE   FALSE

26. Social psychologists should take into consideration ethnicity as a variable when considering self-perception.   TRUE   FALSE

27. Sexism is a widely accepted form of discrimination.   TRUE   FALSE

28. It is not possible to be prejudice without being discriminatory.   TRUE   FALSE

29. Tokenism perpetuates discrimination.   TRUE   FALSE

30. According to the social learning theory, a prejudice is passed down from one generation to the next.   TRUE   FALSE

31. In our psychological study of individuals, it is possible to teach people not to hold prejudices and to avoid stereotypes.   TRUE   FALSE

32. The number of people in a group when studying conformity is not a crucial variable to consider.   TRUE   FALSE

33. A person's position in a group is important because it affects the self-esteem of that person, causing him or her to react and behave independently or insecurely.   TRUE   FALSE

34. The nature of public behavior does not affect the way we set up our public voting in this country because each vote is kept confidential.   TRUE   FALSE

35. Attribution is a helpful way to explain why people conform.   TRUE   FALSE

36. Independence is a factor of why people conform.   TRUE   FALSE

37. Expediency does not conserve mental energy.   TRUE   FALSE

38. Often people are willing to comply with the wishes of others if they see the person giving the commands as an authority figure.   TRUE   FALSE

39. Harvard University served as the background authority in the obedience experiment conducted by Milgram.   TRUE   FALSE

40. Volunteers bring with them undetected biases when they participate in experiments.   TRUE   FALSE

41. Researchers have proven a genetic link or defect that predisposes individuals toward aggression.   TRUE   FALSE

42. Children are indiscriminate television watchers; therefore, it serves as a major source of negative imitative behavior.   TRUE   FALSE

43. Children who watch more violent television programs are likely to be more aggressive.   TRUE   FALSE

44. Men are more physically aggressive than women.   TRUE   FALSE

45. Both men and women use psychological aggression such as verbal abuse and angry gestures.   TRUE   FALSE

46. People under 30 are more likely to engage in domestic violence than are older adults.   TRUE   FALSE

47. Edward Wilson argued that humans have genetic material that underlies all behavior.   TRUE   FALSE

48. Bystanders are often misled by the apparent lack of concern shown by others.   TRUE   FALSE

49. Often bystanders experience diffusion of responsibility because they did not cause the situation to happen.   TRUE   FALSE

50. People are more likely to develop a relationship with a person who is within a close proximity.   TRUE   FALSE

51. People will respond more favorably to an attractive person in the business world than to a person who is less attractive.   TRUE   FALSE

52. People have a tendency to be drawn to people who like them and who share similar attitudes and ideas.   TRUE   FALSE

53. Equity plays an important role in a balanced friendship.   TRUE   FALSE

54. Love is a state of being, but also a series of behaviors.   TRUE   FALSE

55. Culture does not affect the kind of love relationships people experience.   TRUE   FALSE

56. A fear of evaluation brings about social facilitation.   TRUE   FALSE

57. Men are more cautious than women in the interpretation of nonverbal messages sent to them by the opposite sex.   TRUE   FALSE

58. You would be more likely to attribute a person's behavior to internal factors if you believe that most people would have behaved the same way in a similar situation.   TRUE   FALSE

Fill-In-The-Blanks

1. There are three traditional concepts of social psychology: _____, _____ _____, and _____ _____.

2. The _____ dimension of an attitude consists of thoughts and beliefs.

3. The _____ dimension of an attitude involves evaluative feelings, such as like and dislike.

4. The _____ _____ of an attitude determines how people actually show their beliefs and evaluative feelings.

5. The three learning theories that help to explain attitude formation are _____ _____, _____ _____, and _____ _____.

6. To be persuasive, a _____ must project integrity, credibility, and trustworthiness.

7. The way in which communication is presented, its _____, influences people's receptiveness to new ideas.

8. Within the elaboration likelihood model, the _____ _____ emphasizes conscious, thoughtful consideration and elaboration of arguments concerning a given issue.

9. The six techniques to induce attitude change are: _____, _____, _____, _____, _____, and _____.

10. According to the _____ _____ theory, people feel compelled to change their attitudes or their behaviors when there is a conflict between them.

11. According to the _____ _____ theory, people define their attitudes when they stop and examine their own behavior.

12. When people feel their freedoms are restricted, they often react negatively and try to reestablish their freedom. This negative influence is known as _____.

13. When we interpret the world around us, make sense of events, and process our feelings about other people, we are completing the thought process of _____ _____.

14. When we try to guess how other people feel and what their intentions are, we are sizing them up by the process of _____ _____.

15. We are able to quickly classify individuals and events that are representative of their members as a group by using the rule of thumb known as _____.

16. _____ is an easy way to bring to mind a category, a type, or an idea to describe an event.

17. Sometimes people have a tendency to believe that others believe exactly what they believe to be true. This rule of thumb is known as _____ _____ _____.

18. The way people present or _____ information helps others to process it and accept it easily.

19. When people use their body, especially their face, to communicate, they are using _____ _____.

20. _____ _____ is an important way to show others your mood and attitude through gestures and various body positions.

21. The eyes convey enormous amounts of information. This kind of information is passed on through _____ _____.

22. Looking at another person's behavior in order to determine his or her intentions and motives is called _____.

23. The causes of one's behavior can be _____(internal) or _____ (external).

24. In order to determine whether a person's behavior is caused by internal or external causes, one can base their decision on three criteria: _____, _____, and _____.

25. When we attribute the behavior of others to dispositional causes, and we attribute our own behavior to situation causes, we call this tendency the _____ effect.

26. When a person takes credit for their positive behaviors, but blames their negative traits on outside factors, this person is illustrating the _____ _____.

27. Often, people need to develop their _____ _____, so they develop a self-serving bias.

28. According to Binion's study of African American women and white women, African American women were more than twice as likely to characterize themselves as _____.

29. A negative evaluation of an entire group of people based on stereotypes or unfavorable ideas is known as _____.

30. When a person takes his or her prejudice of a group and decides to act on those negative feelings, it is known as _____.

31. A _____ _____ is a person who holds a prejudice, but does not act out or discriminate based on his or her behavior.

32. An attempt to over compensate and be overly kind to a group that is typically discriminated against is called _____ _____.

33. There are four theories to explain prejudice: _____ _____ _____, _____ _____, _____ _____, and _____ _____.

34. According to the _____ _____, people learn to develop negative feelings and prejudices toward their competitors.

35. An attempt to make sense of the world by grouping people according to their origin is called the _____ _____.

36. Personality psychologists who study people with prejudices often find that people have " _____ _____ _____ ."

37. The ability for another person to alter your attitude or behavior is known as _____ _____.

38. Peer groups and family groups often influence people socially to _____.

39. The _____ _____ _____ provided when making a decision is an important conformity variable.

40. People are more likely to conform to a group if the _____ _____ of the group is perceived to be high.

41. People feel stigmatized in a group when they are wrong, different from the rest of the group, or out of line. Therefore, the _____ _____ approach attempts to explain this phenomenon of not wanting to be wrong, thereby forcing people to conform.

42. The _____ _____ of even one or two people within a group often help to sway the opinion of the group.

43. People who are _____ comply or go along with the orders of another person or group.

44. It is important to _____ participants in an experiment, informing them of the hypotheses, methods, and expected outcomes of the experiment.

45. Often people feel they are not able to control situations in their lives, thereby displaying _____ or harmful behavioral patterns.

46. There are two explanations of domestic violence: _____ _____ and _____ _____.

47. Although not supported by data, male assaults on their female partners are often attributed to _____ _____.

48. One approach, the _____ _____ _____, views people as growing and developing with a social context.

49. Behavior that is described as being helpful to the community, but not necessarily beneficial to the person doing the act, is _____ _____.

50. When a person behaves in a way that is beneficial to others, without expecting a reward, this person is described as being _____.

51. Day to day behaviors being determined by genetic material is known as the theory of _____.

52. There are many horrible stories of people who as bystanders are not willing to help in a situation. That unwillingness to help is known as _____ _____.

53. A special relationship in which two people equally contribute is called a _____.

54. Within the realm of friendship, the _____ theory suggests that people attempt to maintain a balanced relationship of equal contributions from each person.

55. A willingness to open oneself to another person by disclosing and expressing important feelings is known as _____.

56. According to Sternberg, love has three components: _____, _____, and _____ _____.

57. According to David McClelland, there are two sources that exist for understanding love: _____ _____ _____ and _____ _____.

58. A group of people, whether large or small, working together for a common goal or because of common ties is referred to as a _____.

59. A change in performance that comes from the idea of being in the presence of other people is known as _____ _____.

60. If individual performance decreases because of relying on the group, this decrease in productivity is known as _____ _____.

61. Often there are shifts within a group which polarize or force people to choose sides. This is known as _____ _____.

62. In order to develop the best solution to a problem, often members of a group will seek validation or concurrence with one another. This concept of _____ affects the decisions made within the group.

63. Because groups are made up of several people, individuals often loose their sense of self-awareness. This lose of distinctive personality within a group is known as _____.

Applications

1. Describe the following techniques.
   A. Foot in the door effect _____
   _____

   B. Door in the face technique _____
   _____

   C. Ask and you shall receive _____
   _____

   D. Low balling _____
   _____

   E. Modeling _____
   _____

   F. Incentive _____
   _____

2. In the table below, Kelly's criteria for determining whether the causes of a behavior are due to internal characteristics of an individual or to external factors is presented. Kelly's criteria for internal vs. external attribution are based on consensus, consistency, and distinctiveness.

INTERNAL

1. _____ _____:_____
others act the same way.
2. _____ _____: Person
acts the same way in other _____
situations.
3. _____ _____:
Person acts in the same way on other
occasions.

EXTERNAL

1. _____ _____:
_____ act the _____ way.
2. _____ _____:
Person acts the same way in other
_____ situations.
3. _____ _____:
Person acts differently in other situations.

SQ3R*plus*

RECITE: When you have finished reading the assigned material in your text and you have completed the exercises in your study guide, turn back to the chapter outline. Read each learning objective and recite out loud everything you can remember in support of each objective.

REVIEW: Check to see if you have answered all the questions you wrote during the *Survey* stage. Complete all sections of your study guide and check your answers for accuracy. If you are having trouble with specific topics ask you instructor for help.

WRITE: Read the learning objective again and then, in your own words, write down everything you can remember about this chapter. Summarize the main points and the concepts introduced in this chapter.

REFLECT: After each study period, take a break and reflect on what you have just studied. Ask yourself how this newly acquired information can be used in the future.

CHAPTER SIXTEEN SELF-TEST

1. Which of the following is *not* of major concern to social psychology?
    A. How and why people establish cultures.
    B. Why people sometimes use the standards of others to measure their own feelings of self-worth.
    C. How one adult can influence the behavior of another adult.
    D. How to minimize or maximize the factors that affect behavior that are present when two or more people are together.

2. Attitudes:
   A. may or may not be displayed in overt, public behavior.
   B. when combined with one's perception of the environment, determine behavior.
   C. are determined by experience.
   D. all of the above

3. Attitude formation that occurs as a result of classical conditioning occurs:
   A. because a person is reinforced for having particular belief.
   B. with such little effort, it frequently goes unnoticed.
   C. when someone watches the behavior of another whom they hold in high esteem and then imitates it.
   D. if the person has the opportunity to practice the attitude with strangers.

4. Which of the following does *not* tend to contribute to a speaker's effectiveness in promoting attitude change?
   A. The speaker is attractive.
   B. The audience believes the speaker is powerful and prestigious.
   C. The speaker is able to surprise the audience with new and unexpected ideas.
   D. The speaker uses a layman's vocabulary when speaking to people not closely related to his or her own field.

5. According to Petty and Cacioppo, peripheral processes involved in attitude change:
   A. lead to rational decisions.
   B. allow a person to attend to how logical a communication actually is.
   C. have an indirect, but powerful effect.
   D. all of the above

6. According to research, when people experience discomfort because there is a discrepancy between their held beliefs and their actual behaviors they:
   A. experience dissonance.
   B. change the belief or the behavior to regain consistency.
   C. engage in activities that help reduce the dissonance without changing the beliefs or behaviors that cause the inconsistency.
   D. all of the above are supported by research

7. According to the self-perception view put forth by Bem and Schachter, the situations individuals find themselves in lead to:
   A. the experience of dissonance and ultimately decisions that will influence their future behavior.
   B. inferences concerning their emotions, attitudes, and the causes of their behaviors.
   C. paying attention to the reinforcements and punishments associated with change.
   D. establishing friendships that allow them to maintain a consistency in their belief systems.

8. If Barb's mother tells Barb that she has to go to college, and Barb responds by moving out of the house, taking a full-time job in a restaurant, and spending her free time doing aerobic exercises, *reactance theory* would suggest that Barb:
    A. has a rebellious attitude.
    B. needed to maintain consistency with her beliefs and behaviors.
    C. behaved as she did in order to maintain a sense of autonomy.
    D. was not open to parental advice or suggestions.

9. The effects of gender on nonverbal communication are apparent in the observation that:
    A. men are better than women at interpreting facial expressions.
    B. women are more cautious than men in interpreting nonverbal messages from the opposite sex.
    C. men are more likely than women to send nonverbal facial messages.
    D. all of the above

10. When psychologists examine the internal motivations for a person's behavior they:
    A. focus on behavioral genetics.
    B. must look at behaviors that have only one cause.
    C. decide whether to attribute the behavior to internal or external causes.
    D. ask the person to give an evaluation of his or her own behavior.

11. According to Kelly, we attribute behavior to *internal* causes when we evaluate a behavior and situation and find:
    A. low consensus, consistency, and distinctiveness.
    B. high consensus, consistency, and distinctiveness.
    C. low consensus and distinctiveness, with high consistency.
    D. high consensus and distinctiveness, with low consistency.

12. When Carolyn walked in the door, home late from work, Steve lost his temper. According to attribution studies:
    A. Steve will explain his behavior by reference to some situational factor such as his concern that the company would show up before his wife did.
    B. Carolyn will explain his behavior by reference to some internal characteristic such as Steve is too dependent.
    C. Steve and Carolyn will realize that the world is not always a just world.
    D. A and B

13. People make errors when they attribute motives to someone's behavior because acknowledging the truth threatens their:
    A. belief that people get what they deserve.
    B. sense of control.
    C. self-esteem.
    D. all of the above

14. Solomon Asch's conformity/line discrimination experiment:
    A. made use of collaborators who actively pressured a naive subject.
    B. involved a fairly difficult task of distinguishing between two lines of almost equal length.
    C. involved deception.
    D. all of the above

15. In Asch's experiment the naive subject gave a correct answer concerning the length of the lines:
    A. about fifty percent of the time.
    B. even when the ten collaborators gave the incorrect answer.
    C. when one out of ten collaborators gave the correct answer.
    D. none of the above

16. Dissenting opinions within a group:
    A. generally strengthen the group's influence upon individuals.
    B. can have a substantial influence on the decision making of a large group even if only two people are dissenting.
    C. become influential only when a majority of the members agree with the opposition.
    D. do not influence the group unless they come from a consistent minority that holds power and is considered highly competent.

17. Which of the following does NOT provide an explanation for why people conform?
    A. Through attribution processes an individual is able to identify causes for the behavior of people in the group.
    B. People want to do whatever is generally accepted as "right."
    C. The risks of being independent are high.
    D. People want to avoid the stigma of being different or deviant.

18. Social learning theories of aggression suggest that nonaggressive behaviors can occur:
    A. when people exercise cognitive control over their actions.
    B. if people observe others being punished for aggressive acts.
    C. if people are provided with plenty of nonaggressive models to imitate.
    D. B and C

19. Which of the following statements concerning research investigating television's relationship to aggressive behavior is *false*?
    A. People who observe TV violence are more likely to intervene and help victims of real violence.
    B. Most studies show that TV violence increases the incidence of real-life violence.
    C. Aggressive children tend to watch more television than nonaggressive children.
    D. Television can be beneficial in establishing positive social and personal behaviors.

20. According to scientific evidence, you are most likely to be attracted to:
    A. your neighbors and work associates.
    B. people you have met only once.
    C. people you have met and have difficulty visiting often.
    D. people who have ideas very different from your own.

21. When it comes to liking someone, people tend to:
    A. keep a distance until they have evidence about the person they like.
    B. assume that the person they like is like them and likes them.
    C. almost always choose people who have personalities very similar to their own.
    D. seek friends who are less attractive and socially skilled than they perceive themselves to be.

22. Physical attractiveness seems to play a role in attraction:
    A.   only in your youth-oriented culture.
    B.   in the Western world, but not in primitive and agricultural societies.
    C.   at least at first.
    D.   to men in all cultures, but not to women in all cultures.

23. People are motivated to feel attracted to those they believe share similar attitudes in order to:
    A.   avoid cognitive dissonance.
    B.   guarantee equity.
    C.   have something to talk about.
    D.   experience a sense of love.

24. Shared attitudes lead to attraction and liking as long as the attitudes are:
    A.   genuine.
    B.   ingratiating.
    C.   for the sole purpose of gain.
    D.   all of the above

Congratulations, you have completed Chapter 16. Now, proceed to the Exam Preparation Section in the back of your study guide for your final review, but don't forget to review the Enrichment Glossary for help understanding difficult words.

LANGUAGE ENRICHMENT GLOSSARY

Some students who reviewed the textbook listed the following words as difficult to understand. Use this list, your dictionary, and teachers and friends to learn the meaning of words you do not understand

Page	Term	Explanation	Page	Term	Explanation
556	nonverbal messages	communication without talking	575	collaborating	working together
556	array	many different types	576	deviant	different
557	Shroud of Turin	believed by many to be the burial cloth of Jesus Christ	576	stigma	being thought of in a certain way
558	socializing	getting them to behave	577	sort out	analyze, interpret
558	mimic	copy, do the same	576	incinerator	a container that burns trash
558	situations	way things are around you	576	relevant	important
559	integrity	having good values	577	compliance	agrees with
560	susceptible	open	577	draw lots	take an object to make a choice by chance
560	Southern	area in lower part of U.S.	579	debriefing	discussing the experiment after it is over
560	instilling	firmly putting an idea in your mind	579	gossip	repeating personal information to others
560	peripheral	additional, surroundings	579	rumors	information from unknown sources
562	low stakes	not much will happen as a result of making decision	581	combativeness	with anger and fighting
564	infer	conclude	582	exploits	takes advantage of
564	coercion	force	581	unsympathetic	not care
565	pragmatic	practical, logical	583	socioeconomic status	level in society based upon how much money you make
565	shortcuts	a quick way of doing things	583	domestic	in the home
565	grimace	make an angry face	584	bystander	someone nearby
567	deceitful	involved with lying	584	discernible	understandable difference
567	amputations	cutting off body parts	585	darts	quickly runs
567	genuinely	real	585	deed	action
567	multifaceted	having to do with many categories of behavior	585	apathetically	they do not care
567	intentions	what they want to do	586	embarrassment	feeling a little foolish
568	straightforward	direct	587	proximity	how close you are to a person
570	venture	go, explore	587	ascribe	give or attribute
570	reckless	not careful, dangerous	588	predicator	the telling of the future
571	androgynous	has male and female traits	588	qualifications	your skills and abilities
571	enormous diversity	great differences	588	candidate	someone running for office
586	masculinity	acting like a man	588	persuasive	able to talk into something
570	mountain folk	people living in mountain	588	politicians	people who hold elected government positions
572	bigots	people who hate other races	588	minimize	make less
572	token gesture	comment with little value	588	slogan	an easy to remember phrase used to advertise
573	shortcuts	quick way to do something	588	defeated	won victory over
573	roots	beginning	588	dissonance	a lack of agreement
573	prayed	worship, talk to God	588	equals	at the same level
573	worthwhile	good, valuable	589	essentials	the most important parts
574	instill	to place, to create	589	frequently	often
574	celebrity	famous person	589	differ	are not the same as
574	slaughtered	killing many people	589	Apologies	saying you are sorry
575	experimenter	person doing experiment	589	self-disclose	to share important personal information
574	hazing	initiate, mistreat	589	moonlit walks	walking at night
574	mob	crowd of people acting badly	590	despair	feeling hopeless
575	refraining	holding back	591	discern	consider or decide on
575	naive participant	person who seems to believe everything	591	tackle	take on and understand
575	exerted	puts forth, slow	596	reestablishing	create or begin again

CHAPTER 17

Applied Psychology

Efficiency	620		17.6	Describe how human factors psychologists are involved in helping people and machines work together more efficiently.
Safety	621		17.7	Discuss the three categories of designs used to enhance the safety of the work environment.
Psychology and the Law	622	**3**	17.8	Describe the multiple roles that psychologists play in the legal system, as researchers, policy or program evaluators, advocates, and expert witnesses.
Environmental Psychology	623	**4**	17.9	Describe the research interests of environmental psychologists.
Environmental Variables	624		17.10	Discuss how temperature, noise, and environmental toxins act as environmental stressors and have the potential to affect performance.
Crowding	625		17.11	Characterize the conditions that contribute to the psychological state of crowding and discuss the variations in needs for personal space.
Preserving the Environment	629		17.12	Discuss the findings concerning how people can be encouraged to conserve natural resources and protect the environment.
Community Psychology	630	**5**	17.13	Discuss the general aims of community psychology, describe the key elements involved in efforts to bring about social change, and identify the three levels of prevention programs utilized by community psychologists.

Chapter 17 Overview

This chapter examines a multitude of fields in which psychology is applied to modern life. Industrial/Organizational psychology is divide into four broad areas: human resources, motivating job performance, job satisfaction, and leadership. Human resource psychologists work in the personnel area to select, train, promote, evaluate performance and determine benefits of employees.

Motivating people on the job requires a unique approach to understanding human behavior. Humans have desires more complex than basic needs. The goal-setting theory states that people given specific, clear, attainable goals will perform better. Expectancy theory asserts that goal-directed behavior is determined by expectancy of outcomes. Vroom adds that employees must first have willingness and ability. Others state that role perceptions play a role in job motivation. Equity theory states that if people are treated fairly compared to coworkers then they will be satisfied and perform well. Three basic approaches exist to managing motivation. The paternalistic approach is to take care of employees' needs in a fatherly fashion. The behavioral approach assumes people will work if they are rewarded. The participatory approach empowers people to become part of the organization.

Job satisfaction differs from job motivation. Motivation is the internal drive, and satisfaction is an attitude that may not be reflected in job behavior. Although factors that contribute to job satisfaction are numerous, they cluster into five general categories: the work itself, the rewards, supervision, coworker support, and the work setting. Leadership is an important contributor to job satisfaction and motivation. Two major theories that describe leadership effectiveness are the Fiedler contingency model and Vroom's leadership model. A description of a transformational leader is also provided.

Human factors psychologists are concerned with the relationship between humans and machines. Their goals are to provide efficiency and safety on the job.

Psychologists are providing assistance in the legal arena in a variety of ways. They are being employed as researchers, policy or program evaluators, advocates, and expert witnesses. Although psychologists and lawyers do not always agree, the psychologist is being recognized as a key player in both the private and public sector.

Environmental psychologists are interested in how the physical setting affects human behavior. Variables such as temperature, noise, toxins, and crowding are discussed. In the discussion on crowding, personal space, culture, and territoriality are examined. Lefton examines the role of environmental psychology in changing people's behaviors toward preservation of the environment.

Community psychology provides primary, secondary, and tertiary prevention programs to entire communities. Educational psychology combines instructional techniques and classroom management principles into working systems models for school settings. The relatively new field of sport psychology applies psychological principles such as motivation, an understanding of arousal and anxiety, and relaxation training to helping athletes maximize performance.

SQ3R*plus*

SURVEY THE LESSON: Read learning objectives 17.1 through 17.18 and, in the text, examine the chapter headings, tables, and pictures on pages 602-637 in the text to *form an idea of what you should learn and to set goals for your study time.*

WRITE DOWN QUESTIONS: *While surveying and reading the text, write down questions* about the information being presented. *Write your questions* in the space below or on a separate piece of paper and try to find answers to these questions in the text.

ACTIVELY READ PAGES 602-637: The following exercise is designed to facilitate this process. Complete the following questions as you read, and when you are done, check your answers with those printed in the back of this study guide.

YOUR QUESTIONS:

Matching
Match the following terms or concepts from your textbook with the appropriate description.

1. _____ anxiety
2. _____ Applied psychology
3. _____ arousal
4. _____ cognitive interventions
5. _____ Community psychology
6. _____ crowding
7. _____ developmental change
8. _____ Educational psychology
9. _____ empowerment
10. _____ Environmental psychology
11. _____ equity theory
12. _____ ergonomics
13. _____ expectancy
14. _____ expectancy theories
15. _____ Fred Fiedler
16. _____ functional job analyses
17. _____ goal setting theory
18. _____ human factors
19. _____ hypnosis
20. _____ Industrial/Organizational psychology
21. _____ instrumentality
22. _____ intrinsically motivated behavior
23. _____ job analyses
24. _____ job satisfaction
25. _____ leaders

26. _____ lost letter technique
27. _____ meditation
28. _____ mental imagery
29. _____ Occupational Safety and Health Act (OSHA)
30. _____ perceptual research
31. _____ performance appraisal
32. _____ personal space
33. _____ policy or program evaluators
34. _____ primary prevention
35. _____ privacy
36. _____ progressive relaxation
37. _____ secondary prevention
38. _____ selection procedures
39. _____ social density
40. _____ spatial density
41. _____ Sport psychology
42. _____ strategic planning
43. _____ stressor
44. _____ territorial behavior
45. _____ tertiary prevention
46. _____ training
47. _____ transformational leaders
48. _____ valence
49. _____ Victor Vroom

a. branch of psychology that uses the principles of psychology to help solve practical problems of every day living

b. study of how individual behavior is affected by the work environment, by co-workers, and by organizational practices

c. high level planning which emanates from the top of an organization

d. careful descriptions of the various tasks and activities that are required of employees

e. describes each type of work and the level of complexity of each job

f. predict the success of job candidates

g. process by which organizations' employees systematically teach skills to improve their job performance

h. process by which a supervisor periodically evaluates the job of a subordinate

I. behavior engaged in strictly because it brings pleasure

j. asserts that setting specific, clear, attainable goals for a given task will lead to better performance

k. suggest a worker's effort and desire to maintain goal directed behavior is determined by expectations regarding the outcomes of work

l. suggested that job performance is determined by both motivation and ability

m. belief that hard work will lead to improved performance

n. a worker's belief that a good performance will be rewarded

o. value placed on rewards that are offered

p. asserts that what people bring to work a situation should be balanced by what they receive compared with other workers

q. a person's attitude about the work and workplace

r. persuade and motivate employees

s. developed a contingency model of leadership

t. provide inspiration, intellectual stimulation, and individual care to followers

u. study of how physical settings affect human behavior

v. a stimulus that affects an organism in an injurious way

w. the perception that your space is too limited

x. number of people in a given space

y. amount of space allocated to a fixed number of people

z. unmailed letters are purposely dropped in dormitory corridors

aa. area of invisible boundary around an individual that the person considers private

bb. result of the process of controlling boundaries between people so access is limited

cc. behavior involved in establishing, maintaining, personalizing, and defending a delineated space

dd. the study of the relationship of human beings to machines and to workplaces

ee. the study of the fit between people, their anatomy or physiology, the demands of a particular task or piece of equipment, and the environment in which the task occurs

ff. established standards for health and safety in the workplace

gg. focuses on light levels that are appropriate for reading computer screens

hh. psychologists who help governments and other institutions determine whether policies, agencies, or programs have actually worked

ii. a branch of psychology that seeks to reach out to society to provide services

jj. helping people in the community to enhance their own existing skills and to develop new skills

kk. reducing the risk of new cases of disorder or counteracting harmful circumstances before they lead to maladjustment

ll. involves catching problems and identifying new cases in the early stage

mm. focuses on the treatment of full blown psychological problems

nn. systematic application of psychological principles in sports

oo. focus on how and when individuals develop physically, socially, and intellectually

pp. the systematic application of psychological principles in sports

qq. a performance enhancer

rr. feelings of fear, stress, or apprehension

ss. a technique used by athletes to slowly relax as time passes

tt. the state of encouraging critical acceptance of suggestions

uu. the focus of energy and attention on a single though or idea

vv. used as a form of relaxation to psyche up or practice mentally what will happen

ww. a form of relaxation by changing the thought processes

True or False

1. Applied psychologists help people learn to manage their behavior. TRUE FALSE

2. Industrial/Occupational psychologists must consider culture differences when analyzing operational problems. TRUE FALSE

3. Human resources psychology focuses on finding people to fill positions, but ends after the personnel has been hired. TRUE FALSE

4. Motivation of job performance is an area that focuses on workers' rewards, successes, and influence. TRUE FALSE

5. Leadership is key when discussing influence on others attempting to attain a goal. TRUE FALSE

6. Personnel psychologists must consider the internal and external conditions of an organization. TRUE FALSE

7. Job analysis examines what gets done and how it gets done. TRUE FALSE

8. Functional job analysis is difficult to study because it is not concrete, observable, or measurable. TRUE FALSE

9. Employers use analysis instruments to ensure the appropriateness of jobs and that they have the correct scope or direction. TRUE FALSE

10. Industrial/organizational psychologists have the tasks of creating jobs that are motivating. TRUE FALSE

11. Industrial/organizational psychologists help frustrated individuals point out biases, discrimination, and unfair practices by employers.　　TRUE　　FALSE

12. Tests that measure personality and interests can be misleading when determining job placement.　　TRUE　　FALSE

13. Positive information always outweighs negative information in sizing up a candidate.　　TRUE　　FALSE

14. It is more difficult to find constructive mentors to train women in the workplace.　　TRUE　　FALSE

15. Training is an ongoing process which helps identify strengths, weaknesses, obstacles, and opportunities.　　TRUE　　FALSE

16. Relationships should not and do not enter into one's appraisal of performance.　　TRUE　　FALSE

17. A rater, in hope of avoiding confrontation, may rate an employee leniently, giving them higher ratings than they deserve.　　TRUE　　FALSE

18. Central ratings surface when the rater feels it is insensitive and unfair to rate people as "high" or "low."　　TRUE　　FALSE

19. The halo effect is difficult to remove because once a person is labeled as doing well in one area, this opinion is carried to other areas.　　TRUE　　FALSE

20. Cognitive processes are not crucial in performance appraisals.　　TRUE　　FALSE

21. The diaries in the DeNisi, Robbins, and Cafferty experiment proved to be useful tools.　　TRUE　　FALSE

22. People are motivated by different culturally determined values such as money or praise.　　TRUE　　FALSE

23. Money is the single most motivating factor to increase productivity.　　TRUE　　FALSE

24. Industrial/organizational psychologists help employers find ways to motivate employees.　　TRUE　　FALSE

25. Goals are most successful when they are challenging, yet attainable.　　TRUE　　FALSE

26. Motivation is not determined by what people expect to experience in performing a task.　　TRUE　　FALSE

27. According to Porter and Lawler, performance is also determined by role perceptions.　　TRUE　　FALSE

28. The recipe for success in setting goals is to have high challenges accompanied by high expectations.	TRUE	FALSE
29. Most people feel they are above average.	TRUE	FALSE
30. The paternalistic approach views the company as a father figure, taking care of its employees' needs.	TRUE	FALSE
31. According to the goal setting and expectancy theories, behavior approaches do not work.	TRUE	FALSE
32. Participation by all workers does not increase the levels of motivation, it only creates confusion.	TRUE	FALSE
33. Job motivation is shown in behavior; job satisfaction may not be shown in behavior.	TRUE	FALSE
34. All leaders are assertive.	TRUE	FALSE
35. Women are more employee oriented; men are more task oriented.	TRUE	FALSE
36. Employee oriented leaders have the best overall effect on motivating and satisfying employees.	TRUE	FALSE
37. Good leaders stick to their original plans and do not vary their plans according to the situation.	TRUE	FALSE
38. Workers who work under a boss-centered leadership hierarchy have little choice in decisions.	TRUE	FALSE
39. Both men and women are capable of being effective, transformational leaders.	TRUE	FALSE
40. Environmental psychologists make connections between people and their interactions with the environment.	TRUE	FALSE
41. Temperature affects academic performance.	TRUE	FALSE
42. The number of wife beatings decreases when the temperature drops.	TRUE	FALSE
43. Noise overstimulates people.	TRUE	FALSE
44. Respiratory problems caused by toxins can decrease work performance.	TRUE	FALSE
45. Crowding is a psychological state.	TRUE	FALSE
46. Social density is correlated to the perception of crowding.	TRUE	FALSE
47. Students who live in high density dorms are less likely to mail a letter they find in the hallway.	TRUE	FALSE
48. Personal space, according to Hall, is a form of communication.	TRUE	FALSE

49. People are able to maintain a sense of privacy by changing their environment.   TRUE   FALSE

50. In order to maintain privacy, people perform territorial behaviors.   TRUE   FALSE

51. Changing tax laws does not encourage people to conserve energy.   TRUE   FALSE

52. Human factors research can help reduce accidents.   TRUE   FALSE

53. Failsafe designs help reduce the consequences of an accident.   TRUE   FALSE

54. Environmental research proves that low level noises improve safety.   TRUE   FALSE

55. As researchers, psychologists help determine why people behave the way they do in ways that are not acceptable to society.   TRUE   FALSE

56. Lawyers always like having psychologists as expert witnesses in the courtroom.   TRUE   FALSE

57. Since psychologists have extended their services to the community, the general health of the community has improved.   TRUE   FALSE

58. The most important factor in social change is involvement.   TRUE   FALSE

59. Primary prevention usually targets individuals rather than groups.   TRUE   FALSE

60. Prevention is a process that dips into existing programs, creates new programs, and teaches people to live independently.   TRUE   FALSE

61. Community psychologists focus on change.   TRUE   FALSE

62. Parental marital status is an environmental condition that affects learning.   TRUE   FALSE

63. Psychologists examine the classroom to ensure the learning environment is following the appropriate behavioral principles of learning.   TRUE   FALSE

64. In studying cognitive processes, psychologists study how students are influenced by others.   TRUE   FALSE

65. Teachers should learn to pace a class and establish clear rules as a way of allocating and measuring time.   TRUE   FALSE

66. Each of the four elements of classroom management help teachers be effective.   TRUE   FALSE

67. In studying motivation of athletes, it is important to consider the goal, the person who sets the goal, the self perception of the athlete, and if the goals, means, and outcomes are realistic.   TRUE   FALSE

68. The four step analysis of motivation examines what motivates athletes and in turn what sustains their desire to be athletes.   TRUE   FALSE

69. It is difficult to predict a corresponding increase in performance due to an increase in arousal.   TRUE   FALSE

Fill-in-the-Blanks

1. In order to help people cope with solving everyday problems, companies turn to _____ _____.

2. _____ _____ provide research based answers to pressing organizational problems.

3. Industrial/organizational psychology can be divided into four broad areas: _____ _____ _____, _____ _____ _____, _____ _____, and _____.

4. _____ _____ _____ are used to ask employees, who know most about a job, to analyze the job.

5. The position analysis questionnaires address questions in six areas: _____ _____, _____ _____, _____ _____, _____ _____ _____, and _____.

6. Selection procedures can help employers choose candidates by measuring _____ _____ _____ abilities, motivation, or personality variables.

7. Tests that measure _____ are sometimes seen as controversial when determining the level of a candidate's integrity.

8. The problems that are often associated with performance appraisals when objective measures are used are _____, _____ _____, _____ _____, and _____.

9. Performance appraisals are cognitive tasks which are affected by _____ _____ _____.

10. In measuring performance appraisals, industrial/occupational psychology helps employers to be _____, _____, and _____.

11. The hierarchy in a company or the _____ _____ is the extent to which there is a rigid pecking order.

12. Employees often have a lack of patience and tolerance or _____ _____ in the workplace.

13. In different cultures, _____ or the emphasis of work goals rather than interpersonal goals, varies according to the people.

14 According to Vroom, the expectancy theory has three parts: _____, _____, and _____.

15. The three basic approaches to motivation in the workplace are _____, _____, and _____.

16. The five categories of job satisfaction are: _____ _____ _____, _____ _____ _____ _____, _____ _____ _____ _____, _____ _____, and _____ _____ _____.

17. When studying leadership, industrial/occupational psychologists must consider _____ _____ _____.

18. It is important to consider the _____ when deciding if direction or leadership is needed.

19. The two major categories to define leadership are: _____ _____ _____ and _____ _____ _____.

20. People who study how physical settings such as homes a neighborhoods affect behavior are called _____ _____.

21. The three easily controlled environment variables are _____, _____, and _____ _____.

22. _____ acts as a stressor because it interferes with communication and raises psychological arousal.

23. Hall defined four spatial zones in reference to personal space: _____, _____, _____, and _____ _____.

24. An _____ _____ examines machinery to see what can be changed to make it more efficient.

25. _____ equipment is a more important focus of efficiency research than operating.

26. There are three human factor considerations: _____, _____, and _____.

27. The three categories that define safe work environments are: _____ _____, _____ _____, and _____ _____ _____.

28. _____ _____ seeks to improve existing social networks within a community and to create new networks.

29. Prevention operates at three levels: _____, _____, and _____.

30. A _____ _____ was created in response to the growing need for a primary prevention service agency that targets mental health problems.

31. _____ _____ _____ are centers which help people deal with short term situations that require immediate therapeutic counseling.

32. _____ _____ help teachers become better classroom managers.

33. _____ psychologists focus on intervention with individuals whereas _____ psychologists focus on strategies to improve overall learning in the classroom.

34. Educational psychologists consider the whole child and his or her background to examine how _____ _____ affect the learning process.

35. _____ _____ can be put into place to relieve anxiety and arousal.

Applications

1. Describe crowding and social density and spatial density.
    A. Crowding _____
    _____
    B. Social density _____
    _____
    C. Spatial density _____
    _____

2. Describe Hall's four spatial zones as they are found in Western cultures.
    A. Intimate distance
        1. Distance involved _____
        2. Acceptable for _____
        3. Sensory events experienced _____
        4. Reserved for _____
    B. Personal distance
        1. Distance involved _____
        2. Acceptable for _____
    C. Social distance
        1. Distance involved _____
        2. Commonly found _____
        3. Purpose served _____
        4. Controls used _____
    D. Public distance
        1. Distance involved _____
        2. Commonly found _____
        3. Purpose served _____

SQ3R*plus*

RECITE: When you have finished reading the assigned material in your text and you have completed the exercises in your study guide, turn back to the chapter outline. Read each learning objective and recite out loud everything you can remember in support of each objective.

REVIEW: Check to see if you have answered all the questions you wrote during the *Survey* stage. Complete all sections of your study guide and check your answers for accuracy. If you are having trouble with specific topics ask you instructor for help.

WRITE: Read the learning objective again and then, in your own words, write down everything you can remember about this chapter. Summarize the main points and the concepts introduced in this chapter.

REFLECT: After each study period, take a break and reflect on what you have just studied. Ask yourself how this newly acquired information can be used in the future.

CHAPTER SEVENTEEN SELF-TEST

1. By developing standardized measures for personnel selection, industrial/organizational psychologists:
   A. encourage employers to use uniform procedures in predicting the success or failure of prospective employees.
   B. help employers predict personal and motivational changes that may occur in a prospective employee over time.
   C. motivate prospective employees to obtain skill enrichment training before they apply for a job.
   D. attempt to predict academic and job success.

2. People are motivated to work productively *primarily* through:
   A. receiving monetary rewards.
   B. the social affiliation that comes with a job.
   C. having feelings of self-worth.
   D. a variety and unique combination of emotional and social needs being fulfilled.

3. According to Vroom's expectancy theory, people are motivated by:
   A. doing what they are expected to do.
   B. what they expect to get from performing an assigned task.
   C. having the ability to make an assigned task a rewarding experience.
   D. B and C

4. According to Lawler and Porter,
   A. ability, effort, and role perception determine work performance.
   B. the values of a reward and the probability of success with a task affect motivation levels.
   C. an individual is motivated when he or she fully understands all that is required in performing the job.
   D. all of the above

5. Job satisfaction:
   A. is a person's attitude about his or her job.
   B. is directly related to job performance.
   C. is solely determined by one's ability to do the job.
   D. A and B

6. Most psychologists see the paternalistic management style as being self-defeating because this style:
   A. prevents slower workers from receiving rewards.
   B. prevents employees from having any influence in establishing goals for the company.
   C. does not encourage hard work because rewards are given without contingency.
   D. requires hard work without adequate rewards.

7. Employees tend to experience a sense of self-determination and competence when they work under:
   A. behavioral management styles.
   B. participatory management styles.
   C. boss-centered leadership.
   D. task-oriented leadership styles.

8. Which of the following leadership styles would be the *least* effective? A leader:
   A. perceives the goals and needs of the organization and acts accordingly.
   B. finds a comfortable style and uses it in all situations.
   C. uses an employee-orientation when employees need external support concerning the importance of their job.
   D. uses a task-orientation when the organization is in trouble and quick, direct action is necessary.

9. An environmental psychologist probably *would not*:
   A. be conducting all his research in a laboratory.
   B. investigate behaviors like cognitive dissonance or group polarization.
   C. focus on applied problems and their solutions.
   D. be interested in how humans make changes in their environment.

10. Research investigating the effects of temperature shifts on performance indicate that when temperatures become uncomfortably high:
    A. experimental subjects become more willing to administer shock to other subjects.
    B. people become more concerned with their own discomfort than with performance or goal-oriented activity.
    C. adaptive behaviors counteract the effects of the temperature.
    D. people show more aggression.

11. If a psychologist observes a group of 100 people in a 1,000 square foot room and then moves the group to a 10,000 square foot room and observes them there, he is studying the effects of:
    A. crowding.
    B. social density.
    C. spatial density.
    D. social and spatial density.

12. The spatial zone that Hall called social distance:
    A. is usually maintained by using some kind of physical barrier.
    B. allows good eye contact and a sense of being personal.
    C. is commonly found in contact sports.
    D. eliminates personal communication between individuals.

13. Which of the following is *not* considered a privacy-regulating mechanism?
    A. territorial behavior
    B. the design and layout of one's office or home
    C. choosing to read a book while your roommate reads the newspaper
    D. nonverbal communications and body positions

14. The most recent concern of environmental psychologists is the study of:
    A. how natural environments affect behavior.
    B. how man-made environments affect behavior.
    C. how behavior affects the environment.
    D. development of lifelong behaviors that will help maintain environmental quality.

LANGUAGE ENRICHMENT GLOSSARY

Some students who reviewed the textbook listed the following words as difficult to understand. Use this list, your dictionary, and teachers and friends to learn the meaning of words you do not understand

Page	Term	Explanation	Page	Term	Explanation
609	reluctant	holding back your actions	626	bathroom	room with toilet/bathtub
618	reluctance	holding back your actions	626	lounge	a rest area in a building
624	crowded	many people small place	627	unobtrusively	without being noticed
624	New England	region in northeast U.S.	627	stairwells	the area around stairs
625	chirping	sound a bird makes	627	stamped	an envelop with a postage stamp on it
625	exhilarating	excited and alive	627	encroachment	closing in on
626	throngs	crowds of people	628	receptionist	person who welcomes you in an office building
626	ambiance	atmosphere, setting	628	adaptations	behavioral changes
626	dormitories	student housing on campus	629	turf	their own area
626	hallways	passage between rooms	630	socioeconomic status	level in society based upon how much money you make
			634	multi-dimensional	in many parts

Appendix

Statistical Methods

Appendix Overview

The appendix describes how descriptive and inferential statistics are used by psychologists. Descriptive statistics are used to summarize and describe data. These statistics help researchers organize vast amounts of information into manageable and understandable formats. Measures of central tendency include the mean, mode, and median. Measures of variability like the range and the standard deviation are how scores differ from the average (mean).

Inferential statistics allow psychologists to make decisions about the meaning of their research data. The normal curve is used as a reference from which judgments about significant differences are made. A correlation coefficient is used to describe the relationship between two variables. The strength of a correlation is determined by the magnitude of the statistic. A positive correlation exists when two variables differ in the same direction and a negative correlation means that two variables have an inverse relation. Correlation does not show cause.

SQ3R*plus*

SURVEY THE LESSON: Read learning objectives A.1 through A.6 and, in the text, examine the chapter headings, tables, and pictures on pages 641-651 in the text to *form an idea of what you should learn and to set goals for your study time*.

WRITE DOWN QUESTIONS: *While surveying and reading the text, write down questions* about the information being presented. *Write your questions* in the space below or on a separate piece of paper and try to find answers to these questions in the text.

ACTIVELY READ PAGES 641-651: The following exercise is designed to facilitate this process. Complete the following questions as you read, and when you are done, check your answers with those printed in the back of this study guide.

YOUR QUESTIONS:

Matching

1. _____ correlation coefficient
2. _____ frequency polygon
3. _____ inferential statistics
4. _____ mean
5. _____ median

6. _____ mode
7. _____ normal curve
8. _____ range
9. _____ standard deviation
10. _____ variability

a. arithmetic average
b. most frequent data point
c. point at which 50% of all scores occur above and 50% below
d. the extent to which scores differ from one another, especially differ from the mean
e. measure of variability that describes the spread between the lowest and highest scores
f. measures the variance from the mean
g. bell shaped frequency distribution
h. frequency distribution that shows data points connected by lines
i. procedure used to generalize conclusions from sample to larger population
j. number used to describe degree and direction of relationship between two variables

True or False

1. Statistics are commonly used by psychologists to discover causes of behavior.   TRUE   FALSE

2. Frequency polygons are meaningful ways to arrange data into the range of all possible results.   TRUE   FALSE

3. The mean, mode, and median are descriptive statistics that each tell the researcher something about the average (typical) subject.   TRUE   FALSE

4. A standard deviation gives information about all the members of a group, not just an average number.   TRUE   FALSE

5. Knowledge of the standard deviation does little to aid the psychologist in making predictions.   TRUE   FALSE

6. Generally, psychologists assume that a difference is statistically significant if the likelihood of its occurring by chance is less than 5 out of 100 times.   TRUE   FALSE

7. Inferential statistics are used to predict confidence intervals.   TRUE   FALSE

8. A scatter plot is a diagram that shows the positive correlation of two variables.   TRUE   FALSE

9. A correlation of +.7 is stronger than a correlation of -.7.   TRUE   FALSE

10. Variables that show no correlation are expressed by a   TRUE   FALSE
negative number.

Fill-in-the-Blanks

1. _____ statistics are procedures used to summarize samples of data.

2. A graphical representation of data showing the range of possible data is called a frequency
_____.

3. The _____ is the most frequent score in a score distribution.

4. Half of the scores in a distribution fall below the _____.

5. If all scores are the same, then their _____ is equal to zero.

6. The _____ _____ gives information about all of the scores in a
distribution.

7. If you know the _____ and the standard deviation, you can estimate where an
individual score lies relative to the sample.

8. _____ statistics are used by researchers to state conclusions and the significance
of the results.

9. When one variable increases and the second variable decreases the variables are
_____ correlated.

10. A correlation coefficient of -0.5 is _____ than a correlation of +0.4.

SQ3R*plus*

RECITE: When you have finished reading the assigned material in your text and you have
completed the exercises in your study guide, turn back to the chapter outline. Read each learning
objective and recite out loud everything you can remember in support of each objective.

REVIEW: Check to see if you have answered all the questions you wrote during the *Survey*
stage. Complete all sections of your study guide and check your answers for accuracy. If you
are having trouble with specific topics ask you instructor for help.

WRITE: Read the learning objective again and then, in your own words, write down everything
you can remember about this chapter. Summarize the main points and the concepts introduced in
this chapter.

REFLECT: After each study period, take a break and reflect on what you have just studied.
Ask yourself how this newly acquired information can be used in the future.

1. Researchers use descriptive statistics to:
    A. reach conclusions about a set of data.
    B. show cause and effect relationships.
    C. detect direction and strength of relationships.
    D. summarize, condense, and describe data.

2. Which of the following is a measure of central tendency?
    A. median
    B. correlation
    C. standard deviation
    D. all of the above

3. A statistic that describes the extent to which scores differ from one another in a distribution is called a:
    A. median.
    B. correlation.
    C. measure of central tendency.
    D. measure of variability.

4. If you subtract the lowest score from the highest score, you will be calculating the:
    A. mean.
    B. mode.
    C. median.
    D. range.

5. A researcher would use _____ to gain information concerning how an average score related to scores above and below the mean.
    A. standard deviations
    B. a correlation
    C. a normal curve
    D. a median

6. When describing a characteristic common to a number of subjects that results in a normal distribution a researcher would use:
    A. inferential statistics.
    B. a correlation coefficient.
    C. a normal curve.
    D. the mode score, but not the median or mean score.

7. A scholastic aptitude test has a mean score of 500 and a standard deviation of 100. Bill scored 600. Approximately what percentage of the students scored lower than Bill?
    A. 13 percent
    B. 26 percent
    C. 68 percent
    D. 84 percent

8. Inferential statistics are used to:
    A. replicate experiments.
    B. summarize, condense, and describe data.
    C. reach conclusions about a set of data.
    D. measure the relationships among variables.

9. A zero correlation represents:
    A. no relationship between variables.
    B. a positive correlation.
    C. a negative correlation.
    D. a perfect relationship between variables.

10. A difference between two or more groups in an experiment is thought to be a significant difference when the probability that it occurred by chance is less than:
    A. 1 percent.
    B. 5 percent.
    C. 10 percent.
    D. A or B, it depends on the researcher

11. When one variable shows an increase and a second variable also shows a consistent increase, a researcher can feel confident that:
    A. a cause-and-effect relationship exists.
    B. a positive correlation exists.
    C. two perfectly correlated variables have been found.
    D. all of the above

Keeping Pace Plus

Examination Preparation Section

Flash Cards, Crossword Puzzles
& Practice Tests

EXAM PREPARATION SECTION

HOW TO PASS YOUR EXAMS

FACING EXAMS. I have questioned thousands of my students about using study guides and what features they like the most. Students dread preparing for exams and suggest to me thousands of grading methods that do not include taking exams. However, students recognize that the most prevalent method of assessing acquired knowledge is to administer exams. Test anxiety can interfere with your ability to learn, as well as with accuracy of recall during the exam itself. There are a number of methods to relieve you of test-anxiety. They all have one common goal--*to help you be relaxed and confident going into the exam*. Many students in survey-type courses find that the amount of material requires many more hours of study than they had anticipated, thus many more hours of exam preparation. Students also feel that preparing for an exam covering several chapters is anxiety provoking, and they come to the exam with a great deal of tension. Achieving top scores on exams requires preparation and practice. One way of mitigating the tension is to give the student a chance to simulate the exam without the pressure of failing or the shock of a tough question causing the student to block on the correct answer. This Exam Preparation Section is designed to provide you practice exams in a tension-free environment and prepare you for the real thing.

PREPARING FOR EXAMS. Preparing for exams should be an ongoing process. As you read your text, listen in class, and take lecture notes, keep in mind--an exam is coming. Then, about one week before an exam, begin your study sessions. Do not wait until the day before because time pressure, low energy, and unexpected events are too likely to interfere with your ability to prepare well. About a week before the exam you should take the following steps:

1. Ask your instructor what the exam will cover, what material will be omitted, and what kinds of questions will be used.
2. Make a list of things you must know and rank them according to their importance. You will want to give the most important and difficult concepts more preparation time.
3. Spend some time predicting test questions: How might they be worded? How general or detailed might they be? How might two or more concepts be combined into one question?
4. Begin reviewing. Your text, lecture notes, *study guide questions and answers*, *chapter learning objectives*, *practice tests*, and *self-test* will become extremely useful tools at this time.
5. Schedule group study sessions with other students. Sharing ideas about what might be covered on the test and talking out loud about the things you have learned will help clarify and solidify your understanding.
6. Make up practice exams and test yourself before the test day. If you don't know it all yet you still have time to get the answers or clarification from your instructor.

ANSWERING ESSAY TEST QUESTIONS. Essay test questions require that you know the material well enough to be able to recall from memory, in an organized way, both major and minor points that will provide an answer. The Crossword Puzzles in the Exam Preparation Section will let you know if you have grasped the concepts beyond rote memorization. When presented with an essay test, keep these steps in mind.

1. Before you begin to answer any test questions, read all of the questions and make some quick notes about the major and minor points you will want to cover when answering them.
2. Estimate how much time you should give to each question and try to stick to your schedule. You will want to allow more time for difficult questions and questions that carry more points toward scoring of the test. If possible, plan to have some time in the last minutes of the class session to review and polish your answers.
3. Answer the easier questions first.
4. Answer each question as directly as possible and avoid wandering and writing too much or too little.
5. Leave a few blank lines between answers so that you can go back if time allows and add ideas.

ANSWERING OBJECTIVE TEST QUESTIONS. Objective test questions include multiple-choice, true-false, and matching questions. These questions require you to recognize and discriminate between correct and incorrect answers. The *self-tests* at the end of each chapter, and the *practice tests* in the Exam Preparation Section should give you good practice at this. When taking an objective test keep the following in mind.

1. Read each question carefully and completely; do not jump to conclusions and assume that you have the correct answer until you have read and considered the entire question.
2. Give careful thought to questions that include words such as *always, never, all, tendency*, or *sometimes*. The first three terms may indicate that the statement is too extreme and perhaps false; the last two terms show more qualified conditions, suggesting that the statement may be true; however, these rules are not absolute.
3. Treat each alternative in a multiple-choice question as a true-false statement. Eliminate those alternatives that are definitely false and if more than one answer seems to be true, choose the one that most thoroughly and directly answers the question.
4. Do not spend too much time on any one question. If you are unsure of an answer, put a check mark in the margin next to the question and go back to it later.
5. The rule of thumb about changing answers is to stick with your original answer unless you have *strong* second thoughts about it. If you feel reasonably sure that your second thoughts are correct then go ahead and change the answer.

SIMULATING YOUR EXAMS In the Exam Preparation Section you are provided with three techniques for exam review and preparation. The first will be to use the *Flash Cards* to enhance your memory for the marginal definitions in *Psychology*. This technique is a proven way to increase your ability to recall the correct test answer in many test formats such as matching or short answer type questions. The next, more difficult task is to recognize the correct answer when you are given less than the complete definition, as in multiple-choice items or scenarios, where the item stem is lengthy, and you need to determine what the salient points are before attempting to answer. What if you could be given bits of information about specific topics and asked to correctly identify and spell the topic? What if you could learn difficult concepts, increase your confidence and also have some fun doing it? The *Crossword Puzzle* for each chapter will test your ability to recognize key terms and definitions by reading clues that contain key information about the topic but challenge you to infer the correct answer from this limited information. Finally, I have provided a sample of multiple-choice test items selected from the computerized testbank that your instructor may be using. These *Practice Tests* items are real and an excellent method of practicing for an exam.

Although Lefton's *Psychology sixth edition* is written in a very logical format, many instructors choose to alter the chapter sequence to better fit individual desires. Preparing for a multiple chapter exam is difficult, but there is a way to put together your own practice exam and build your confidence prior to the real exam. For example, if your instructor assigns Chapters 1, 2 and 5 as the readings covered on the next exam, you would remove the *Flash Cards* for Chapters 1, 2, and 5; then remove the *Crossword Puzzles* for Chapters 1, 2, and 5; then the *Practice Tests* for Chapters 1, 2, and 5 and combine them to make a simulated exam covering the same material as your instructor's exam. You can mix and match the cards, puzzles, and tests in any way you choose. Combine them in whatever fashion most closely resembles your real exam. Be sure to grade yourself on the simulated exam and keep up with how this practice helps you on the real exam. If you feel like you need to practice more than once, simply make copies of the pages before you begin, and scramble them for subsequent practice exams.

Keeping Pace Plus

Flash Cards

CUT-OUT FLASH CARDS CHAPTER ONE

psychology	theory
introspection	psychoanalytic approach
behaviorism	cognitive psychology
eclecticism	Psychologist
Psychoanalyst	participant
experiment	variable
independent variable	dependent variable
hypothesis	case study

CUT-OUT FLASH CARDS CHAPTER ONE

In psychology, a collection of interrelated ideas and facts put forward to explain and predict behavior and mental processes.	The science of behavior and mental processes.
The school of psychological thought developed by Freud, which assumes that psychological maladjustment is a consequence of anxiety resulting from unresolved conflicts and forces of which a person may be unaware; includes therapeutic technique known as psychoanalysis.	Description and analysis by a person of what he or she is thinking and feeling. Also known as *self-examination*.
The school of psychological thought that focuses on the mental processes and activities involved in perception, memory, learning, and thinking.	The school of psychological thought that rejects the study of the contents of consciousness and focuses on describing and measuring only that which is observable directly or through assessment instruments.
Professional who studies behavior and uses behavioral principles in scientific research or in applied settings.	In psychology, a combination of theories, facts, or techniques; the practice of using whatever clinical and counseling techniques are appropriate for an individual client rather than relying exclusively on the techniques of one school of psychology.
Individual who takes part in an experiment and whose behavior is observed for research data collection. Also known as a *subject*.	Psychiatrist or, occasionally, nonmedical practitioner who has studied the technique of psychoanalysis and uses it in treating people with emotional problems.
Condition or characteristic of a situation or person that is subject to change (that varies) within or across situations or individuals.	Procedure in which a researcher systematically manipulates and observes elements of a situation in order to answer a question and, usually to test hypotheses and make inferences about cause and effect.
The variable in a controlled experiment that is expected to change because of the manipulation of the independent variable.	The variable in a controlled experiment that the experimenter directly and purposely manipulates to see how the variables under study will be affected.
Method of interviewing participants to gain information about their background, including data on such things as childhood, family, education, and social and sexual interactions.	Tentative statement or idea expressing a causal relationship between two events or variables that are to be evaluated in a research study.

CUT-OUT FLASH CARDS CHAPTER TWO

nature	nurture
gene	nervous system
neuron	synapse
refractory period	neurotransmitter
peripheral nervous system	somatic nervous system
autonomic nervous system	sympathetic nervous system
parasympathetic nervous system	electroencephalogram
hormones	hypoglycemia

CUT-OUT FLASH CARDS CHAPTER TWO

An individual's experiences in the environment.	An individual's genetically inherited characteristics.
The structures and organs that act as the communication system for the body, allowing all behavior and mental processes to take place.	The unit of heredity transmission carried in chromosomes and consisting of DNA and protein.
The microscopically small space between the axon terminals of one neuron and the receptor sites of another neuron.	The basic unit (a single cell) of the nervous system, comprising dendrites, which receive neural signals; a cell body, which generates electrical signals; and an axon, which transmits neural signals. Also known as a *nerve cell*.
Chemical substance that resides in the axon terminals and within synaptic vesicles and that, when released, moves across the synaptic space and binds to a receptor site on adjacent neurons.	The recovery period of a neuron after it fires, during which time it cannot fire again; this period allows the neuron to reestablish electrical balance with its surroundings.
The part of the peripheral nervous system that carries information to skeletal muscles and thereby affects bodily movement; it controls voluntary, conscious sensory and motor functions.	The part of the nervous system that carries information to and from the central nervous system through a network of spinal and cranial nerves.
The part of the autonomic nervous system that becomes most active in response to emergency situations; it calls up bodily resources as needed for major energy expenditures.	The part of the peripheral nervous system that controls the vital and automatic processes of the body, such as the heart rate, digestive processes, blood pressure, and functioning of internal organs.
Record of electrical brain-wave patterns obtained through electrodes placed on the scalp.	The part of the autonomic nervous system that controls the ongoing maintenance processes of the body, such as heart rate, digestive processes, and blood pressure.
A condition in which overproduction of insulin results in very low blood sugar.	Endocrine gland chemicals that regulate the activities of specific organs or cells.

CUT-OUT FLASH CARDS CHAPTER THREE

sensation	perception
electromagnetic radiation	myopic
hyperopic	photoreceptors
visual cortex	dark adaptation
saccades	saturation
opponent-process theory	size constancy
shape constancy	accommodation
sound	kinesthesis

CUT-OUT FLASH CARDS CHAPTER THREE

Process by which an organism selects and interprets sensory input so that it acquires meaning.	Process by which the sense organ receptor cells are stimulated and relay their initial information to higher brain centers for further processing.
Able to see things that are close but having trouble seeing objects at a distance. Also known as *nearsighted*.	The entire spectrum of waves initiated by the movement of charged particles.
The light-sensitive cells in the retina: rods and cones.	Having trouble seeing things that are nearby but able to see objects at a distance. Also known as *farsighted*.
Increased sensitivity to light in a dark environment; when a person moves from a light environment to a dark one, chemicals in the rods and cones regenerate and return to their inactive and sensitivity increases.	The most important area of the brain's occipital lobe, which receives information from the lateral geniculate nucleus. Also known as the *striate cortex*.
The depth of hue of reflected light, as determined by the homogeneity of the wavelengths contained in the light. Also known as *purity*.	Rapid voluntary movements of the eyes, to focus on different points.
The ability of the perceptual system to recognize that an object remains constant in size regardless of its distance from the observer or the size of its image on the retina.	The theory, proposed by Herring, that color is coded by stimulation of three types of paired receptors; each pair of receptors is assumed to operate in an antagonistic way so that stimulation by a given wavelength produces excitation in one receptor of the pair and inhibition in the other receptor.
The change in the shape of the lens of the eye to keep an object in focus on the retina when the object is moved closer to or farther away from the observer.	The ability to recognize a shape despite changes in the orientation or angle from which it is viewed.
The awareness aroused by movements of the muscles, tendons, and joints.	A psychological term describing changes in pressure through a medium; the psychological experience that occurs when changes in air pressure take place at the receptive organ for hearing and that vary in frequency and amplitude.

CUT-OUT FLASH CARDS CHAPTER FOUR

consciousness	sleep
NREM (no rapid eye movement) sleep	REM (rapid eye movement) sleep
dream	manifest content
latent content	biofeedback
hypnosis	age regression
meditation	addictive drug
substance abusers	psychological dependence
withdrawal symptoms	tolerance

CUT-OUT FLASH CARDS CHAPTER FOUR

Nonwaking state of consciousness characterized by general unresponsiveness to the environment and general physical immobility.	The general state of being aware of and responsive to events in the environment, including one's own mental processes.
Stage of sleep characterized by high-frequency, low-voltage brain-wave activity, rapid and systematic eye movements, and dreams.	Four distinct stages of sleep during which no rapid eye movements occur.
The overt story line, characters, and setting of a dream—the obvious, clearly discernible events of the dream.	A state of consciousness that occurs largely during REM sleep and is usually accompanied by vivid visual, tactile, and auditory imagery.
Technique by which individuals can monitor and learn to control the involuntary activity of some of the body's organs and functions.	The deeper meaning of a dream, usually involving symbolism, hidden content, and repressed or obscured ideas and wishes.
The reported ability, sometimes induced by hypnosis, to "return" to an earlier time in one's life and to recount events that occurred at that time.	Altered state of consciousness brought about by procedures that may induce a trance.
A drug that causes a compulsive physiological need and that, when withheld, produces withdrawal symptoms.	State of consciousness induced by a variety of techniques and characterized by concentration, restriction of incoming stimuli, and deep relaxation to produce a sense of detachment.
A compelling desire to use a drug, along with an inability to inhibit that desire.	People who overuse drugs and rely on them to deal with stress and anxiety.
Progressive insensitivity to repeated use of a specific drug in the same dosage and at the same frequency of use.	Physiological reactions that occur when an addictive drug is no longer administered to an addict.

CUT-OUT FLASH CARDS CHAPTER FIVE

stimulus generalization	operant conditioning
shaping	reinforcer
positive reinforcement	negative reinforcement
primary reinforcer	secondary reinforcer
superstitious behavior	punishment
primary punisher	secondary punisher
variable-interval schedule	variable-ratio schedule
extinction	observational learning theory

CUT-OUT FLASH CARDS CHAPTER FIVE

Conditioning in which the probability that an organism will emit a response is increased or decreased by the subsequent delivery of a reinforcer or punisher. Also known as *instrumental conditioning*.	Occurrence of a conditioned response with a stimulus that is similar but not identical to the original conditioned stimulus.
Any event that increases the probability of a recurrence of the response that preceded it.	Gradual training of an organism to give the proper responses through selective reinforcement of behaviors as they approach the desired response.
Removal of an aversive stimulus after a particular response to increase the likelihood that the response will recur.	Presentation of a rewarding or pleasant stimulus after a particular response, to increase the likelihood that the response will recur.
A neutral stimulus with no intrinsic value for an organism initially but that can become rewarding when linked with a primary reinforcer.	A reinforcer (such as food, water, or the termination of pain) that has survival value for an organism and thus its value does not have to be learned.
The process of presenting an undesirable or noxious stimulus, or removing a desirable stimulus, to decrease the probability that a particular preceding response will recur.	Behavior learned through coincidental association with reinforcement.
A neutral stimulus with no intrinsic effect on an organism that acquires punishment value through repeated pairing with a punishing stimulus.	Any stimulus or event that is naturally painful or aversive to an organism.
A reinforcement schedule in which a reinforcer (reward) is delivered after a predetermined but variable number of responses has occurred.	A reinforcement schedule in which a reinforcer (reward) is delivered after predetermined but varying intervals of time, provided that the required response occurrs at least once after each interval.
Theory that suggests that organisms learn new responses by observing the behavior of a model and then imitating it. Also known as *social learning theory*.	In operant conditioning, the process by which the probability of an organism's emitting a conditioned response is reduced when reinforcement no longer follows the response.

CUT-OUT FLASH CARDS CHAPTER SIX

memory	sensory memory
short-term memory	rehearsal
chunks	working memory
long-term memory	procedural memory
declarative memory	state-dependent learning
schema	interference
proactive interference	retroactive interference
amnesia	consolidation

CUT-OUT FLASH CARDS CHAPTER SIX

The mechanism that performs initial encoding and brief storage of stimuli. Also known as the *sensory register*.	The ability to remember past events, images, ideas, or previously learned information or skills; the storage system that allows for retention and retrieval of previously learned information.
The process of repeatedly verbalizing, thinking about, or otherwise acting on information in order to keep the information in memory.	The memory storage system that temporarily holds current or recently attended to information for immediate or short-term use.
A different conception of short term memory that focuses on several subsystems, a component to encode and rehearse auditory information, a visual-spatial scratch pad, and a central processing mechanism, or executive, that balances and controls information flow.	Manageable and meaningful units of information that can be easily encoded, stored, and retrieved.
Memory for the perceptual, motor, and cognitive skills required to complete a task.	The memory storage system that keeps a relatively permanent record of information.
The tendency to recall information learned in a particular physiological state most accurately when one is again in that physiological state.	Memory for specific facts.
Suppression or confusion of one bit of information with another that was received either earlier or later.	A conceptual framework that organizes information and makes sense of the world by laying out a structure in which events can be encoded.
Decrease in accurate recall of information as a result of the subsequent presentation of different information. Also known as *retroactive inhibition*.	Decrease in accurate recall of information as a result of the effects of previous learned information interfering with its recall. Also known as *proactive inhibition*.
The evolution of a temporary neural circuit into a more permanent circuit.	Inability to remember information (typically all events within a specific period) usually due to physiological trauma.

CUT-OUT FLASH CARDS CHAPTER SEVEN

reasoning	concept
problem solving	functional fixedness
brainstorming	convergent thinking
divergent thinking	heuristics
means-end analysis	backward search
linguistics	phonemes
morpheme	syntax
transformational grammar	syllogism

CUT-OUT FLASH CARDS CHAPTER SEVEN

Mental category used to classify an event or object according to some distinguishing property or feature.	The process by which people generate logical and coherent ideas, evaluate situations, and reach conclusions.
The inability to see that an object can have a function other than its stated or usual one.	The behavior of individuals when confronted with a situation or task that requires some insight or some unknown elements to be determined.
In problem solving, the process of narrowing down choices and alternatives to arrive at a suitable answer.	A problem solving technique that involves considering all possible solutions without making prior evaluative judgments.
Sets of strategies, not strict rules, that act as guidelines for discovery-oriented problem solving.	In problem solving, widening the range of possibilities and expanding the options for solutions.
Heuristic procedure in which a problem solver starts at the end of a problem and systematically works in reverse steps to discover the subparts necessary to achieve a solution.	Heuristic procedure in which the problem solver tries to move closer to a solution by comparing the current situation with the desired goal and determining the most efficient way to get from one to the other.
A basic unit of sound in a language.	The study of language, including speech sounds, meaning, and grammar.
The way words and groups of words are related and combine to form phrases and sentences.	A basic unit of meaning in a language.
A sequence of statements, or premises (usually two), followed by a conclusion; the task is to decide (deduce) whether the conclusion is warranted.	An approach to the study of language that assumes that each surface structure of a sentence has a deep structure associated with it.

CUT-OUT FLASH CARDS CHAPTER EIGHT

intelligence	factor analysis
mental age	standardization
norms	representative sample
normal curve	raw score
standard score	percentile score
deviation IQ	reliability
validty	halo effect
mental retardation	mainstreaming

CUT-OUT FLASH CARDS CHAPTER EIGHT

A statistical procedure designed to discover the mutually independent elements (factors) in any set of data	According to Wechsler, "the aggregate or global capacity of the individual to act purposefully, to think rationally, and to deal effectively with the environment."
The process of developing uniform procedures for administering and scoring a test and for establishing norms.	The age level at which a child is functioning cognitively, regardless of chronological age.
A sample of individuals who match the population with whom they are to be compared with regard to key variables such as socioeconomic status and age.	The scores and corresponding percentile ranks of a large and representative sample of individuals from the population for which a test was designed.
An examinee's score that has not been transformed or converted in any way.	A bell-shaped graphic representation of data arranged to show what percentage of the population falls under each part of the curve.
A score indicating what percentage of the test population would obtain a lower score.	A score that expresses an individual's position relative to the mean, based on the standard deviation.
A test's ability to yield the same score for the same individual through repeated testing.	A standard IQ test score for which the mean and standard deviation remain constant at all ages.
The tendency for one of an individual's characteristics to influence the evaluation of other characteristics.	The ability of a test to measure what it is supposed to measure and to predict what it is supposed to predict.
The administrative practice of placing children with special needs in regular classroom settings with the support of special education services.	Below-average intellectual functioning, as measured on an IQ test, accompanied by substantial limitations in functioning that originates before age 18.

CUT-OUT FLASH CARDS CHAPTER NINE

motivation	drive theory
anorexia nervosa	bulimia nervosa
vasocongestion	orgasm phase
motive	learned helplessness
extrinsic rewards	social need
arousal	need for achievement
cognitive theory	intrinsically motivated behaviors
self-actualization	emotion

CUT-OUT FLASH CARDS CHAPTER NINE

An explanation of behavior emphasizing internal factors that energize organisms to attain, reestablish, balance, or maintain some goal that helps with survival.	Any internal condition that appears by inference to initiate, activate, or maintain an organism's goal-directed behavior.
An eating disorder characterized by repeated episodes of binge eating (and a fear of not being able to stop eating) followed by purging.	An eating disorder characterized by an intense fear of becoming obese, dramatic weight loss, concern about weight, disturbances in body image, and an obstinate and willful refusal to eat.
The third phase of the sexual response cycle, during which autonomic nervous system activity reaches its peak and muscle contractions occur throughout the body, but especially in the genital area, in spasms.	In the sexual response cycle, engorgement, particularly in the genital area, due to increased blood flow.
The behavior of giving up or not responding, exhibited by organisms exposed to negative consequences or punishment over which they have no control; the major cause is an organism's belief that its response will not affect what happens to it in the future.	A specific (usually internal) condition, usually involving some sort of arousal, that directs an organism's behavior toward a goal.
An aroused condition that directs people toward establishing feelings about themselves and others and toward establishing and maintaining relationships.	Rewards that come from the external environment.
A social need that directs people to strive constantly for excellence and success.	Activation of the central nervous system, the autonomic nervous system, and the muscles and glands; according to some motivational theorists, organisms seek to maintain optimal levels of arousal by actively varying their exposure to arousing stimuli.
Behaviors engaged in for no apparent reward except the pleasure and satisfaction of the activity itself.	In motivation, an explanation of behavior that emphasizes the role of thought and individual choices regarding life goals and the means of achieving them.
A subjective response, usually accompanied by a physiological change, which is interpreted by an individual and then readies the individual for some action that is associated with a change in behavior.	In humanistic theory the final stage of psychological development, in which one realizes one's uniquely human potential; the process of achieving everything one is capable of achieving; this includes attempts to minimize ill-health, to have a superior perception of reality, and to feel a strong sense of self-acceptance.

CUT-OUT FLASH CARDS CHAPTER TEN

zygote	embryo
fetus	teratogen
labor	bonding
temperment	assimilation
accommodation	sensorimotor stage
egocentrism	decentration
concrete operational stage	conservation
formal operational stage	morality

CUT-OUT FLASH CARDS CHAPTER TEN

The human organism from the 5th through the 49th day after conception.	A fertilized egg.
Substance than can produce developmental malformations (birth defects) in a fetus.	The human organism from the 49th day after conception until birth.
A special process of emotional attachment that may occur between parents and babies in the minutes and hours immediately after birth.	The process in which the uterus contracts and the cervix opens so that the fetus can descend through the birth canal to the outside world.
According to Piaget, the process by which new concepts and experiences are incorporated into existing mental frameworks so as to be used in a meaningful way.	Long-lasting individual differences in the intensity and especially quality of a person's emotional reactions.
The first of Piaget's four stages of cognitive development (covering roughly the first 2 years of life), during which the child begins to interact with the environment and the rudiments of memory are established.	According to Piaget, the process by which new concepts and experiences modify existing cognitive structures and behaviors.
The process of changing from a totally self-oriented point of view to one that recognizes other people's feelings, ideas, and viewpoints.	The inability to perceive a situation or event except in relation to oneself. Also known as *self-centeredness*.
The ability to recognize that something that has changed in some way (such as the "shape" of a liquid put in a different container) still has the same weight, substance, or volume.	Piaget's third stage of cognitive development (lasting from approximately age 6 or 7 to age 11 or 12), during which the child develops the ability to understand constant factors in the environment, rules, and higher-order symbolism.
A system of learned attitudes about social practices, institutions, and individual behavior used to evaluate situations and behavior as being right or wrong, good, or bad.	Piaget's fourth and final stage of cognitive development (beginning at about age 12), during which the individual can think hypothetically, can consider all future possibilities, and is capable of deductive logic.

CUT-OUT FLASH CARDS CHAPTER ELEVEN

puberty	gender schema theory
gender role stereotyping	androgynous
ageism	dementia
Alzheimer's disease	thanatology
adolescence	gender identity
glass ceiling	gender role
wage gap	life structures
terminal drop	menopause

CUT-OUT FLASH CARDS CHAPTER ELEVEN

The theory that children and adolescents use gender as an organizing theme to classify and understand their perceptions about the world.	The period during which the reproductive system matures; it begins with an increase in sex hormone production and occurs at (and signals) the end of childhood.
Having both typically male and typically female characteristics.	Typical beliefs about gender based behaviors that are expected, regulated, and reinforced by society.
Long standing impairment of mental functioning and global cognitive abilities in otherwise alert individuals, causing memory loss and related symptoms.	Prejudice against the elderly and the discrimination that follows from it.
The study of the psychological and medical aspects of death and dying.	A chronic and progressive disorder of the brain that is a major cause of degenerative dementia and may actually be a group of related disorders tied together loosely under one name.
A person's sense of being male or female.	The period extending from the onset of puberty to early adulthood.
The full range of behaviors generally associated with one's gender, which help one establish who one is. Also know as sex role.	An allusion to the idea that the top is visible but blocked, or the inability of women to rise to very senior positions, is sometimes referred to as the *glass ceiling*.
Unique patterns of behavior and ways of interacting with the world, the "themes" of one's life at a given time, as reflected in the two to three major areas of chosen commitment.	Women in the United States earn about 72 cents of each dollar that a man earns -- this is referred to as the *wage gap*.
Midlife changes in hormones lead to the cessation of ovulation and menstruation about 50 years of age in women.	A rapid decline in intellectual functioning in the year before death.

CUT-OUT FLASH CARDS CHAPTER TWELVE

oral stage	Oedipus complex
genital stage	fixation
defense mechanism	repression
projection	denial
reaction formation	rationalization
Neo-Freudians	self-actualization
self	ideal self
assessment	projective tests

CUT-OUT FLASH CARDS CHAPTER TWELVE

Occurring during the phallic stage, feelings of rivalry with the parent of the same sex and love of the parent of the opposite sex, ultimately resolved through identification with the parent of the same sex; in girls this process is called the *Electra complex*.	Freud's first stage of personality development, from birth to about age 2, during which infants obtain gratification primarily through the mouth.
An excessive attachment to some person or object that was appropriate only at an earlier stage of development.	Freud's last stage of personality development, from the onset of puberty through adulthood, during which the sexual conflicts of childhood resurface (at puberty) and are often resolved (during adolescence).
Defense mechanism by which people block anxiety-provoking feelings from conscious awareness and push them into the unconscious.	A largely unconscious way of reducing anxiety by distorting perceptions of reality.
Defense mechanism by which people refuse to recognize the true source of their anxiety.	A defense mechanism by which people attribute their own undesirable traits to other people or objects.
Defense mechanism by which people reinterpret undesirable feelings or behaviors in terms that make them appear acceptable.	A defense mechanism by which people behave in a manner opposite to their true but anxiety-provoking feelings.
The fundamental human need to strive to fulfill one's potential; from a humanist's view, a final level of psychological development in which a person attempts to minimize ill-health, be fully functioning, have a superior perception of reality, and feel a strong sense of self acceptance.	Personality theorists who have proposed variations on the basic ideas of Freud, usually attributing a greater influence to cultural and interpersonal factors than did Freud.
The self that a person would ideally like to be.	In Rogers theory of personality, the perceptions individuals have of themselves and of their relationships to other people and to various aspects of life.
Personality-assessing devices or instruments in which examinees are shown a standard set of ambiguous stimuli and asked to respond in an unrestricted manner.	The process of evaluating individual differences among human beings by means of tests and direct observation of behavior.

CUT-OUT FLASH CARDS CHAPTER THIRTEEN

stressor	anxiety
stress	frustration
conflict	approach-approach conflict
avoidance-avoidance conflict	approach-avoidance conflict
burnout	Type A behavior
Type B behavior	Posttraumatic stress disorder
coping	coping skills
stress inoculation	health psychology

CUT-OUT FLASH CARDS CHAPTER THIRTEEN

A generalized feeling of fear and apprehension that may be related to a particular event or object and is often accompanied by increased physiological arousal.	An environmental stimulus that affects an organism in physically or psychologically injurious ways, usually producing anxiety, tension, and physiological arousal.
The emotional state or condition that results when a goal—work, family, or personal—is thwarted or blocked.	A nonspecific, often global, response by an organism to real or imagined demands made on it (a person must appraise a situation as stressful for it to be stressful).
The conflict that results from having to choose between two equally attractive alternatives or goals.	The emotional state or condition in which a person has to make difficult decisions about two or more competing motives, behaviors, or impulses.
The conflict that results from having to choose an alternative or goal that has both attractive and repellent aspects.	The conflict that results from having to choose between two equally distasteful alternatives or goals.
Behavior characterized by competitiveness, impatience, hostility, and constant efforts to do more in less time.	State of emotional and physical exhaustion, lowered productivity, and feelings of isolation, often caused by work-related pressures.
Mental disorder that may become evident after a person has undergone extreme stress caused by some type of disaster; common symptoms include vivid, intrusive recollections or reexperiences of the traumatic event and occasional lapses of normal consciousness.	Behavior characterized by more calmness, more patience, and less hurrying than that of Type A individuals.
Techniques people use to deal with stress and changing situations.	Process by which a person takes some action to manage environmental and internal demands that cause or might cause stress and that will tax the individual's inner resources.
Subfield concerned with the use of psychological ideas and principles in health enhancement, illness prevention, diagnosis and treatment of disease, and rehabilitation processes.	Procedure of giving people realistic warnings, recommendations, and reassurances to help them prepare for and cope with impending dangers or losses.

CUT-OUT FLASH CARDS CHAPTER FOURTEEN

abnormal behavior	anxiety
phobic disorder	specific phobia
obsessive-compulsive	conversion disorders
hypochondriasis	dissociative identity disorder
personality disorders	antisocial personality disorder
bipolar disorders	learned helplessness
psychotic	hallucinations
affect	concordance rate

CUT-OUT FLASH CARDS CHAPTER FOURTEEN

A generalized feeling of fear and apprehension that might be related to a particular event or object and is often accompanied by increased physiological arousal.	Behavior characterized as atypical, socially unacceptable, distressing, maladaptive, or the result of distorted cognitions.
An anxiety disorder characterized by irrational and persistent fear of an object or situation, along with a compelling desire to avoid it.	Anxiety disorder characterized by unreasonable fear of, and consequent attempted avoidance of, specific objects or situations.
Somatoform disorders characterized by the loss or alteration of physical functioning for no apparent physiological reason.	Anxiety disorders characterized by persistent and uncontrollable thoughts and irrational beliefs that cause the performance of compulsive rituals that interfere with daily life.
Dissociative disorder characterized by the existence within an individual of two or more distinct personalities, each of which is dominant at particular times and directs the individual's behavior at those times.	Somatoform disorder characterized by an inordinate preoccupation with health and illness, coupled with excessive anxiety about disease.
Personality disorder characterized by egocentricity, behavior that is irresponsible and that violates the rights of other people (lying, theft, delinquency, and other violations of societal rules) a lack of guilt feelings, an inability to understand other people, and a lack of fear of punishment.	Disorders characterized by inflexible and long-standing maladaptive ways of dealing with the environment, which typically cause stress and social or occupational problems.
The behavior of giving up or not responding, exhibited by people or animals exposed to negative consequences or punishment over which they have no control.	Mood disorders characterized by vacillation between two extremes: mania and depression. Originally known as manic-depressive disorders.
Compelling perceptual (visual, tactile, olfactory, or auditory) experiences without a real physical stimulus.	Suffering from a gross impairment in reality testing that interferes with the ability to meet the ordinary demands of life.
The percentage of occasions when two groups or individuals show the same trait.	A person's emotional responses.

CUT-OUT FLASH CARDS CHAPTER FIFTEEN

psychotherapy	placebo effect
free association	interpretation
resistance	transference
client-centered therapy	behavior therapy
symptom substitution	token economy
time-out	counterconditioning
systematic desensitization	aversive counterconditioning
rational-emotive therapy	brief therapy

CUT-OUT FLASH CARDS CHAPTER FIFTEEN

A nonspecific therapeutic change that occurs as a result of a person's expectations of change rather than as a direct result of any specific treatment.	The treatment of emotional or behavioral problems through psychological techniques.
In Freud's theory, the technique of providing a context, meaning, or cause of a specific idea, feeling, or set of behaviors; the process of tying a set of behaviors to its unconscious determinant.	Psychoanalytic technique in which a person reports to the therapist his or her thoughts and feelings as they occur, regardless of how trivial, illogical, or objectionable their content may appear.
Psychoanalytic phenomenon in which a therapist becomes the object of a patient's emotional attitudes about an important person in the patient's life, such as a parent.	In psychoanalysis, an unwillingness to cooperate by which a patient signals a reluctance to provide the therapist with information or to help the therapist understand or interpret a situation.
A therapy based on the application of learning principles to human behavior and focuses on changing overt behaviors rather than on understanding subjective feelings, unconscious processes, or motivations. Also known as *behavior modification*.	An insight therapy, developed by Carl Rogers, that seeks to help people evaluate the world and themselves from their own perspective by providing them with a nondirective environment and unconditional positive regard for the client. Also known as *person-centered therapy*.
An operant conditioning procedure in which individuals who engage in appropriate behavior receive tokens that they can exchange for desirable items or activities.	The appearance of one symptom to replace another that has been eliminated by treatment.
A process of reconditioning in which a person is taught a new, more adaptive response to a familiar stimulus.	A punishment procedure in which a person is physically removed from a desired or reinforcing situation to decrease the likelihood that an undesired behavior will recur.
A counterconditioning technique that seeks to teach a new response by pairing on aversive or noxious stimulus with the stimulus that elicits on undesirable response so that the subject will learn to adopt a new, more worthwhile behavior in response to the familiar stimulus and cease the undesirable behavior.	A counterconditioning procedure in which a person first learns deep relaxation and then imagines a series of progressively fearful situations; with each successive experience, the person learns relaxation rather than fear as a new response to a formerly fearful stimulus.
A therapeutic approach that focuses on identifying the client's current problem and solving it with the most effective treatment as quickly as possible. Also known as *brief intermittent therapy*.	A cognitive behavior therapy that emphasizes the importance of logical, rational thought processes.

CUT-OUT FLASH CARDS CHAPTER SIXTEEN

social psychology	attitudes
cognitive dissonance	self-perception theory
balance theory	social cognition
impression formation	nonverbal communication
attribution	fundamental attribution error
actor-observer effect	reactance
self-serving bias	social influence
obedience	debriefing

CUT-OUT FLASH CARDS CHAPTER SIXTEEN

Long lasting patterns of feelings and beliefs about people, ideas, or objects that are based in a person's past experiences, shape his or her future behavior, are evaluative in nature, and serve certain functions.	The study of how individuals influence and are influenced by the thoughts, feelings, and behaviors of other people.
Approach to attitude formation in which people are assumed to infer their attitudes on the basis of observations of their own behavior.	A state in which individuals feel uncomfortable because they hold two or more thoughts, attitudes, or behaviors that are inconsistent with one another.
The thought process involved in making sense of events, people, oneself, and the world in general through analyzing and interpreting them.	An attitude theory stating that people prefer to hold consistent beliefs and try to avoid incompatible beliefs.
Information provided by cues or actions that involve movements of the body, especially the face.	The process by which a person uses the behavior and appearance of others to infer their internal states and intentions.
The tendency to attribute other people's behavior to dispositional (internal) causes rather than situational (external) causes.	The process by which someone infers other people's motives and intentions through observing their behavior and deciding whether the causes of the behavior are dispositional (internal) or situational (external).
Patterns of feelings and subsequent behaviors aimed at reestablishing a sense of freedom when there is an inconsistency between a person's self image as being free to choose and the person's realization that someone is trying to force him/her to chose a particular alternative.	The tendency to attribute the behavior of others to dispositional causes but to attribute one's own behavior to situational causes.
The way in which one or more people alter the attitudes or behavior of others.	People's tendency to evaluate their own positive behaviors as due to their own internal traits and characteristics, but their failures and short comings to external, situational factors.
A procedure to inform participants about the true nature of an experiment after its completion.	Compliance with the orders of another person or group of people.

CUT-OUT FLASH CARDS CHAPTER SIXTEEN

conformity	group
social facilitation	social loafing
group polarization	deindividuation
aggression	prosocial behavior
prejudice	stereotypes
discrimination	altruism
bystander apathy	interpersonal attraction
sociobiology	

CUT-OUT FLASH CARDS CHAPTER SIXTEEN

Two or more individuals who are loosely or cohesively related and who have some common characteristics and goals.	People's tendency to change attitudes or behaviors to be consistent with other people or with social norms.
Decrease in productivity that occurs when an individual works in a group instead of alone.	Change in performance that occurs when people believe they are in the presence of other people.
The process by which individuals in a group lose their self-awareness and concern with evaluation.	Exaggeration of an individual's preexisting attitudes as a result of group discussion.
Behavior that benefits someone else or society but that generally offers no obvious benefit to the person performing it and that may even involve some personal risk or sacrifice.	Any behavior designed to harm another person or thing.
Fixed, overly simple, often wrong, and often negative ideas about traits, attitudes, and behaviors attributed to groups of people.	Negative evaluation of an entire group of people, typically based on unfavorable (and often wrong) ideas about the group.
Behaviors that benefit other people and for which there is no discernible extrinsic reward, recognition, or appreciation.	Behavior targeted at individuals or groups, with the aim of holding them apart and treating them differently.
The tendency of one person to evaluate another person (or a symbol or image of another person) in a positive way.	The unwillingness of witnesses to an event to help, an effect that increases when there are more observers.
	The theory that even everyday behaviors are determined by the process of natural selection; that social behaviors that contribute to the survival of a species are passed on genetically from one generation to the next and account for mechanisms producing behaviors such as altruism.

CUT-OUT FLASH CARDS CHAPTER SEVENTEEN

crowding	personal space
territorial behavior	job analysis
performance appraisal	goal setting theory
expectancy theory	equity theory
transformational leader	stressor
privacy	human factors
ergonomics	empowerment
educational psychology	sports psychology

CUT-OUT FLASH CARDS CHAPTER SEVENTEEN

The area around an individual that is considered private and around which the person feels an invisible boundary.	The perception that one's space is too restricted.
Careful descriptions of the various tasks and activities that will be required for employees to do their jobs, along with the necessary knowledge, skills, and abilities; such analyses describes what gets done and *how* it gets done.	Behavior involved in establishing, maintaining, personalizing, and defending a delineated space.
The theory that asserts that setting specific, clear, attainable goals for a given task will lead to better performance.	The process by which a supervisor periodically evaluates the job-relevant strengths and weaknesses of subordinates.
Theory that suggests that what people bring to a work situation should be balanced by what they receive compared with other workers; thus, input should be balanced by compensation, or rewards, or workers will adjust their work level and potentially their job satisfaction.	Theories that suggest that a worker's effort and desire to maintain goal-directed behavior (to work) is determined by expectancies regarding the outcomes of that work.
A stimulus that affects an organism in physically or psychologically injurious ways and usually elicits feelings such as anxiety, tension, and physiological arousal.	Charismatic leader who inspires and provides intellectual stimulation to re-create an organization.
The study of the leadership of human beings to machines and to workplaces and other environments.	The result of the process of controlling the boundaries between people so that access is limited.
Facilitating the development of skills, knowledge, and motivation in individuals so they can act for themselves and gain control over their own lives.	The study of the fit between human anatomy or physiology, the demands of a particular task or piece of equipment, and the environment in which the task occurs.
The systematic application of psychological principles in sports.	The systematic application of psychological principles to learning and teaching.

CUT-OUT FLASH CARDS APPENDIX A

statistics	mean
mode	median
normal distribution	frequency polygon
measure of central tendency	descriptive statistics
frequency distribution	variability
range	standard deviation
inferential statistics	significant difference
replicating	correlation coefficient

CUT-OUT FLASH CARDS APPENDIX A

A measure of central tendency that is calculated by dividing the sum of the scores by the total number of scores. Also known as the *arithmetic average*.	The branch of mathematics that deals with collecting, classifying, and analyzing data.
A measure of central tendency that is the data point having 50 percent of all the observations (scores) above it and 50 percent below.	A measure of central tendency, the most frequently observed data point.
Graph of frequency distribution that shows the number of instances of obtained scores, usually with the data points connected by straight lines.	The approximately expected distribution of scores when a sample is drawn from a large population, drawn as a frequency polygon that often takes the form of a bell-shaped curve. Also known as a *normal curve*.
A general set of procedures used to summarize, condense, and describe samples of data.	A descriptive statistic that tells which result or score best represents an entire set of scores.
The extent to which scores differ from one another, especially the extent to which they differ from the mean.	A chart or array, usually arranged from the highest to the lowest score, showing the number of instances of each obtained score.
A descriptive statistic that measures the variability of data from the mean of the sample.	A measure of variability that describes the spread between the highest and the lowest scores in a distribution.
An experimentally obtained statistical difference that is unlikely to have occurred because of chance alone.	Procedures used to reach conclusions (generalizations) about larger populations from small samples of data.
A number that expresses the degree and direction of a relationship between two variables, ranging from -1 (a perfect negative correlation) to +1 (a perfect positive correlation).	Repeating an experiment to verify the results.

CROSSWORD PUZZLES

Word List

BEHAVIORISM
BIOLOGICAL
CASE
COGNITIVE
CONTROL
DEBRIEFING
DEPENDENT
ECLECTICISM
ETHICS
EXPERIMENT
EXPERIMENTAL
FUNCTIONALISM
GESTALT
HAWTHORNE
HUMANISTIC
HYPOTHESIS
INDEPENDENT
INTERVIEW
INTROSPECTION
NATURALISTIC
OPERATIONAL
PARTICIPANT
PSYCHOANALYST
PSYCHIATRIST
PSYCHOLOGIST
PSYCHOLOGY
QUESTIONNAIRE
SAMPLE
STRUCTURALISM
THEORY
VARIABLE

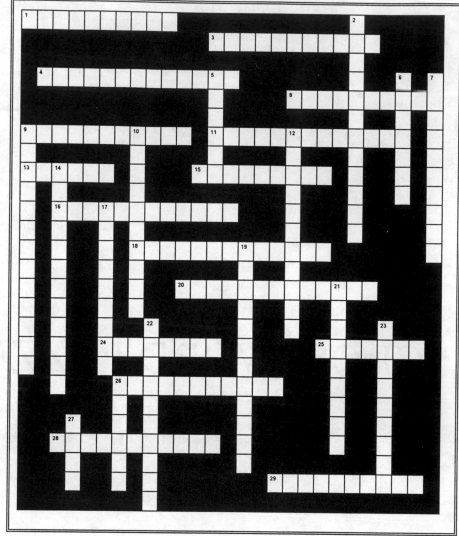

Across

1. uniqueness and free will
3. describes and measures observable behaviors
4. organized structure of conscious experience
8. human behavior & mental processes
9. variable that is manipulated
13. collection of ideas
11. practices psychoanalysis
15. variable expected to change
16. medical doctor
18. studies how & why conscious mind works
20. also known as survey
24. condition of experiment
25. sum of parts greater than whole
26. combining techniques
28. also known as subject
29. permits inferences & tests hypotheses

Down

2. uses behavioral principles
5. represents population
6. the comparison group
7. statement of relationship
9. self-examination
10. information about experiment
12 definition: set of procedures
14. group where IV is manipulated
17. focus on mental processes
19. without observer intervention
21. face-to-face
22. also neuroscience perspective
23. effect; observation changes behavior
26. rules of proper conduct
27. study: interviews participants

CHAPTER 2

Word List

ACTION POTENTIAL
AFFERENT
AGONIST
ALLELE
ALL-OR-NONE
AMYGDALA
ANTAGONIST
AUTONOMIC
AXON
BRAIN
CEREBELLUM
CHROMOSOMES
CNS
CONVOLUTION
CORTEX
DENDRITES
DIABETES
EEG
EFFERENT
ENDOCRINE
FOREBRAIN
FRATERNAL
GENE
GENETICS
HINDBRAIN
HORMONES
HYPOGLYCEMIA
HYPOTHALAMUS
IDENTICAL
INSULIN
NEURON
NEUROTRANSMITTER
PKU
PONS
SYMPATHETIC
SYNAPSE

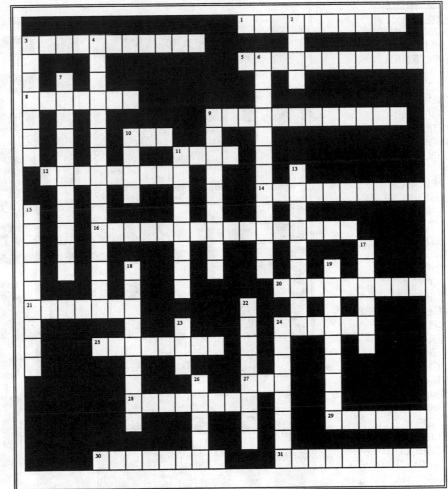

Across

1. opposes neurotransmitter
3. responds to emergencies
5. strand of DNA
8. mimics neurotransmitter
9. eating, drinking, & sexual behavior
10. phenylketonuria
11. consists of DNA & protein
12. firing rate of neuron (3 words)
14. controls balance, coordination & movement
16. chemical substance
20. ductless gland
21. facilitates sugar transport
24. member of pair of genes
25. endocrine gland chemicals
27. electroencephalogram
28. sends messages to body
29. basic unit of nervous system
30. sends messages to brain
31. controls automatic processes

Down

2. transmits from cell body
3. juncture between neurons
4. also known as spike discharge (2 words)
6. overproduction of insulin
7. folds in brain tissue
9. most primitive part of brain
10. connects medulla & cerebellum
11. study of heredity
13. 2 ova fertilized by 2 sperm
15. result of split zygote
17. also known as neocortex
18. receives signals
19. largest part of brain
22. too little insulin
23. brain & spinal cord
24. controls emotion
26. part of CNS

CHAPTER 3

Word List

ACCOMMODATION
AMPLITUDE
BINOCULAR
BRIGHTNESS
CHIASM
CONDUCTION
CONVERGENCE
DICHROMATS
ENDORPHINS
FREQUENCY
HUE
HYPEROPIC
ILLUSION
KINESTHESIS
LIGHT
MONOCHROMATS
MONOCULAR
MYOPIC
OLFACTION
PERCEPTION
PHOTORECEPTORS
PITCH
PRAGNANZ
RECEPTIVE
SACCADES
SATURATION
SENSATION
SENSORINEURAL
SOUND
SUBLIMINAL
THRESHOLD
TRANSDUCTION
TRICHROMATS
VESTIBULAR

Across

2. also known as purity
4. changes in the shape of the lens of the eye
7. fields of the retina that produce changes in firing
9. movement of the eyes toward each other
11. also known as coding
12. rapid eye movement
13. also known as color
14. natural painkillers
19. rods and cones
21. cycles per second (Hz)
22. color blindness
25. movement awareness
26. Gestalt principle of grouped stimuli
27. perception differing from normal
30. the lightness or darkness of light
31. seeing only two basic hues

Down

1. sense of bodily orientation
2. deafness from damage to higher audio processes
3. minimum level of stimulation to excite
5. deafness resulting from interference with transmission to the inner ear
6. also known as nearsighted
8. tone
10. optic nerve crossover
12. stimulation of sense organs
13. also known as farsighted
15. sensory input acquires meaning
16. depth cues not dependent on two eyes
17. normal color vision
18. perception below the threshold
20. smell
23. also known as intensity
24. perception by use of both eyes
28. electromagnetic spectrum
29. changes in frequency and amplitude

CHAPTER 4
Word List
ADDICTIVE
ALCOHOLIC
ALTERED STATE
BIOFEEDBACK
CIRCADIAN
CONSCIOUSNESS
DEPENDENCE
DREAM
DRUG
EEG
HYPNOSIS
INSOMNIA
LATENT
LUCID
MANIFEST
MEDITATION
NREM
OPIATES
PSYCHEDELICS
PSYCHOACTIVE
PSYCHOSTIMULANT
REGRESSION
REM
SEDATIVE-HYPNOTIC
SLEEP
TOLERANCE
WITHDRAWAL

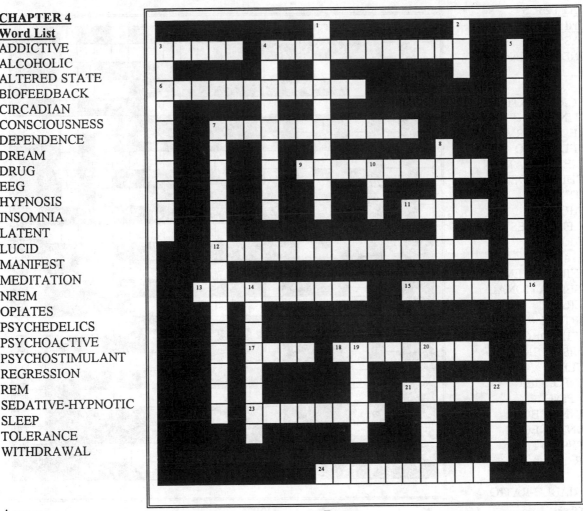

Across
3. REM sleep
4. dramatically different from ordinary
6. affect moods, thoughts, memory, judgment, & perception
7. alters behaviors, thought, emotions
9. control of body's organs and functions
11. unresponsiveness and physical immobility
12. drugs that relax and calm
13. physiological reaction to addictive drugs
15. storyline, characters, and setting
17. without rapid eye movement
18. problem drinker with physiological & psychological need to consume
21. internally generated cycles
23. inability to sleep
24. hypnotic return to an earlier age

Down
1. relaxation and restricted stimulation
2. rapid eye movement
3. desire to use a drug
4. physiological need and withdrawal
5. awareness and responsiveness
7. reduces fatigue, increases alertness, & elevates mood
8. symbolic meaning of a dream
10. electroencephalogram
14. state of trance
16. progressive insensitivity
19. dream awareness
20. pain relieving and sedative drugs
22. chemical substance

CHAPTER 5

Word List

CLASSICAL
CONDITIONING
CR
CS
DISCRIMINATION
EXTINCTION
FIXED-INTERVAL
FIXED-RATIO
GENERALIZATION
HIGHER ORDER
LATENT
LEARNED
HELPLESSNESS
LEARNING
NEGATIVE -
   REINFORCEMENT
OBSERVATIONAL
OPERANT
POSITIVE -
   REINFORCEMENT
PUNISHMENT
REFLEX
REINFORCER
SHAPING
SKINNER BOX
SPONTANEOUS
SUPERSTITIOUS
UCR
UCS
VARIABLE-RATIO

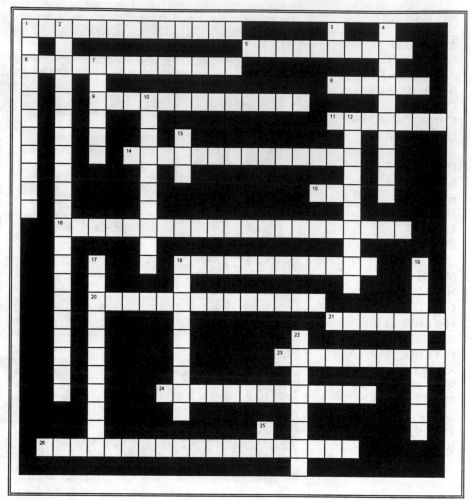

Across

1. behavior learned through coincidence
5. response rate is rapid
6. also known as social learning theory
8. occurs in the absence of direct reinforcement
9. timed reinforcement schedule
11. also known as instrumental conditioning
14. response specificity
15. produces involuntary response
16. removal of an aversive stimulus
18. systematic learning procedures
20. response to a similar stimulus
21. gradual training of organism
23. event that increases probability of recurrence
24. reinforcement after predetermined but variable responses
26. giving up after exposure to negative consequences

Down

1. recurrence of extinguished response
2. presentation of a rewarding stimulus
3. elicited response elicited by CS
4. response-dependent reinforcement schedule
7. automatic response to stimuli
10. reduction in probability of CR
12. event that decreases probability of recurrence
13. unlearned or involuntary response
17. conditioning through pairing with a CS
18. also known as Pavlovian conditioning
19. device for administering reinforcement
22. relatively permanent change
25. neutral stimulus that elicits a CR

CHAPTER 6

Word List

AMNESIA
ANTEROGRADE
CHUNKS
CONSOLIDATION
DECAY
DECLARATIVE
ELABORATIVE
ENCODING
EPISODIC
EXPLICIT
IMAGERY
IMPLICIT
INTERFERENCE
LTM
MAINTENANCE
MEMORY
PDP
PRIMACY
PROACTIVE
PROCEDURAL
RECENCY
REHEARSAL
RETRIEVAL
RETROACTIVE
RETROGRADE
SCHEMA
SEMANTIC
SENSORY MEMORY
SPAN
STATE-DEPENDENT
STM
STORAGE

Across

1. inhibition as a result of previous information
2. repetitive review of information
5. memory for perceptual motor and cognitive skills
8. memory for specific events, objects, & situations
11. memory for specific facts
12. ability to remember past
14. long-term memory
16. evolution of temporary circuit into permanent neural circuit
18. physiologically based recall
20. brief and limited number of items that can be reproduced
21. loss of memory for adults following trauma
23. electrochemical memory process
28. manageable and meaningful units of information
29. process by which information is recovered
30. recall of items presented first
31. suppression or confusion due to received information

Down

1. parallel distributed processing
3. mental picture of sensory event
4. voluntary active memory process
6. decrease in recall due to subsequent presentation of information
7. loss of information due to time
9. memory for ideas, rules, and general concepts
10. short-term memory
13. loss of memory for experiences prior to trauma
15. inability to remember past events
17. also known as sensory register
19. rehearsal involving repetition and association
21. recall of items presented last
22. repetitive actions on information
24. passive, unconscious memory processing
25. process of maintaining information
27. conceptual framework

CHAPTER 7
WORD LIST
ALGORITHM
BRAINSTORMING
COGNITIVE
CONCEPT
CONSERVATIVE
CONVERGENT
CREATIVITY
DIVERGENT
FIXEDNESS
GRAMMAR
HEURISTICS
LINGUISTICS
LOGIC
MEANS-ENDS
MORPHEME
PHONEME
PSYCHO-LINGUISTICS
REASONING
SEMANTICS
SURFACE
SYLLOGISM
SYNTAX
TRANSFORMA-
    TIONAL

Across
2. study of speech, sounds, meaning, & grammar
5. strategies, not rules, for problem-solving
10. association between surface and deep structure
12. problem-solving through identifying set goals
13. how language is acquired, perceived, understood, & produced
14. all possible solutions without prior judgments
17. generation of logical possibilities
18. elimination of alternative possibilities
19. sequence of statements followed by conclusion
20. procedure used to reach valid conclusion
21. inability to see multiple uses of objects
22. original, novel, and appropriate problem solving

Down
1. how word groups are related
3. study of learning, perception, and thought
4. basic unit of sound
6. closest to written or spoken form of a sentence
7. rules and patterns for generating sentences
8. mental categories used to classify
9. solution of the problem after a step-by-step analysis
11. generation and evaluation of situations
12. basic unit of meaning
15. analysis of the meaning of language
16. selective narrowing into answer

WORD LIST

FACTOR ANALYSIS
HALO EFFECT
INTELLIGENCE
IQ
MAINSTREAMING
MR
NORMAL CURVE
NORMS
PERCENTILE SCORE
RAW SCORE
RELIABILITY
SAMPLE
SS
STANDARDIZATION
VALIDITY

Across

5. statistic to discover mutual independence
8. position relative to mean based on standard deviation
9. bell-shaped graphic representative of the population
10. below average intellectual functioning
11. test's ability to yield same scores repeatedly
12. process for establishing norms
13. standard deviation score with equal means and standard deviation for all ages
14. percentage of population obtaining the lower score

Down

1. exceptional children's placement in regular classroom settings
2. scores and percentiles from the population
3. characteristic influence on evaluation
4. score on a test not transformed
6. global capacity to act purposefully, think rationally, & deal with environment
7. ability to measure what is intended
12. individuals who match the population

ANOREXIA
AROUSAL
BULIMIA
COGNITIVE
DRIVE
EMOTION
EXCITEMENT
EXPECTANCY
EXTRINSIC
HUMANISTIC
INTRINSICALLY
MOTIVATION
MOTIVE
NEED
ORGASM
PLATEAU
RESOLUTION
SOCIAL NEED
VASO-CONSTRICTION

Across

2. theory that focuses on expectations of success in reaching goals
6. specific conditions of goal directed behavior
8. condition that directs people toward establishing relationships
10. the phase to which the body naturally returns after orgasm
11. focuses on human dignity, choice, and self-worth
13. condition directed to satisfy physiological need
15. engorgement of the blood vessels
16. behaviors engaged in for no apparent reward
18. autonomic nervous system activity reaches its peak
19. bingeing followed by purging

Down

1. physiological imbalance accompanied by arousal
3. second phase of sexual response cycle
4. intense fear of becoming obese
5. emphasis on the role of thought
7. first phase of sexual response cycle
9. subjective response that readies individuals for action
12. internal conditions of goal directed behavior
14. external rewards
17. activation of the CNS, ANS, muscles, and brain

CHAPTER 10
WORD LIST

ACCOMMODATION
ATTACHMENT
ASSIMILATION
BABINSKI
BONDING
CONCRETE
CONSERVATION
DECENTRATION
EGOCENTRISM
EMBRYO
FETUS
FORMAL
GRASPING
LABOR
MORALITY
MORO
PLACENTA
PREOPERATIONAL
ROOTING
SENSORIMOTOR
SUCKING
TEMPERMENT
TERATOGENS
ZYGOTE

Across

4. experiences are incorporated into existing mental framework
5. emotional tie toward another person
6. substance that may produce malformations
11. ability to recognize changes in weight, substance, or volume
12. the process of changing from a totally self-oriented point of view
14. reflex response to loud noise or abrupt change in environment
18. stage when symbolic thought is developed
19. infant reflex after touching palm or fingers
21. infant turns head when cheeks or lips are stimulated
22. system for evaluating right or wrong
23. emotional attachment in the early minutes after birth

Down

1. 5th through the 49th day after conception
2. process in which the uterus contracts to open the cervix
3. uterine tissue for the exchange of nutrients and waste products
4. new concepts modify existing cognitive structures
7. motions when lips are stimulated
8. period from 49th day until birth
9. third stage of cognitive development (age 6 to 12)
10. also known as self-centeredness
13. individual differences in emotional reactions
15. first two years of cognitive development
16. final stage of cognitive development
17. reflex when the soles of the feet are touched
20. a fertilized egg

Word List

adolescence
ageism
Alzheimers
androgynous
dementia
gender identity
gender role
gender schema
puberty
thanatology

Across
1. also known as sex role
2. study of death and dying
3. period following puberty
5. sense of being male or female
6. chronic and progressive disorder of the brain
7. period of increase in sex hormone production
8. prejudices against the elderly

Down
1. organizing theme to classify and understand perceptions of the world
3. having male and female characteristics
4. impairment in mental functioning

CHAPTER 12
Word List
ANAL
ARCHETYPES
ASSESSMENT
CONSCIOUS
DENIAL
EGO
FIXATION
FULFILLMENT
GENITAL
ID
IDEAL SELF
LATENCY
LIBIDO
NEO-FREUDIANS
OEDIPUS
ORAL
PERSONALITY
PHALLIC
PRECONSCIOUS
PROJECTION
PROJECTIVES
PSYCHIC
DETERMINISM
RATIONALIZATION
REACTION
FORMATION
REPRESSION
SELF
SELF-EFFICACY
SHYNESS
SUBLIMINATION
SUPEREGO
TRAIT
TYPES
UNCONSCIOUS

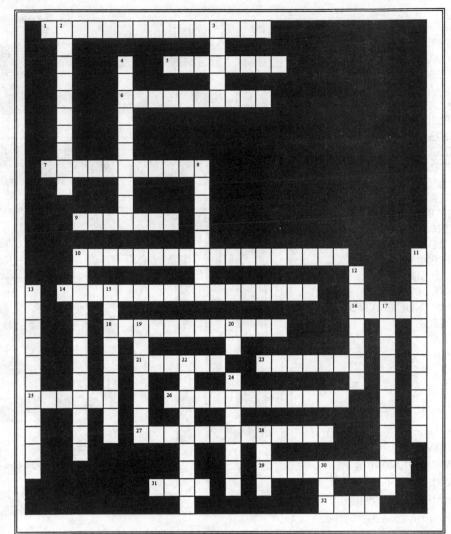

Across
1. reinterpretation of undesirable feelings
5. excessive attachment to object or person
6. attribution of undesirable traits to other people
7. mental activities beyond normal awareness
9. anxiety often leading to avoidance
10. all behaviors are caused by past events
14. behavior in a manner opposite to true behaviors
16. broad collection of traits
18. proposed variations of Freudian theory
21. refusal to accept the true source of anxiety
23. stage in which gratification is primarily from the genitals
25. instinctual life force that energizes the id
26. belief that one can succeed and execute specific behaviors
27. unacceptable impulses redirected into acceptable ones
29. Jung's collective unconscious
31. perception individuals have of themselves
32. stage in which gratification is primarily through the mouth

Down
2. evaluation of individual differences
3. identifiable stable behavior
4. blocking of anxiety provoking feelings
8. moral aspect of mental functioning
10. Freud's second level of awareness
11. set of relatively enduring behavioral characteristics
12. inactive stage of personality development
13. obtaining potential
15. 1st level of awareness
17. tests with ambiguous stimuli
19. complex feelings of rivalry with same sex parent
20. source of instinctual energy
22. the self a person wants to be
24. Freud's last stage of personality development
28. Freud's second stage of personality development
30. in accordance with reality

CHAPTER 13

Word List

ANXIETY
APPROACH-APPROACH
APPROACH-AVOIDANCE
AVOIDANCE-AVOIDANCE
BURNOUT
CONFLICT
COPING
COPING SKILLS
FRUSTRATION
HEALTH PSYCHOLOGY
POSTTRAUMATIC STRESS
PRESSURE
PSYCHO-
  NEUROIMMUNOLOGY
RESILIENCE
SOCIAL SUPPORT
STRESS
STRESS INOCULATION
STRESSOR
TYPE-A
TYPE-B

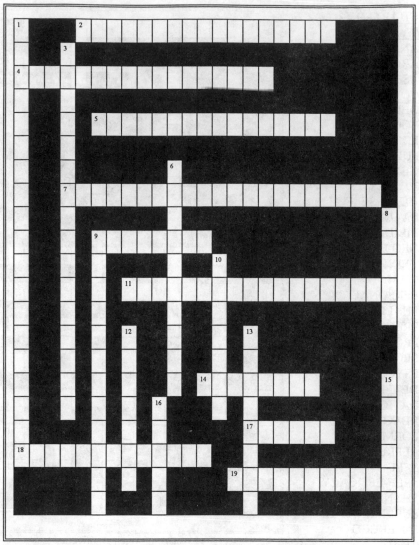

Across

2. conflict that results from having to choose an alternative
4. preparing for and coping with impending dangers or losses
5. conflict that results from having two attractive alternatives
7. psychological process of the immune system
9. emotional state requiring difficult decisions
11. conflict that results from having to choose between two distasteful alternatives
14. environmental stimulus
17. nonspecific response to real or imagined demands
18. availability of comfort, recognition, approval, and encouragement
19. emotional state when goals are blocked

Down

1. post traumatic stress disorder
3. field concerned with health enhancement
6. extent to which people are flexible
8. competitiveness, impatience, & hostilities
9. techniques for managing stress
10. generalized feeling of fear and apprehension
12. emotional and physical exhaustion
13. feelings that result from coercion
15. management of stress
16. calmness, patience, and less hurried

CHAPTER 14
Word List
ABNORMAL
AFFECT
AGORAPHOBIA
ANTISOCIAL
ANXIETY
BIPOLAR
CATATONIC
CHILD ABUSE
CONCORDANCE
CONVERSION
DELUSIONS
DEPRESSIVE
DISSOCIATIVE
DOUBLE BIND
FREE-FLOATING
GENERALIZED
HALLUCINATIONS
HYPOCHONDRIASIS
LEARNED HELPLESSNESS
MODEL
OCD
PARANOID
PHOBIC
PREVALENCE
PSYCHOTIC
RAPE
RESIDUAL
SCHIZOPHRENIC
SOCIAL PHOBIA
SOMATIZATION
SOMATOFORM
UNDIFFERENTIATED
VULNERABILITY

Across
1. percentage of population displaying disorder
2. person's diminished ability to deal with demands
3. sudden, but temporary alteration in consciousness
5. fear of being scrutinized by others
6. obsessive compulsive disorder
7. generalized feeling of fear and apprehension
9. percentage of individuals showing the same traits
10. inordinate preoccupation with illness
15. giving up after exposure to uncontrollable negative consequences
17. anxiety not clearly related to specific objects or situations
18. also known as manic depressive
19. fear of being alone or unable to escape
21. years of recurrent and multiple physical complaints
24. mood disorders with extreme sadness and despair
26. egocentric, irresponsible, and violates people's rights
27. atypical, socially unacceptable, distressing, and maladaptive
29. two different inconsistent messages
30. excited or violent motor activity

Down
1. gross impairment in reality testing
3. false beliefs inconsistent with reality
4. real physical symptoms not under voluntary control
5. lack of reality testing; intellectual deterioration
8. schizophrenia characterized by a mixture of symptoms
11. perceptual experiences
12. loss of physical functioning with no physiological reason
13. persistent anxiety for at least 6 months
14. physical, emotional, or sexual mistreatment of children
16. person's emotional responses
20. schizophrenic disorder with patient generally in touch with reality
22. respective or approach derived from data
23. delusions and hallucinations of persecution
25. fear and subsequent avoidance of objects or situations
28. forceful sexual assault

CHAPTER 15
Word List

BEHAVIOR
BRIEF INTERMITTENT
CLIENT-CENTERED
COUNTER-
    CONDITIONING
ECT
EGO ANALYST
ENCOUNTER
FAMILY
FREE ASSOCIATION
GESTALT
GROUP
INSIGHT
INTERPRETATION
NONDIRECTIVE
PLACEBO EFFECT
PSYCHOANALYSIS
PSYCHODRAMA
PSYCHOTHERAPY
RESISTANCE
RET
TIME-OUT
TOKEN ECONOMY
TRANSFERENCE

Across

1. also known as ego psychologists
5. group therapy where members act out feelings
7. also known as Freudian therapy
9. treatment of emotional or behavioral problems
10. _____ therapy: insight therapy that emphasizes awareness
11. _____ _____ therapy: also known as brief therapy
15. _____ _____ therapy: also known as person centered therapy
16. appropriate behavior receives tokens for exchange
18. therapist becomes object of patient's problem
20. unwillingness to cooperate while a patient
21. teaching of more adaptive responses
22. _____ therapy: relationship between unconscious motivations and current behaviors

Down

2. _____ therapy: psychotherapeutic processes with several people
3. _____ therapy: therapy committed to changing people's interactions
4. electronconvulsive shock therapy
6. _____ therapy: client determines direction of therapy
7. therapeutic change as a result of expectations
8. _____ therapy: also known as behavior modification
12. process of tying behaviors to unconscious determinants
13. technique of reporting one's thoughts and feelings as they occur
14. physical removal from desired situation
17. _____ group: people needing to learn about feelings, behavior, and interactions
19. emphasizes rational thought

CHAPTER 16

Word List

ATTITUDES
ATTRIBUTION
ATTRIBUTION-ERROR
COGNITIVE DISSONANCE
CONFORMITY
DEBRIEFING
DEINDIVIDUATION
DISCRIMINATION
EQUITY
GROUP
GROUPTHINK
INTIMACY
NONVERBAL
OBEDIENCE
POLARIZATION
PREJUDICE
PROSOCIAL
REACTANCE
SELF-PERCEPTION
SOCIAL COGNITION
SOCIAL FACILITATION
SOCIAL LOAFING
SOCIAL PSYCHOLOGY
SOCIOBIOLOGY
STEREOTYPES

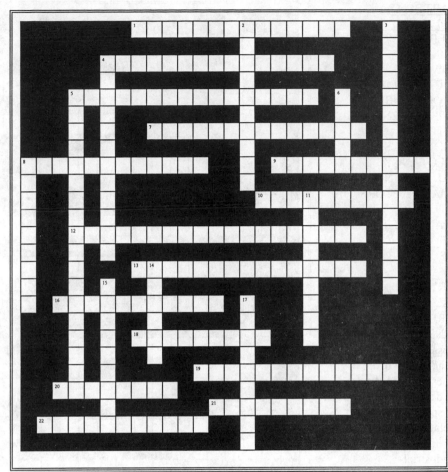

Across

1. theory: infer attitudes on the basis of observations of their own behavior
4. process of making sense of the world through analysis
5. study of how individuals are influenced by others
7. different treatment for targeted individuals or groups
8. exaggeration of pre-existing attitudes
9. group reinforcement and concurrence
10. procedure to inform subjects
12. thoughts, attitudes, or behaviors that are inconsistent
13. group loses sense of self-awareness and concern for evaluation
16. inference of other people's motives
18. long lasting patters of feelings and beliefs
19. decrease in productivity by member of group
20. willingness to self disclose
21. communication via the body, especially the face
22. fixed overly simple negative ideas

Down

3. tendency to blame on disposition rather than situation
4. termination by the process of natural selection
5. change due to belief that others are present
6. individuals who share same characteristics and goals
8. act that benefits others
11 behaviors aimed at reestablishing a sense of freedom
14. _____ theory: attempt to maintain stable, consistent, interpersonal relationships
15. negative evaluation of an entire group
17. compliance with the orders of another person or group

CHAPTER 17

Word List
APPLIED PSYCHOLOGY
COMMUNITY
CROWDING
EDUCATIONAL
EMPOWERMENT
ENVIRONMENTAL
EQUITY
ERGONOMICS
EXPECTANCY
GOAL-SETTING
HUMAN FACTORS
IO
JOB ANALYSIS
PERFORMANCE
PERSONAL SPACE
PRIVACY
SPORT
STRESSOR
TERRITORIAL
TRANSFORMATIONAL

Across
2. behavior involved in establishing and defending a delineated space
4. relationship between humans and machines
5. industrial-organizational psychology
6. facilitating the development of skills, knowledge, and motivation
8. ____ _____ theory: goals for a given task will lead to better performance
10. _____ psychology: psychology to solve everyday living problems
11. invisible boundary
13. descriptions of tasks required to do the job
15. _____ psychology: how physical settings affect human behavior
16. _____ theories: work effort determined by expected outcome of work
17. result of controlling boundaries
18. the fit between people and the environment

Down
1. perception that one's space is being too restricted
2. _____ leader: charismatic leader who inspires and stimulates to recreate an organization
3. _____ psychology: provides mental health service to effect social change
7. stimulus that elicits feelings of anxiety, tension, physiological arousal
9. _____ psychology: systematic application of psychology to learning and teaching
11. _____ appraisal: periodic evaluation of a subordinate
12. _____ theory: balance of what people bring with what they receive in comparison to others
14. _____ psychology: systematic application of psychology in sport

CHAPTER 1

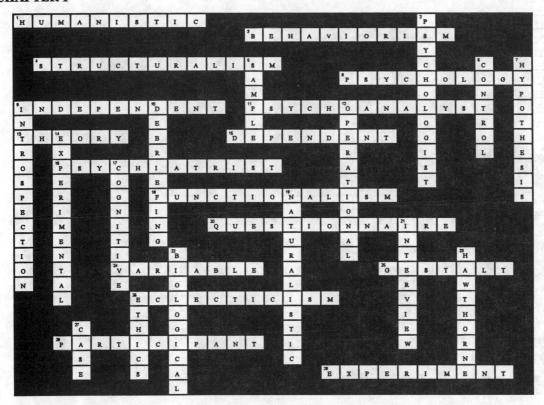

CHAPTER 2

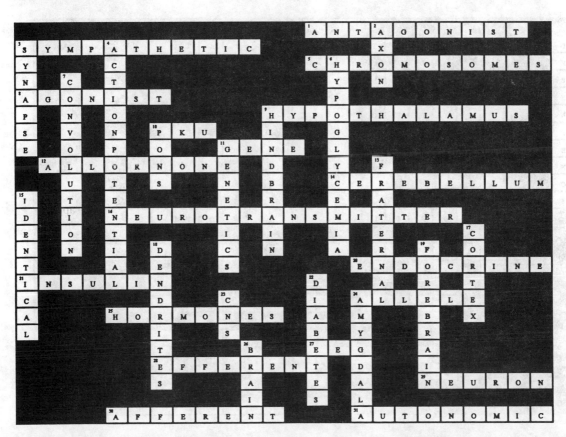

CHAPTER 3

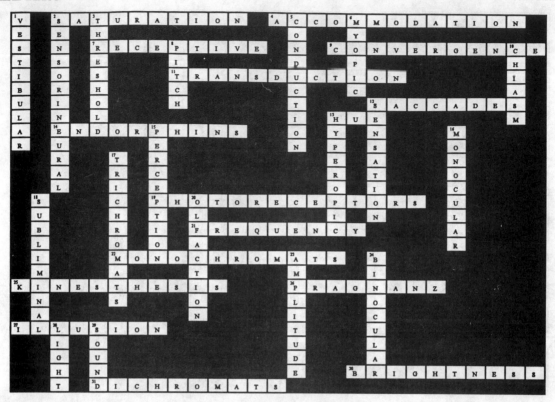

CHAPTER 4

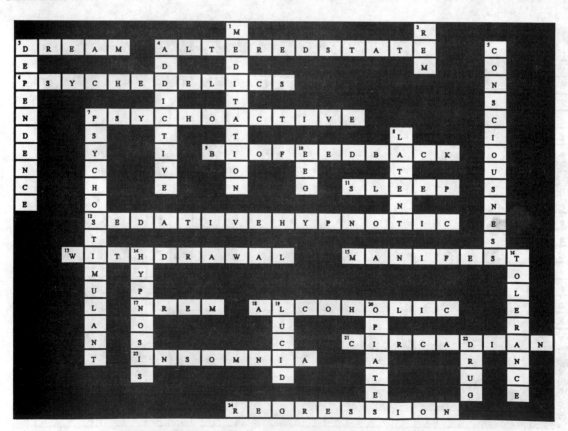

CHAPTER 5

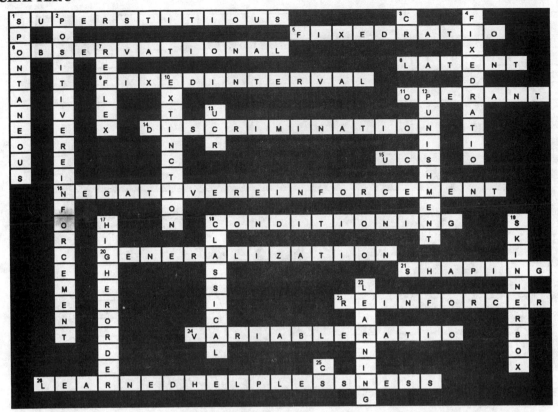

CHAPTER 6

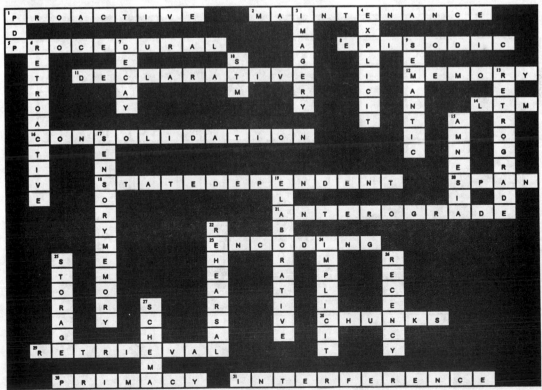

CHAPTER 7

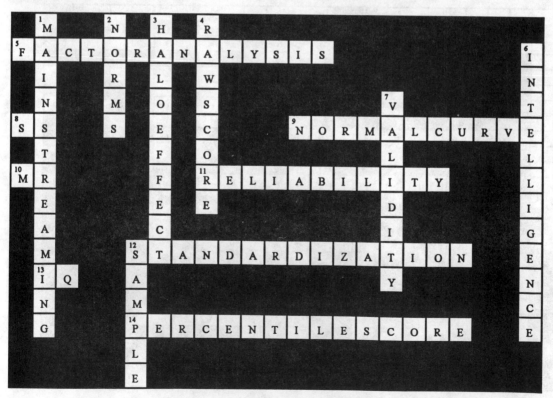

CHAPTER 8

CHAPTER 9

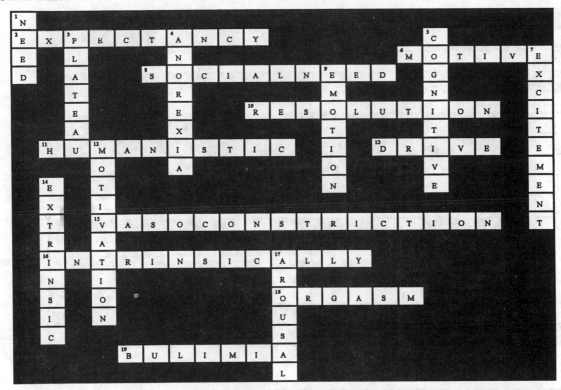

CHAPTER 10

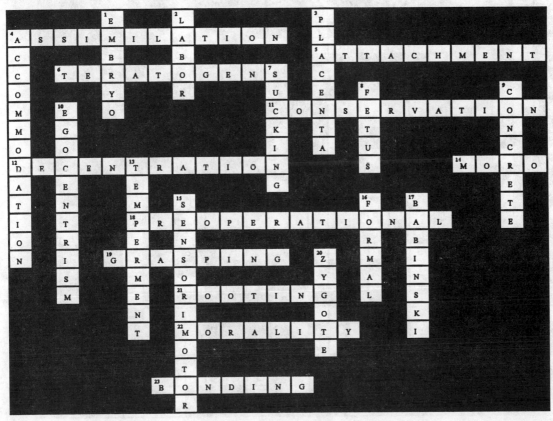

CHAPTER 11

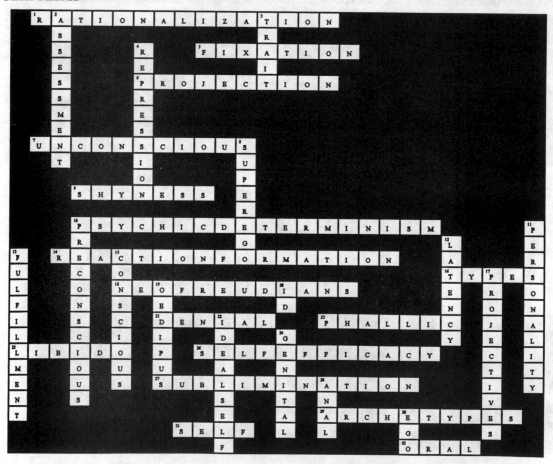

CHAPTER 12

CHAPTER 13

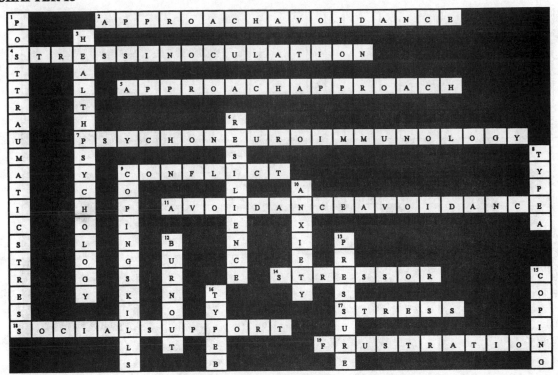

CHAPTER 14

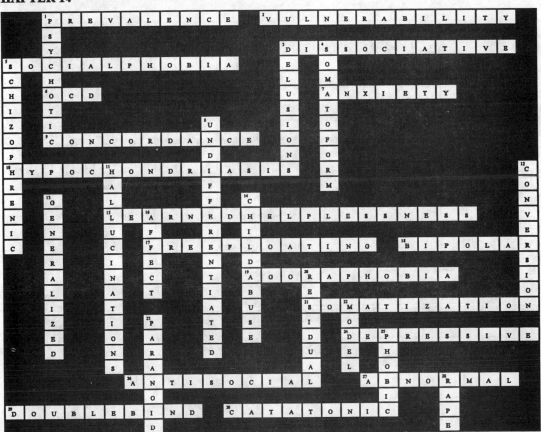

CHAPTER 15

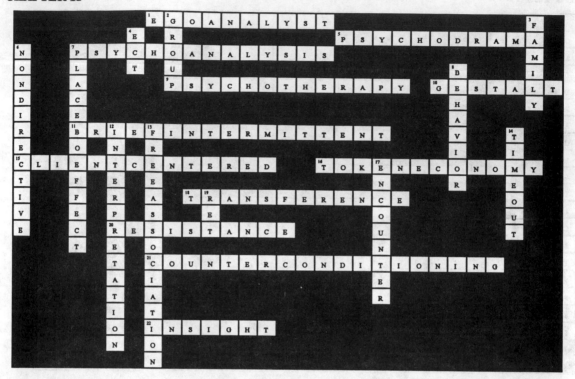

CHAPTER 16

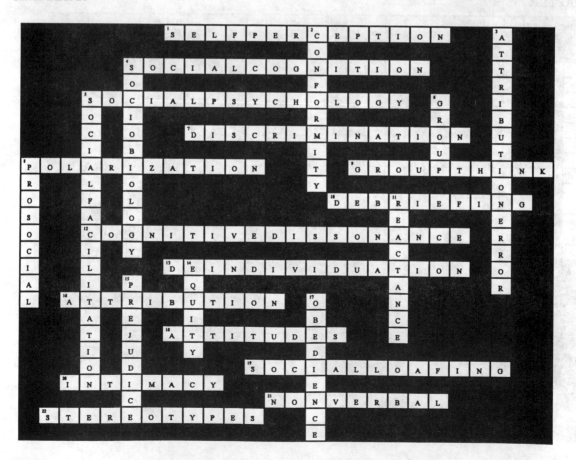

CHAPTER 17

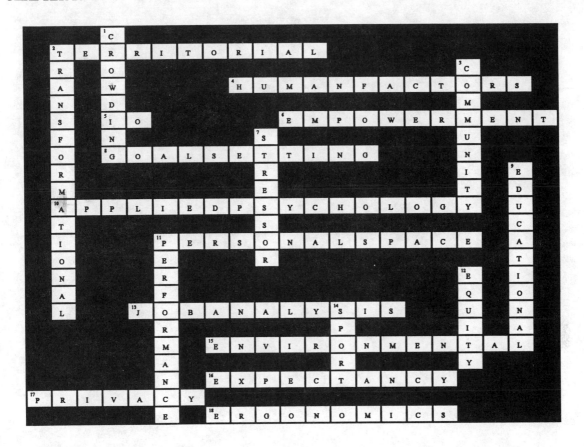

KEEPING PACE PLUS

PRACTICE TESTS

CHAPTER ONE

1. A psychologist who makes detailed records of a teacher's words and actions in the classroom and how they affect students' test scores is studying.
   A. biological processes.
   B. mental processes.
   C. physiological reactions.
   D. overt behavior

2. When Alice was pulled over by a police officer because she was speeding, her heart started to pound and her hands started to shake. These are examples of
   A. social relationships.
   B. mental processes.
   C. clairvoyance.
   D. physiological reactions.

3. A factor in an experiment that might affect the results but is not of interest to the experimenter is called a(n)
   A. hypothesis
   B. extraneous variable.
   C. replication.
   D. theoretical condition.

4. Compared to a psychiatrist, a clinical psychologist's training makes him or her better prepared to
   A. engage in research about psychological problems.
   B. prescribe the appropriate medications for a patient.
   C. understand the biological causes of disorders.
   D. explain psychological disorders to their patients.

5. A psychologist who tries to help those with chronic pain, such as from a bad back, learn how to manage and control that pain is most likely a _____ psychologist.
   A. psychiatric
   B. counseling
   C. human factors
   D. behavioral medicine

6. A condition or characteristic of a situation or person that can change over time or that can be different between different situations or people is called a(n)
   A. variable.
   B. hypothesis.
   C. correlation.
   D. experiment.

7. A student researcher collecting data on how attractive a photograph is to a number of people would smile and nod when given the answer he expected, but would frown when given a different answer and wait until they changed their response. This is an extreme example of a(n)
   A. demand characteristic.
   B. double-blind experiment.
   C. operational definition.
   D. statistical significance.

8. Which of these is an important reason for using animals as research subjects in psychology?
   A. Their short life spans make it easier to study changes over several generations.
   B. There are no ethical rules that limit what research can be performed with animals.
   C. Their mental processes are practically identical with those of humans.
   D. Animals don't feel pain, loneliness, or stress the same way humans do.

9. When a researcher uses deception as part of a research project, it is especially important that there should be
   A. no animals or children used in the research.
   B. both informed consent and debriefing.
   C. a second piece of research that does not use deception.
   D. a careful record of all responses.

10. Cognitive psychology is a school of psychological thought that emphasizes the importance of
    A. biological and chemical processes in the brain.
    B. measuring overt, observable behaviors.
    C. mental processes such as thought and memory.
    D. unresolved conflicts and forces in the unconscious.

CHAPTER TWO

1. The new field that focuses on how much of our abilities and actions are due to our biological inheritance is called
   A. psychoneurology.
   B. physiological psychiatry.
   C. cerebral anatomy.
   D. behavior genetics.

2. How is it possible to have two people in which the genetic heritage is the same but the environment is not?
   A. Paternal twins, reared apart
   B. Identical twins, reared apart
   C. Monoclonal twins, reared apart
   D. Nothing; this is NOT possible

3. The long slim fiber that extends from a neuron and that carries its message out to other neurons is called the
   A. dendrite.
   B. glia.
   C. myelin.
   D. axon.

4. When a postsynaptic potential (PSP) is received by a cell, if it is excitatory it will _____ while if it is inhibitory it will _____.
   A. trigger then release of neurotransmitters; trigger the absorption of neurotransmitters.
   B. trigger the absorption of neurotransmitters; trigger the release of neurotransmitters.
   C. make the cell fire more easily; make the cell fire less easily.
   D. make the cell fire less easily; make the cell fire more easily.

5. The peripheral nervous system consists of two parts, which are
   A. the brain and the spinal cord.
   B. the parasympathetic and sympathetic nervous systems.
   C. the somatic and the autonomic nervous systems.
   D. the afferent and the efferent fibers.

6. The sympathetic nervous system is primarily responsible for
   A. helping relax and conserve energy.
   B. processing sensory inputs to the brain.
   C. muscular coordination and movements.
   D. coping with an emergency situations.

7. Which of the following parts of the brain is most heavily involved in regulating emotions?
   A. The cerebellum
   B. The reticular formation
   C. The limbic system
   D. The corpus callosum

8. A CAT scan (computerized axial tomography) is created using
   A. electrodes attached to the outside of someone's head.
   B. Computer controlled and processed X-ray pictures.
   C. radiochemicals injected into the patient's blood.
   D. the magnetic fields of varying strength and direction.

9. The relationships between the endocrine glands, the brain, and behavior can best be summarized by saying
   A. the endocrine glands control the brain through the hormones they secrete into the bloodstream.
   B. the brain controls the endocrine glands and the hormones they produce through nerve signals.
   C. Hormones produced by the endocrine glands affect behavior through their effect on the brain.
   D. The endocrine glands, the brain, and behavior all interact and affect each other.

10. One way in which men and women use their brains differently when performing the same task is that
    A. men process language primarily on the right side, women primarily on the left.
    B. men's brains process more tasks at lower levels, women more at higher levels.
    C. men's brains are less affected by hormones than women's brains are.
    D. women use both sides of their brains more equally on some cognitive tasks.

CHAPTER THREE

1. An absolute threshold is
   A. a statistically determined minimum level of stimulation needed to excite a perceptual system.
   B. the smallest amount of change in a stimulus needed for most people to detect the change.
   C. a relatively permanent change in the level of sensitivity in a sense organ due to experience.
   D. the shortest amount of time a stimulus can exist before it will be detected by the perceptual system.

2. The theory of selective attention that states that all incoming information is analyzed, but only certain information is chosen to be passed on to higher levels for more complex processing, is called the
   A. localization theory.
   B. filter theory.
   C. attenuation theory.
   D. threshold theory.

3. When a sense organ processes stimuli and converts them into electrical impulses, it is called.
   A. lateralization.
   B. localization.
   C. papillation.
   D. transduction.

4. The experiment with kittens raised to see only one kind of line who, as adult cats, were unable to see any other kinds of lines supports which view of the visual system?
   A. Biological factors have no effect on our ability to see; it is completely controlled by our experience.
   B. Biological abilities are present from birth, but without proper experience they do not develop normally.
   C. Experience has no effect on our ability to see; it is completely controlled by biological factors.
   D. The biological structures we need to see are created as a result of our experience.

5. In the opponent-process theory of color, our experience of a color is controlled by
   A. its position on three dimensions (red-green, blue-yellow, black-white).
   B. the relative activations of three different kinds of cones (red, green, and blue).
   C. the frequency of firing in the optic nerve, corresponding to the frequency of the light.
   D. an automatic process that triggers the opposite color for any wavelength of light.

6. An object that is moving appears more three-dimensional than one that is perfectly still. This is called the _____ effect.
   A. visual motion
   B. shape constancy
   C. optical localization
   D. kinetic depth

7. Cross-cultural research on the perception of illusions indicates that people whose culture does not include many straight lines or sharp corners will
   A. have more trouble seeing many illusions.
   B. be fooled more easily by many illusions.
   C. be unable to interpret the pictures at all.
   D. see the illusions exactly as Americans do.

8. The three major parts of the ear are the
   A. hammer, anvil, and stirrup.
   B. timbre, pitch, and loudness detectors.
   C. rods, cones, and hair cells.
   D. outer ear, middle ear, and inner ear.

9. The first bite of Joe's soup seemed very salty. After eating continuously for several minutes, it seemed less salty. This is probably due to the phenomenon of
   A. sensory overload.
   B. chemical deterioration.
   C. sensory adaptation.
   D. gustatory amnesia.

10. When a police officer asks a suspected drunk drive "How many fingers do you see?" it is a test of vision. When the officer asks the driver to touch his finger to the tip of his nose with his eyes closed, which sense is being tested?
    A. Kinesthesis
    B. Olfaction
    C. Gustation
    D. Orientation

CHAPTER FOUR

1. One topic on which psychologists who study conscious are still unresolved is the controversy over whether consciousness
   A. displays profound differences or is all one thing.
   B. reflects more than simply our observable behaviors.
   C. is affected by our culture and expectations.
   D. varies along a continuum or reflects totally different states.

2. When you have to stay up all night you may find yourself feeling chilled at two in the morning, even if the thermostat is keeping the room as a constant temperature. This is probably because
   A. it is such a long time since you have eaten anything hot.
   B. lower light levels at night make the room look cooler.
   C. you feel depressed at having to stay up all night.
   D. your circadian rhythms have lowered your body temperature.

3. REM sleep is often called paradoxical sleep because
   A. no one knows what purpose it serves.
   B. it occurs at unpredictable times during the night.
   C. it is in some ways deep and in some ways active.
   D. some people experience it but others don't.

4. Both cocaine and amphetamines act on the nervous system by
   A. decreasing the activity in the pain and sleep centers.
   B. calming the central nervous system and stimulating the brain.
   C. reducing the activity in the sympathetic nervous system.
   D. increasing the activity in the sympathetic nervous system.

5. In one study that compared the dreams of elderly Hispanic people with those of elderly citizens of the U.S., what was discovered about how often people in these groups remember their dreams?
   A. Hispanic people remembered many more dreams.
   B. U.S. citizens remembers many more dreams.
   C. People in all cultures remembered equal numbers of dreams.
   D. There were no consistent patterns in the memory for dreams.

6. Biofeedback is a technique that allows individuals to
   A. gain control over the content of their dreams.
   B. alter the patterns of their sleep cycles.
   C. interpret the true meanings of their dreams.
   D. control some of the body's involuntary responses.

7. A psychoactive drug causes _____, while an addictive drug causes _____.
   A. tolerance; psychological dependence
   B. psychological dependence; tolerance
   C. changes in behavior, thought, or mood; physical compulsion
   D. physical compulsion; changes in behavior, thought, or mood

8. The fact that early childhood behavior problems can predict later addiction, and the fact that many addicts don't really want to give up their addiction, lead some researchers to believe that
   A. there is really no such thing as drug addiction.
   B. some people have addiction-prone personalities.
   C. withdrawal symptoms are much more serious than we think.
   D. addiction is largely caused by one's cultural experience.

9. Suppose two people are put in a situation where they both experience equal amounts of stress, and both of them are given alcohol to drink. If one of these people has a family history of alcoholism (high risk) and the other has no alcoholics in the family (low risk), how will their stress reactions be affected?
   A. The alcohol will increase stress reactions for both of them.
   B. Reactions will increase for the high risk person and decrease for the low risk person.
   C. Reactions will decrease for the high risk person and increase for the low risk person.
   D. The alcohol will have no effect on either person's stress reactions.

10. The most common dreams are
    A. very disturbing and frightening.
    B. psychologically important to the dreamer.
    C. related to common, everyday events.
    D. part of a pattern of recurring dreams.

CHAPTER FIVE

1. A systematic procedure through which associations and responses to specific stimuli are learned is called
   A. cognition.
   B. conditioning.
   C. operationalization.
   D. stimulus control.

2. The Garcia taste-aversion effect is a type of classical conditioning that CONTRADICTS the traditional principle that
   A. understanding the situation is important for conditioning.
   B. conditioning only works with very short time intervals.
   C. stimuli must be paired over and over for conditioning.
   D. conditioning has no real effect on important behaviors.

3. The presentation of a rewarding or pleasant stimulus after some behavior, to increase the likelihood of the behavior, is
   A. positive reinforcement.
   B. negative reinforcement.
   C. stimulus discrimination.
   D. stimulus generalization.

4. Maritta bought her weekly lottery ticket at a different store than usual one week, and that was the week she won a respectable prize. She now prefers to buy her tickets at that store. This is an example of
   A. stimulus generalization.
   B. superstitious behavior.
   C. an unconditioned response.
   D. a conditioned response.

5. Punishment can be administered in two ways:
   A. delivering a pleasant stimulus or removing an unpleasant stimulus.
   B. delivering an unpleasant stimulus or removing a pleasant stimulus.
   C. through classical conditioning or operant conditioning principles.
   D. either before or after the behavior that is being conditioned.

6. A dental insurance company will reimburse claims for regular checkups only if at least six months have passed since the last checkup. This is an example of a _____ schedule of reinforcement.
   A. fixed ratio
   B. variable ratio
   C. fixed interval
   D. variable interval

7. When an organism receives a reinforcer for correctly discriminating between two stimuli, it illustrates
   A. stimulus generalization.
   B. stimulus discrimination.
   C. classical conditioning.
   D. primary reinforcement.

8. A hospital-based program for helping heart attack patients follow their new lifestyle requirements has the patients chart their own behaviors, observe their progress, and reward their achievements with rewards of their choice. This program uses principles of
   A. classical conditioning.
   B. spontaneous recovery.
   C. continuous reinforcement.
   D. behavioral regulation.

9. The learning-to-learn course for college students discussed in the text not only benefited the students, it also benefited the field of psychology as a whole, because it showed that psychology
   A. can be helpful to people in their daily lives.
   B. is concerned about more than rats.
   C. uses scientific techniques in its research.
   D. is a well-paid profession to go into.

10. Research by Bandura and others on how children respond to witnessing aggressive actions, for instance on TV, shows that watching aggression will make children act more aggressively
    A. in almost every case that was tested.
    B. only under the most unusual conditions.
    C. unless the observed aggressive person is punished.
    D. if parents and teachers put too much emphasis on it.

CHAPTER SIX

1. Which of these basic memory processes is most central to the operation of sensory memory?
   A. Encoding
   B. Storage
   C. Retrieval
   D. Consolidation

2. The process of repeating information over and over to hold it in short-term memory is called _____, while the process of associating it with other information and analyzing its meaning is called _____.
   A. consolidation; metamemory
   B. metamemory; consolidation
   C. maintenance rehearsal; elaborative rehearsal
   D. elaborative rehearsal; maintenance rehearsal

3. Marcia sets up her coffee maker to brew the coffee correctly every morning, but she can't explain the procedure to her roommate. This information is held in Marcia's _____ memory.
   A. procedural
   B. episodic
   C. declarative
   D. semantic

4. Memories that are conscious and relatively easy to access are _____ memories, while those that are more automatic and do not require conscious awareness are _____ memories.
   A. explicit; implicit
   B. implicit; explicit
   C. sensory; procedural
   D. procedural; sensory

5. Which of these students is using active learning to study for a biology test?
   A. One who thinks of possible exam questions and writes out answers to them in his own words.
   B. One who never sits still, but walks around the room as she reads the chapters in the book.
   C. One who reads over the material in the assigned chapters at least five times before the test.
   D. One who tape-records the lectures and listens to them while cooking or doing the laundry.

6. If you are going to study four hours for a quiz, what is probably the most efficient way to spend that time?
   A. Four hours the night before the test, so it will be fresh.
   B. Two hours a day for the two days before the test.
   C. Two hours in the morning and two in the evening on the day before the test.
   D. A half hour at a time, twice a day, on the four days before the test.

7. When a crime victim is shown a series of photos and asked to pick out the picture of the criminal, it is which measure of memory?
   A. Reconstruction
   B. Relearning
   C. Recall
   D. Recognition

8. If information learned in the past is making it harder to learn some new information, it is called _____, while if information you are learning now makes it harder to recall something you once knew it is called _____.
   A. procedural memory; declarative memory
   B. declarative memory; procedural memory
   C. retroactive interference; proactive interference
   D. proactive interference; retroactive interference

9. According to the principle of state-department learning, if you have to take an early morning exam, you should do your studying for the exam
   A. the night before, so the facts will be fresh.
   B. early morning on several days before the test.
   C. after lunch, when your energy level is high.
   D. in one long session, to minimize interference.

10. In experiments that provided some animals with enriched environments full of toys, structures for climbing and burrowing, and challenges to meet, while providing others with small, plain cages, what differences were measured in the enriched animals?
    A. Their brain processes became more efficient.
    B. They depended less on social contact with other animals.
    C. Their stimulating environment created stress.
    D. Their brain cells developed more interconnections.

CHAPTER SEVEN

1. When do humans begin to develop concepts?
   A. late childhood
   B. infancy
   C. early adolescence
   D. early childhood

2. Once we've solved a problem a particular way, we tend to stick to this strategy even when more efficient approaches exist. This is known as
   A. functional fixedness.
   B. psychological set.
   C. metacognition.
   D. means-end analysis

3. When leaders are accused of lacking creative solutions to problems, they may find it a good idea to try:
   A. means-end analysis.
   B. computer simulation.
   C. brainstorming.
   D. functional fixedness.

4. Select the major disadvantage of using heuristics to solve problems.
   A. No solution is guaranteed.
   B. They are time consuming and inefficient.
   C. They involve so much effort.
   D. They only apply to a specific problem.

5. A stroke patient knows that a picture has a keyboard and a screen but cannot identify it as a computer. What key zone has been corrupted?
   A. divergence
   B. semantic
   C. convergence
   D. parallel

6. In what aspect of language would a psycholinguist most likely be interested?
   A. phonology
   B. evolution
   C. origins
   D. acquisition

7. What are the basic units of sound that compose the words in a language?
   A. phonemes
   B. morphemes
   C. graphemes
   D. phones

8. Name the smallest units of speech that contain meaning.
   A. semantics
   B. morphemes
   C. cognates
   D. phonemes

9. Select the sentence that has two deep structures.
   A. Happiness is a warm blanket.
   B. People who live in glass houses shouldn't throw stones.
   C. The student council was told that they should stop drinking on campus.
   D. Mary was bitten by the dog that belonged to the man who lived next door and had three dogs and a cat.

10. There are specific areas of the brain that are specialized for processing language. This fact supports the view of language acquisition that emphasizes the importance of
    A. innate biological factors.
    B. operant conditioning.
    C. illness and nutrition.
    D. classical conditioning.

CHAPTER EIGHT

1. The psychologist who minimized the importance of individual differences was:
   A. John Watson.
   B. Robert Sternberg.
   C. David Wechsler.
   D. Lewis Terman.

2. What kind of intelligence does Sternberg call the ability to readily adapt your skills to new or novel tasks?
   A. componential
   B. crystallized
   C. experiential
   D. contextual

3. What is standardization used to determine?
   A. achievement
   B. test norms
   C. reliability
   D. validity

4. What will the standard error of measurement be on a highly reliable standardized test?
   A. significant
   B. variable
   C. valid
   D. small

5. When one particular or outstanding characteristic about an individual is allowed to influence evaluations, this is called a:
   A. singular advantage.
   B. blooming effect
   C. corona significance
   D. halo effect

6. Name the first widely used individual intelligence test in the United States.
   A. Wechsler scales
   B. Stanford-Binet test
   C. Kaufman Assessment Battery for Children
   D. Army Alpha test

7. In Sternberg's triarchic theory, the ability to adapt to changing environmental conditions and to adapt in order to accomplish one's goals is referred to as _____ intelligence.
   A. componential
   B. experiential
   C. contextual
   D. crystallized

8. What is measured by the two major scales of the Wechsler tests?
   A. verbal ability and performance
   B. cognitive skills and memory
   C. production and comprehension
   D. verbal reasoning and arithmetic reasoning

9. What happens to IQ scores during adulthood?
   A. steadily decrease
   B. usually show significant increases
   C. remain relatively stable
   D. change more than during childhood

10. The term that refers to the influence of genetic factors on intelligence is _____; the term that refers to the influence of living standards and educational opportunities is _____.
    A. kinship; confluence
    B. heredity; kinship
    C. nature; nurture
    D. confluence; nurture

CHAPTER NINE

1. One of the four aspects of the definition of motivation is that it is
    A. biologically significant
    B. a response to an incentive
    C. an internal condition
    D. a conditioned response.

2. Select a "quick fix" for hunger.
    A. milk
    B. candy
    C. chicken
    D. cheese

3. What part of the brain regulates eating behavior?
    A. hypothalamus
    B. amygdala
    C. superior colliculus
    D. reticular formation

4. What disorder is characterized by an obstinate and willful refusal to eat?
    A. anoxia praecox
    B. telesthesia
    C. anorexia nervosa
    D. neurasthenia

5. Name the stage of the sexual response cycle in which the body returns to its normal state.
    A. post-orgasmic
    B. refractory
    C. recovery
    D. resolution

6. Which of the following is a key element in expectancy theory?
    A. Thoughts guide behavior.
    B. Physiological drives guide behavior.
    C. Emotions can be motives.
    D. Motives can be reinforced.

7. Which term refers to behavior that people engage in for no reward other than the pleasure of the activity itself?
    A. achievement motivated
    B. power motivated
    C. extrinsically motivated
    D. intrinsically motivated

8. How would early motivation theorists have described the needs at the base of Maslow's pyramid?
    A. social motives
    B. drives
    C. expectations
    D. incentives

9. What theory of emotion suggests that smiling can make people happy?
    A. Cannon-Bard
    B. Shoaf-Strouss
    C. James-Lange
    D. Schacter-Singer

10. What do polygraphs measure?
    A. arousal
    B. honesty
    C. lies
    D. confusion

CHAPTER TEN

1. What branch of psychology focuses on change in an individual's lifetime?
   A. social
   B. developmental
   C. motivational
   D. personality

2. Which of the following situations will cause the Moro reflex to occur in newborn infants?
   A. a touch on the cheek
   B. pressure on the kneecap
   C. a touch on the bottom of the foot
   D. a sudden change in environmental stimulation

3. What did Frantz use his "viewing box" to study?
   A. the visual preferences of infants
   B. recognition memory in infants
   C. stimulus generalization in infants
   D. the depth perception of infants

4. What was the focus of Piaget's research and theory?
   A. individual differences
   B. the content of the mind
   C. thought processes
   D. motivation

5. A child who begins to engage in make-believe play is in which of Piaget's cognitive stages?
   A. sensorimotor
   B. concrete operational
   C. formal operational
   D. preoperational

6. In which of Piaget's cognitive stages would an individual develop the ability to engage in abstract reasoning about hypothetical events that are not directly experienced?
   A. concrete operational
   B. preoperational
   C. formal operational
   D. sensorimotor

7. According to Piaget, the best way to encourage a child's cognitive development is to
   A. provide stimulation appropriate to the child's level.
   B. create structured educational activities at an early age.
   C. avoid situations that are overstimulating for the child.
   D. treat the child as a small inexperienced adult.

8. Gilligan's research on moral development suggests that a _____ might respond to a question on lying by saying that it is all right to lie if telling the truth would hurt the feelings of another person.
   A. male
   B. female
   C. religious person
   D. nonreligious person

9. What is the focus of Lawrence Kohlberg's moral development theory?
   A. the morality of young children
   B. the morality of adults
   C. moral behavior
   D. moral reasoning

10. Select the central concept in Kohlberg's theory of morality.
    A. justice
    B. property rights
    C. truth
    D. reciprocity

CHAPTER ELEVEN

1. In which period of life are people most likely to become extreme in their orientation toward stereotypical maleness?
   A. early adulthood
   B. early childhood
   C. middle childhood
   D. adolescence

2. Which of the following activities would make one suspect that Susan is an androgynous individual?
   A. dancing with another girl
   B. changing the spark plugs in her car
   C. helping her father clean the kitchen
   D. helping her mother do the grocery shopping

3. Which of the following concepts was originated by Erik Erikson?
   A. mid-life crisis
   B. hospice
   C. identity crisis
   D. androgyny

4. In comparison to men, women experience their transitions and life events
   A. completely unpredictably.
   B. much earlier in their lives.
   C. later and more irregularly.
   D. in reaction to other people

5. Select the ethnic group that most fears the consequences of a poor education.
   A. Asian-American
   B. White American
   C. African-American
   D. Hispanic-American

6. According to Haan, Millsap, and Hartka, when does personality change the most?
   A. childhood and adolescence
   B. adulthood
   C. childhood
   D. adolescence

7. What did Levinson believe was the first task of early adulthood?
   A. figuring out one's identity and life purpose
   B. becoming intimate with another person
   C. acquiring an educational or career direction
   D. establishing one's independence

8. Multiple infarct dementia is caused by
   A. insulin deficiency.
   B. radiation.
   C. toxins released into the bloodstream from the small intestine.
   D. ruptures of small blood vessels in the brain.

9. It is predicted that John will have a long life because his parents are presently over 85. This prediction is based on the _____ theory of aging.
   A. congenital
   B. heredity
   C. familial
   D. homologous

10. What common change occurs in the nervous system of older people?
    A. loss of spinal reflexes
    B. random neural activity in the brain
    C. stereotypical scanpaths
    D. increased reaction time

CHAPTER TWELVE

1. Choose the best description of the id.
   A. practical and unsympathetic
   B. irrational and selfish
   C. devious and scheming
   D. pragmatic and opportunistic

2. What is the primary function of the ego?
   A. promote behavior that is unselfish and ethical
   B. satisfy the desires of the id in a socially acceptable way
   C. deny and overpower the id
   D. shift energy from the id to the superego

3. How is the Oedipus complex resolved in both sons and daughters?
   A. repression of sexual feelings
   B. attachment to the opposite-sex parent
   C. identification with the same-sex parent
   D. displacement of sexual urges into substitute objects

4. Select the term used by Jung to refer to the store of images and ideas that we inherit from our ancestors and share with all human beings.
   A. primal representation
   B. racial memory
   C. psychic structure
   D. collective unconscious

5. What term did Adler use to refer to unrealistic goals that are unlikely to be achieved?
   A. fictional finalism
   B. personal myth
   C. "hitching your wagon to a star"
   D. fantasy aspirations

6. Select the most basic level of Maslow's hierarchy of needs.
   A. safety needs
   B. physiological needs
   C. acceptance needs
   D. esteem needs

7. Which of the following theories has been criticized for failing to provide an account of personality development?
   A. trait
   B. psychoanalytic
   C. humanistic
   D. behavioral

8. Mike always rationalizes his failures by blaming them on bad luck or the influence of other people. According to Rotter, he is demonstrating
   A. low self-efficacy.
   B. faulty encoding strategies.
   C. negative expectancies.
   D. an external locus of control.

9. A test with clinical scales that includes hypochondriasis, paranoia, hypomania, and psychoasthenia is the
   A. Rorschach Ink Blot Test.
   B. 16 Personality Factor Questionnaire (16PF).
   C. California Personality Inventory (CPI).
   D. Minnesota Multiphasic Personality Inventory-2 (MMPI-2).

10. Select an example of a projective test of personality.
    A. Minnesota Multiphasic Personality Inventory-2 (MMPI-2).
    B. 16 Personality Factor Questionnaire (16PF)
    C. Rorschach Ink Blot Test
    D. California Personality Inventory (CPI)

CHAPTER THIRTEEN

1. Which emotion is most likely to be experienced when a loved one is dying and no prevention is possible?
   A. apprehension
   B. frustration
   C. conflict
   D. pressure

2. Which of the following groups would most likely feel stress due to time pressure?
   A. customer service agents
   B. housewives
   C. auto mechanics
   D. assembly-line workers

3. What do the physiological changes that accompany stress include?
   A. elevation of blood pressure
   B. constriction of the pupils
   C. increased production of gastric enzymes
   D. warmer hands and feet

4. In which stage of the general adaptation syndrome is arousal level the highest?
   A. alarm
   B. exhaustion
   C. recovery
   D. resistance

5. Which of the following life events would probably be the most stressful?
   A. having trouble with your boss
   B. moving to a new residence
   C. getting married
   D. going on vacation

6. Which term refers to the frequently occurring, repetitive sources of stress that happen to us on an almost daily basis?
   A. burnout
   B. hassles
   C. stressors
   D. overload

7. Research into ethnic effects on stress that compared Hispanics with non-Hispanic Americans found that Hispanics are more likely to be
   A. victims of crime.
   B. unemployed.
   C. economically disadvantaged.
   D. experiencing marital problems.

8. Maggie is considering leaving her abusive husband. Leaving would bring her physical security, but she has no job skills to support herself. Maggie is faced with a(n) _____ conflict.
   A. approach-approach
   B. avoidance-avoidance
   C. approach-avoidance
   D. double approach-avoidance

9. The condition that is frequently involved in the health consequences of stress is
   A. muscular dysfunction.
   B. a hormone imbalance.
   C. a weakened immune system.
   D. disturbed patterns of eating and sleeping.

10. Work-site stress is likely to be high for jobs in which the demands are _____ and the workers have _____ control over the speed, flow, and level of work.
    A. high; low
    B. low; high
    C. low; low
    D. high; high

CHAPTER FOURTEEN

1. Which of the following is emphasized in the humanistic explanation of abnormality?
   A. balanced archetypes
   B. effective coping skills
   C. techniques for constructive self-criticism
   D. a realistic self-concept

2. Select the criterion used by the law to define "insane."
   A. statistical frequency
   B. intellectual competence
   C. responsibility for behavior
   D. social acceptability

3. What is the acronym for the most widely accepted system for identifying psychological disorders?
   A. TAT
   B. K-ABC
   C. EVE
   D. DSM-IV

4. One goal of the DSM-IV is to
   A. organize disorders into categories on the basis of etiological evidence.
   B. improve the reliability of diagnosis.
   C. introduce a common terminology into the mental health field.
   D. describe preventative measures.

5. When is anxiety described as "free-floating?"
   A. It spreads to other people.
   B. It accompanies agoraphobia.
   C. There is no obvious source or cause.
   D. It is not accompanied by autonomic nervous system arousal.

6. Select a common symptom of conversion disorder.
   A. paralysis
   B. headaches with blurred vision
   C. depression
   D. memory loss

7. Which of the following disorders can produce unscrupulous business persons, deceptive salespeople, and violent criminals?
   A. paranoid
   B. antisocial
   C. avoidant
   D. histrionic

8. The best predictor of whether parents will abuse their children is:
   A. socioeconomic status of the parents
   B. the behavior patterns of their children.
   C. the mental and physical health of the parents.
   D. whether the parents were abused as children.

9. What is the most frequently occurring psychological disorder?
   A. depression
   B. schizophrenia
   C. bipolar disorder
   D. phobias

10. In which type of schizophrenia are symptoms the most severe and bizarre?
    A. undifferentiated
    B. paranoid
    C. disorganized
    D. catatonic

CHAPTER FIFTEEN

1. Which of the following involves using psychological principles to treat emotional and behavioral problems?
   A. behavioral medicine
   B. biotherapy
   C. psychiatry
   D. psychotherapy

2. The factor most important in long-lasting effects from treatment is:
   A. hope.
   B. expectations.
   C. efforts.
   D. placebo effects

3. The therapist whose main goal is to provide patients with insight into their repressed inner conflicts is a:
   A. humanistic therapist.
   B. cognitive therapist.
   C. behavioral therapist.
   D. psychoanalyst.

4. How can client-centered therapy be best described?
   A. ahistorical
   B. evaluative
   C. structured
   D. nondirective

5. A major goal of Gestalt therapy is to
   A. teach people to use anxiety in constructive ways.
   B. make people aware of current feelings and situations.
   C. help people develop critical thinking skills.
   D. overcome barriers that block the path to self-actualization.

6. The codependent person is likely to
   A. express clear feelings of shame, fear, anger, and pain.
   B. dwell constantly on his or her own feelings.
   C. assume responsibility for other people.
   D. avoid being with people who have problems.

7. A technique often used with young children is
   A. time-out:
   B. systematic desensitization.
   C. aversive conditioning.
   D. psychoanalysis.

8. A goal of encounter groups is to
   A. release floodgates of emotion.
   B. help people reach self-actualization.
   C. gather insight into unconscious motivations.
   D. confront clients on problems they have been denying.

9. What is the primary aim of family therapy?
   A. identifying maladaptive behavior in family members.
   B. changing the way the family interacts.
   C. restructuring the organization of the family.
   D. balancing the power in the family.

10. Which of these is an antipsychotic drug?
    A. imipramine
    B. benzodiazephine
    C. barbiturates
    D. chlopromazine

CHAPTER SIXTEEN

1. What branch of psychology focuses on the influences that other people have on our thoughts and behaviors?
   A. social
   B. developmental
   C. clinical
   D. personality

2. What has been the effect of fear messages about AIDS?
   A. decreased use of condoms among college students who fear AIDS
   B. no change in condom use among college students
   C. decreased use of condoms among all college students
   D. increased condom use among college students who fear AIDS

3. Bianca used to think that all Oriental food was better for you than American food. However, she recently read several articles claiming health risks from Oriental food. After carefully weighing the arguments on both sides, Bianca has changed her attitude. According to the elaboration likelihood model, this illustrates the _____ route to attitude change.
   A. rational
   B. central
   C. primary
   D. peripheral

4. What is meant by the term "social facilitation?"
   A. negative effects on one's performance due to the presence of others
   B. both positive and negative effects on one's performance due to the presence of others
   C. positive effects on one's performance due to the presence of others
   D. negative effects on the performance of others due to one's presence with them.

5. Which of these people is MOST likely to experience cognitive dissonance?
   A. Someone who loves Italian food but is allergic to it.
   B. Someone who is deeply religious but too ill to go to church.
   C. Someone who hates jazz but listens to all-jazz radio.
   D. Someone who loves stamps and collects many of them.

6. Who is associated with the self-perception theory?
   A. Stanley Milgram
   B. Solomon Asch
   C. Leon Festinger
   D. Daryl Bem

7. TV advertisers indicate awareness of the reactance phenomenon when they
   A. emphasize that the buyer has a choice.
   B. are careful in their criticism of competing products.
   C. use messages that make the audience feel good about themselves.
   D. limit the amount of information in commercials.

8. Name the process that people use to infer the internal states and intentions of others from their behavior and appearance.
   A. social interpretation
   B. interpersonal perception
   C. impression formation
   D. social facilitation

9. Prejudice is best defined as
   A. a negative evaluation of an entire group of people.
   B. treating people differently because of race or color.
   C. attributing personality traits to members of a group.
   D. the belief that one's own group is superior to all others.

10. Randy helped a homeless family because he would be featured in the newspaper. His behavior was motivated largely by personal rewards. Larry helped a homeless family because he was concerned for their welfare. What motivated Larry's behavior?
    A. egoism
    B. bystander apathy
    C. sociobiology
    D. altruism

CHAPTER SEVENTEEN

1. Which of the following psychologists would be interested in techniques developed by architects and landscape gardeners to make small areas appear more open and spacious?
   A. ecological
   B. environmental
   C. habitat
   D. organizational

2. A family that lives near an airport is at significant risk for experiencing
   A. noise-related stress.
   B. low income levels.
   C. an airplane crash into their house.
   D. jet fuel spills in their yard.

3. How do environmental psychologists define crowding?
   A. in terms of volume of space per person
   B. as a situational variable
   C. in terms of area of floor space per person
   D. as a psychological state

4. Why might anthropologist Edward Hall say that people on a crowded elevator rarely speak or make eye contact with other passengers?
   A. Their personal space is being invaded.
   B. All humans have a mild case of claustrophobia.
   C. They believe other passengers are evaluating them.
   D. Their freedom of movement is restricted.

5. Much of the research dealing with the effects of high temperature on aggression uses the correlational method. The correlation method permits the research to
   A. draw conclusions about cause-and-effect relationships.
   B. examine the effects of manipulating one variable on another.
   C. discover which levels of one variable are associate with which levels of another.
   D. make use of control groups to make statistical comparisons.

6. The study of how a worker's behavior is affected by the work environment, by coworkers, and by organizational practices is called
   A. collective/productional psychology.
   B. industrial/organizational psychology.
   C. union/management psychology.
   D. economic/managerial psychology.

7. One way in which job motivation is different from job satisfaction is that job motivation
   A. is always reflected in the worker's behavior.
   B. is NOT always reflected in the worker's behavior.
   C. is more difficult to measure or control.
   D. is generally lower than job satisfaction.

8. Which of the following situations is likely in an organization that has paternalistic management?
   A. Workers compete for challenging jobs.
   B. Bosses socialize with workers
   C. Workers take pride in the product they produce.
   D. Pay is based on length of service.

9. Susan is paid by the number of boxes of apples she picks. This is an example of the _____ approach to motivating workers.
   A. behavioral
   B. traditional
   C. participatory
   D. extrinsic

10. The manager of a shipping department believes that the most important part of her job is to see that the packages get out to the right places on time. This manager is
    A. appraisal-oriented.
    B. administration-oriented.
    C. employee-oriented.
    D. task-oriented.

APPENDIX

1. The *modal* score on a psychology pop quiz was 63. This means that
    A. equal numbers of students scored over 63 and under 63.
    B. most students failed the quiz.
    C. the arithmetic mean on the quiz was 63.
    D. 63 was the most commonly received score.

2. The difference between the highest and lowest scores is called the _____ of the scores.
    A. variance.
    B. range.
    C. standard deviation.
    D. normal distribution.

3. Why are descriptive statistics used?
    A. draw inferences from data
    B. transform data
    C. summarize data
    D. make predictions from data

4. A table that shows scores on a final exam and the number of students make each score is called a:
    A. spread sheet.
    B. frequency distribution.
    C. statistical polygon.
    D. score matrix.

5. Which of the following samples would probably show the greatest variability of height?
    A. newborn infants
    B. elementary school children
    C. college basketball players
    D. pregnant women

6. The standard deviation of a score gives information about how far the score is from the
    A. mean.
    B. lowest score.
    C. highest score.
    D. median.

7. What kind of statistics are used to reach conclusions about whether one set of conditions creates different results than another set of conditions?
    A. descriptive statistics
    B. experimental statistics
    C. inferential statistics
    D. interpretive statistics

8. Which of the following is true of the normal curve?
    A. Most scores fall in the low or high extremes of the range.
    B. The mode is larger than the median which is greater than the mean.
    C. The mean, mode, and median are all the same.
    D. Every score occurs with the same frequency.

9. Jan noticed that as the weather got colder she saw more clients in her counseling practice. Which of the following is a reasonable conclusion for her to make?
    A. People have more mental disorders in the winter than in summer.
    B. Jan will work with more clients in January than in August.
    C. People don't seek the professional help they need in hot weather.
    D. Shorter days cause more depression.

10. Assume that a researcher has found a strong negative correlation between two variables. A strong negative correlation means that
    A. there is no relationship between the two variables.
    B. persons who obtain high scores on the first variable also tend to obtain high scores on the second variable.
    C. persons who obtain high scores on the first variable tend to obtain low scores on the second variable.
    D. persons who obtain low scores on the first variable also tend to obtain low scores on the second variable.

Chapter 1 Answers

1.	D	6.	A
2.	D	7.	A
3.	B	8.	A
4.	A	9.	B
5.	D	10.	C

Chapter 2 Answers

1.	D	6.	D
2.	B	7.	C
3.	D	8.	B
4.	C	9.	D
5.	C	10.	D

Chapter 3 Answers

1.	A	6.	D
2.	C	7.	A
3.	D	8.	D
4.	B	9.	C
5.	A	10.	A

Chapter 4 Answers

1.	D	6.	D
2.	D	7.	C
3.	C	8.	B
4.	D	9.	C
5.	B	10.	C

Chapter 5 Answers

1.	B	6.	C
2.	B	7.	B
3.	A	8.	D
4.	B	9.	A
5.	B	10.	C

Chapter 6 Answers

1.	A	6.	D
2.	C	7.	D
3.	A	8.	D
4.	A	9.	B
5.	A	10.	D

Chapter 7 Answers

1.	B	6.	D
2.	D	7.	A
3.	C	8.	B
4.	A	9.	C
5.	C	10.	A

Chapter 8 Answers

1.	A	6.	B
2.	C	7.	C
3.	B	8.	A
4.	D	9.	C
5.	D	10.	C

Chapter 9 Answers

1.	C	6.	A
2.	B	7.	D
3.	A	8.	B
4.	C	9.	C
5.	D	10.	A

Chapter 10 Answers

1.	B	6.	C
2.	D	7.	A
3.	A	8.	B
4.	C	9.	D
5.	D	10.	A

Chapter 11 Answers

1.	D	6.	B
2.	B	7.	D
3.	C	8.	D
4.	D	9.	B
5.	A	10.	D

Chapter 12 Answers

1.	B	6.	B
2.	B	7.	A
3.	C	8.	D
4.	D	9.	D
5.	A	10.	C

Chapter 13 Answers

1.	B	6.	B
2.	D	7.	C
3.	A	8.	C
4.	A	9.	C
5.	C	10.	A

Chapter 14 Answers

1.	D	6.	A
2.	C	7.	B
3.	D	8.	D
4.	B	9.	A
5.	C	10.	C

Chapter 15 Answers

1.	D	6.	C
2.	C	7.	A
3.	D	8.	B
4.	D	9.	B
5.	B	10.	D

Chapter 16 Answers

1.	A	6.	D
2.	D	7.	A
3.	B	8.	C
4.	B	9.	A
5.	C	10.	D

Chapter 17 Answers

1.	B	6.	B
2.	A	7.	A
3.	D	8.	D
4.	A	9.	A
5.	C	10.	D

Appendix Answers

1.	D	6.	A
2.	B	7.	C
3.	C	8.	C
4.	B	9.	B
5.	B	10.	C

Keeping Pace Plus
Study Guide Answers

Chapter 1

Matching

	Answer	Word	Page
1.	e	accuracy	5
2.	p	correlation	14
3.	n	counseling psychologist	11
4.	s	debriefing	24
5.	j	educational	11
6.	d	emotional response	5
7.	i	engineering	11
8.	k	forensic	11
9.	l	health	11
10.	g	hypothesis	6
11.	o	industrial/organizational	11
12.	c	objectivity	5
13.	b	overt actions	5
14.	a	psychology	4
15.	h	replication	7
16.	r	sample	16
17.	m	sports	11
18.	f	theory	6
19.	q	variables	14

True or False

1. TRUE (4)	2. TRUE (11)	3. TRUE (12)	4. FALSE (7)	5. FALSE (13)
6. TRUE (14)	7. FALSE (16)	8. FALSE (21)	9. TRUE (22)	10. TRUE (18,19)
11. FALSE (18,19)	12. FALSE (17)	13. TRUE (29)	14. FALSE (23)	15. FALSE (31)

Fill-in-the-Blanks

	Answers	Page
1.	explain and predict	6
2.	psychiatrists	8
3.	individuals	12
4.	approach	12
5.	neuropsychologists	13
6.	causally	14
7.	variables	14
8.	comparison	15
9.	population	16
10.	double-blind	17
11.	Hawthorne	17
12.	within	20-21
13.	unethical	23
14.	deception	24
15.	eclectism	31

Applications

1. A. a) background noise; b) time (14,15)
    B. a) eating breakfast; b) academic performance (14, 15)
    C. a) reward; b) rate of cooperative behavior (14, 15)

2. A. interview (21)
    B. case study (22)
    C. naturalistic observation (21,22)
    D. experiment (13)
    E. questionnaire (21)

3. (pp. 18-19)
    1. What is the purpose of the study?
    2. Was methodology appropriate?
    3. Was sample properly chosen?
    4. Are the results replicable?
    5. What are the conclusions?

4. (pp. 21-22)

Research	Strength	Weakness
Questionnaire	Used to gather information from a large number of people.	Impersonal, responses limited; gathers only information asked.
Interview	Ask questions other than standard ones to explore a wider range of responses.	Time-consuming.
Naturalistic Observation	Data is largely uncontaminated by the presence of the researcher.	Time-consuming; Little opportunity to control variables
Case Study	Information it provides is complete	Information describes only one individual; can't generalize
Experiment	Can make causal inferences about 2 variables	Lab environment is artificial; limited generalizability; ethical concerns

5. (pp. 25-31)

School of Psychological Thought	Focus	Early Leader(s)
Structuralism (25)	organized structure of immediate, consciouse experience	Wundt, Titchner
Functionalism (25-26)	how and why the mind functions	James
Gestalt (27)	total experience	Wertheimer,Kofpka
Psychoanalysis (28)	unconscious mental processes	Freud
Behaviorism (28-29)	how observable responses are learned	Watson, Skinner
Humanistic (29-30)	free will, desire for self-actualization & fulfillment	Maslow, Rogers
Cognitive (30-31)	mental processes and activities in learning	Bandura, Ellis
Biological	physical mechanisms affect feeling, thoughts, desires, sensory exporsure	Gazzanna, Kety

Self Test

1. A (28)	2. D (8)	3. B (9)	4. A (11)	5. A (23)	6. A (13-14)
7. C (15)	8. A (16)	9. B (17)	10. D (18-21)	11. B (21-22)	

Chapter 2

Matching

	Answer	Word	Page
1.	i	agonists	48
2.	b	Allele	39
3.	j	antagonist	48
4.	f	axon	44
5.	l	CNS	42
6.	e	dendrite	43
7.	t	EEG	56
8.	k	endocrine gland	63
9.	a	genetics	39
10	q	hippocampus	54
11.	r	hormones	62
12.	s	hypoglycemia	66
13.	o	hypothalamus	54
14	p	limbic system	54
15.	h	neuromodulator	48
16.	d	neuron	42
17.	c	PKU	40
18.	m	pons	53
19.	g	synapse	44
20.	n	thalamus	54

True or False

1. TRUE (38)	2. FALSE (39)	3. TRUE (39)	4. TRUE (39)	5. TRUE (40)
6. FALSE (42)	7. FALSE (43)	8. TRUE (45)	9. TRUE (46)	10. FALSE (48)
11. TRUE (49)	12. FALSE (49)	13. TRUE (52)	14. FALSE (57)	15. TRUE (57-59)
16. TRUE (53)	17. TRUE (53)	18. FALSE (54)	19 TRUE (54).	20. TRUE (54)
21. TRUE (58-59)	22. TRUE (58-59)	23. TRUE (58-59)	24. FALSE (59)	25. TRUE (62)
26. FALSE (63)	27. TRUE (66)	28. TRUE (66)	29. FALSE (64-65)	

Fill-in-the-Blanks

	Answers	Page
1.	gene	39
2.	dominant	39
3.	too few too many	40
4.	neuron	42
5.	glial	43
6.	axon	43-44
7.	polarization	45
8.	threshold	45-46

9.	refractory period	46
10.	postsynaptic potential	46
11.	neurotransmittor	47
12.	psychopharmacology	48
13.	anagonist, agonist	48
14.	sympathetic	50
15.	spinal cord	52
16.	reticular formation	53
17.	cerebellum	53
18.	corpus collosum	54
19.	cortex	55
20.	plastic	60-61
21.	neurotransplants	60-62
22.	endocrine	63
23.	pituitary	64
24.	epinephrine	66
25.	insulin	65-66

Applications

1. (pp. 38-41)
   - A. Both
   - B. Nature
   - C. Nuture
   - D. Nature
   - E. Both

2. (pp. 65-66)

ENDOCRINE GLAND	HORMONE	EFFECT
Anterior lobe	Somatotrophic	Controls rate of protein synthesis and release of fat stores
Posterior Pituitary	Antidiuretic Hormone	Controls retention of fluids
Posterior Pituitary	Oxytocin	Stimulates uterine contractions and lactation
Pancreas	Insuline	Regulates use of sugar and storage of carbohydrates
Adrenal Medulla	Adrenaline	Changes metabolic activity

3.
   - A. Somatic (49)
   - B. Sympathetic (50)
   - C. Central (51-52)
   - D. Parasympathetic (50-51)

Self Test

1. B (38)	2. D (38-39)	3. A (39)	4. D (40)	5. A (41)
6. C (41-42)	7. C (43)	8. B (45)	9. B (46-47)	10. C (48)
11. A (47)	12. C (50)	13. B (49-50)	14. A (52)	15. D (55)
16. D (54)	17. D (53)	18. C (58-59)	19. D (61-62)	20. D (66)
21. B (65-66)				

Chapter 3

Matching

	Answer	Word	Page
1.	h	absolute threshold	73
2.	o	accommodation	91
3.	x	amplitude	97
4.	p	convergence	92
5.	n	dichromats	87
6.	w	endorphin	107
7.	t	frequency	96
8.	q	illusion	92
9.	v	kinesthesis	109
10.	d	light	77
11.	m	monochromats	86
12.	e	myopic	77
13.	u	olfaction	103
14.	i	optic chiasm	81
15.	f	photoreceptors	77
16.	s	pitch	96
17.	a	psychophysics	73
18.	k	purity	84
19.	j	saccades	83
20.	b	sensation	72
21	r	sound	96
22.	c	subliminal perception	74
23.	g	transduction	77
24.	l	trichromatic theory	85

True or False

1. TRUE (73)	2. FALSE (72)	3. FALSE (73)	4. FALSE (76)	5. TRUE (77)
6. FALSE (78)	7. FALSE (79)	8. TRUE (80)	9. FALSE (80)	10. TRUE (82)
11. TRUE (82)	12. TRUE (82)	13. FALSE (83)	14. TRUE (83)	15. TRUE (83)
16. FALSE (84)	17. FALSE (85)	18. FALSE (85)	19. TRUE (87)	20. FALSE (88)
21. TRUE (89)	22. FALSE (91)	23. FALSE (92)	24. TRUE (92)	25. FALSE (97)
26. TRUE (97)	27. TRUE (97)	28. FALSE (98)	29. TRUE (100)	30. TRUE (74)
31. FALSE (74)	32. TRUE (75)	33. FALSE (75)	34. TRUE (101)	35. TRUE (102)
36. TRUE (102)	37. TRUE (105)	38. TRUE (104-105)	39. FALSE (105)	40. TRUE (106-107)
41. TRUE (108)	42. TRUE (109)	43. FALSE (107)		

Fill-in-the-Blanks

	Answers	Page
1.	perception	72
2.	difference threshold	73
3.	method of limits	73
4.	Signal detection	73
5.	subliminal perception	74-75
6.	filter, attenuation	75
7.	Myopic, hyperodic	77

8.	cones, rods	79
9.	movement	82
10.	fixation	83
11.	hue, brightness, saturation	84
12.	trichromats	86
13.	monochromats, dichromats	86-87
14.	size constancy	88
15.	depth	90-92
16.	retinal disparity	91-92
17.	law of Pragnanz	94-96
18.	Sound	96
19.	high	96
20.	ossicles	98
21.	sound localization	100
22.	sensorineural	101
23.	sweet, sour, bitter, salty	102
24.	olfaction	103
25.	Pheromones	104
26.	endorphins	107
27.	pain	106-107
28.	vestibular sense	109
29.	Precognition	109-110
30.	Psychokinesis	110

Applications

1. A.1. goggles (orientation of receptive fields) (82)
   A.2. response to horizontal/vertical objects (82)
   B.1. presenting pictures in experimental groupings (83)
   B.2. fixation and scan paths (83)

2. A. When a moving observer stares at a fixed point, the objects behind that point seem to move in the same direction as the observer (91).
   B. Objects that appear flat when stationary look 3 dimensional when put into motion. (91)
   C. Distant objects appear to be closer together than nearer objects. (91)
   D. When one object blocks out part of another, the first appears to be closer. (91)
   E. Surfaces that have little detail or texture appear to be in the distance. (91)
   F. Highlighted objects appear close. (91)
   G. Distant mountains often look blue because long (red) wavelengths are scattered in the air allowing more short (blue) wavelengths to reach our eyes. (91)
   H. The change in lens shape that allows the observer to keep an object in focus when the object is moved or when the choice of objects for focus changes. (91)

3. A. The slight difference between the images projected on the 2 retinas. (91)
   B. The movement of the eyes toward each other in order to keep information on corresponding points on the retina as an object moves closer to the observer. (92)

4. A. 2 equal length lines with arrows attached to their ends appear to be of different lengths (93); this occurs because of the angle and shape of the arrows attached to the ends of the lines. (93)
   B. (The railroad illusion) 2 horizontal lines of the same length bracketed by slanted lines which appear to be different lengths (93); accounted for by the linear perspective provided by the slanted background lines (93)

C. In a matter of minutes, the size of the moon appears to change from quite large to quite small (93); when the moon is overhead it has a featureless background -- at the horizon, objects are close to it. (93)

5.   A. common fate (96)
      B. closure (96)
      C. proximity (95)
      D. continuity (96)
      E. similarity (95)

6.   A. inner ear (98)
      B. external ear (98)
      C. middle ear (98)

7.

A. monocular depth cue (90)	B. monocular depth cue (90)	C. binocular depth cue (91)
D. Gestalt laws (93)	E. monocular depth cue (90)	F. illusion (92)
G. Gestalt laws (93)		

Self Test

1. D (72)	2. D (73)	3. C (77)	4. A (77)	5. D (79)
6. A (81)	7. B (82)	8. B (82)	9. B (84)	10.C (85)
11. A (85)	12. A (86)	13. D (88)	14. B (91)	15. A (93)
16. D (93)	17. C (95)	18. B (97)	19. C (98)	20. A (97)
21. C (102)	22. D (103)	23. C (109)	24. C (107)	25. B (109)
26. D (104-105)	27. C (105)			

Chapter 4

Matching

	Answer	Word	Page
1.	n	addictive drug	134
2.	p	alcoholic	137
3.	j	biofeedback	130
4.	b	circadian rhythms	119
5.	a	consciousness	117
6.	g	dream	127
7.	m	drug	134
8.	d	eletroencephalogram	121
9.	k	hypnosis	131
10.	f	insomnia	125
11.	h	lucid dream	127
12.	i	manifest content	128
13.	l	meditation	133
14.	q	opiants	141
15.	r	psychedelics	141
16.	s	psychostimulants	142
17.	e	REM	121
18.	c	sleep	120
19.	o	tolerance	135

True or False

1. FALSE (117)	2. TRUE (117)	3. TRUE (119)	4. TRUE (120)	5. TRUE (122)
6. TRUE (125)	7. TRUE (127)	8. TRUE (128)	9. FALSE (129)	10. TRUE (130)
11. FALSE (130)	12. TRUE (132)	13. FALSE (132)	14. TRUE (134)	15. FALSE (134)
16. FALSE (135)	17. TRUE (135)	18. FALSE (135)	19. TRUE (136)	20. TRUE (136)
21. FALSE (137)	22. FALSE (138-139)	23. TRUE (138)	24. TRUE (140)	25. TRUE (141)
26. FALSE (141)	27. FALSE (143)	28.TRUE (143)		

Fill-in-the-Blanks

	Answers	Page
1.	consciousness	117
2.	altered state	117
3.	circadian rhythm	119
4.	Sleep	120
5.	core, optional	120
6.	electroencephalograms	121
7.	NREM-no rapid eye movement	121
8.	REM-rapid eye movement	121
9.	sleep spindle	121
10.	K complex	121
11.	delta waves	121
12.	narcolepsy	124
13.	sleep apnea	125
14.	insomnia	125
15.	Night terrors	125
16.	sleepwalking	125
17.	dream	127
18.	lucid	127
19.	manifest content	128
20.	latent content	128
21.	collective unconscious	129
22.	Biofeedback	130
23.	hypnosis	131
24.	hypnotic susceptibility	131
25.	age regression	131
26.	phantom	132
27.	cognitive-behavioral viewpoint	132
28.	meditation	133
29.	mindful, concentrative	133
30.	drug	134
31.	psychoactive	134
32.	addictive drug	134
33.	substance abusers	134
34.	Psychological dependence	134-135
35.	withdrawal symptoms	135
36.	tolerance	135
37.	polydrug	135
38.	sedative-hypnotic	136
39.	alcoholic	136-137
40.	alcohol	136

41.	tranquilizers	140
42.	Opiates	141
43.	psychodelics	141
44.	psychostimulates	142

Applications

1. A.1. the active-verbal-rational mode (118)
    A.2. automatic (118)
    A.3. shut out experiences, events, and stimuli that do not directly relate to their ability to survive (118)
    B.1. the receptive spatial mode
    B.2. people need to gain perspective and judgment (118)
    B.3. expanding normal awareness (118)

2. A. sleep apnea (125)
    B. night terrors (125)
    C. insomnia (125)
    D. narcolepsy (124)

3. A.   A dream expressed desires, wishes, and unfulfilled needs that exist in the unconscious. (128)
    A.1. consists of overt story line, characters, and setting. (128)
    A.2. is the deep meaning of the dream (128)
    B. focused on the meaning of the dream to understand human nature (129)
    C. believe dreams have a physiological basis. During REM sleep, parts of the brain are spontaneously activated from cells in the hindbrain. (129)

4. A. dependence (134)
    B. withdrawal symptoms (135)
    C. tolerance (135)

5. A.1. abstinence (138)
    A.2. an alcoholic is an alcoholic forever; alcoholism is a disease. (138)
    B.1. limited, non problem drinking (139)
    B.2. alcohol abuse is learned behavior and can be unlearned (140)
    C. is an important part of treatment for an alcoholic (140)
    D. many modes of treatment (138-140)

6. A.1 impaired functioning of the respiratory system (141)
    A.2 detrimental changes in the heart, arteries, and veins, constipation and loss of appetite (141)
    B.1 from snorting lethal doses of pure heroin or a mixture (141)
    B.2 from disease (141)

7. A. is an addicting drug that blocks the effects of heroine (141)
    B. methodone must be combined with treatment programs and must be consumed daily to avoid withdrawal symptoms (141)

8. A.1 increase excitability, depress appetite, and increase alertness and talkativeness (143)
    A.2 stimulates the nervous system and serves as an anesthetic, dilation of pupils, increased heart rate, blood pressure (142-143)
    B.1 cause cravings for the drug, the user experiences exhaustion, lethargy, and depression (142-143)
    B.2 is addictive, produces irritability, eating and sleeping disturbances, can cause panic attacks, and several mental disorders (142-143)

Self Test

1. D (117)	2. A (118)	3. A (119)	4. C (120)	5. B (122)
6. C (123)	7. D (125)	8. D (130-131)	9. B (131)	10. D (133)
11. D (135)	12. C (135)	13. D (135)	14. A (136)	15. C (136)
16. A (138-139)	17. D (138-139)	18. B (140)	19. A (141)	20.A (141)
21. C (141)				

Chapter 5

Matching

	Answer	Word	Page
1.	g	conditioned response	153
2.	f	conditioned stimulus	152-153
3.	b	conditioning	151
4.	h	extinction	158
5.	p	fixed interval schedule	172
6.	r	fixed ratio	172
7.	t	latent learning	182
8.	a	learning	150
9.	m	negative reinforcement	166
10.	o	punishment	168
11.	c	reflex	151
12.	l	reinforcer	165
13.	k	shaping	164
14.	i	spontaneous recovery	158
15.	j	stimulus generalization	159
16.	n	superstitious behavior	167
17.	e	unconditioned response	151
18.	d	unconditioned stimulus	151
19.	q	variable interval	172
20.	s	variable ratio	172

True or False

1. TRUE (151)	2. FALSE (151)	3. TRUE (150-153)	4. FALSE (151)	5. FALSE (151)
6. TRUE (154-155)	7. FALSE (155-156)	8. TRUE (156)	9. FALSE (158)	10. TRUE (159-160)
11. TRUE (162-163)	12. TRUE (164-165)	13. TRUE (166-167)	14. TRUE (166)	15. FALSE (166)
16. FALSE (168)	17. FALSE (168)	18. TRUE (169-170)	19. FALSE (169-170)	20. TRUE (170)
21. TRUE (171)	22. FALSE (173-174)	23. TRUE (174)	24. FALSE (175)	25. TRUE (176)
26. TRUE (182)	27. TRUE (186)	28. TRUE (186-187)	29. FALSE (187)	

Fill-in-the-Blanks

	Answers	Page
1.	learning	150
2.	experience, change, permanence	150
3.	conditioning	151
4.	conditioning	151
5.	reflex	151
6.	Pavlov; classical conditioning	151

7.	Classical conditioning	151
8.	unconditioned	151
9.	unconditioned response	151
10.	neutral	151
11.	conditioned	152-153
12.	acquisition	153
13.	higher-order conditioning	154
14.	similarity frequency	154
15.	strength, timing, frequency	155
16.	predictability	156
17.	Garcia effect	157
18.	extinction	158
19.	spontaneous recovery	158
20.	stimulus generalization	159
21.	stimulus discrimination	159-160
22.	The Behavior of Organism	162
23.	Operant conditioning	162
24.	Instrumental conditioning	162
25.	reinforcer	163
26.	punisher	163
27.	Skinner Box	163
28.	cummulative recorder	164
29.	shaping	164-165
30.	successive approximating	165
31.	reinforcer	165
32.	positive reinforcement	165-166
33.	negative reinforcement	166
34.	escape avoidance	166
35.	probable behavior	166
36.	primary reinforcer	167
37.	secondary reinforcer	167
38.	superstitious behavior	167
39.	remove a desirable	168
40.	primary punisher	168
41.	secondary punisher	168
42.	learned helplessness	170
43.	schedule of reinforcement	172
44.	continuous reinforcement	172
45.	interval ratio	172
46.	ratio	172
47.	variable-ratio	172
48.	extinction	174
49.	resistance to extinction	175
50.	extrinsic; intrinsic	176
51.	insight	181
52.	latent learning	182
53.	generative process	182
54.	Metacognition	183
55.	Observational learning	186

Applications

1. (pp. 150-154)
   A. 1. bell, 2. startled response, 3. chalk, 4. apprehension (fear)
   B. 1. food, 2. salivation, 3. can opener, 4. stand under foot

2. (pp. 150-154)
   parent tells child to say "thank you"
   child responds with "thank you"
   positive reinforcement, parent says "Good"

3. (pp. 168-170)
   A. The process of presenting an undesirable or noxious stimulus or removing a desirable stimulus, to decrease the probability that a particular response will recur. When a dog growls at visitors, it's owner chastises it or chains it to a post.
   B. This is not defined; it's just a type of punishment. The example is a time-out.
   C. The removal of a pleasant environment or an environment containing positive events or reinforcers. A child who hits and kicks may be put in a room without toys, TV, or people.
   D. A stimulus that is naturally painful to an organism. Electric shock or visible parental rage to a small child.
   E. A neutral stimulus that takes on punishing qualities. A verbal no or a shake of the head.

4. p. 150-170

UP	DOWN
DOWN	UP

5. p. (170-174)
   A. The reward will follow the first required response that occurs after a specified interval of time. A scalloped pattern. Both animals and humans typically respond slowly; just before the reinforcer is due, there is an increase in performance.
   B. The reinforcement is delivered after predetermined but varying amounts of time as long as an appropriate response is made at least once after each interval. Work slow at a regular rate without showing the scalloped effect of those on a fixed interval schedule.
   C. The subject is reinforced for a specified number of responses (amount of work). The subject will work at a fast regular rate for the regular delivery of the reinforcer.
   D. The subject is reinforced for a predetermined but varying number of responses (amount of work). The subject works at a regular high rate, generating the highest available rate of response.

6. p. 150-170
   A. extinction
   B. negative reinforcement
   C. positive reinforcement
   D. time-out
   E. shaping
   F. spontaneous recovery
   G. punishment

7. p. 170-174
   A. fixed-ratio
   B. variable-ratio
   C. variable interval
   D. fixed interval

8. (pp. 150-187)
  A. classical conditioning
  B. operant conditioning
  C. classical conditioning
  D. observational learning

Self Test

1. D (150)	2. D (151)	3. A (151-153)	4. D (153)	5. B (154-155)
6. A (151)	7. D (158)	8. A (158-160)	9. C (159-160)	10. B (156)
11. D (157)	12. D (160-161)	13. C (162)	14. B (163)	15. B (167-168)
16. D (166-167)	17. A (169)	18. C (172)	19. C (174)	20. D (178)

Chapter 6

Matching

	Answer	Word	Page
1.	x	amnesia	222
2.	h	chunks	201
3.	y	consolidation	223
4.	u	decay	217
5.	m	declarative memory	205
6.	j	elaborative rehearsal	201
7.	b	encoding	195
8.	n	episodic memory	205
9.	s	imagery	208
10.	p	implicit	207
11.	v	interference	217
12.	k	long term memory (LTM)	204
13.	i	maintenance rehearsal	201
14.	a	memory	194
15.	q	primacy effect	208
16.	l	procedural memory	204
17.	r	recency effect	208
18.	g	rehearsal	200
19.	d	retrieval	196
20.	t	schema	215
21.	o	semantic memory	206
22.	e	sensory memory	198-199
23.	f	short term memory (STM)	200
24.	w	state defendant learning	220
25.	c	storage	196

True or False

1. FALSE (195)	2. TRUE (196)	3. TRUE (198-199)	4. TRUE (202)	5. TRUE (201)
6. FALSE (204)	7. FALSE (205)	8. FALSE (208)	9. TRUE (206-207)	10. TRUE (206-207)
11. TRUE (208-209)	12. FALSE (210)	13. TRUE (220)	14. TRUE (217-218)	15. FALSE (212-213)
16. TRUE (213-214)	17. TRUE (213)	18. TRUE (214)	19. FALSE (215)	20. FALSE (218)
21. FALSE (222)	22. FALSE (222)	23. TRUE (223)	24. FALSE (224)	25. TRUE (222-223)
26. TRUE (224)	27. TRUE (225)			

Fill-in-the-Blanks

	Answers	Page
1.	memory	194
2.	encoding	195
3.	storage	196
4.	retrieve	196
5.	parallel distributed processing	197
6.	short-term memory	200-201
7.	rehearsal	200
8.	memory span	201
9.	chunks	201
10.	maintenance rehearsal	201
11.	elaborative rehearsal	201
12.	working memory	202
13.	long-term memory	204
14.	procedural	204
15.	declarative	205
16.	episodic	205
17.	semantic	206
18.	Explicit	207
19.	primacy	208
20.	recency	208
21.	imagery	208-211
22.	schemas	215
23.	Decay	217
24.	interference	217
25.	proactive interference	217-218
26.	retroactive interference	218
27.	encoding specificity principle	220
28.	state dependent learning	220
29.	amnesia	222
30.	retrograde amnesia, anterograde amnesia	222
32.	consolidation	222-224

Applications

1. (pp. 215)
   A. a conceptual framework that organizes and makes sense of the world
   B. to shorten and simplify details
   C. to focus or over emphasize certain ideas
   D. to alter facts to make stories fit your own world view

2. (pp. 217-222)
   A. suppression or confusion of one bit of information with another that was learned earlier or later.
   B. the decrease in accurate recall as a result of previous information interfering with recall.
   C. the decrease in accurate recall as a result of subsequent presentations of different information.
   D. the inability to remember events preceding the trauma
   E. the inability to remember events since the time of trauma

3. (pp. 217-222)

    A. retroactive inhibition
    B. primary effect
    C. anterograde amnesia
    D. decay
    E. proactive inhibition
    F. recency effect
    G. motivated forgetting
    H. retrograde amnesia

Self Test

1. B (194)	2. D (195)	3. C (198-199)	4. D (201)	5. B (204-205)
6. A (208)	7. D (207)	8. D (211)	9. A (210-211)	10. C (213)
11. A (215)	12. C (217)	13. B (218)	14. A (219)	15. C (220)
16. C (222)	17. D (216)	18. D (216)	19. B (223)	20. C (223)
21. A (223)	22. C (224)	23. B (224)	24. D (224-225)	

Chapter 7

Matching

	Answer	Word	Page
1.	j	algorithm	247
2.	h	brainstorming	244
3.	a	concept	233
4.	i	creativity	244
5.	e	decision making	238
6.	u	deep structure	256
7.	g	functional fixedness	243
8.	s	grammar	255
9.	k	heuristics	248
10.	m	linguistics	252
11.	c	logic	238
12.	p	morpheme	253
13.	o	phoneme	253
14.	f	probelm solving	242
15.	n	psycholinguistics	252
16.	b	reasoning	238
17.	q	semantics	253
18.	l	subgoal analysis	248
19.	t	surface structure	255
20.	d	syllogism	238
21.	r	syntax	253

True or False

1. TRUE (233)	2. TRUE (234)	3. TRUE (236)	4. FALSE (236)	5. FALSE (236)
6. TRUE (241)	7. TRUE (239)	8. TRUE (239)	9. FALSE (240)	10. FALSE (242)
11. TRUE (242)	12. FALSE (243)	13. TRUE (243)	14. TRUE (245)	15. TRUE (244)
16. TRUE 246)	17. FALSE (247)	18. FALSE (248)	19. TRUE (253)	20. FALSE (253)
21. FALSE (253)	22. FALSE (255-256)	23. TRUE (256)	24. TRUE (257)	25. TRUE (257)
26. TRUE (257)	27. TRUE (258)	28. TRUE (257)		

Fill-in-the-Blanks

	Answers	Page
1.	cognitive psychology	232
2.	concepts	233
3.	hypothesis testing theory	237
4.	conservation focusing	237
5.	reasoning	238
6.	logic	238
7.	Decision making	238
8.	syllogisms	238
9.	problem solving	242
10.	functional fixcdness	243
11.	brainstorm	245
12.	Creativity	244
13.	convergent thinking	245
14.	Divergent thinking	245
15.	Algorithms	247
16.	heuristics	248
17.	subgoal analysis	248
18.	means-end analysis	248
19.	backward search	248
20.	linguistics	252
21.	Psycholinguistics	252
22.	Phonemes	253
23.	morphemes	253
24.	semantics	253
25.	syntax	253
26.	grammar	255
27.	transformational grammar	255
28.	surface structure	255
29.	deep structure	256
30.	referential naming	260

Applications

1. (p. 238)

   A. the process by which we generate logical and coherent ideas, evaluate situations, and reach conclusions

   B. the procedure we use to reach a valid conclusion

   C. assessing and choosing among alternatives

2. a procedure for solving a problem by using a set of rules to implement particular steps over and over until the problem is solved (p. 247)

3. a set of strategies that act as flexible guidelines -- not strict rules and procedures -- for discovering oriented problem solving (p. 248)

4. (p. 246)

   1. increase your knowledge
   2. automate some tasks
   3. follow a plan
   4. draw inferences and develop subgoals
   5. work backwards

6. look for contradictions/relations
7. reformulate the problem and represent it physically
8. practice

5. (pp. 237-244)
    A. dimension checking
    B. hypothesis checking
    C. conservative focusing
    D. brainstorming
    E. global focusing

6. (pp. 252-255)
    A. phonology
    B. morpheme
    C. phoneme
    D. psycholinguistics
    E. grammar
    F. syntax
    G. semantics

7. (pp. 255-256)
    A. each sentence has both surface and deep structure
    B. the organization of a sentence that is closest to its written or spoken form
    C. the underlying meaning of the sentence

Self Test

1. B (233)	2. D (237)	3. C (238)	4. D (241)	5. C (243)
6. D (245)	7. A (247)	8. B (246)	9. D (251)	10. B (251)
11. A (253)	12. C (253-254)	13. B (253)	14. C (255-256)	15. D (257)
16. D (260)	17. B (258)	18. A (259)		

Chapter 8

Matching

	Answer	Word	Page
1.	j	halo effect	277
2.	a	intelligence	267
3.	g	IQ	275
4.	l	mainstreaming	294
5.	k	mental retardation	291
6.	c	norms	274
7.	f	percentile score	275
8.	d	raw score	275
9.	h	reliability	276
10.	e	standard score (SS)	275
11.	b	standardization	274
12.	i	validity	277

True or False

1. FALSE (266)	2. TRUE (268)	3. TRUE (268)	4. FALSE (268)	5. TRUE (270)
6. FALSE (273)	7. TRUE (274)	8. FALSE (275)	9. TRUE (276)	10. TRUE (278)
11. TRUE (282)	12. TRUE (282)	13. TRUE (283)	14. TRUE (282)	15. FALSE (285)
16. TRUE (284)	17. TRUE (284)	18. FALSE (287)	19. FALSE (290)	20. TRUE (289)
21. FALSE (291)	22. TRUE (291)	23. FALSE (293)	24. FALSE (294)	

Fill-in-the-Blanks

	Answers	Page
1.	Intelligence	267
2.	John Watson	267
3.	factor analysis	268
4.	two factor theory of intelligence	268
5.	standardization	274
6.	norm	274
7.	representative sample	274
8.	normal curve	274
9.	raw score	275
10.	percentile score	275
11.	Deviation IQ	275
12.	reliability	276
13.	Validity	276-277
14.	halo effect	277
15.	David Wechsler	280
16.	nature, nurture	282-283
17.	gifted	290-291
18.	mental retardation	291
19.	biological vs. environmental	291
20.	mild retardation	292
21.	moderate	292
22.	mainstreaming	294
23.	inclusion	294

Applications

1. (pp. 267-272)
   - A. Jenson
   - B. Thurstone
   - C. Piaget
   - D. Spearman
   - E. Wechsler
   - F. Wechsler
   - F. Sternberg
   - G. Guilford
   - H. Gardner and Hatch

2. (pp. 274-275)
   - A. representative sample
   - B. norms
   - C. standardization
   - D. raw score
   - E. normal curve

F. percentile score
G. intelligence quotient
H. deviation IQ
I. standard score

3. (pp. 291-293)
   A. mild
   B. severe
   C. moderate
   D. profound

4. (p. 276)
   1. Administer the same test to the same person two or more occasions.
   2. Give two different versions of the same test.
   3. Divide the test into two parts. On a reliable test, the scores from the two halves will yield similar if not identical results.

5. (pp. 276-277)
   A. A test's ability to measure the knowledge or behavior it is intended to measure.
   B. The ability to predict future achievements accurately.
   C. The extent to which a person can judge a tests appropriateness by examining the test items.
   D. The extent to which a test actually measures a particular trait.

6. (p. 285)

Criticism	Response (Rebuttal)
1. Intelligence cannot be measured because no clear, agreed-upon measure of intelligence exits.	Although different IQ tests seem to measure different abilities, the major tests have face validity.
2. IQ tests consist of learned information and reflect the quality of a child's schooling rather than actual intelligence.	Most vocabulary items on IQ tests are learned in the general environment -- not in school and the ability to learn vocabulary depends on ability to reason.
3. Because of the Halo effect, a test administrator can develop positive or negative feelings about individuals, classes, or groups of students that can influence test scores.	This effect may happen -- but it's less powerful than opponents think.
4. Some people are test wise.	Items on IQ tests are unfamiliar even to experienced test takers and the effects of practice are seldom or never evident.
5. IQ scores often depend on motivation to succeed; minority groups often do not have the same motivation to succeed as do members of the majority.	IQ tests do not influence motivation.

7. (pp. 278-281)
   A. WISC-III
   B. K-ABC
   C. Stanford-Binet

8. (pp. 291)
  - A. deprived environment
  - B. physical trauma
  - C. genetic abnormality
  - D. infectious disease

Self Test

1. B (273)	2. D (267)	3. C (267)	4. B (269)	5. D (270)
6. C (273)	7. B (273-274)	8. C (275)	9. D (277)	10. B (278-281)
11. D (280)	12. B (282)	13. D (282)	14. C (282-286)	15. D (287)
16. C (288)	17. B (290)	18. A (291)	19. D (291)	20. C (293)
21. A (294)				

Chapter 9

Matching

	Answer	Word	Page
1.	i	anorexia nervosa	315
2.	d	arousal	302
3.	j	bulimia nervosa	316
4.	b	drive	301
5.	p	emotion	324
6.	g	extrinsic rewards	307
7.	o	learned helplessness	323
8.	a	motivation	300
9.	e	motive	304
10.	c	need	301
11.	m	orgasm phase	319
12.	l	plateau phase	319
13.	n	resolution phase	319
14.	h	self actualization	308
15.	f	social need	304
16.	k	vasocongestion	318

True or False

1. FALSE (301)	2. FALSE (301)	3. FALSE (313)	4. TRUE (313)	5. FALSE (315-316)
6. TRUE (316)	7. TRUE (310)	8. FALSE (317)	9. TRUE (318)	10. FALSE (302)
11. TRUE (302)	12. FALSE (302)	13. TRUE (303)	14. TRUE (322)	15. FALSE (304)
16. FALSE (324)	17. TRUE (305)	18. FALSE (307)	19. TRUE (308-309)	20. TRUE (326)
21. FALSE (326)	22. FALSE (328)	23. TRUE (330)	24. TRUE (331)	25. TRUE (329)
26. FALSE (329)	27. FALSE (333)	28. TRUE (333)		

Fill-in-the-Blanks

	Answers	Page
1.	motivation	300
2.	internal condition, inference, initiation, goal directed behavior	300
3.	Drive theory	300
4.	drive	301

5.	arousal	302
6.	expectancy theories	303
7.	social need	304
8.	cognitive theory	305
9.	Intrinsically motivated behaviors	306
10.	extrinsic rewards	307
11.	humanistic theory	308
12.	Self actualization	308
13.	homeostasis	310
14.	glucostatic	310
15.	eating disorders	314
16.	anorexia nervosa	315
17.	bulimia nervosa	316
18.	sexual response cycle	318
19.	excitement phase	318
20.	vascogestion	318
21.	plateau phase	319
22.	orgasm phase	319
23.	resolution	319
24.	need for achievement	322
25.	Learned helplessness	323
26.	emotion	324

Applications

1. (p. 300)
   1. internal condition
   2. inference
   3. initiation, activation, or maintenance
   4. goal directed behavior

2.
   1. excitement (318)
   2. plateau (319)
   3. orgasm (319)
   4. resolution (319)

3.
   A. plateau (319)
   B. resolution (319)
   C. excitement (318)
   D. orgasm (319)

4.
   A. James Lange (326)
   B. Schachter-Singer (330)
   C. self-regulation (333)
   D. Cannon-Bard (328)

Self Test

1. C (300)	2. A (300-301)	3. B (311)	4. A (314-315)	5. B (315-316)
6. C (316)	7. B (302)	8. A (303)	9. A (304)	10. B (304)
11. D (304)	12. C (305)	13. B (306)	14. C (309)	15. D (308-309)
16. C (324)	17. A (324)	18. B (326-327)	19. D (330)	20. C (330)
21. C (331)	22. D (324-325)	23. C (329)		

Chapter 10

Matching

	Answer	Word	Page
1.	m	accommodation	351
2.	l	assimilation	351
3.	v	attachment	363
4.	g	Babinski reflex	348
5.	w	bonding	364
6.	r	concrete operational	354
7.	s	conservation	354
8.	q	decentration	354
9.	p	egocentrism	354
10.	b	embryo	342
11.	c	fetus	343
12.	t	formal operational	355
13.	k	grasping reflex	348
14.	f	labor	345
15.	u	morality	359
16.	h	moro reflex	348
17.	d	placenta	343
18.	o	preoperational stage	354
19.	i	rooting reflex	348
20.	n	sensorimotor stage	353
21.	j	sucking reflex	348
22.	x	temperament	366
23.	e	teratogen	345
24.	a	zygote	342

True or False

1. FALSE (341)	2. TRUE (341)	3. FALSE (342-343)	4. FALSE (343)	5. TRUE (345)
6. FALSE (345)	7. TRUE (346)	8. TRUE (348)	9. FALSE (348)	10. TRUE (351)
11. FALSE (351)	12. FALSE (351)	13. TRUE (353)	14. FALSE (354)	15. FALSE (353)
16. FALSE (356)	17. TRUE (356-357)	18. FALSE (357)	19. TRUE (357)	20. TRUE (359)
21. TRUE (362)	22. TRUE (366)	23. FALSE (365)	24. TRUE (367)	25. FALSE (368)
26. FALSE (368)	27. FALSE (371)	28. FALSE (372-373)	29. TRUE (372)	30. TRUE (371)

Fill-in-the-Blanks

	Answers	Page
1.	reductionist	341
2.	organismic	341
3.	contextual	341
4.	zygote	342
5.	embryo	342
6.	fetus	343
7.	placenta	343
8.	Teratogens	345
9.	Labor	345
10.	Babinski	348

11.	moro	348
12.	rooting	348
13.	sucking	348
14.	grasping	348
15.	visual cliff method	350
16.	Assimilation	351
17.	accommodation	351
18.	sensorimotor	353
19.	preoperational	354
20.	egocentrism	354
21.	decentration	354
22.	concrete operational	354
23.	Conservation	354
24.	formal operational	354
25.	Morality	359
26.	gender differences	362
27.	attachment	363
28.	bonding	364
29.	Temperment	366
30.	gender stereotyping	369

Applications
1. (pp. 342-343)
   1. A fertilized egg.
   2. The name given to an organism from conception until the 49th day.
   3. The name given to an organism from the 8th week until birth.

2. (p. 343)

   The mass of tissue in the uterus that acts as the life-support system for the fetus by supplying it with oxygen, food, and antibodies from the mother and by eliminating wates by way of the mother.

3. (p. 345)

   The process in which the uterus contracts to open the cervix so the fetus can descend through the birth canal to the outside world.

4. (pp.345-346)
   A. early labor
   B. active labor
   C. transition

5. (p. 351)

   A. The process by which a person absorbs new ideas and experiences, incorporates them into existing cognitive structures and behaviors and uses them later in similar situations. A child who learns to grasp a spoon demonstrates assimilation by later grasping similar objects.
   B. The process of modifying previously developed cognitive structures and behaviors to adapt them to a new concept. The child can learn the new, more complex behavior of grasping a sphere (a ball) by modifying the earlier response and widening the grasp.

6. (pp. 353-358)

	Stage	Age	Major Accomplishment
1.	sensorimotor	Birth - 2	Develop some motor coordination, rudimentary memory for past events, begin to manipulate their environment, object permanence, use language
2.	preoperational	2 - 6 or 7	represent the world symbolically, egocentrism, decentration
3.	concrete operational	6 or 7 - 11 or 12	higher order symbolism math/geography, learn rules and understand the reasons, conservation
4.	formal operational	about 12 +	hypothetic thought, new egocentrism

7. (pp. 353-358)
   A. Rudimentary memory for past events.
   B. They try to manipulate their environment and make interesting events recur.
   C. The ability to realize that objects continue to exist even when they are out of sight.
   D. Walking
   E. Talk about objects and events.

8. (p. 354)
   A. The inability to perceive a situation or event except in relation to oneself. Children are unable to understand that the world does not exist solely to satisfy their interests.
   B. The understanding of the difference between ones ideas, feelings and interests, and those of others.

9. (pp. 360-361)
   A. preconventional morality/condemn or justify
   B. conventional morality/conform in order to avoid disapproval
   C. post conventional morality/concerned with contracts moral conscience and laws

10. (pp. 351-355)
    A. egocentrism
    B. accommodation
    C. assimilation
    D. conservation
    E. decentration

Self Test

1. B (341)	2. D (343)	3. D (343)	4. A (345)	5. B (345)
6. D (345)	7. C (348)	8. B (348)	9. C (346)	10. C (350)
11. B (343)	12. D (351)	13. C (354)	14. B (354)	15. C (351-353)
16. B (354)	17. B (356)	18. D (356-357)	19. A (358)	20. C (357)
21. C (357)	22. C (361)	23. D (362)	24. A (365)	25. D (366-367)
26. B (368)	27. B (370-371)			

Chapter 11

Matching

	Answer	Word	Page
1.	a	adolescence	380
2.	f	ageism	398
3.	h	Alzheimer	401
4.	e	androgynous	386
5.	g	dementia	400
6.	c	gender identity	384
7.	d	gender role	386
8.	b	puberty	380
9.	i	thanatology	402

True or False

1. TRUE (381)	2. FALSE (381)	3. FALSE (381)	4. FALSE (382)	5. TRUE (383)
6. TRUE (385)	7. FALSE (386)	8. TRUE (386)	9. TRUE (386)	10. TRUE (386)
11. TRUE (392)	12. TRUE (393)	13. FALSE (394)	14. FALSE (392)	15. FALSE (390)
16. FALSE (391)	17. TRUE (391)	18. TRUE (392)	19. TRUE (393)	20. TRUE (397)
21. TRUE (398)	22. FALSE (399)	23. TRUE (400)	24. TRUE (401)	25. TRUE (401)
26. FALSE (399)	27. TRUE (402)	28. TRUE (403)		

Fill-in-the-Blanks

	Answers	Page
1.	chronological age	380
2.	functional age	380
3.	adolescence	380
4.	Puberty	380
5.	secondary sex characteristics	382
6.	formal operations	382
7.	peer group	384
8.	gender identity	384
9.	gender schema theory	385
10.	gender roles	386
11.	gender role stereotype	386
12.	androgynous	386
13.	strict	386
14.	identity vs. role confusion	389
15.	life structures	390
16.	early	391
17.	middle	391
18.	late	391
19.	transition	392
20.	crisis	392
21.	primary aging	395
22.	Secondary aging	395
23.	ageism	398
24.	Dementias	400
25.	Alzheimer's disease	401

26.	thanatology	402
27.	hospice	403

Applications

1. (pp. 389-390)

Age 1, Successful Completion: Discovers the world is a living and comfortable place.

Age 2-3, Successful Completion: Masters toilet training with little or no punishment; views self as having control over things.

Age 4-5, Result of Conflict: Fails and/or is punished for achievements; has problems identifying with parent of same sex.

Age 6-11, Successful Completion: Is able to feel confident with people and tasks.

Age 12-18, Successful Completion: Develops an identity, knows who he is and what he wants.

Age 16-25, Result of Conflict: Unable to Establish a close loving relationship.

Age 20-40, Result of Conflict: Sees life as boring and unexciting.

Age 40-, Successful Completion: Sees life as being meaningful.

2. (pp. 390-391)

A. (11-17) Young people enter the adult world but are still immature and vulnerable.

B. (18-45) The first major life choices are made regarding family, occupation, and style of living.

C. (46-65) Adults now live with the decisions they made. Career and family are usually well established. People experience either a sense of satisfaction, self worth, and accomplishment, or a sense that much of their life has been wasted.

D. (65-on) Covers the years from sixty-five on. During retirement many people relax and enjoy the fruits of their labors.

3. (p. 402)

A. serves as a buffer against the shocking news

B. is directed against family, friends, or medical staff

C. a person tries to gain more time by making a deal with God, themselves, or their doctors

D. often caused by the pain of their illness and guilt over inconveniencing their family

E. in which a person stops fighting and accepts death

Self Test

1. C (380)	2. D (381)	3. B (381)	4. C (384)	5. D (384)
6. C (385)	7. B (386)	8. D (386)	9. A (387)	10. A (389)
11. B (387)	12. C (393)	13. C (394)	14. A (392)	15. C (392)
16. A (390)	17. C (390)	18. C (391)	19. B (396-397)	20. B (398-399)
21. A (399)	22. B (394)	23. B (395)	24. C (400)	25. D (400)
26. D (401)	27. A (401)	28. D (402)	29. B (403)	

Chapter 12

Matching

	Answer	Word	Page
1.	j	anal stage	415
2.	w	archetypes	420
3.	ff	assessment	439
4.	c	conscious	412
5.	p	defense mechanism	416
6.	s	denial	416
7.	g	ego	412

8.	o	fixation	416
9.	x	fulfillment	423
10.	n	genital stage	416
11.	f	id	412
12.	z	ideal self	423
13.	m	latency stage	415
14.	b	libido	411
15.	l	Oedipus complex	415
16.	i	oral stage	413
17.	a	personality	410
18.	k	phallic stage	415
19.	d	preconscious	412
20.	r	projection	416
21.	gg	projective tests	441
22.	v	rationalization	417
23.	t	reaction formation	417
24.	q	repression	416
25.	y	self	423
26.	aa	self actualization	423
27.	ee	self efficacy	434
28	hh	self monitoring	443
29.	dd	shyness	434
30	u	sublimation	417
31.	h	superego	413
32.	bb	trait	425
33.	cc	types	425
34.	e	unconscious	412

True or False

1. TRUE (410)	2. FALSE (411)	3. FALSE (412)	4. FALSE (413)	5. FALSE (417)
6. FALSE (419)	7. FALSE (419)	8. TRUE (420)	9. TRUE (422)	10. FALSE (422)
11. TRUE (425)	12. FALSE (425)	13. FALSE (428)	14. FALSE (428)	15. TRUE (429)
16. TRUE (431)	17. TRUE (432)	18. FALSE (434)	19. TRUE (434)	20. FALSE (436)
21. TRUE (439)	22. TRUE (440)	23. TRUE (441)	24. TRUE (442)	25. TRUE (443)

Fill-in-the-Blanks

	Answers	**Page**
1.	personality	410
2.	Psychic determinism	411
3.	unconscious motivation	411
4.	conscious	412
5.	preconscious	412
6.	unconscious	412
7.	id	412
8.	ego	412
9.	superego	413
10.	oral	413
11.	anal	415
12.	phallic	415
13.	Oedipus complex	415
14.	latent stage	415

15..	genital stage	416
16.	fixation	416
17.	defense mechanism	416
18.	Repression	416
19.	projection	416
20.	denial	416
21.	Reaction formation	417
22.	sublimation	417
23.	rationalization	417
24.	neo Freudians	419
25.	collective unconscious	420
26.	ideal self	423
27.	self actualization	423
28.	traits	425
29.	Shyness	434
30.	Self efficacy	434

Applications

1. (p. 412)
    - A. Conscious
    - B. Preconscious
    - C. Unconscious

2. (pp. 412-413)
    - A. Id
    1. It is the source of a person's instinctual energy.
    2. The id works on the pleasure principle, seeking complete and immediate gratification without regard to morals, society, or others.
    3. The id is demanding, irrational, and selfish.
    - B. Ego
    1. It grows out of the id.
    2. It seeks to satisfy instinctual needs in accordance with reality.
    3. It is patient, reasonable, and works by the reality principle.
    - C. Superego
    1. It can be thought of as the moral branch of mental functioning.
    2. It tells the id and ego whether gratification in a particular instance is ethical.
    3. It helps control the id by internalizing parental authority through the process of socialization.

3. (pp. 416-417)
    - A. rationalization
    - B. denial
    - C. projection
    - D. reaction formation
    - E. repression
    - F. Sublimation

4. (p. 419)
    - A. Harry Sullivan
    - B. Alfred Adler
    - C. Karen Horney
    - D. Erich Fromm
    - E. Carl Jung

5. (pp. 425–427)

    A. are ideas and behaviors that determine the direction of a person's life

    B. are reasonably easy to identify behaviors that characterize a person's daily interactions

    C. are specific behaviors that occur in response to specific situations

6. (pp. 427–428)

Trait Categories	Description
Extroversion-introversion	the extent to which people are social/unsocial, talkative/quiet, affectionate, reserved
Agreeableness-antagonism	the extent to which people are good-natured or irritable, courteous or rude, flexible or stubborn, lenient or critical
Conscientiousness-undirectedness	the extent to which people are reliable, careful, punctual, or organized
Neuroticism-stability	the extent to which people are worriers, nervous, or insecure
Openness to experience	the extent to which people are open to experience or closed, original or conventional, independent or conforming, creative or uncreative, daring or timid

7. (pp. 439–443)

    A. IQ: provide specific information about a person's level of intellectual functioning, provides good predictor of academic success.

    B. CPI: it examines personality traits such as sociability, self-control, and responsibility.

    C. MMPI-2: Consist of 567 true/false statements that focus on attitudes, feelings, motor disturbances, and bodily complaints.

    D. Rorschach test: is a projective test that uses ten, symmetrical in design, inkblots; subjects are asked to tell what they see in the inkblot.

    E. TAT: is a projective test that uses black and white pictures of one or more people in a variety of situations. Subjects are asked to tell a story about the picture.

8. (pp. 442–443)

    A. Tend to be systematic and structured, focusing on overt and current behavior and paying attention to the situations in which behaviors occur.

    B. Involves two or more observers entering a client's natural environment and recording the occurrence of specified behaviors at predetermined intervals.

    C. A procedure in which a person systematically counts and records the frequency and duration of specific behaviors themselves.

9. (pp. 416–417)

    A. Reaction formation

    B. Repression

    C. Denial

    D. Rationalization

    E. Projection

Self Test

1. C (410)	2. D (411)	3. B (412)	4. B (415)	5. A (417)
6. B (417)	7. D (419)	8. A (419–420)	9. B (421)	10. D (422)
11. B (422)	12. D (424)	13. B (424)	14. D (425)	15. C (425)
16. B (427–428)	17. C (428)	18. C (429–430)	19. A (430)	20.B (431)
21. A (432–433)	22. D (434)	23. D (434)	24. D (436–437)	25. B (444)

Chapter 13

Matching

	Answer	Word	Page
1.	b	anxiety	450
2.	g	burnout	455
3.	e	conflict	451-452
4.	i	coping	462
5.	k	coping skills	463
6.	d	frustration	451
7.	n	health psychology	466
8.	f	pressure	452
9.	m	psychoneuroimmunology	466
10.	h	PTSD	461
11.	j	resilience	463
12.	c	stress	450
13.	l	stress inoculation	465
14.	a	stressor	450

True or False

1. TRUE (450)	2. FALSE (452)	3. TRUE (454)	4. TRUE (455)	5. TRUE (455)
6. TRUE (456)	7. TRUE (458)	8. TRUE (459)	9. FALSE (460)	10. FALSE (461-462)
11. FALSE (462)	12. FALSE (463)	13. FALSE (464)	14. TRUE (465)	15. FALSE (466-467)
16. FALSE (467)	17. TRUE (470-471)	18. TRUE (469)		

Fill-in-the-Blanks

	Answers	Page
1.	stressor	450
2.	anxiety	450
3.	Stress	450
4.	frustration	451
5.	conflict	452
6.	approach-approach conflict	452
7.	avoidance-avoidance conflict	452
8.	approach-avoidance conflict	452
9.	pressure	452
10.	emotional, physiological, and behavioral	454
11.	burnout	455
12.	alarm stage, resistance, exhaustion	456-457
13.	stressful life events	457
14.	autonomy	460
15.	Type A behaviors	460
16.	Type B behaviors	460
17.	Reactivity	460
18.	post traumatic disorder	461
19.	Coping	463
20.	resilience	463
21.	coping skills	463
22.	Social support	463
23.	defense oriented coping strategies	463

24.	rationalization	463
25.	reaction formation	463
26.	stress inoculation	465
27.	Psychoneuroimmunology	466
28.	physical fitness	466-467
29.	Health psychology	466-467
30.	The sick role	469-470

Applications

1. (p. 450)
   1. how familiar people are with an event
   2. how much they have anticipated the event
   3. how much they can control the events and themselves

2. (p. 452)
   1. Approach-approach: Arise when a person must choose one of two equally pleasant alternatives.
   2. Avoidance-avoidance: Occur when a choice involves two equally distasteful alternatives.
   3. Approach-avoidance: Occur when a particular situation has both appealing and repellent aspects.

3. (p. 452)
   1. The closer a subject is to a goal, the stronger the tendency is to approach the goal.
   2. When two incompatible responses are available, the stronger one will be expressed.
   3. The strength of the tendency to approach or avoid is correlated with the strength of the motivating drive.

4. (p. 454)
   A. Emotionally: people become frustrated, aroused, anxious, angry, annoyed, irritable and/or hostile.
   B. Physiologically: the autonomic nervous system is aroused.
   C. Behaviorally: various levels or arousal lead to optimal, ineffective, or disorganized behaviors.

5. (p. 461)
   A. Post-traumatic stress disorder is a category of mental disorder evident after a person has undergone some type of trauma.
   B. Include vivid, intrusive recollections or reexperiences of the traumatic event and occasional lapses of normal consciousness. People may develop anxiety, depression, or exceptionally aggressive behavior.
   C. Such behaviors eventually interfere with daily functioning, family interactions, and health.

6. (p. 462)
   1. Coping is constantly changing and being evaluated, and is therefore a process.
   2. Coping involves managing situations, not necessarily bringing them under control.
   3. Coping requires effort; it does not happen automatically.
   4. Coping aims to manage both behavioral and cognitive events.
   5. Coping is a learned process.

7. (p. 463)
   A. Are the techniques people use to deal with stress and changing situations.
   B. Have found that rewards and punishment are not contingent on their behavior, learn not to cope.
   C. Is the availability of comfort, recognition, approval, and encouragement.

8. (p. 464-465)
   A. These include biofeedback, hypnosis, and meditation; exercise is also a way to relax.
   B. Prepare people for pressure through gradual exposure to increasingly higher stress levels.
   C. Helps people confront stressors, cope with pain and the feelings of being overwhelmed because they can gain control over emotions, arousal, and stress reaction.

Self Test

1. A (450)	2. C (451)	3. D (452)	4. C (454)	5. B (455)
6. C (457)	7. D (457)	8. A (459)	9. D (461)	10. B (463)
11. C (464-465)	12. B (465)	13. A (466)	14. D (466-467)	15. B (466)
16. D (469)	17. C (470-471)	18. D (469)	19. A (469)	20. A (472)
21. B (472)				

Chapter 14

Matching

	Answer	Word	Page
1.	v	affect	506
2.	f	agoraphobia	486
3.	c	anxiety	484
4.	q	bipolar disorders	496
5.	o	child abuse	494
6.	x	concordance rate	508
7.	k	conversion disorders	490
8.	s	delusions	498
9.	r	depressive disorders	497
10.	m	dissociative disorder	490
11.	y	double bind	511
12.	d	free floating anxiety	485
13.	u	hallucinations	506
14.	l	hypochondriasis	490
15.	a	model	479
16.	h	obsessive/compulsive disorder	487
17.	n	personality disorders	492
18.	e	phobic disorder	485
19.	b	prevalence	482
20.	t	psychotic	505
21.	p	rape	495
22.	w	schizophrenia	504-507
23.	g	social phobia	486
24.	j	somatization disorder	489
25.	i	somatoform disorder	489
26	z	vulnerability	512

True or False

1. TRUE (478)	2. TRUE (482)	3. FALSE (482)	4. FALSE (485)	5. TRUE (485)
6. FALSE (486)	7. FALSE (487)	8. FALSE (490)	9. TRUE (491)	10. TRUE (493)
11. TRUE (493)	12. TRUE (494-495)	13. TRUE (495)	14. TRUE (492)	15. TRUE (500-501)
16. TRUE (497)	17. FALSE (497)	18. TRUE (498)	19. TRUE (500)	20. FALSE (505)
21. FALSE (505-506)	22. FALSE (505)	23. TRUE (507)	24. TRUE (510)	25. TRUE (511-512)

Fill-in-the-Blanks

	Answers	Page
1.	abnormal behavior	478
2.	model	479
3.	abnormal psychology	479
4.	prevalence	482
5.	anxiety	484
6.	generalized anxiety disorder	485
7.	free floating anxiety	485
8.	phobic disorder	485
9.	agoraphobia	486
10.	social phobia	486
11.	specific	487
12.	obsessive-compulsive disorder	487
13.	somatoform	489
14.	somatization disorder	489
15.	conversion disorder	490
16.	hypocondriasis	490
17.	dissociative disorder	490
18.	dissociative amnesia	490
19.	dissociative identity disorder	490
20.	sexual deviation	491
21.	personality disorder	492
22.	antisocial personality disorder	493
23.	child abuse	494
24.	rape	495
25.	bipolar	496
26.	Depressive disorders	497
27.	major depressive disorder	497
28.	delusions	498
29.	learned helplessness	500
30.	Schizophrenic disorder	505

Applications

1. (pp. 485-487)

A. An anxiety disorder involving the excessive, unreasonable, and irrational fear of, and consequent attempt to avoid, specific objects or situation.

B. Fear and avoidance of being alone or isolated in open and public places.

C. Fear and desire to avoid of being where you can be under scrutiny of others and might behave in an embarrassing or humiliating way.

D. Irrational and persistent fear of specific object or situation along with a compelling desire to avoid.

2. (pp. 489-490)

A. Involve real physical symptoms that are under voluntary control and for which no apparent physical cause exists.

B. Disorder involving recurrent and multiple physical complaints for which medical attention has been ineffective, often beset with anxiety and depression.

C. Loss or alteration of physical functioning (blindness for example).

D. A sudden but temporary alteration in consciousness, identity or memory.

E. Inability to recall important, personal information.

F. When 2 or more distinct personalities, each of which is dominant at particular times, exists in a single person.

3. (pp. 492-494)
   A. Unwarranted feelings of persecution and mistrust everyone. These people are hypersensitive to criticism.
   B. Fearful and anxious, afraid of making decisions.
   C. Dramatic, emotional, and erratic behaviors, attention seeking usually having stormy interpersonal relationships.
   D. Superficially charming but are destructive and reckless usually unwilling to live by society's rules.

4. (pp. 491-492)
   A. Sexual gratification from objects rather than people.
   B. Gratification from dressing in opposite sex's clothing.
   C. Watching other people as a way of gratification.
   D. Exposing one's genitals to others.
   E. Sexual contact with children.
   F. Gratification from experiencing pain inflicted by someone else.
   G. Gratification from inflicting pain on someone else.

5. (pp. 504-512)
   A. catatonic
   B. disorganized
   C. undifferentiated
   D. paranoid
   E. residual

6. (pp. 484-490)
   A. dissociative disorder
   B. somatization disorder
   C. generalized anxiety disorder
   D. agoraphobia
   E. conversion disorder
   F. specific phobia
   G. obsessive-compulsive disorder
   H. social phobia

Self Test

1. A (479)	2. D (481)	3. C (482)	4. D (485)	5. A (487)
6. D (487)	7. A (489)	8. D (489)	9. B (493)	10. B (493)
11. C (495)	12. D (491)	13. D (492)	14. A (498)	15. A (498)
16. C (499)	17. C (500)	18. B (505)	19. A (505)	20. B (507)
21. C (507)	22. D (511)	23. C (510)	24. D (512)	

Chapter 15

Matching

	Answer	Word	Page
1.	k	behavior therapy	532
2.	q	brief therapy	542
3.	i	client centered therapy	528
4.	o	counter conditioning	535
5.	t	ECT	546-547

6.	s	encounter group	543
7.	e	free association	525
8.	j	Gestalt therapy	529
9.	d	insight therapy	524
10.	f	interpretation	525
11.	b	placebo effect	520
12.	c	psychoanalysis	524
13.	r	psychodrama	543
14.	a	psychotherapy	519
15.	g	resistance	525
16.	p	RET	539
17.	l	symptom substitution	533
18.	n	time out	535
19.	m	token economy	533
20.	h	transference	525

True or False

1. TRUE (520)	2. TRUE (520)	3. TRUE (524)	4. TRUE (522-523)	5. TRUE (524)
6. TRUE (526)	7. FALSE (528)	8. TRUE (532)	9. FALSE (532)	10. FALSE (533)
11. TRUE (533-535)	12. FALSE (537)	13. TRUE (539)	14. TRUE (543)	15. FALSE (545)

Fill-in-the-Blanks

	Answers	Page
1.	psychotherapy	518
2.	placebo effect	520
3.	psychoanalysis	524
4.	psychodynamically based	524
5.	Insight therapy	524
6.	free association	525
7.	Dream analysis	525
8.	interpretation	525
9.	resistance	525
10.	transference	525
11.	working through	526
12.	ego analysis	526
13.	client-centered therapy	528
14.	Non-directive therapy	528
15.	Gestalt therapy	529
16.	behavior therapy	532
17.	Symptom substitution	533
18.	token economy	533
19.	Time-out	535
20.	counterconditioning	535
21.	Systematic desensitization	536
22.	Aversive counterconditioning	536
23.	rational-emotive therapy	539
24.	Brief intermittent therapy	542
25.	Group therapy	543
26.	encounter groups	543
27.	family therapy	544

28.	codependence	545
29.	Electroconvulsive therapy	546-547
30.	psychotropic drugs	547

Applications

1. (pp. 524-526)
    A. transference
    B. dream analysis
    C. resistance
    D. interpretation
    E. free association

2. (pp. 533-535)
    A. the withholding of reinforcers for a behavior that has been reinforced in the past. The behavior decreases as a result.
    B. the presentation of an aversive stimulus for undesired behaviors. The behaviors decrease as a result.
    C. The person is removed from a desired, reinforcing situation when undesired behaviors are emitted. The undesired behaviors decrease as a result.

3. (pp. 547-549)
    1. Drug: antianxiety; effect: reduce stressful feelings, calm patients, lower excitability; disorder treatment: high anxiety
    2. Drug: antidepressant; effect: raise optimism, less sad, redevelop sense of purpose; disorder treatment: major depression.
    3. Drug: antimania; effect: relieve manic episodes; disorder treated: bipolar disorders
    4. Drug: antipsychotic; effect: reduce hostility, reduce aggression, reduce delusions; disorder treated: schizophrenia

Self Test

1. C (518-519)	2. B (524)	3. D (524-525)	4. C (525)	5. C (526)
6. C (526-527)	7. A (528)	8. D (529)	9. A (529-530)	10. D (529-530)
11. B (532)	12. C (533)	13. D (534)	14. A (534)	15. C (536)
16. B (536-537)	17. D (539)	18. D (545)	19. D (543)	B (544)

Chapter 16

Matching

	Answer	Word	Page
1.	o	aggression	579
2.	q	altruism	584
3.	b	attitudes	556
4.	i	attribution	567
5.	d	cognitive dissonance	563
6.	m	conformity	574
7.	n	debriefing	579
8.	aa	deindividuation	595
9.	l	discrimination	570
10.	c	elaboration likelihood model	560
11.	t	equity theory	589
12.	j	fundamental attribution error	569

13.	v	group	592
14.	y	group polarization	593
15.	z	groupthink	594
16.	h	impression formation	565
17.	s	interpersonal attraction	586
18.	u	intimacy	589
19.	k	prejudice	570
20.	p	prosocial behavior	584
21.	f	reactance	564
22.	e	self perception theory	564
23.	g	social cognition	565
24.	w	social facilitation	592
25.	x	social loafing	593
26.	a	social psychology	556
27.	r	sociobiology	585
28.	bb	Solomon Asch	575

True or False

1. TRUE (558)	2. FALSE (558)	3. TRUE (559)	4. TRUE (559)	5. FALSE (559)
6. TRUE (567-568)	7. TRUE (570)	8. TRUE (577-578)	9. TRUE (589-591)	10. TRUE (566)
11. TRUE (567-568)	12. TRUE (567)	13. TRUE (569)	14. TRUE (570)	15. FALSE (570)
16. TRUE (563)	17. TRUE (563)	18. TRUE (564)	19. TRUE (564)	20. FALSE (565)
21. TRUE (566)	22. TRUE (567)	23. TRUE (568)	24. TRUE (571)	25. TRUE (571)
26. TRUE (571)	27. TRUE (570)	28. FALSE (570)	29. TRUE (572)	30. TRUE (572-573)
31. TRUE (573)	32. FALSE (576)	33. TRUE (576)	34. FALSE (576)	35. TRUE 576
36. TRUE (576)	37. FALSE (576)	38. TRUE (577)	39. FALSE (577)	40. TRUE (578)
41. FALSE (580)	42. TRUE (582)	43. TRUE (582)	44. TRUE (581-582)	45. TRUE (582)
46. TRUE (583)	47. TRUE (585)	48. TRUE (585-586)	49. FALSE (585-586)	50. TRUE (587)
51. TRUE (587)	52. TRUE (588)	53. TRUE (588-589)	54. TRUE (589)	55. FALSE (591)
56. TRUE (592)	57. FALSE (566)	58. TRUE (568)		

Fill-in-the-Blanks

	Answers	Page
1.	attitudes, social cognition, and social interactions	556
2.	cognitive	556
3.	emotional	556
4.	behavioral dimension	557
5.	classical conditioning, operant conditioning, and observational learning	557-558
6.	communicator	559
7.	medium	559-560
8.	central route	560
9.	the foot in the door, the door in the face, the ask and you shall receive approach, low balling, modeling, incentives	562
10.	cognitive dissonance	563
11.	self perception	564
12.	reactance	564
13.	social cognition	565
14.	impression formation	565
15.	representativesness	565
16.	Availability	565
17.	false consensus effect	565

18.	frame	565
19.	nonverbal communication	565
20.	Body language	566
21.	eye contact	566
22,	attribution	567
23.	dispositional; situational	567-568
24.	consensus, consistency, and distinctiveness	568-569
25.	actor-observer	569
26.	self-serving bias	570
27.	self esteem	570
28.	androgynous	571
29.	prejudice	570
30.	discrimination	570
31.	cautious bigot	572
32.	reverse discrimination	572
33.	social learning theory, motivational theory, cognitive theory, personality theory	572-573
34.	motivational theory	573
35.	cognitive theory	573
36.	prejudice prone personalities	573
37.	social influence	574
38.	conform	574-575
39.	amount of information	576
40.	relative competence	576
41.	social conformity	576
42.	dissenting opinions	577
43.	obedient	577
44.	debrief	579
45.	aggression	579
46.	mental disorders; biological dispositions	583
47.	social rules	583
48.	nested ecological approach	583
49.	prosocial behavior	584
50.	altruistic	584
51.	sociobiology	585
52.	bystander apathy	585
53.	friendship	588
54.	equity	589
55.	intimacy	589
56.	commitment, passion, consumate love	590
57.	analytical self reports; emotional reports	591
58.	group	592
59.	social facilitation	592
60.	social loafing	593
61.	group polarization	593
62.	groupthink	594
63.	deindividuation	595

Applications

1. (p. 562)

    1. Foot in the door - the asking of a small favor first then ask for the larger favor.
    2. Door in the face - first ask for something outrageous, then the more reasonable.
    3. Ask and you shall be given - asking a simple request in the name of a good cause.
    4. Low balling - compliance is given because of a low-risk factor.
    5. Modeling - show by example the behavior desired.
    6. Incentives - offering payment of some kind of a desired behavior.

2. (pp. 567-569)

INTERNAL	EXTERNAL
1. low, consensus, few	1. high, consensus, most, same
2. high, consistency, similar	2. high, consistency, similar
3. low, distinctiveness	3. high, distinctiveness

Self Test

1. A (556)	2. D (556-557)	3. B (557-558)	4. C (559)	5. C (560-561)
6. D (563)	7. B (564)	8. C (564)	9. B (567)	10. C (567-569)
11. C (569)	12. D (569)	13. B (569)	14. C (575)	15. C (575-576)
16. B (577)	17. A (577)	18. D (580-581)	19. A (582)	20. A (587)
21. B (588)	22. C (587)	23. A (588)	24. A (588)	

Chapter 17

Matching

	Answer	Word	Page
1.	rr	anxiety	635
2.	a	Applied psychology	602
3.	qq	arousal	635
4.	ww	cognitive interventions	636
5.	ii	Community psychology	630
6.	w	crowding	625-626
7.	oo	developmental change	632
8.	nn	Educational psychology	631
9.	jj	empowerment	630
10.	u	environmental psychology	623
11.	p	equity theory	612
12.	ee	ergonomics	620
13.	m	expectancy	611
14.	k	expectancy theories	610
15.	s	Fred Fiedler	617
16.	e	functional job analyses	603
17.	j	goal setting theory	610
18.	dd	human factors	619
19.	tt	hypnosis	636
20.	b	Industrial/organizational psychology	602
21.	n	instrumentality	611
22.	i	intrinsically motivated behavior	609

23.	d	job analyses	603
24.	q	job satisfaction	614
25.	r	leaders	615
26.	z	lost letter technique	626
27.	uu	meditation	636
28.	vv	mental imagery	636
29.	ff	Occupational Safety and Health Act (OSHA)	621
30.	gg	perceptual research	621
31.	h	performance appraisal	607
32.	aa	personal space	627
33.	hh	policy or program evaluators	622
34.	kk	primary prevention	630
35.	bb	privacy	628
36.	ss	progressive relaxation	636
37.	ll	secondary prevention	631
38.	f	selection procedures	604
39.	x	social density	626
40.	y	spatial density	626
41.	pp	Sport psychology	634
42.	c	strategic planning	603
43.	v	stressor	624
44.	cc	territorial behavior	629
45.	mm	tertiary prevention	631
46.	g	training	606
47.	t	transformational leaders	618
48.	o	valence	611
49.	l	Victor Vroom	611

True or False

1. TRUE (602)	2. TRUE (602-603)	3. FALSE (603)	4. TRUE (603)	5. TRUE (603)
6. TRUE (603)	7. TRUE (603)	8. FALSE (603)	9. TRUE (603-604)	10. TRUE (604)
11. TRUE (605)	12. TRUE (605-606)	13. FALSE (606)	14. TRUE (606)	15. TRUE (606)
16. FALSE (607)	17. TRUE (608-609)	18. TRUE (609)	19. TRUE (609)	20. FALSE (608)
21. TRUE (608)	22. TRUE (609-610)	23. FALSE (610)	24. TRUE (610)	25. TRUE (610)
26. FALSE (611)	27. TRUE (611)	28. TRUE (612)	29. TRUE (612)	30. TRUE (613)
31. TRUE (614)	32. FALSE (614)	33. TRUE (614)	34. FALSE (616)	35. TRUE (617)
36. TRUE (617)	37. FALSE (617-618)	38. TRUE (618)	39. TRUE (619)	40. TRUE (624)
41. TRUE (624)	42. FALSE (625)	43. TRUE (625)	44. TRUE (625)	45. TRUE (626)
46. TRUE (626)	47. TRUE (626-627)	48. TRUE (627)	49. TRUE (628)	50. TRUE (629)
51. FALSE (629)	52. TRUE (621)	53. TRUE (621)	54. TRUE (622)	55. TRUE (622)
56. FALSE (623)	57. TRUE (630)	58. TRUE (630)	59. FALSE (630)	60. TRUE (630-631)
61. TRUE (631)	62. TRUE (632)	63. TRUE (632)	64. FALSE (632)	65. TRUE (633)
66. TRUE (633)	67. TRUE (634)	68. TRUE (634-635)	69. TRUE (635)	

Fill-in-the-Blanks

	Answers	Page
1.	applied psychologists	602
2.	industrial/organizational psychologists	602
3.	human resources psychology, motivation of job performance, job satisfaction, leadership	602-603
4.	position analysis questionnaires	604

5.	information sources, mental processes, work output, relationships with others, job context, and other	604
6.	general or specific	604-605
7.	integrity	606
8.	leniency, central tendency, halo effects, and reliability	608-609
9.	traditional cognitive variables	608
10.	fair, professional, and accurate	608
11.	power distance	609
12.	uncertainty avoidance	609
13.	masculinity	609
14.	expectancy, instrumentality, and valence	611
15.	paternalistic, behavioral, and participatory	613-614
16.	the work itself, the quality of supervision, the support of coworkers, the work setting, perceived rewards	616
17.	traits, behaviors, situations	616-617
18.	situation	617
19.	Fiedler contingency model and Vroom's leadership model	617
20.	environmental psychologists	624
21.	temperature, noise, and environmental toxins	624-625
22.	Noise	625
23.	intimate, personal, social, and public	627
24.	industrial/organizational researcher	620
25.	Controlling	620
26.	accuracy, productivity, and safety	621
27.	exclusion designs, prevention designs, and fail safe designs	621
28.	Community psychology	630
29.	primary, secondary, and tertiary	630-631
30.	neighborhood clinic	630
31.	Crisis intervention centers	631
32.	Educational psychologists	631
33.	School, educational	631-632
34.	environment conditions	633
35.	Intervention strategies	636

Applications

1. (pp. 625-626)

    A. a psychological state; the perception that one's space is too restricted

    B. the number of people in a given space (experimental manipulations the space stays the same, the number of people in the space is varied)

    C. the size of a space with a given number of people in it (in experimental manipulations the number of people is held constant while the size of the space is varied)

2. (p. 627-628)

    A. intimate distance

        1. 0 to 18 inches

        2. acceptable for comforting someone, lovers, contact sports

        3. sensory events included hearing another's breathing, smelling the other person, examining every physical detail of the other person

        4. reserve for people who have great familiarity with one another

    B. personal distance

        1. 1 1/2 feet to 4 feet

        2. acceptable for close friends and everyday social interactions

C. social distance
1. 4 to 12 feet
2. found in business interactions and interactions with strangers
3. allows people to be close enough to communicate while remaining separated
4. social zone is controlled by the use of physical barriers such as a desk

D. public distance
1. 12 to 25 feet
2. found when people speak or perform for an audience
3. eliminates any personal communication

Self Test

1. D (604)	2. D (609)	3. B (611)	4. A (611-612)	5. A (614)
6. C (613)	7. B (614)	8. B (617-619)	9. A (624)	10. D (624-625)
11. C (626)	12. A (627-628)	13. C (628-629)	14. D (629)	

Appendix

Matching

	Answer	Word	Page
1.	j	correlation coefficient	650
2.	h	frequency polygon	642
3.	I	inferential statistics	649
4.	a	mean	642
5.	c	median	642
6.	b	mode	642
7.	g	normal curve	647-648
8.	e	range	645
9.	f	standard deviation	646
10.	d	variability	645

True or False

1. TRUE (640)	2. TRUE (642)	3. TRUE (642)	4. TRUE (645)	5. FALSE (646)
6. TRUE (649)	7. FALSE (649)	8. FALSE (650)	9. FALSE (651)	10. FALSE (651)

Fill-in-the-Blanks

	Answers	Page
1.	Descriptive	641
2.	polygon	642
3.	mode	642
4.	median	642
5.	variability	645
6.	standard deviation	646
7.	mean	642
8.	Inferential	649
9.	negatively	651
10.	stronger	651

Self Test

1. D (641)	2. A (642)	3. D (645)	4. D (645)	5. A (646)	
6. C (647-648)	7. D (647)	8. C (649)	9. A (651)	10. D (649)	11. B (650)

Thank you for using Keeping Pace Plus.